SACRIFICING THE SALMON

A Legal and Policy History of the Decline of Columbia Basin Salmon

SACRIFICING THE SALMON

A Legal and Policy History of the Decline of Columbia Basin Salmon

Michael C. Blumm

VANDEPLAS PUBLISHING, LLC

UNITED STATES OF AMERICA

Sacrificing the Salmon: A Legal and Policy History of the Decline of Columbia Basin Salmon

Blumm, Michael C.

Cover sketch by Roger A. Long. His Salmon Banner monoprints are available from Roger A. Long, 756 Evergreen Rd., Lake Oswego, OR 97034. (503) 635-2677. Proceeds benefit the Native Fish Society.

This book was originally published in 2002 by BookWorld Publications, The Netherlands with ISBN: 978-90-75228-25-0

Published by:

Vandeplas Publishing, LLC – July 2013

801 International Parkway, 5th Floor
Lake Mary, FL. 32746
USA

www.vandeplaspublishing.com

ISBN 978-1-60042-197-6

PREFACE

I have been writing and teaching about Columbia River salmon and the law for over twenty years, beginning with editing the *Anadromous Fish Law Memo* published by the Oregon State University Sea Grant Program from 1979 to 1990. In the ensuing decade, I continued to follow the law affecting Pacific salmon, writing mostly in legal journals, and co-directing the Northwest Water Law and Policy Project. This book draws on several of those writings, but leaves none of them unchanged, and more than half of the chapters here are not based on earlier writings.

This book is neither a doctrinal legal analysis, nor a conventional history, but it does contain a large amount of both legal analysis and history. Because as a whole it does not attempt a chronological history, chapter 1 provides a capsule history, which seeks to put into context the disparate aspects of salmon law and policy discussed in the succeeding chapters. Some readers may want to proceed from the capsule history directly to the chapter analyzing the issue of particular interest, or to the final two chapters, which draw lessons from the earlier chapters. The book's principal use may well be as a reference source on the numerous discrete aspects of salmon history, law, and policy it discusses. A detailed table of contents, an extensive index, and table of cases aim to aid researchers.

Another means to give structure to what otherwise might seem to be an unconnected series of legal and policy analyses is the promise metaphor. Salmon and those who depend upon salmon for culture, commerce, and recreation have received a variety of promises over the last century and a half, beginning with the 19th century Stevens Treaties, which promised Native Americans a "right of taking fish" to preserve their way of life and supply them with a commercial livelihood. Over the years since, other promises were made, such as the international promise in the Pacific Salmon Treaty to fairly apportion harvests and rebuild run sizes. Another promise was that the Pacific Northwest could have developed rivers and cheap hydropower while also maintaining salmon runs through hatchery construction. Later, the promise of having both hydropower and salmon was continued in the Northwest Power Act's salmon restoration program. More recently, the Endangered Species Act promised that salmon would not go extinct and in fact would recover from the threat of extinction, although there remain numerous questions about whether the statute can achieve those goals. Two largely overlooked promises are the Clean Water Act's promise of fishable water quality and the Federal Power Act's promise of re-licensing nonfederal hydroelectric dams with conditions protective of salmon.

One reason for writing this book is to explain these promises, what they have and have not accomplished, and what they may offer for the future. This is not a simple story, and at times involves some technical legal explanations. But oversimplifications, which are common in the salmon world, do a greater disservice than technical arguments, for they provide the public with misinformation. I've often claimed that, given the vast scientific uncertainty and potential economic consequences of various salmon recovery options, virtually anything anyone says about salmon has at least some kernel of truth to it. Thus, the public can be easily misled by self-serving statements that are not entirely false, but highly improbable. A badly informed public cannot participate effectively in debates about the salmon's future, and the species has never fared particularly well when decisions have been made by policymakers without public pressure. This book hopes to increase public pressure on those responsible for land and water policies affecting salmon at least to make them explain clearly the probable effects of their decisions on the salmon's future in the Columbia Basin.

The book has clear points of view on several issues, and does not shy away from advocacy. As Judge Robert Belloni once said, when granting a state motion to disqualify himself from hearing further arguments concerning Columbia River treaty fishing rights, he was not biased when he first began to preside over the proceedings. But twenty years of experience had educated him on the weakness of the states' reasoning and the strength of the tribal claims. More recently, one of Judge Belloni's successors, Judge Malcolm Marsh, also disqualified himself for similar reasons after presiding over treaty rights issues for over a decade. I too have formed opinions about the cogency of the tribes' rights, the effect of hydroelectric development on salmon, the breaching of the Lower Snake River dams, and other issues central to the story of the past and future of salmon in the Columbia Basin, and my opinions are evident in the text.

Although the focus of this book is on the Columbia Basin, it occasionally strays beyond its confines to consider issues of relevance, such as Judge Boldt's decision on the equal sharing formula imposed by the Stevens Treaties, the international Pacific Salmon Treaty, and the effects of the implementation of the Northwest Forest Plan, which is not confined to the Columbia Basin. But most of the focus of attention is on the Columbia Basin — once home to the largest salmon runs in the world — although a concluding chapter attempts to draw generic lessons from the Columbia experience that may be useful to other resources in other locations.

Pacific salmon law, once an obscure backwater of the law, is now expanding at a breathtaking pace. There is never an easy way to decide to end an ongoing story like the Columbia River Basin saga. This book ends with the end of 2000, with new Endangered Species and Northwest Power Act plans, and with a new president who campaigned against removing the four Lower Snake River dams, which many biologists think is necessary to restore Snake River salmon runs. The book leaves to others the chore of evaluating events in 2001 and beyond.

In earlier writings, I included copious footnotes, literally thousands of them. After a while I became convinced that the footnotes detracted from the readability of the text. But I have been convinced by several reviewers, who felt that documentation was essential, to include endnotes. Nevertheless, I have confined the notes by limiting them to the end of paragraphs, restricting the references to a few sources, and sometimes indicating where more thorough documentation can be found in my earlier writings.

I owe many people large thanks for helping me complete this book. First and foremost is the late William Q. Wick, long-time Director of the Oregon Sea Grant Program, who had the vision and courage to fund a different approach to analysis of

Columbia Basin issues, one centered around salmon, when he approved the Anadromous Fish Law Project at Lewis & Clark Law School in 1979, and he continued to fund it for over a decade. Second, over the years the deans at my law school — Art LaFrance, Steve Kanter, and Jim Huffman — supported the project and my other writings with summer stipends. Third, a grant from the Rocky Mountain Mineral Law Foundation helped finance research assistants. Fourth, Charles Wilkinson, whose writings speak to the soul of the American West, encouraged this project at an early stage. Fifth, many reviewers helped me refine the text and avoid mistakes, including Nina Bell, Chip McConnaha, Dan Rohlf, John Volkman, and Jim Weber, all of whom read portions of the manuscript. My greatest debt, however, is to John Shurts and Jay Taylor, both prominent natural resource historians, whose detailed review of the entire manuscript was particularly helpful. None of these individuals should be blamed for any remaining mistakes, and not all endorse everything that is written here.

In addition, the efforts of several of my co-authors in earlier endeavors are represented in one way or another in the text, including Chris Beckwith, Lorraine Bodi, Greg Corbin, Brad Johnson, Laird Lucas, Don Miller, Dan Rohlf, Andy Simrin, Michael Schoessler, and Glenn Spain. Half of those co-authors were my students, indicative of what a collective effort of Lewis & Clark Law School this project and the *Anadromous Fish Law Memo* have been. Literally dozens of former students were involved, reflected in the dozens of citations to former students' publications in the endnotes. However, trying to name them all here would be hazardous because I would surely forget someone. But I especially want to thank Scott Althouse, Chuck Bonham, Melissa Powers, Mike Newhouse, and Bill Warnock, who worked on the final stages of the manuscript. The late Lenair Mulford typed and retyped the manuscript with great care. Tami Gierloff was a superb indexer. Jane McDowell not only assisted with word processing and indexing, but also edited the manuscript. And Shirley Johansen and Andy Marion solved the layout problems caused by incompatible word processing programs, when it seemed the manuscript would never be published. I also wish to thank the following publishers for allowing me to use portions of material contained in earlier publications: *Ecology Law Quarterly, Environmental Law, Oregon Sea Grant and Oregon State University Press,* the *Idaho Law Review, The Michie Company (*a division of *Mathew Bender and Co.),* the *University of Colorado Law Review,* and the *Washington Law Review.*

Finally, I want to thank my wife, Jo, and my kids, Nicky and Aria, for putting up with this project much longer than I promised them they would have to. My five-year old son will be especially pleased that we can spend more time at what really is important: baseball practice. And I would be remiss in not remembering my parents, who always valued education even more than baseball.

Michael C. Blumm
Sisters, Oregon
January 2001

SUMMARY OF CONTENTS

DETAILED TABLE OF CONTENTS

TABLE OF MAPS, CHARTS AND FIGURES

1— CAPSULE HISTORY

As they have been for thousands of years, salmon remain the cultural and spiritual soul of the Pacific Northwest, a region whose outlines have been described as "anywhere a salmon can get to." From Alaska's Kotzebue Sound to California's Monterey Bay, the rivers of the Northwest once teemed with wild salmon. These magnificent animals are born in freshwater, ride the rivers' spring freshet to the sea as juveniles, spend two to five years in the ocean, then, almost miraculously, return to their natal streams as adults to mate and die. On Lewis and Clark's expedition in 1805, William Clark remarked that "the number of dead fish on the shores and floating in the river is incredible." This ritualized fornication, as Timothy Egan has called it, brings not merely death but also essential marine nutrients to fresh water. The salmon's spawned-out bodies supply food for riparian wildlife, ranging from eagles and bears to insects. These oceanic proteins — a treasure from the sea — are the salmon's gift to the rivers which produced them.[1]

The salmon returning to the rivers of the Pacific Northwest consist of several different species. They are part of a vast migration throughout the North Pacific, stretching across the Bering Sea to Siberia and to the northern islands of Japan. These Pacific salmon (*Oncorhyuchus*) were separated from their Atlantic cousins (*Salmo*) a million years ago in the Great Ice Age, when the Arctic ice cap joined the North American continent and blocked the marine Northwest Passage. During the Ice Age, with ice blockading most of the North Pacific, salmon survived in refuges low in river basins. When the ice began to retreat as global temperatures rose, glacial rivers flooded the oceans with fresh water, diluting oceanic salinity and encouraging the salmon to range far into the ocean in search of rich feeding grounds populated by crustacea that thrived in the frigid seas. However, while the ocean provided fertile feeding grounds, it was not a fit environment for young salmon. In order to perpetuate the species, the ocean travelers returned to their natal rivers. Salmon thus are anadromous fish: they migrate from the sea up rivers to spawn.[2]

The life cycle of Pacific salmon is both awe-inspiring and shrouded in some mystery. Although blocked from much of their historic habitat during the last century, the largest and longest travelers, sockeye and chinook salmon, still can ascend 900 miles inland from the sea, gaining over a mile in elevation. The athleticism of these mountain-climbing fish remains a wonder. Surprisingly little is known about the salmon's ocean travels, however. Chinook can travel more than 10,000 miles in the Pacific, often making several circuits before returning to spawn, usually four years after descending to the ocean. However, biologists know relatively little about the routes salmon pursue in the marine environment, although it seems likely that some fish originating in American and Canadian waters spend some time mingling with their relatives from Siberia and Japan.[3]

Chapter 2 of this book provides a kind of layman's guide to Pacific salmon, explaining the characteristics of various salmon species and discussing their life cycles in greater detail.

The First Fishers

The mysteries associated with the salmon's immense migrations — its magical return and its imminent death — were attributed to supernatural forces by native populations throughout the North Pacific. For these people the most important ritual of the year was the First Salmon Ceremony, marking the return of salmon in the spring. This ceremony included prayers and incantations expressing joy, relief, and thanksgiving to the creator who restored the fish which had died so visibly the year before. Some tribes treated the first-caught salmon as if it were a visiting chief of great renown.[4]

The importance of the return of the salmon to the native peoples of the Pacific Northwest is difficult to overstate. There is some evidence suggesting that it was the abundance of fish and fresh water that attracted the first natives to cross the Asian land bridge and settle in the Northwest. Federal District Judge George Boldt, after examining three years of evidence, including exhaustive anthropological studies, concluded that all the Northwest tribes shared a "universal and paramount dependence" on salmon.

Native life was intrinsically linked to the salmon's migrations; the fish were not only vital to their diet, they were also a major trade good. Through trade, surplus fish could be converted to wealth. In fact, the salmon economy made the natives of the Pacific Northwest America's wealthiest aboriginals north of Mexico. Millions of pounds of salmon were harvested annually. Little wonder, then, that long before the arrival of whites, some Northwest natives called themselves "The Salmon People." The salmon was the equivalent of the buffalo to the natives of the plains, of the reindeer to the Inuit.[5]

Although salmon were abundant, the natives did not take that abundance for granted. They employed elaborate procedures to cure and preserve salmon for winter food. Wasting salmon was generally proscribed, and refuse was never deposited in streams during salmon season. One tribe even beached its canoes to bail them to avoid polluting the salmon's waters. These "laws" were enforced by peer pressure and religious taboos, which usually were strong enough to ensure that they were respected. Or perhaps it is more accurate to say that the native ways of relating to salmon and water were so fundamental as to be an essential part of cultural and spiritual norms. In short, just as the salmon adapted to the post-Ice Age ecosystem, the natives adapted their lifestyles to the salmon.[6]

White Settlement

By the time European explorers, seeking the Northwest Passage, began to arrive in the region in the late 18th century, the natives of the Northwest had been harvesting salmon for around 10,000 years. Before it was drowned behind The Dalles Dam in 1957, the Indian fishing community near Celilo Falls was the oldest continuously inhabited community on the North American continent, dating back some eight millennia. That fifteen-mile stretch of river supported a permanent population in excess of 1,000 people. Recent estimates place total native Columbia Basin harvests at around 41 million annual pounds, comparable to white harvests in the era between 1883 and 1919. However, the native harvest did not have the same adverse effects, since it was dispersed throughout the basin, not concentrated in the lower river.

Because of salmon, Northwest natives had the highest aboriginal population density north of Mexico. Northwest natives generally lived in settled communities, preferred trade to war, and quickly developed a mutual dependency with white traders. Whites brought horses, gems, metals, cloth, and blankets, which they exchanged for furs and salmon. Although whites had little effect on the Northwest environment prior to the Oregon Trail settlement era of the mid-1800s, white contact quickly proved disastrous for the natives. Even before the Lewis and Clark expedition in 1805, smallpox brought by whites had already reduced native populations by an estimated 33 to 50 percent. By 1834, there was a 90 percent population decline of Chinook Indians on the Lower Columbia, due to non-endemic diseases introduced by whites. In 1851, the Commission of Indian Affairs estimated that only 8,260 Columbia River Indians remained, just one-sixth of the pre-contact population.[7]

Despite the declining numbers of natives, white settlement after the peace treaty with Great Britain in 1846 and the creation of the Oregon Territory two years later induced the natives to harvest more salmon to meet increased white demand and to provide money for the purchase of white goods. But the influx of white settlers, who had been promised free land by the 1850 Oregon Land Donation Act, also led to increased friction between the two cultures. This migration gave lie to the Oregon Territorial Act's assurances of "good faith" dealings and preservation of the natives' properties.[8]

The Stevens and Palmer Treaties

To forestall conflict and facilitate white settlement, Washington territorial governor Isaac Stevens and Oregon territorial governor Joel Palmer negotiated a series of treaties in the mid-1850s under which the natives conveyed some 64 million acres of what are now the states of Idaho, Oregon, and Washington. In return, natives received a series of small land reserves, some schools and missionaries, and the right to continue to harvest salmon "in common with" whites at all the native "usual and accustomed" fishing grounds. This treaty right to continue to fish as they always had was the basis of one of the largest real estate transactions in history. Both government negotiators and the natives clearly intended that the tribes would continue to fish as they had before the treaties. Through their salmon harvests, the tribes were to become an integral element of the Northwest economy. Salmon were seen as a means to achieve tribal economic self-sufficiency.[9]

Chapter 3 examines the origins of the treaty-guaranteed right to fish, which this book considers the "first promise" concerning salmon. Chapter 4 explains the evolution of the treaty promise in court decisions beginning in the nineteenth century and continuing through the 1970s.

The Great Salmon Free-For-All

For about twenty years, the intent of the treaty negotiators was largely realized: native fishing indeed became a vital part of the pioneer economy of the Northwest. True, some settlers fenced natives out of their fishing grounds, but such exclusions were not commonplace, and ultimately they were ruled illegal by the Washington territorial court in 1887.[10]

The seeds of white preemption of native fisheries were sown when the canning process was perfected, making salmon an export product. The first Pacific salmon cannery began on the Sacramento River in 1864. Within a few years, as increasing amounts of canned salmon were shipped to the East Coast, Great Britain, and other distant markets, the Sacramento runs were quickly decimated. The canning industry then turned its attention northward to the Columbia, where the first cannery opened in 1867. By 1883, completion of the transcontinental railroad to Portland allowed canned salmon to be shipped throughout the continent. Aided by huge fish traps, fish wheels, drift nets, and weirs, the Columbia River harvest peaked at 43 million pounds of chinook. This proved to be an unsustainable harvest level because, unlike the native harvest prior to white settlement, it was concentrated in the lower river, not spread throughout the basin. This concentrated, unselective lower river harvest was more likely to overharvest individual runs. Seven years later, in 1890, the Columbia's salmon runs were in decline, many canneries had closed, and the pack of salmon fell by nearly one-half.[11]

In this era, which Charles Wilkinson has labeled the "frenzied free-for-all," the response to declining harvests was simply to move farther north. The first cannery was built on Puget Sound in 1887; by 1905, there were twenty-four. Although at first native harvests contributed to the canneries, technological and legal developments quickly combined to effectively preempt native fisheries. New saltwater fishing technologies, such as gasoline-powered boats with purse seines and gill nets, pushed salmon harvests out into the ocean and Puget Sound. This shift in harvest effort robbed many traditional native fishing sites of their locational advantages.[12]

State Regulation

Especially after Washington achieved statehood in 1889, the law was increasingly used to restrict native commercial harvests by closing freshwater areas but leaving saltwater open to fishing. These so-called "salmon preserves" outlawed fishing at numerous traditional fishing sites of many Puget Sound tribes. In effect, the preserves foisted the burden of salmon conservation on the tribes, while allowing white fisheries in the sound and ocean to continue largely unrestrained.[13]

State regulation helped to disenfranchise native fishers, but it utterly failed to halt run-size declines. The first timid efforts at regulating harvests occurred in 1871, when the Washington territory banned fish-traps, weirs, or nets that extended two-thirds of the way across fresh water streams and lakes if they prevented the upstream or downstream passage of fish. Six years later, in 1877, Washington closed the Columbia to fishing during four months of the year. In 1878, Oregon also closed the Columbia during specified periods, established net size limits and spacing between traps, and required traps and weirs to have openings allowing fish passage during closed seasons. But neither state attempted to coordinate with the other, and neither employed any fish biologists. Worse, there was little or no enforcement. For example, Oregon originally had only one enforcement agent, and its law did not prohibit ships or railroads from receiving or transporting fish during closed seasons, thus crippling enforcement efforts.[14]

For the next half century, regulation was ineffective at overcoming the effects of overfishing. 1938, the year the Bonneville Dam was completed, ushered in the era of large federal dams in the Columbia Basin. That year, the director of research for the Oregon Fish Commission noted that the number of adult salmon which escaped harvest was well below that necessary to produce maximum sustained yield. The director complained of the ineffectiveness of closed fishing seasons, which he believed were offset by increased harvest intensity during open seasons. Most intensive had been fish wheels — large waterwheels that literally scooped salmon out of the river twenty-four hours a day, which first appeared on the Columbia River in 1879. By the turn of the century, there were seventy-six of these devices, collecting five percent of harvest. They were not banned until 1926 in Oregon, and not until 1934 in Washington.[15]

Perhaps an even more glaring shortcoming of state regulation was its failure to restrict a wide variety of activities that were destroying salmon habitat. Mining, timber harvesting, livestock grazing, dredging and filling wetlands, and dam building continued unrestrained as the salmon runs declined. Hydraulic gold mining, which flushed thousands of tons of earth down mountains and buried spawning beds, contributed to the decimation of the Sacramento River runs. Logging on nearly every watershed in British Columbia changed runoff patterns, gouging river beds and choking spawning grounds with silt. Miners and loggers compounded their transgressions by building dams that often completely wiped out salmon runs.[16]

Early Hatcheries

Instead of curtailing the harvest or restricting habitat damage, the conventional wisdom was that artificial propagation would maintain the salmon runs. The first salmon hatchery was built on the Sacramento River in 1872. It exported salmon eggs to the East Coast, Europe, Australia, and New Zealand. Five years later, in 1877, the first Columbia Basin hatchery was sited on the Clackamas River. But it was not until the 1890s that extensive hatchery construction began. Between 1895 and 1900 hatchery production tripled, then tripled again during the next five years. By 1905, some 62 million hatchery smolt were being released in the Columbia Basin. That year the magazine *Pacific Fisherman* claimed that fully 75 percent of the Columbia River run was artificially propagated.[17]

Nevertheless, in a harbinger of things to come, by 1909 the salmon harvest declined by more than one-third, from 38 to 24 million pounds. Despite limited knowledge of fish diet and frequent outbreaks of disease, fish managers in the Columbia Basin pursued an increasing commitment to hatcheries throughout the early years of the twentieth century. But hatcheries failed to sustain harvests, due to primitive rearing practices, disease, and the adverse effects of hatchery fish on wild fish (due to competition for limited food and habitat and interbreeding which diluted the wild stocks' genetic integrity). Between 1900 and 1935, for example, the state of Washington increased production of hatchery fish from 25 to 90 million fish. During the same 35-year period, however, the state's commercial salmon harvest fell to 15 million pounds, more than a 300 percent decline.[18]

The Dam-Building Era

But the worst was yet to come. The era of large dam building began in the 1930s. The first mainstem dam, Rock Island Dam, was completed near Wenatchee, Washington by Puget Sound Power and Light in 1933. That same year, spurred by the New Deal philosophy of government projects putting people back to work, the federal government began constructing the Bonneville and Grand Coulee Dams. Bonneville on the Lower Columbia was finished in 1938, the year after Congress created the Bonneville Power Administration to market the electricity produced by the project. Three years later, in 1941, the massive Grand Coulee storage project, impounding over sixty times more water than Bonneville Dam, destroyed the salmon runs of the Upper Columbia by forever blocking access to their spawning grounds. No longer would salmon reach the Columbia's Canadian headwaters.[19]

Some adult salmon were able to surmount the run-of-river dam at Bonneville (as they could at Rock Island), because fish ladders were included in the project at the request of federal and state fish agencies. But little thought was given to downstream juvenile salmon passage, and downstream passage losses killed up to 15 percent of salmon at each dam. The Assistant Chief of the Army Corps of Engineers, which built Bonneville Dam, erroneously told Congress that the dam's power turbines were "absolutely incapable" of harming migrating salmon. Failure to adequately address the downstream passage problem would prove to be, next to completely sealing off salmon runs as at Grand Coulee and inundating spawning grounds with other dams, the most damaging legacy of the dam-building era.[20]

Before the dam-building era ended — with the completion of the last mainstem dam on the Snake River in 1975 — the dam builders constructed nearly twenty mainstem dams on the Columbia and its principal tributary, the Snake, and many more on tributary streams. (See map 1.) Most of these dams were authorized and constructed in the post-war period, intending to produce a multiplicity of benefits: 1) providing work for returning soldiers; 2) helping sustain an electricity-intensive aluminum industry, which the federal government brought to the Northwest during the war; and 3) aiding agriculture by providing cheap irrigation water and electricity and a slack-water navigation channel that would make Lewiston, Idaho a seaport.[21]

The cumulative effect of these dams on the salmon runs was devastating. After completion of the four Lower Snake River dams — whose benefits, the Corps admitted, amounted to just 15 percent of their costs — the average death rate for Upper Snake River juvenile salmon jumped from 5 to 75 percent.[22]

Dam building did more than just inflict salmon mortalities at each dam, however. Large storage projects in the upper basin — like Grand Coulee on the mainstem Columbia and Idaho Power's Brownlee Dam on the mainstem Snake — enabled dam operators to substantially alter Columbia Basin river flows, especially after completion of four large storage projects authorized by the 1964 Columbia River Treaty between the U.S. and Canada, which doubled the basin's storage capacity. Dam operators could now store the spring freshet in reservoirs to produce hydropower in the fall and winter, when demand was higher. For the last thirty-five years, the Columbia River hydropower system has been operated to store spring flows in this manner. Unfortunately, the salmon depend on this freshet for efficient transport to the ocean. The lost freshet would prove to be an even more intractable issue for salmon recovery efforts than dam passage mortalities.

Chapter 5 explores the dam-building era and explains the consequences for salmon.

More Hatcheries

In the Columbia Basin, dams are responsible for roughly 80 percent of human-caused mortalities of some salmon species, notably fall chinook. And that figure might actually understate the dams' true effect, because the dams were the principal reason for the basin's overwhelming commitment to hatcheries. In fact, in 1938, the year that Bonneville Dam was completed, Congress enacted the Mitchell Act. That statute authorized federal funding of hatcheries to compensate for dam-induced salmon mortalities. Hatcheries were perceived as the way to preserve the salmon runs without losing the benefits accompanying maximum hydroelectric development.[23]

Map 1 — Major Columbia Basin Dams

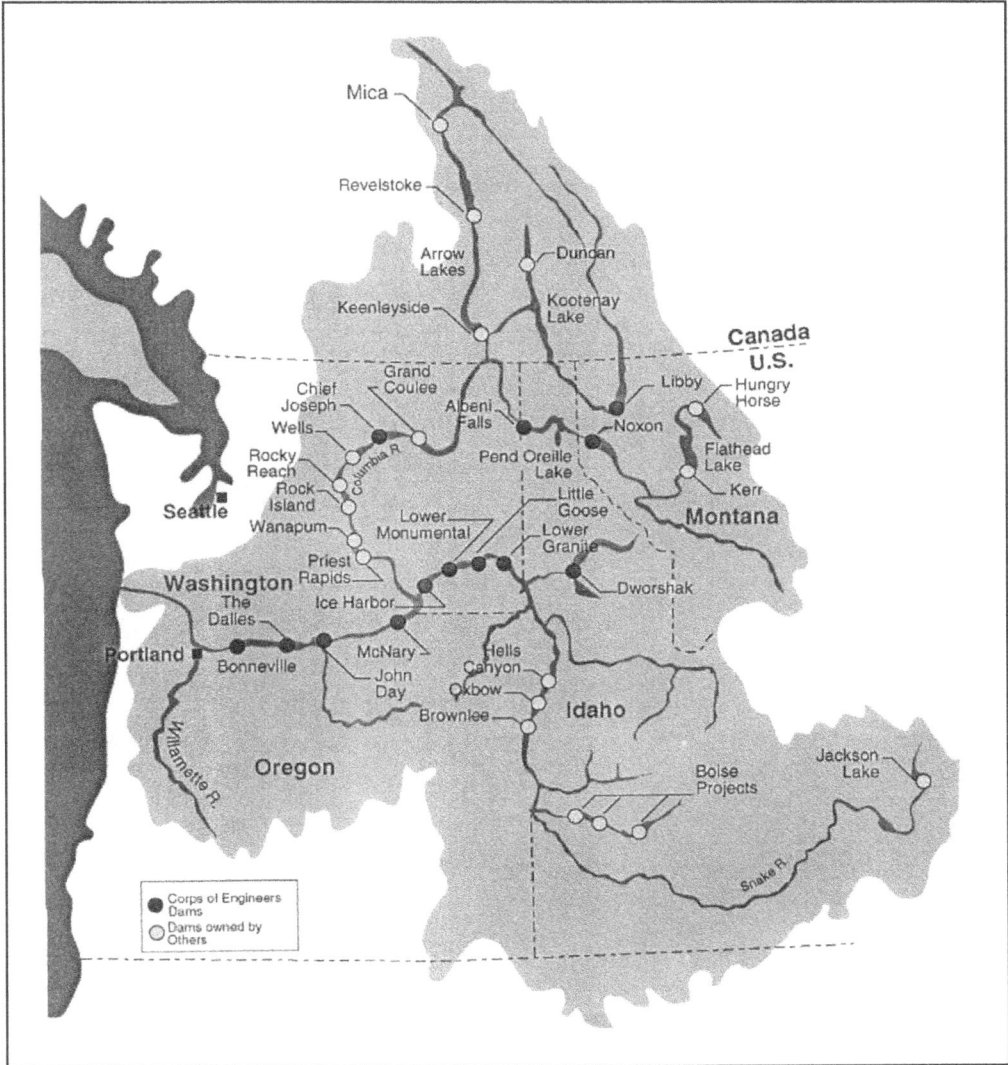

Courtesy of the U.S. Army Corps of Engineers

Over the next half century, $200 million in Mitchell Act funds supported construction of roughly 40 hatcheries, nearly all of which were situated below Bonneville Dam. While this location made sense in terms of avoiding dam-related mortalities, it served to shift salmon migration to below Bonneville Dam, away from the fishing grounds of the Columbia Basin Indian treaty tribes. Moreover, lower basin hatcheries encouraged the harvest effort to move toward the ocean. Ocean harvests are necessarily unselective; fish from many rivers swim together in the ocean, including those from streams predominated by hatchery fish and those producing only wild fish. Because far fewer fish are necessary to produce eggs to sustain a hatchery than the number of wild fish necessary to maintain a spawning wild run, hatcheries encouraged harvest managers to set high ocean harvest levels. Increased ocean harvests produced overharvests of wild runs. This incidental overharvest of wild salmon, due to inundating the ocean with hatchery fish, went largely unnoticed until biologists began to focus on the importance of salmon genetics in the 1970s.[24]

The Columbia Basin's overwhelming commitment to hatcheries was extended to the Snake River in the late 1970s. Congress authorized a $70 million hatchery program designed to compensate for salmon losses resulting from the construction and operation of the four Corps of Engineers' dams on the Lower Snake that made Lewiston a deepwater port. Unfortunately, this investment was not accompanied by a commitment to change dam operations to restore streamflows to facilitate the downstream migration of the hatchery-produced salmon. Further, scientists began to question whether hatcheries were capable of rebuilding salmon runs. Studies showed that hatchery fish damaged wild salmon by transmitting diseases, competing for limited food and habitat, and jeopardizing the genetic integrity of wild fish through interbreeding. Other studies demonstrated that hatchery fish do not perform nearly as well in the river environment as wild fish. Many biologists began to consider hatcheries as a narcotic, serving to conceal the true magnitude of the problems that dam-induced alterations in streamflows pose for wild salmon.[25]

The marriage of hatcheries to dam building in the Columbia Basin is perhaps best illustrated by comparing the Columbia to the Fraser River in British Columbia. The Fraser, which has supplanted the Columbia as the world's largest salmon producer, is undammed. Although hatcheries proliferated on the Fraser until 1925, they were thereafter phased out, due to budgetary constraints as well as questions about their effectiveness. British Columbia renewed its interest in hatcheries in the late 1960s, but situated most of them on Vancouver Island, not on the Fraser. The salmon runs of the undammed Fraser are now growing without hatcheries due to a large-scale commitment of constructing spawning channels, fishways, gravel box incubators, and maintaining natural river flows. Meanwhile, the hatcheries on the Columbia have been unable to revive what were once the world's largest salmon runs.[26]

The failed promise of salmon hatcheries is the subject of Chapter 6, which this book considers the salmon's "second promise."

The End of Dam Building

The 1960s, still in the era of the Columbia Basin's headlong commitment to dam construction, also saw the region's first rejection of a dam. Oddly enough, the rejection came from the U.S. Supreme Court, in a remarkable 1967 decision by that Court's first (and thus far perhaps only) environmentalist, Justice William O. Douglas. Justice Douglas's opinion overturned the Federal Power Commission's grant of a license to construct the High Mountain Sheep Dam at the confluence of the Salmon and Snake Rivers in Idaho. Justice Douglas interpreted federal law to impose an affirmative obligation on the Commission to preserve salmon runs, writing:

> [t]he importance of salmon and steelhead in our outdoor life as well as commerce is so great that there certainly comes a time when their destruction might necessitate a halt in so-called 'improvement' or 'development' of waterways. The destruction of anadromous fish in our

western waters is so notorious that we cannot believe that Congress . . . authorized their ultimate demise.

This decision effectively saved from destruction, for a time at least, Idaho's remaining salmon runs. The result was confirmed by Congress in 1975, when it established the Hells Canyon National Recreation Area, which prohibited dam construction and required preservation of the area's free-flowing rivers and its fish and wildlife.[27]

But blocking new dams would not be sufficient to save the Columbia Basin salmon; the operation of existing dams had to be changed. The need for changed operations became apparent in the drought year of 1977, when a hundred-year record low snowpack produced a record low spring runoff. Faced with the prospect of disastrous juvenile salmon losses due to low streamflows, fish and wildlife officials convinced the Northwest governors to intervene and persuade federal water managers — the Bonneville Power Administration, the U.S. Army Corps of Engineers, and the Bureau of Reclamation — to release water from storage and manipulate the resulting streamflows to aid salmon migration. As a result, 1.4 million acre-feet of water was released on the mainstem Columbia, but no additional water was made available on the Snake, where a futile attempt was made to trap and haul downstream migrating salmon in trucks. Although the salmon mortalities in 1977 proved to be disastrous, the emergency "fish flow '77" indicated that salmon mortalities on the Columbia might be reduced through systematic changes in dam operations. This lesson would prove to be an important one when Congress began to seriously consider a salmon restoration program three years later as part of the Northwest Power Act.[28]

Indian Treaty Fishing Rights

For most of the 1970s, however, the paramount salmon issue was not restoring salmon runs but allocating harvest rights. Using the same 19th century treaties which the Supreme Court interpreted to guarantee access to their traditional fishing grounds more than 60 years before, the region's Indian tribes challenged state harvest regulations, which they claimed unfairly restricted their harvest rights. In 1969, federal district judge Robert Belloni struck down Oregon regulations that he found deprived the tribes of a "fair share" of the salmon harvest. The next year Puget Sound tribes sought to define a "fair share" in a Washington case in which they also claimed environmental protection for salmon under their treaties. Federal district judge George Boldt declined to rule on the environmental issue, but in 1974 he concluded that the treaty language guaranteeing the "right of taking fish in common" with non-Indians entitled the tribes to half of the harvestable salmon destined for traditional native fishing sites.[29]

The "Boldt Decision," as it came to be called, was reviled by non-Indian fishermen and state regulators, especially in Washington where a minor "fish war" saw shots fired. The decision — which was twice affirmed by federal appeals courts and eventually, in 1979, by the U.S. Supreme Court — substantially reallocated salmon harvests despite, as one judge noted, "the most concerted official and private efforts to frustrate a decree of a federal court witnessed in this century. . . . except for some desegregation cases."[30]

Judge Boldt determined that the tribal harvest of Puget Sound salmon was just two percent of the total harvest; after the decision the tribes had a judicially enforceable right to 50 percent. This had the effect of reallocating some of the harvest from the ocean (where non-Indians dominated) to the rivers and estuaries (where the tribes' traditional fishing sites were located). This reallocation required a much more sophisticated understanding of the migration patterns of individual salmon runs. Thus, the Boldt Decision ushered in the modern era of salmon management, in which biologists sought to understand the salmon's complete life cycle — from spawning to river and ocean migration back to spawning. "Gravel to gravel" management became the focus of attention.[31]

The sophistication of salmon biology increased when courts subsequently recognized Indian tribes as co-managers of the salmon resources, and tribes began hiring their own biologists to work with federal and state biologists. Although sometimes they disagreed, federal, state, and tribal biologists often found themselves advocating the same measures, particularly with respect to habitat protection and streamflow restoration.[32]

In 1980, the year after the Supreme Court affirmed the Boldt Decision, the tribes went back to federal court in an effort to resolve the environmental protection issue that Judge Boldt had deferred. In what was called the "Phase 2" case, federal district judge William Orrick determined that there was indeed a right of environmental protection for salmon implicit in the treaties, but five years later an appeals court vacated his decision as premature. Although the appellate court did not reach the merits of Judge Orrick's reasoning, it vacated his decision, concluding that deciding the issue in the absence of a concrete factual controversy involving environmental degradation of salmon habitat was unwise. In the ensuing decade, the tribes decided to concentrate their efforts to protect and restore salmon habitat on the fish and wildlife program created by the Northwest Power Act rather than in court. Thus, the question of whether the treaties entitle the tribes to environmental protection of salmon habitat remains unresolved to this day.[33]

Chapter 12 examines the modern treaty fishing rights decisions, labeled here as the "ultimate promise" to salmon, focusing on whether the treaties promise the tribes that there will be fish to harvest.

The Northwest Power Act

The 1980 Northwest Power Act was a pathbreaking piece of legislation because it promised to protect and restore Columbia Basin salmon runs (as well as other fish and wildlife) "to the extent affected by the development and operation" of the basin's dams. The Act's legislative history made clear the statute's goal was to elevate the status of fish and wildlife to that of a "coequal partner" with hydropower, "on a par" with the other authorized purposes of the dams. The vehicle for achieving this operational equality was a basinwide restoration program, the Columbia Basin Fish and Wildlife Program, to be developed by a new interstate agency, the Northwest Power Planning Council. The statute directed the Council to formulate this program based on the "best available" scientific knowledge. However, it cautioned that biological outcomes were favored over economic ones and specifically called for restoring river flows sufficient to "improve the protection, migration and survival" of salmon runs.[34]

The Council promulgated its program in 1982, after the region's fish and wildlife agencies and Indian tribes submitted some 700 pages of recommendations for program measures. The program called for increased river flows in the spring to facilitate salmon migration, improvements in fish bypass at the dams, habitat protection and restoration measures, and use of hatcheries where they would not conflict with the program's preference for preserving and restoring spawning salmon. But the river flows in the program were not the fixed flows the fish and wildlife agencies and tribes recommended. Instead, the Council adopted what it called a "water budget," a dedicated volume of water that would be in addition to "base power flows," and placed it under the control of representatives of the region's fish and wildlife agencies and Indian tribes. Unfortunately, this water budget contained too little water to produce biologically sound river flows, the base power flows turned out to be unreliable, and the federal agencies operating the dams frequently ignored the flows called for by the fish and wildlife agencies and tribes. For example, during one spring the water budget was met only six of twenty-six days during the critical migration season.[35]

Despite its inability to significantly restructure hydroelectric operations, the Columbia Basin Fish and Wildlife Program and the statute which created it marked a considerable change in salmon law and policy. The statute established a goal of regionwide salmon restoration, and the Northwest Power Planning Council supplied an open regional forum in which hydropower/ salmon tradeoffs as well as other salmon restoration issues, such as the feasibility of relying on hatcheries to supplement wild fish runs, could be publicly discussed and debated. The program's provisions that called for sensitivity to genetic issues, development of fish bypass systems at mainstem dams, and protection of areas from future hydroelectric development, made important contributions to salmon restoration efforts.

Nonetheless, the statute and the program promised more than they were able to deliver. The Act's limited scope — focusing exclusively on the hydroelectric system while overlooking harvest regulation, federal land management activities, and irrigation diversions — made a comprehensive approach to salmon restoration impossible. Moreover, the Act contained weak enforcement language that encouraged federal water management agencies like the Army Corps of Engineers and the Bonneville Power Administration to consider the program's measures as merely advisory, so they often failed to carry out the program's mainstem flow provisions. The Council also proved to be a poor overseer of program implementation, as was Congress. Thus, while the program charted an innovative, systematic approach to salmon restoration, it failed to achieve its basic goal of producing substantial improvements in salmon run sizes. The Northwest Power Act experience is emblematic of a recurrent theme in Columbia Basin salmon restoration efforts: a statute is passed or an agreement is reached, based on assumptions that eventually turn out to be false or half-truths; then, as time passes, the institutional framework established by the statute or agreement becomes rigid and part of the problem.[36]

Chapter 7 analyzes the Northwest Power Act and the salmon restoration program it spawned, considered here as the "third promise" to preserve salmon.

Extending Harvest Regulation

Efforts to rebuild Columbia Basin salmon runs in the 1980s did not focus exclusively on implementing the Northwest Power Act, however. Two important agreements were reached concerning harvest rights. First, in 1977, some nine years after Judge Belloni ordered the states of Oregon and Washington to ensure that tribes with treaty rights had a "fair share" of the Columbia harvest, the states and tribes finally agreed to a management plan for harvests. The resulting Columbia River Management Plan set run-by-run harvest rights and fish spawning goals. This plan went beyond ensuring the tribes' harvest rights; it was the first approach to in-river harvest management aimed at ensuring that sufficient salmon would escape harvest to spawn and begin rebuilding the runs. However, the scope of the plan was limited to Columbia Basin harvests in state-regulated waters of Oregon and Washington; it had no effect on distant fisheries controlled by Alaska and Canada. Moreover, the plan was premised on hatchery production, which is now largely discredited as a restoration mechanism.[37]

The second agreement aimed to extend the reach of coordinated management to those Alaskan and Canadian harvests that intercept Columbia-bound salmon. Most Columbia Basin salmon migrate north to mature in the cold North Pacific in waters offshore of Alaska and British Columbia, where they intermingle with salmon from Puget Sound, the Fraser, and other rivers. In this "mixed stock" fishery there are strong economic incentives to intercept salmon spawned in other jurisdictions, and interceptions have been commonplace since the beginning of non-Indian fisheries in the late nineteenth century. In the early 1980s, however, a number of developments motivated Canada and the United States to reach a treaty whose goal was to reduce salmon interceptions. Both countries were undertaking large-scale expansions in hatchery production, and neither wanted to share the fruits of its efforts with intercepting fishermen. Moreover, British Columbia was implementing an aggressive habitat improvement program that promised to double Fraser River sockeye runs, which since 1930 had been shared equally with the United States under the terms of the Fraser River Convention. Another impetus was that in the early 1980s, biologists noticed a startling decline in both U.S. and Canadian chinook and coho, illustrating the need for a joint management plan.[38]

The result, after more than a decade of negotiations, was the Pacific Salmon Treaty of 1985. The treaty sought to ensure that each country's interceptions were roughly equivalent through 1) conserving the salmon resource by preventing overfishing and providing for optimum production, and 2) equitably apportioning harvests by assuring each country that it would receive benefits equivalent to its salmon production. Unfortunately, another treaty provision, cautioning against "undue disruption" of existing fisheries, made curtailing interceptions difficult. Thus, major interception fisheries in southeast Alaska and off of Vancouver Island continued under the treaty, resulting in considerable harvests of Columbia River salmon. Moreover, even though the treaty committed both countries to a coastwide rebuilding program for chinook salmon, the treaty was never interpreted to restrain habitat-damaging activities like logging, irrigation, and other contributors to water pollution. As a result, the treaty proved to be largely a disappointment, requiring amendments in 1999 that initiated a new "abundance-based" regime for managing harvests, promising significant, if overdue, conservation improvements.[39]

Chapter 8 considers as the "fourth promise" to salmon the attempt of the Pacific Salmon Treaty and its 1999 amendments to reduce international salmon interceptions.

The Endangered Species Act

The 1990s saw attention shift from the Northwest Power Act and the Pacific Salmon Treaty to the Endangered Species Act (ESA). Actually, the seeds of the ESA role were sown in the late 1970s, when salmon were first considered for ESA listing, and again in 1987, when a conservation biologist working for the Northwest Power Planning Council reported that over twenty salmon runs in the Snake River Basin were in danger of extinction, and that the Snake River coho were already extinct. (See chart 1.) This unsettling information focused concern on the weakest salmon runs, rather than the aggregate number of salmon coastwide. Public attention soon centered on the ESA, under which the first "threatened species" listing of a salmon run, the Sacramento River winter chinook, occurred in 1989.[40]

In March 1990, after a year in which only two sockeye spawners returned to Idaho's Redfish Lake, the Shoshone-Bannock tribe sought to include Snake River sockeye under the ESA's protections by filing a petition with the National Marine Fisheries Service (NMFS). Two months later, a coalition of environmental groups filed ESA petitions seeking listing of spring, summer, and fall runs of Snake River chinook and Lower Columbia River coho. The petitions ushered in a new era of salmon law and policy. Senator Mark Hatfield of Oregon immediately asked federal and state fishery agencies for a status report on the petitioned salmon runs. The ensuing report painted a chilling picture of salmon runs in drastic decline. For example, in 1989 the Snake river

Chart 1 — Columbia Basin Salmon Runs: An Historical Perspective

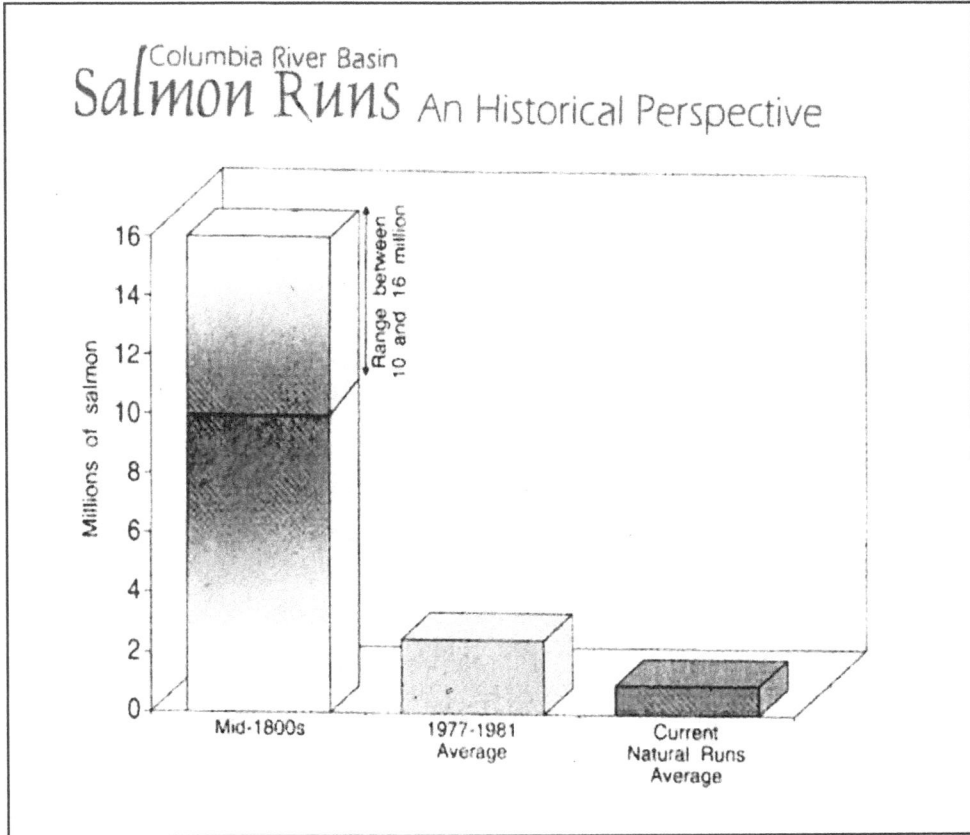

Courtesy of the Northwest Power Planning Council

spring chinook redd (nest) count was only six percent of what it had been in 1961.[41]

Senator Hatfield convened a series of meetings among the major users of Columbia Basin streamflows — representatives of hydropower, irrigation, and navigation interests and also environmental groups and Columbia Basin Indian tribes — to consider measures to aid the imperiled salmon runs. These meetings, dubbed the "Salmon Summit," ultimately were unable to produce a recovery plan for the petitioned stocks. However, the summit did give birth to a proposal, championed by Idaho Governor Cecil Andrus, to draw down the four reservoirs on the Lower Snake River during the spring migration to increase river flows, and thereby benefit the salmon runs. This reservoir drawdown proposal was quickly embraced by a coalition of environmentalists, fishery groups, and Indian tribes, but it was vigorously opposed by hydropower, irrigation, and navigation interests. Another notable initiative was a Bureau of Reclamation study that examined a variety of options for securing water from the Upper Snake River Basin, including using the Snake Basin water bank to lease water for fish flows. This too drew opposition, this time from Idaho irrigators. After Governor Andrus left office, Idaho began to oppose any increase in streamflows for salmon which would require storage releases from reservoirs located in Idaho.[42]

In March 1991, five months after the Salmon Summit failed to reach an agreement to increase Columbia Basin streamflows, the American Fisheries Society reported that the salmon crisis was not limited to the Columbia Basin but was in fact a coastwide problem. Its report, *Pacific Salmon at the Crossroads*, suggested that the imperiled Columbia runs were only the tip of an iceberg, with over 100 runs of wild salmon facing "a high risk of extinction" from central California to the Canadian border.[43]

While the NMFS was considering the ESA petitions, the Northwest Power Planning Council began amending its fish and wildlife program to provide increased protection for migrating salmon. These amendments, which offered the first improvements in mainstem flows since 1982, were approved in late 1991. They were too late to deter the ESA process, however: Snake River sockeye were listed as endangered in November 1991, and Snake River chinook were listed as threatened in April 1992. By 2000, NMFS had listed 12 Columbia Basin salmon runs and a total of 26 Pacific salmon species from central California to the Canadian border.[44]

Under the ESA, once a species has been listed all federal actions that might significantly adversely affect the species or its habitat are scrutinized by NMFS in "biological opinions" to ensure that such activities will not jeopardize the continued existence of the species. For ESA-listed salmon, this scrutiny has included annual hydroelectric operation and harvest management plans, hatchery operations, and also timber harvests and grazing on federal lands. For a time, the ESA listings even led to a court injunction barring most federal land management activities such as timber harvesting, grazing, and road building. The ESA thus had the effect of broadening the activities subject to scrutiny beyond hydroelectric operations to include all aspects of the salmon life cycle.[45]

The ESA's wider scope of inquiry also broadened the opposition to salmon measures, as an alliance of utilities, industries, irrigators, and ports — named the Columbia River Alliance — was formed to provide a united front among water users. Interestingly, the alliance did not claim to oppose the goal of salmon restoration, merely the means. It especially opposed restructuring Columbia River dam operations to increase river flows for salmon and rested this opposition on grounds of science, claiming a lack of scientific proof of the benefits of increased flows. The alliance's preferred salmon restoration plan relied heavily on trucking and barging juvenile salmon, a program which federal dam operators have been pursuing with little apparent success since the 1970s. The controversial barging program would become a target of fishery advocates in the 1990s.[46]

Strangely, although the prospect of ESA listing prompted the Northwest Power Planning Council to boost river flows under its program, the ESA biological opinions actually produced few changes in hydroelectric operations beyond those called for by the Council's program. Despite widespread complaints from groups like the Columbia River Alliance about the inflexibility of decision making under the ESA, there was apparently sufficient flexibility in the ESA to justify making few changes in river operations beyond those called for by the Northwest Power Planning Council.[47]

Court Intervention

This preference for incremental change would not stand, however. NMFS's 1993 biological opinion on hydroelectric operations was challenged by a coalition of states and Indian tribes, and the Northwest Power Planning Council's 1991 amendments were challenged by a coalition of environmental groups and tribes. Both challenges met with success, as the courts found that both actions failed to satisfy statutory requirements calling for increased salmon protection. One judge described the management of the hydroelectric system as "seriously, 'significantly,' flawed because it is too heavily geared toward a status quo that has allowed all forms of river activity to proceed in a deficit situation." He decried undertaking only "relatively small steps, minor improvements and adjustments — when the situation literally cries out for a major overhaul."[48]

The response to the court decisions was confusion, as two separate plans were developed. The Northwest Power Planning Council's amended program included a phased drawdown of several reservoirs to improve salmon flows. Similarly, the plan advocated by Idaho Governor Andrus called for an additional one million acre-feet of storage water for fish flow augmentation and imposed limits on trucking and barging juvenile salmon. NMFS's revised biological opinion, on the other hand, made no commitments to reservoir drawdowns, called for no additional storage water for flow augmentation, imposed no immediate limits on trucking and barging salmon, and instead relied on detailed dam operational changes that, the Service contended, would give priority to fish flows over hydropower production. Throughout the 1990s, it was the Service's plan which governed river operations. In 2000, NMFS promulgated a new five-year BiOp which again rejected reservoir drawdowns or dam breaching in favor of an improved transportation program and "offsite mitigation" measures which emphasized protection and restoration of habitat to be undertaken mostly by entities other than federal water agencies.[49]

Chapter 9 explores the listings of Columbia Basin salmon under the Endangered Species Act and the resulting restoration efforts, the "fifth promise" of salmon preservation.

Congressional Intervention

1995 also witnessed the first serious congressional efforts to curtail salmon restoration efforts. With a new Republican congressional majority calling for reductions in or elimination of environmental regulation, Northwest legislators began to suggest that salmon recovery was too expensive. Senator Slade Gorton of Washington, a prime sponsor of a bill to curtail the reach of the Endangered Species Act, claimed that it was time to recognize that some salmon runs should be allowed to go extinct. Oregon's Senator Mark Hatfield, in an effort to preserve the financial viability of the Bonneville Power Administration (BPA), sponsored a bill that would place a cap on salmon recovery costs. Although neither of these efforts bore legislative fruit, a "salmon budget" was administratively imposed on fish and wildlife measures.[50]

Further, responding to critics who believed that salmon restoration measures like reservoir drawdowns were based on flimsy science, Senator Gorton succeeded in amending the Northwest Power Act to require independent scientific review of fish and wildlife measures funded by BPA revenues. The scientific review process would substantially change the funding of fish and wildlife projects, especially hatchery funding and research. But several scientific studies subsequently concluded that effective restoration of Columbia Basin salmon would require radical restructuring of hydroelectric dam operations and perhaps even elimination of some Columbia Basin dams — hardly the result Senator Gorton anticipated his amendment would produce.[51]

The Clean Water and Federal Power Acts

Although the ESA was widely viewed as the ultimate protection for salmon listed under its provisions, the statute contained enough administrative discretion to permit NMFS to sanction few changes in hydroelectric operations. As a result, salmon advocates pursued other legal mechanisms, such as ensuring that water quality is sufficient to promote salmon spawning and rearing. The federal Clean Water Act's goal is in fact to provide fishable waters, and there have been several recent developments aimed at achieving that objective, including a NMFS decision to subject state water quality standards in Oregon to ESA biological consultation and a judicial determination that the operation of federal dams on the Lower Snake River violates Washington's water quality standards. These issues are taken up in Chapter 10, concerning the Clean Water Act's promise for salmon.

A less obvious vehicle for salmon protection is the relicensing of nonfederal hydroelectric dams under the Federal Power Act. Although the agency responsible for licensing, the Federal Energy Regulatory Commission, historically has been insensitive to fish and wildlife concerns, several Federal Power Act provisions authorize other federal agencies to attach mandatory conditions to decisions to relicense hydroelectric projects. In recent years, these conditions have produced significant changes at many projects, including some which have been or are scheduled for removal because the cost of relicensing them is prohibitive. Chapter 11 explains these developments as a "hidden promise" of salmon protection.

Dam Breaching

The Northwest Power Planning Council's seasonal drawdown program was never implemented, due to changes in Council membership which produced a political stalemate and uncertainties about the program's enforceability. But in 1996, the Council's independent scientific group, asked by the Council to evaluate the scientific underpinnings of its program, issued a report that sharply criticized the program for lacking a coherent conceptual foundation. The scientists concluded that the program amounted to merely a "collection of individual measures proposed by a diverse constituency" and was based on the flawed assumption that "economically desirable fish populations can be managed in isolation from other components of the ecosystem." The report was especially critical of the program's emphasis on technological fixes, like hatcheries and artificial transportation, as substitutes for lost ecosystem functions and concluded that these technologies had failed. The most arresting aspect of the report was its recommendation that restoration efforts be concentrated in alluvial reaches of the mainstem river, which before the dam building era were the most prolific salmon producers, but which are now drowned in reservoirs. The report suggested that permanent drawdowns of reservoirs, like John Day and McNary, to restore salmon spawning areas were the best way to restore the Columbia's salmon runs.[52]

The Council's scientists gave support to calls for permanent, rather than seasonal, reservoir drawdowns, which could require breaching of dams. The call for dam breaching gained momentum when several other scientific studies concluded that the truck and barge transport program was extremely unlikely to recover listed salmon runs. The dam breaching proposal that received the most attention was the proposal to breach the four federal dams on the Lower Snake River. These dams were authorized as make-work projects toward the end of World War II, and today produce relatively little hydropower and no flood control; they supply irrigation for only a dozen or so corporate farms. But the Lower Snake Dams do create a slack-water navigation channel that makes Lewiston, Idaho a seaport, providing some of the most heavily subsidized grain transport in the world. Although several economic studies showed dam breaching to be an affordable option, breaching has been deferred due to significant political opposition.[53]

Chapter 13 examines the issue of breaching the Lower Snake River dams.

Ecosystem Management and the Uncertain Future

If the 1990s was the era of the Endangered Species Act, the first decade of the new millennium is likely to become the era of ecosystem management. The first ecosystem management plan in the Pacific Northwest was a consequence of the ESA listings of the northern spotted owl and the accompanying court injunctions of public land timber harvests. Instead of attempting to lift the court injunctions by amending the ESA or authorizing sales by appropriation rider, which had been the practice of previous administrations, the Clinton Administration devised the Northwest Forest Plan which aimed to allow logging, albeit at much reduced levels, while protecting both owl and aquatic habitat. Courts have ruled that the plan's provisions for wildlife surveys and aquatic protection are judicially enforceable, meaning that timber sales can be enjoined for violating these promises, even where the sales might otherwise satisfy the ESA.[54]

The fact that it took court injunctions to require the land management agencies to implement the provisions of the Northwest Forest Plan is hardly reassuring, however, and the fate of that plan in the Bush Administration is far from clear. Moreover, the plan extends only to the range of the northern spotted owl, which means that public lands east of the Cascades are not included. An effort to devise an ecosystem management plan for that area, the Interior Columbia Basin Ecosystem Management Plan, has run into stiff political opposition and may never be implemented.

On private lands, both the states of Oregon and Washington have attempted ecosystem management plans. Oregon's plan, an overt attempt to ward off ESA listing of Oregon coho, failed at its initial objective when a court invalidated NMFS's decision not to list in deference to the state plan because the plan was based on voluntarily and speculative measures and could not, according to the court, constitute the "adequate regulatory alternative" the ESA required. Moreover, NMFS determined that a centerpiece of the plan, the state's Forest Practices Act, had no "implementing rules that adequately protect coho salmon habitat."[55]*

In Washington, the Timber, Fish and Wildlife Agreement is not actually an ecosystem plan, but rather a consensus-based forum that aims to improve fish and wildlife habitat in managing non-federal forest lands. The agreement has produced new state rules that require fairly large buffer zones protecting fish-bearing streams from the

---

* After this book went to press, federal District Judge Michael Hogan struck down the Oregon coho listing because although NMFS included both hatchery and wild fish in its "evolutionarily significant unit" (ESU) on Oregon coho, it limited its management prescriptions to wild salmon. *Alsea Valley Alliance v. Evans*, 2001 WL 11005100 (D. Or. Sept. 10, 2001). The court decision cast a pall on the role of the ESA in salmon restoration, since most ESUs designated by NMFS have included hatchery fish. As explained in chapter 9, this cloud over the role of the ESA was due to a flawed ESU definition and can be readily lifted if NMFS would redefine the concept to deemphasize reproductive isolation and instead focus on ecological significance.

adverse effects of timber harvests within the critical habitat of listed Columbia and Snake River salmon. NMFS subsequently signaled its approval of the Washington approach in its rules under section 4(d) of the ESA. In addition, several timber companies and utilities have been negotiating habitat conservation plans with federal fish and wildlife agencies that, once approved, will authorize killing of listed species if consistent with the plans. Some of the questions surrounding these plans are discussed at the end of chapter 9.[56]

One harbinger of the role of ecosystem management in the future of Columbia Basin salmon is a basinwide recovery strategy devised by federal agencies to combat all four of the principal causes of salmon mortality: harvest, hatcheries, habitat, and hydropower production (designated as the "all-H" approach). The effect of this all-H approach is to direct attention away from dam breaching and to emphasize the importance of improving habitat in Columbia Basin tributaries and the Columbia River estuary. This alternative focuses attention on changing logging, grazing, and mining practices, and perhaps water diversions instead of breaching the Lower Snake Dams, even though removing the dams would create a 220-mile stretch of free-flowing river which would substantially increase survival of juvenile fish in the mainstem of the river. An undammed Lower Snake River would create potential spawning grounds five times as large as the Hanford Reach on the Mid-Columbia, where the only self-sustaining Columbia Basin salmon now spawn. The basinwide recovery approach will also increase the current costs of maintaining the dams, which exceed $200 million per year, by calling for increased water from Idaho reservoirs and increased enforcement of state and local rules protecting salmon-bearing rivers.[57]

There are several different ways to analyze this new ecosystem management approach to saving Snake River salmon. First, the divergence that the new approach attempts to create between dam breaching and habitat protection/restoration is fanciful, since dam breaching would create many miles of new spawning habitat. Second, the approach may be designed to buy time for the federal government to undertake a five to ten-year study of the costs and benefits of dam breaching, effectively deferring that decision to another generation of federal officials. Or it may buy enough time for some runs to go extinct. Third, if the new ecosystem approach seriously attempts to provide habitat benefits equivalent to dam breaching, a firestorm of political opposition from farm, forestry, and grazing interests — even greater than their opposition to dam breaching — is likely. One suspects that the will to impose such measures may be lacking.

If the resulting habitat protections actually were to prove sufficiently stringent and enforceable, it is possible that the protection may convince Idaho, and perhaps other states, that it is in the interest of water users to negotiate a comprehensive settlement of Indian water right claims. Such a settlement could lead to environmentalist support for impending hydroelectric relicenses, like the Hells Canyon relicensing, which would give stability to water rights holders and hydroelectric licensees in return for water user support of dam breaching. Finally, the new ecosystem approach may simply represent another failure to confront effectively the largest source of Snake River salmon mortalities while making it appear that meaningful recovery efforts are underway. If so, the new recovery approach will join numerous failed initiatives that have been tried over the years to save Columbia Basin salmon. Chapter 14 assesses the new ecosystem approach.

The book's final two chapters consider the future of wild salmon in the Columbia Basin and the lessons the Columbia Basin salmon experience may have for restoration efforts in other places. In order for wild salmon runs to survive the 21st century, both the public and policymakers need to understand the nature of the promises that have been made about salmon in the past, and why they have failed. This in turn requires dispelling a variety of myths that have grown up over the years. Chapter 15 reiterates the promises and exposes the myths. Chapter 16 draws lessons for elsewhere.

2 — THE SALMON

Pacific salmon are members of the family that includes not only their Atlantic cousins but also seagoing steelhead and rainbow trout. All are anadromous fish, beginning their lives in freshwater, migrating to the sea where they spend most of their adult lives, then returning to their natal streams to reproduce. Pacific salmon do not survive spawning, but some Atlantic salmon and steelhead trout do. This urge to spawn in the streams which produced them has been both a source of human wonderment and human wealth, for the salmon's remarkable homing instinct makes them easy to harvest. This chapter examines the origins and life cycles of Pacific salmon and explains some of the distinctive life cycle characteristics of each species of Pacific salmon.[1]

Unlike the other chapters of this book, which focus on salmon law and policy, this chapter is a kind of layperson's guide to the salmon life cycle. Without an adequate grounding in the basics of salmon science, salmon laws and policies are likely to be misguided.

Origins

Scientists think that all species of salmon originated in freshwater and gradually evolved into anadromous fish by following the flows of great glacial rivers seaward. This great freshwater flush diluted the salinity of the oceans sufficiently to encourage salmonids to venture into the marine environment. As the oceans began to cool around 25 million years ago (reaching current temperatures about eight million years ago), salmon developed anadromy to take advantage of increased food sources in the marine environment. But the frigid and turbulent waters of the ocean were inappropriate for nurturing young salmonids, so the fish returned to more sheltered riverine environments to reproduce.[2]

Most scientists believe that the separation of salmonids into Pacific salmon (*Oncorhynchus*) and Atlantic salmon (*Salmo*) occurred long before the onset of anadromy. Prior to the Ice Age, ichthyologists believe that some Atlantic salmon migrated through mild Arctic seas, making their way to the Pacific before there was a land bridge between North America and Asia. When the Ice Age joined the North American continent, blocking the Northwest Passage, Pacific and Atlantic salmon were separated permanently. Over the millennia since, the two types (different genera) of salmon have developed distinct genetic patterns, as the process of natural selection adapted each to the environment in which it exists. For example, Pacific salmon generally have more extensive ocean migrations, probably because they have a larger ocean in which to roam. Similarly, except for steelhead, Pacific salmon do not survive spawning, whereas Atlantic salmon often do.[3]

Life Cycle

The salmon's renowned homing instinct, which gives rise to its immense life cycle, is largely the product of an extraordinary olfactory sense. Salmon literally smell their way home, searching for the unique odor of their natal stream, although scientists believe they also employ salinity and temperature sensors, especially in estuaries. Salmon recently arrived in fresh water from the sea are called "brights." Brights enter fresh water at different times of the year, depending on the particular salmon species. The timing varies according to individual runs destined for particular watersheds. In the Columbia River, brights refer to a group of upriver fall chinook which include the Hanford Reach fall chinook, the last self-sustaining spawning population of salmon in the Columbia Basin. Most Pacific salmon spawn in the autumn.[4]

Once in river, salmon no longer feed; they live off the fat stored during their marine existence, when they eat ravenously. Those that have the farthest to travel upriver generally have the most fat; the famous chinook "June hogs," which once spawned in central Washington and British Columbia above what is now the Grand Coulee Dam, weighed fifty to seventy pounds. Pink salmon, which usually have shorter river migrations and reside in freshwater for shorter periods before spawning, need less body fat and usually weigh only four or five pounds.

When they return to the river, salmon are in the prime of their lives, but they deteriorate as they reach their spawning grounds. They ascend in schools, pausing to rest in river pools. Males change color patterns and, as their sexual organs develop, metamorphose. Male chum salmon, for example, grow canine-like teeth; hence, their popular nickname, dog salmon. (Alternatively, some contend that the name reflects the fact that by the time they reached freshwater, the chum's flesh was inferior, fit only for feeding to dogs.) Scientists speculate that these external changes signify a mature male to a female.[5]

Upon reaching the spawning grounds, females search for a suitable place to build a redd, or nest, in the gravel, usually in riffles or just below logs or boulders. Males congregate around nest-building females, competing with each other and sometimes fighting for the right to mate. An elaborate mating ritual occurs as the female takes as long as three days to prepare several redds. The dominant male is usually accompanied by other mature males as well as underage but sexually precocious salmon, called jacks, that encourage the dominant male to remain vigilant. When at last the female releases her eggs into the redd, the dominant male deposits his sperm, or milt, nearly simultaneously, for the milt is viable only for a very short time, the eggs for less than a minute. Many females deposit up to a thousand eggs in each of three or four different redds, allowing fertilization by the milt of males other than the spent dominant male, including the jacks. This competitive spawning helps to preserve genetic variation within the species. Each fertilized redd is then covered with gravel by the female, who guards the site from other fish until she deteriorates and dies along with her male partner only days later.[6]

As the salmon corpses float downstream in the fall, they supply winter food for scavenging birds like eagles, gulls, and crows, and carnivores like bears, wolves, coyotes, and cougars. But these predators seldom consume all of the carcasses, which, as they rot and decay, provide nutrients from the sea to the rivers, linking the marine environment with the freshwater environment.[7]

Within an hour of fertilization the eggs harden and become sticky, so as to anchor themselves to the stream bottom. The embryo inside forms within a week, first as a rudimentary eye and then a yolk sac, which is the only source of food until the young fish leaves the gravel and begins to feed on larvae and plankton the following spring. In the spring, when it needs more oxygen than the stream can supply, the embryo hatches into an alevin, which is a juvenile salmon that can swim but retains its yolk sac. About 99 percent of embryos in oxygenated streams in redds with porous gravel succeed in hatching, but silting of riverbeds — which reduces oxygen levels — or low water flows can cause premature hatching. In such streams the survival rate is much lower. Alevin are highly temperature-sensitive and remain in the redd for three or four weeks, consuming their yolk sacs in the dark streambed gravel and avoiding light until they leave the gravel to begin a perilous journey.[8]

Leaving the redd and yolk sac behind, the young salmon emerge from the gravel as fry while stream temperatures warm in the spring. Most fry migrate to nursery areas, sometimes downstream, sometimes upstream, although most chum and pink salmon go quickly to sea. Sockeye fry can remain in freshwater lakes up to three years before beginning their seaward migration as fingerlings, or smolt. Coho, too, can live for up to three years in freshwater, although typically they do not linger that long.

Chinook fry, which grow faster than coho, consist of two types: the ocean-type, typically found below the fifty-sixth parallel, which migrate to the sea in the first year (usually within six months, although they may rear in the estuary for an extended time); and the stream-type, which do not migrate to the sea until their second year, although in northern rivers, they may stay in fresh water for two years or more. Salmon fry lead an extremely precarious freshwater existence, subject to predation, starvation, and disease.

It is during this stage of the life cycle in which natural selection is most evident: 80 to 90 percent of salmon fry are lost through predation alone.[9]

The presence of dams can make the oceanward migration of the smolt, beginning in April and extending for some stocks until July, even more hazardous. Dams present passage problems for smolt: up to 15 percent can die at each dam, although mortality rates vary from dam to dam depending on project management, such as spill levels, and the availability of protective screens and sluiceways. In some watersheds, like the Columbia, smolt mortalities can surpass fry mortalities: cumulative mortalities can exceed 95 percent for some upriver runs. Large storage dams also deprive migrating smolt of the spring river flows they need to reach the ocean in a timely fashion. In the pre-dam era, most Columbia Basin smolt took a week to reach the oceans; now that migration can take three times as long.[10]

Little is known about the length of time that surviving smolt remain in the estuary following their downriver migration. However, the critical phase in the salmon's life history is when it adapts from fresh to saltwater. The time varies with species. One estimate, based on marking and recapture techniques, is roughly two weeks. If accurate, the young salmon grow at an astonishing rate during this time.[11]

Ocean migrations remain largely a mystery. Most Pacific salmon migrate north to rich feeding grounds off the coasts of Alaska and British Columbia, although a few turn southward. Some Columbia Basin hatchery fish have been programmed to turn southward to provide fish for Oregon harvests. The distance traveled varies among species and within stocks. Pink salmon can travel over 2,000 miles in just over a year; chum and sockeye, which can spend up to four years in the ocean, can cover up to 10,000 miles. Chinook and coho, the largest Pacific salmon, generally do not travel as far; many runs of chinook and coho cling to protected waters like the nearshore areas off British Columbia and southeast Alaska.[12]

The return to freshwater is highly variable depending on the species and its habitat. Some species, like chinook, coho, sockeye, and steelhead, produce sexually precocious males which return early, after just one year in the sea, instead of two to five years. Biologists think that these "jacks" supply insurance that female eggs will be fertilized; they also provide fishery managers with a preview of the relative abundance of the following year's returning adults, facilitating harvest regulation.

Because all species of Pacific salmon possess distinct life cycles, the following sections discuss some of the most characteristic differences among each. Not considered are two species, the cherry salmon, or masu (*O. masu*) and amago (*O. rhodurus*), because they are found only in Asia.[13]

Chinook

Chinook (*O. tshawytsha*), the largest salmon species, are also called kings, tyee ("chief" in Chinook jargon), springs, and quinnault. Chinook now average from 12 to 25 pounds, but historically some chinook exceeded 100 pounds. Chinook and sockeye are the great river ascenders of the species. Idaho chinook, for example, must surmount eight dams over 900 miles, gaining more than a mile in elevation. Chinook generally spend three to five years in the ocean, although in rare circumstances some stay longer. For example, prior to the construction of the Elwah River dams, the Elwah River chinook on the Olympic Peninsula may have lived a dozen years. Chinook generally spawn in the mainstem of rivers or in larger tributaries.[14]

Although chinook range from the Bering Sea as far south as the Ventura River in southern California, the Columbia River was historically the great breeding ground of chinook salmon. There are more than a thousand different spawning populations within that range, but chinook are actually the least abundant Pacific salmon species in North America. As previously observed, ocean-type chinook migrate during their first year, but stream-type chinook spend up to two years in freshwater. This variation has important management implications for the Columbia River, since it cannot be viewed merely as a transportation corridor for ocean-type chinook but also as essential rearing habitat for stream-type chinook.[15]

Chinook are referred to as spring, summer, or fall chinook, denoting the time of year they reenter freshwater. There is even a winter run of chinook in the Sacramento River. Spring chinook tend to spend some months in freshwater before spawning; they also usually spend at least a year in freshwater as fry before migrating to the ocean. Spring chinook generally spawn in a watershed's highest tributaries. Fall chinook, on the other hand, enter freshwater later in the year and tend to spawn lower in watersheds soon after reentering the river; their fry migrate to the sea some months later. Fall chinook are the only remaining salmon run harvested commercially by Columbia River tribes with treaty fishing rights, and wild fall chinook still spawn in the last free-flowing stretch of the Columbia Basin, known as the Hanford Reach. Parts of all Columbia chinook runs are listed under the Endangered Species Act.[16]

Coho

Coho (*O. keta*), or silver salmon, stay closer to the coast than chinook, traveling neither as far upriver nor as far in the ocean. Coho generally spend one year in freshwater before migrating, then two years in the ocean. Like other Pacific salmon, coho are mostly fall spawners, usually in the upper reaches of small tributary streams, although some coho stocks spawn as late as March. Like chinook, coho are found from the Bering Sea to northern California, although coho are smaller than chinook, averaging around 18 to 20 pounds.[17]

Major coho spawning grounds include coastal Washington and Puget Sound streams, Lower Columbia tributaries, including the Willamette, and Oregon coastal streams. Coho spawn in California as far south as Monterey Bay, but they are rare in the Klamath and Sacramento/San Joaquin Rivers. Snake River coho are now extinct.[18]

Coho harvests have long formed the economic bedrock of many coastal communities in the Northwest; consequently, coastal coho have suffered from overharvest since before the turn of the 20th century. When coho numbers increased in the 1960s and 1970s, harvests increased rapidly until populations in Oregon collapsed in

1977. Harvests declined from 3.9 million fish in 1976 to one million in 1977, and have remained depressed since, with a harvest of just 28,000 in 1997. Because they spend more time as fry in freshwater than most other Pacific salmon, coho are particularly vulnerable to stream degradation, such as siltation from timber harvests. In 1997, the National Marine Fisheries Service listed coho runs in northern California and southern Oregon under the Endangered Species Act. The next year all Oregon coastal coho were listed.[19]

Sockeye

Sockeye (*O. nerka*), also known as blueback or red salmon, are smaller than chinook or coho, averaging six to eight pounds, but are considered by many to be the choicest salmon of all. At spawning, males have bright red bodies. The sockeye's chief characteristic is that it spends most of its freshwater rearing in lakes, spawning in the lakes or in rivers close to them during the months of May to October. Sockeye spend as little as a few days to as long as three years in the lakes. The sockeye's adaptation to lake environments reduces interaction with other species during spawning, incubation, and rearing in freshwater.[20]

Sockeye, like chinook, are great travelers, both in fresh or saltwater, where they spend one to four years. Sockeye spawn as far south as the Sacramento River, but commercially important numbers occur only north of the Columbia River. The greatest producer of sockeye is now the Fraser River in British Columbia. Allocating Fraser River sockeye between Canadian and U.S. harvests was the subject of the 1930 Fraser River Convention, the 1985 Pacific Salmon Treaty, and the 1999 amendments to the treaty (see chapter 8). The sockeye populations of the Columbia Basin have been devastated by the loss of access to their spawning lakes, which mostly were in Canada, as a result of dams. Sockeye were the first Columbia Basin species protected under the Endangered Species Act. Sockeye reaching the only remaining lake accessible in Idaho, Redfish Lake, teeter on the verge of extinction and are now the subject of a multi-million dollar captive breeding program designed to rescue them. The most significant populations in the Columbia Basin are in Lake Osoyoos and Lake Chelan in the upper basin. Fraser River runs, on the other hand, without the obstacles presented by dams, have been healthy and self-sustaining, as have runs on undammed Alaskan rivers. Small landlocked sockeye, called kokanee (*O. nerka Kennerlii*), have been introduced in many places to mitigate salmon losses due to dams. Kokanee tend to become anadromous if they are given the opportunity.[21]

Chum

Chum (*O. keta*), or dog salmon, is the last of the Pacific salmon to return to freshwater in the fall. Chum generally do not travel far upstream to spawn; some spawn just above tidewater, and they rarely travel more than 100 miles inland, except in the Yukon River in Alaska. They enter rivers as early as July and spawn from September to January. Juvenile chum leave the river environment only a few days after emerging from the gravel. However, they are great ocean travelers, sometimes covering 10,000 miles in up to four years at sea.[22]

Chum average about 8 or 9 pounds at maturity, slightly smaller than coho. Their most distinctive characteristic is the development of dog-like teeth as they near spawning and death. Once plentiful in the Columbia and Oregon coastal rivers and spawning as far south as the Sacramento River, chum are now found mostly in Puget Sound and British Columbia streams. But the largest harvests in North America are in Alaska.[23]

Pink

The smallest of the Pacific salmon is the pink (*O. gorbuscha*), also referred to as humpbacks, due to a noticeable hump that adult males develop. Mature pink salmon average just four or five pounds, the smallest of the Pacific salmon species. Like chum, pinks spawn in the lower reaches of streams and leave freshwater almost immediately after emerging, usually within a few days. Unlike the other species, whose life cycle characteristics vary with the watershed, pink salmon always mature in two years.

On many Northwest streams, including those in Puget Sound and the Fraser River, pink salmon return only every other year, and have done so since the beginning of recorded history. Why this occurs is unknown, but it seems likely that it is a consequence of the fixed two-year life cycle in which one year's population never interbreeds with the next year's. On some rivers, like the Fraser, pink salmon spawn only in odd-numbered years; in others, like Bristol Bay tributaries, the major runs are in even-numbered years. Even on streams in which pink salmon spawn in both years, the runs are reproductively isolated and genetically distinct. Pink salmon are now abundant only in streams north of the Columbia River.[24]

Steelhead

Steelhead (*O. mykiss,* formerly *Salmo gairdneri*) is a sea-run rainbow trout that shares many characteristics of salmon. For example, like Atlantic salmon, some steelhead may spawn more than once, although most do not. A typical mature average steelhead weighs about 10 pounds, although some reach 30 pounds. Like coho, steelhead spend a good deal of time in freshwater before migrating to the ocean. Generally, their four-year life cycle is divided evenly between the river and the sea. Steelhead spawn later than salmon, usually in the winter and spring, from December to June, although they may enter rivers in any month of the year. Their historic range was from Alaska to northwestern Mexico, although today their southernmost reach is Malibu Creek in southern California. A total of ten steelhead runs were listed under the Endangered Species Act by 2000.[25]

Unlike salmon, which do not feed after returning to freshwater, steelhead do. This fact, combined with a fierce fighting instinct, has made steelhead perhaps the most prized of game fish. Sportsmen long ago convinced the states of Oregon and Washington to outlaw steelhead harvests by net, and the states' attempt to apply this ban to native harvests occasioned bitter court battles which reached the U.S. Supreme Court more than once (see chapter 4). Native fishermen never distinguished steelhead from salmon, and their late returns provided the tribes with winter food. Historically, the greatest producer of steelhead was the Columbia Basin.[26]

Throughout this book generic references to salmon include steelhead.

The Stock Concept

Cataloguing the various characteristics of the Pacific salmon species is somewhat misleading because, as Jim Lichatowich has shown, these generic life histories are just "central themes around which each population has developed a rich diversity in response to local habitat." The critical population component of salmon is not the species level, but the stock level. Pacific salmon species are composed of populations of fish within particular watersheds that spawn at a particular time, are effectively isolated and self-perpetuating, and do not generally interbreed with other populations. Moreover, because each stock has adapted to local environmental conditions over many years of evolution, they are not readily interchangeable with other stocks. Chinook destined for the same Snake River tributary would not be from the same stock if one began its upriver migration in the spring and the other in the fall. In short, since salmon and their habitat are inextricably linked, efforts to preserve and restore particular salmon species must focus on their individual life histories and habitat.[27]

That stocks were the building blocks of Pacific salmon was recognized in the U.S. as long ago as 1939 by biologist Willis Rich in a report to the Oregon Fish Commission. But that report was largely ignored by fish culturists in the operation of salmon hatcheries, and some biologists disputed the hereditary basis of stock differences. These doubts were laid to rest in a number of studies surveying the life histories and biochemical differences of various salmon stocks, beginning with W.E. Ricker's in 1972. Other studies confirmed that stocks transplanted to foreign streams reduced the survival rate of those fish. All of this was reported in the American Fisheries Society's 1991 report, *Pacific Salmon at the Crossroads*, which concluded that "stocks are the basic building blocks of the Pacific salmon species," and that "[t]he subdivision of a species into local populations which possess genetic differences that are adaptive is the fundamental basis of the stock concept, and it is this concept that must be incorporated into management if fishery resources are to be restored and maintained."[28]

The stock concept explains why some chinook stocks on the Oregon coast migrate north, while others migrate south; and why Oregon coastal chinook stocks vary widely in terms of length of juvenile stay in freshwater, length of stay in saltwater, age composition of spawners, even egg size. It also explains why Bruce Brown could report on two stocks of Dungeness River pink salmon, one of which is an early, upriver spawner, the other of which spawns much later in the lower river.[29]

The stock concept means that each run of salmon is genetically unique, adapted to local watershed conditions. Genetic differences between breeding populations of salmon should have influenced harvest management and attempts to propagate the species artificially through hatcheries. But the stock concept was not accepted until the 1980s, which allowed fishery managers to overlook the fact that harvest regulations led to extirpation of certain breeding populations. Similarly, hatchery operations, which assumed that salmon stocks were fungible, not only failed to maintain local populations but masked declines by allowing harvests to continue in the lower river and the ocean. Worse, hatchery fish can adversely affect spawning populations through interbreeding, disease, and competition for scarce food and habitat (see chapter 6).[30]

It was the stock concept which led the authors of the *Crossroads* report to sound the alarm at the precarious state of Pacific salmon. After surveying stocks in the four Pacific Northwest states, they found no fewer than 214 stocks depleted. Some 101 of these were considered to be at a "high risk of extinction," even though at the time of the 1991 report only one salmon species had been listed under the Endangered Species Act. The report precipitated widespread public recognition of the stock concept and helped to usher in the era of Endangered Species Act management.[31]

Diversity and Metapopulations

Related to the stock concept is diversity, both within and among populations and species. Salmon have diverse life histories, ecological adaptations, and genetic variations which allow them to sustain themselves through natural environmental variations. As long ago as 1938, biologist Willis Rich recognized that where a species is divided into numerous isolated populations, it is important to conserve each individual component group. While Rich was not the only biologist to recognize the significance of conserving diverse populations, the architects of the Lower Columbia Fishery Development Program in the late 1940s believed they could successfully transplant Upper Columbia Basin stocks to the lower river, in apparent ignorance of the need to conserve diverse population stocks adapted to local environments.[32]

Forty years later, in 1996, the National Research Council called for salmon management to recognize the existence of "metapopulations," instead of isolated stocks. The Northwest Power Planning Council's independent scientists concurred, although they noted that information on salmon metapopulations was quite limited and that metapopulation structure remains a hypothesis. The metapopulation concept is an outgrowth of the salmon's fidelity to natal streams, with relatively low but variable levels of straying. Fidelity to natal streams facilitates natural adaptation to local environments through natural selection. Straying among geographically adjacent populations enables recolonization of areas where local extinctions have occurred. Metapopulations are comprised of core populations — large, productive populations occupying high quality habitat — and satellite populations, which are less abundant populations occupying lower quality habitat. Core populations buffer metapopulations against environmental change and also contribute to the resiliency of regional salmon populations by serving as colonists to establish satellite populations in habitats where extirpation has occurred, or where populations have been severely depleted.[33]

An example of a core population is the Hanford Reach fall chinook in the Mid-Columbia, where high quality spawning and rearing habitat remain, and where 40,000 to 50,000 annual spawners have produced a relatively stable population. The independent scientists of the Northwest Power Planning Council speculated that Hanford Reach chinook could colonize adjacent habitats near the confluences of the Snake, Columbia, Yakima, and Umatilla Rivers and as far downriver as the area now inundated by the John Day reservoir. Small spawning populations of fall chinook also exist in the lower mainstem reaches of most tributaries, including the Snake River below Hells Canyon Dam and the lower reaches of the Grande Ronde and Imnaha Rivers in northeastern Oregon. Spring and summer chinook spawning populations are confined to headwater streams where high quality habitat remains, like wilderness areas in Central Idaho and the headwaters of tributaries like the Grand Ronde, the Imnaha, the Yakima, and the John Day Rivers.[34]

Environmental Sensitivity

The salmon's immense migrations, its heroic return to natal streams, and its economic, cultural, and religious value are more than sufficient to make salmon management a topical natural resource study. But the salmon's influence extends beyond its life cycle and the allocation of harvest rights because of its environmental sensitivity. Salmon require high quality cool water; sufficient streamflows to facilitate migration to and from the sea; stable, permeable gravel in the riverbed to promote spawning and incubation; and streamside vegetation and large woody debris in the stream to supply adequate shelter and food. These environmental requirements make salmon the ultimate indicator species of the health of river systems. Like the miner's canary, salmon test the suitability of rivers for a variety of other uses that depend on high quality water.[35]

This environmental sensitivity implicates a host of land and water use activities which lower river flows, increase sediment loadings and water temperatures, reduce riparian vegetation and large woody debris, and impose migration barriers. Thus, dam construction and operations, irrigation diversions, stream channelization, and land developments like logging, grazing, and mining all can damage salmon habitat. Theoretically, effective salmon management could lead to reform of a host of land and water developments, but in reality the multiplicity of causes of the decline of salmon habitat, coupled with the damage attributable to poor harvest management and hatchery practices, has provided a recipe for inaction. Since improvements from reforms in one sector could be canceled out by business-as-usual in another sector, there has been little incentive to change, and every incentive to point in other directions. An even greater obstacle to restoration efforts may be the fact that it is usually impossible to trace the benefits of any particular action throughout the salmon life-cycle due to confounding variables.[36]

Status of the Runs

Over the last century, Pacific salmon have disappeared from roughly 40 percent of their historic range in the Pacific Northwest and California (see maps 2 and 3-6). And many existing salmon runs are threatened with extinction. In fact, if areas with depressed runs are combined with those with extinctions, the total area of loss is two-thirds of the historic salmon range in the four states.[37]

Coastal populations are generally better off than interior salmon runs; runs in the north are usually healthier than those in the south. Those species that spend a greater proportion of their life cycle in freshwater — spring/summer chinook, coho, sockeye, and steelhead — typically are in worse shape than those — like fall chinook, chum, and pink salmon — that spend less of their rearing period in freshwater. However, in the Columbia Basin, fall chinook suffer from the greatest threat, due to an almost total loss of spawning habitat as a result of dams.[38]

The National Academy of Sciences reported in 1996 that slightly more than half of the chinook runs in the Puget Sound Basin were in depressed or critical condition. Slightly fewer than half of the coho runs were classified as depressed, with one stock considered critical. The scientists determined that all remaining sockeye runs were depressed or critical, as were half of the steelhead runs. But many chum stocks were healthy, as were most pink salmon stocks.[39]

The report concluded that coastal chinook salmon runs in Washington and Oregon were in better shape than the Puget Sound runs: it classified some two-thirds of Washington runs as healthy, while only slightly more than half were healthy in Oregon. However, 40 percent of the spring/summer chinook runs in Washington were depressed, and in Oregon 70 percent of southward migrating chinook runs (from the Rogue River southward) were depressed or of special concern. Virtually all known chinook populations in California were at risk of extinction. Most coastal coho runs in Washington were in good condition, although 70 percent relied in part on hatchery stocks. Oregon coho, which constitute the largest coho populations in the U.S. outside of Alaska, were overwhelmingly classified as depressed. California coastal coho, which once numbered in the hundreds of thousands, totaled fewer than 5,000 spawners; most populations were threatened or endangered, and the Sacramento River coho was extinct.[40]

Columbia Basin stocks have suffered some of the most severe declines on the Pacific Coast. In the late 19th century, Snake River sockeye fueled commercial fisheries on many lakes in the Salmon and Wallowa subbasins. However, those fisheries disappeared after dam construction, agricultural diversions, and fish management practices blocked upstream salmon migration. The sockeye runs were so devastated that none reached their last remaining spawning grounds in 1990, the year the Shoshone-Bannock Tribe petitioned for Endangered Species Act (ESA) protection. The major factors for the decline of the species cited by the National Marine Fisheries Service (NMFS) in listing the species were hydropower development and operations, water withdrawals for irrigation and for storage (mostly for irrigation), increased predation (encouraged by the dams), and natural drought cycles. In 1991, the year NMFS listed the species under the ESA, just four sockeye returned to Redfish Lake, their last remaining spawning grounds.[41]

Snake River spring/summer chinook once accounted for over 40 percent of the production for the entire Columbia Basin, producing more than 1.5 million fish annually in the late 19th century. By the mid-20th century, the runs declined to less than 10 percent of their historic strength. Dam development on the Lower Snake in the last forty

Map 2 — Areas of Salmon Extinctions

Range of Pacific
Salmon

Watersheds in which
at least one salmon or
steelhead extinction
has been documented

*During the 20th century, some
232 Pacific salmon stocks
went extinct in the areas
indicated above. Most
extinctions are concentrated
in the southern and eastern
portions of the salmon's range
because there human
activities like irrigation,
logging, grazing, and dam-
building, have been pervasive
and the climate makes them
more vulnerable.*

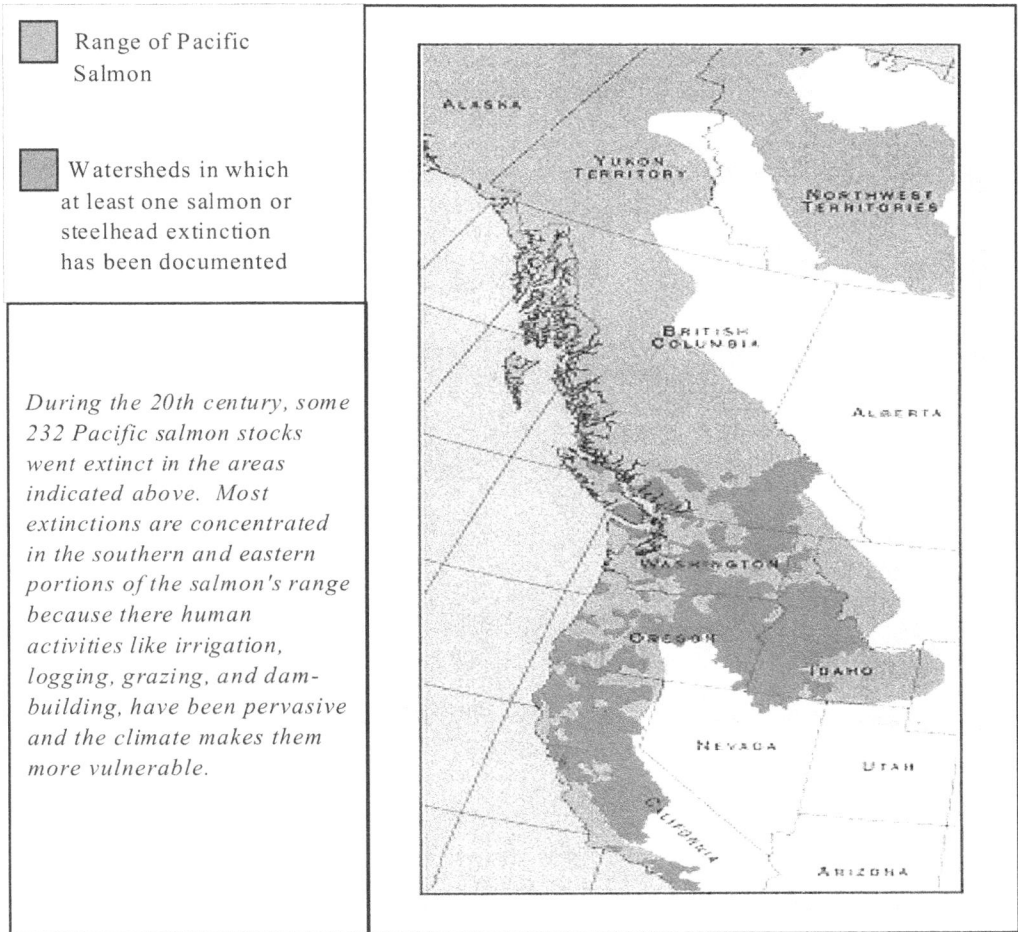

*Map reprinted with the permission of Ecotrust, 721 NW Ninth Ave., Portland, OR 97209.
www.ecotrust.org.*

Maps 3-6 – Current Health of Salmon Runs

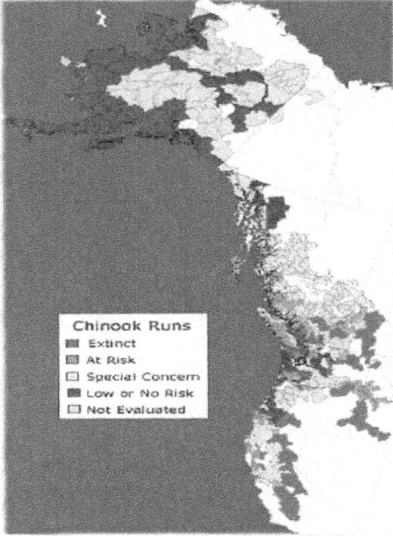

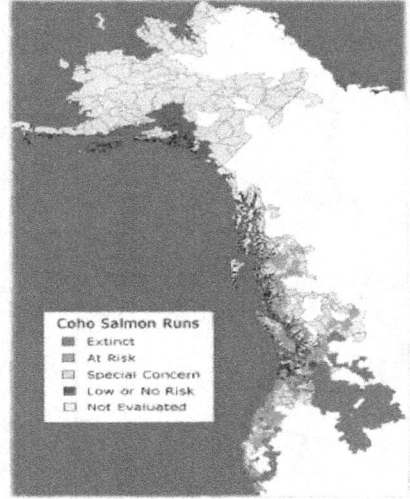

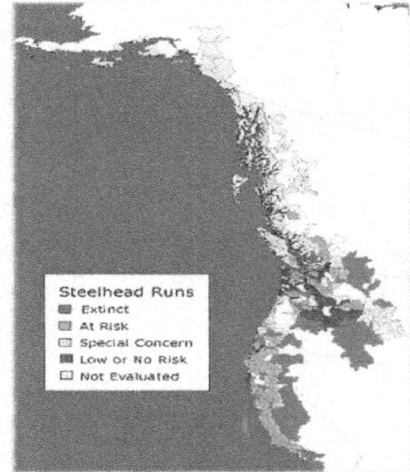

Map reprinted with the permission of Ecotrust, 721 NW Ninth Ave., Portland, OR 97209.
www.ecotrust.org.

years supplied what might be the *coup de grace* for salmon runs already reeling due to habitat degradation and harvest management. In 1991, the year before NMFS listed the Snake River spring/summer chinook under the ESA, the species registered an all-time low, numbering less than one percent of their original 1.5 million.[42]

Snake River fall chinook have fared even worse. The 1901 construction of Swan Falls Dam on the Middle Snake cut off returning adults from over one hundred miles of spawning habitat. Despite this loss, fall chinook populations stabilized around 70,000 adult salmon until the 1950s. At that time construction of three dams in the Hells Canyon reach of the Snake and four dams on the Lower Snake closed off critical habitat and presented serious water quality problems. Altogether, dam building throughout the Columbia Basin destroyed virtually all the fall chinook's mainstem spawning and rearing habitat, except in the Hanford Reach on the Mid-Columbia. In 1990, NMFS estimated that only 78 returning wild fall chinook passed the last of the Lower Snake Dams.[43] In listing both spring/summer and fall chinook under the ESA, NMFS cited many of the same factors which caused the decline of the sockeye: hydropower development, water storage and withdrawals for irrigation, and water pollution, including siltation from poor land use practices. Overharvesting was once a serious problem, but NMFS now considers hydropower development and operations to be the core threat to the species. NMFS noted that the small populations of both species presented significant risk of extinction due to random demographic or genetic events. The agency claimed that existing regulatory mechanisms were inadequate to increase survival chances, noting that the operational changes made to the dams and decreased harvest rates had failed to restore the populations. NMFS also determined that, in addition to the causes listed above, spring chinook population declines could be partially explained by poor ocean conditions. Hatchery operations posed a particular threat to fall chinook.[44]

Ocean conditions can play an overwhelming role in salmon productivity. An adverse ocean environment was almost certainly the reason for population declines beginning in the 1980s. Opponents of freshwater restoration efforts often cite oceanic variability as a reason not to undertake such efforts. But oceanic variations have existed for millennia without risk of widespread species extinctions. Not until the late 20th century did the cumulative effects of freshwater developments in the Columbia Basin reduce the salmon's abundance and diversity to the point where adverse oceanic conditions can produce extinctions.[45]

Snake River steelhead, including runs spawning in tributaries in southeast Washington, northwest Oregon, and Idaho, averaged 71,000 adults between 1990 and 1994. But only 9,400 were wild fish, and the late "B run" had only 2,400 wild fish. NMFS considered the wild runs to have suffered "severe declines" when it listed them under the ESA in 1998, especially the "B run." Over 80 percent of the steelhead passing the uppermost of the Lower Snake Dams were hatchery fish at the time of the listing. In some tributaries, according to NMFS, hatchery operations jeopardize the continued existence of wild steelhead in the Snake and Lower Columbia Rivers. Reduced populations leave Snake River steelhead subject to random genetic and demographic events that can produce extinctions.[46]

NMFS cited hydropower development as a key factor in the steelhead's decline. Other factors included increased in-stream and oceanic predation (the former, exacerbated by conditions created by dams), increased susceptibility to disease (due largely to hatcheries), genetic problems due to hatchery fish, and drought. NMFS pointed to poor land use practices on federal and private land, which produce higher water temperatures and siltation in streams, and which dramatically decrease the number of pool-forming objects in streams like boulders and downed trees. Listed steelhead are also subject to a large tribal harvest — until recently exceeding 30 percent — because the timing of the runs coincides with runs of other nonlisted, hatchery-produced fish subject to commercial harvest. NMFS recognized the inadequacy of existing regulatory structures, pointing to poor federal and state forest practices, weak enforcement of Clean Water Act protections for wetlands and water quality standards, and state harvest and hatchery programs which have had significant adverse effects on steelhead populations.[47]

In the Middle and Upper Columbia River, sockeye runs have fared better than the Snake River sockeye, although Yakima River sockeye went extinct due to the lack of fish passage at irrigation dams. Summer and fall chinook in the Mid-Columbia are now more abundant overall than in the 1930s, due to hatcheries, but five of fourteen wild stocks are depressed. The strongest population in the Columbia Basin is the fall chinook spawning in the last free-flowing stretch of the mainstem river, the Hanford Reach. Spring chinook populations in the Middle or Upper Columbia are all listed under the Endangered Species Act. Coho populations are largely extinct, as they are in the Snake.[48]

Steelhead numbers in the Mid-Columbia are higher in the aggregate than they were in the 1930s, again due to hatcheries. But thirteen of fifteen spawning stocks of summer steelhead are depressed, and another eleven are extinct. By 2000, NMFS had listed Upper, Middle, and Lower Columbia steelhead, Snake River steelhead, and Upper Willamette River steelhead, along with five runs of California steelhead. Upper Columbia steelhead, whose range extends from the Yakima River to the Canadian border, have had their habitat severely restricted by Grand Coulee Dam, which eliminated over 1,100 miles of habitat in 1939. Between 1939 and 1943 fishery agencies trapped all species of salmon at Rock Island Dam, on the Mid-Columbia below Grand Coulee, then transplanted them to hatcheries or released them indiscriminately in tributaries between the two dams, in an effort to produce widespread redistribution. This program redistributed steelhead without regard to their streams of origin and mixed stocks randomly in hatcheries. Since construction of Grand Coulee, wild steelhead in the Upper Columbia have continued to decline, both in absolute numbers and relative to hatchery fish. The remaining wild fish are not reproducing enough surviving offspring to replace themselves. For example, in the mid-1990s, wild steelhead in the Wenatchee and Entiat Rivers were replacing themselves at a rate of only 30 percent, a sure recipe for extinction.[49]

In the Lower Columbia, native coho are extinct, due to habitat loss, overharvest, and hatchery production. The remaining coho are all considered depressed, although fifteen of seventeen chinook runs in Washington tributaries are healthy. Steelhead populations are also depressed. Chum populations, the most abundant of the salmon species until roughly 1940, are severely depressed. They now amount to less than one percent of their historic abundance. Columbia River chum, which were harvested prior to a crash of the population in the 1950s, are also at less than one percent of their historic abundance. Even though there has been no commercial chum fishery since the 1950s, the population remains depressed, both in total numbers and in genetic diversity. In listing the chum as threatened in 1999, NMFS cited freshwater habitat destruction as the major cause of the species' decline, although chum spend relatively little time in freshwater compared to other salmon, making them less susceptible to the deleterious effects of inland human activities that are so devastating to sockeye, chinook, steelhead, and coho. Most damaging to chum was the use of streams for log transport and removal of large woody debris from streams, which actually is true throughout the Columbia Basin, adversely affecting all salmon runs. Other actions contributing to the decline include water withdrawals, loss of riparian habitat, and increased sedimentation in streams from logging, agriculture, and urbanization. Hydropower has played less of a role in the chum's decline than other salmon, but nevertheless has destroyed some chum habitat.[50]

The decline of the salmon has imposed hardships on both commercial and sport fishers, particularly in coastal towns where salmon harvesting has been a way of life for generations. Estimated costs are approximately $500 million per year and 25,000 lost family-wage jobs. But clearly those who have lost the most are Indian tribes, the Northwest's first fishers. This is especially true of the Columbia Basin tribes whose locations upriver make them particularly vulnerable. In 1996, the Chairman of the Columbia River Inter-Tribal Fish Commission reported that the average tribal fisherman *lost* $7,000 annually. Since, as the following chapters show, the tribes' 140-year-old treaties have been interpreted to assure the tribes a livelihood from fishing, it is hard to see how the current situation is not a blatant violation of the treaty promise.[51]

3 — FIRST PROMISE: THE STEVENS AND PALMER TREATIES

Salmon dominated life in the Pacific Northwest before white settlement. Trade in salmon enabled Northwest Indian tribes to become one of the world's few hunting and gathering economies that generated wealth beyond what was needed for subsistence. Salmon gave these tribes the economic prosperity to support a population density higher than anywhere north of Mexico. Salmon were abundant, available for harvest at predictable times, and could be preserved for later consumption. Salmon were the centerpiece of the natives' diet, their lifestyle, and their religion. Seasonal migrations of natives coincided with annual fish runs. Most tribes celebrated a First Salmon Ceremony which, despite regional variations, invariably involved a religious rite thanking the deity for the salmon's return and aimed at ensuring the salmon's continued abundance. These symbolic acts, attitudes of respect, and concern for the well-being of the salmon reflected the interdependence and interrelatedness of all living things that dominated the native world view. This attitude ensured that salmon were never wantonly wasted, and water pollution was generally forbidden.[1]

The Pre-Treaty Fishery

By all accounts, the native harvest of salmon was prodigious. The most recent estimate is 41 million pounds annually, roughly the same harvest that would take place during the "free-for-all" era of the late 19th century. Native harvests were more dispersed, however, and therefore more selective and sustainable. In the Columbia Basin, the most heavily fished sites were waterfalls, such as Celilo Falls and the Cascades on the Lower Columbia, Kettle Falls on the Upper Columbia, and Salmon Falls on the Snake. Native people from all over congregated at these communal fishing sites during the height of a run. The salmon-fishing natives of the Columbia Basin consisted of three distinct cultural groups: 1) the Kalapuya and Chinook Indians of the area west of the Cascades;

2) the Wishram, Umatilla, Walla Walla, Yakama, and Nez Perce tribes of the plateau east of the Cascades and extending into the Lower Salmon River drainage in Idaho; and 3) the Paiute, Shoshoni, and Bannock peoples of the Great Basin, in the Middle and Upper Snake drainages, including the Salmon River's headwaters. Natives used various harvest techniques, including seine nets dragged by canoes, harpoons and spears, small dams or weirs to trap salmon, hook and line, and dip nets; they also built fish platforms from which they could access rapids and narrows with nets and spears.[2]

Trade among these natives was brisk; salmon were exchanged for raw materials and manufactured goods. The accounts of the first white explorers documented the salmon-centered lifestyle of the natives. Both Manuel Quiniper in 1790 and George Vancouver in 1792 reported trading with the natives for salmon. On their overland journey down the Columbia in 1805, Lewis and Clark observed more than a hundred fishing sites, including the great commons like Celilo Falls, where more than five million pounds of salmon were harvested annually (see figure 1). Although these commons dominated inland fishing, most tribes recognized a system of private ownership to moderate harvests. Coastal and Plateau tribes especially recognized individual property rights, but large fishing sites were controlled by villages. While many tribes shared their sites with friends, neighbors and visitors, they were quite clearly granting use rights only, retaining their claim to ownership and monitoring harvests. Similarly, dipnet platforms were alienable, inheritable property.[3]

The Onset of White Settlement

The first white explorers of the Northwest were much more interested in the region's sea otters than its salmon. Following publication of Captain James Cook's *Voyage to the North Pacific Ocean* in 1784, which described the prices paid in China for sea otter pelts, ships of all nations rushed to the North Pacific coast and engaged in a fierce competition for pelts. By the early 19th century, this competition resulted in

Figure 1 — Native Fishing At Celilo Falls

Photo by Roy E. Huffman, 1954
(three years before Celilo Falls was drowned by The Dalles Dam)

the near extinction of sea otters, a half century before similar exploitation decimated the buffalo.

The natives had commercial relations with the fur traders — predominantly the British Hudson's Bay Company — in the early years of the 19th century. By selling their fish to the fur traders, native-harvested salmon reached markets in New York, San Francisco, Hawaii, and even Great Britain, South America, and China by the 1840s. Since there was little fishing by whites, Indian fishing increased to meet the demands of this export market.[4]

But as white settlers began arriving in numbers in the "Great Immigration" beginning in 1843, friction with the natives increased because the settlers wanted land as well as furs. When the United States and Great Britain settled their boundary dispute in the treaty of 1846, the white migration along the Oregon Trail increased, and it soon became apparent that peaceful settlement of the region would require reaching an accommodation with the indigenous populations. Congress affirmed its intention to take the natives' land by treaty, not by force, no fewer than five times between 1848 and 1853, promising, for example, not "to impair the rights of persons or property now pertaining to the Indians" in the Oregon Territorial Act. Yet Congress also authorized white homesteading of Indian land in the Oregon Land Donation Act of 1850. Large-scale homesteading made it imperative to reach an accommodation over land titles to avoid war. Many natives were receptive to a negotiated settlement, since by mid-century white diseases had reduced their numbers by more than 80 percent from the 50,000 who inhabited the region at the time of the Lewis and Clark expedition. A recent estimate suggests that by 1841 malaria had reduced the native population along the Willamette and Columbia Rivers by more than 90 percent in just a decade.[5]

Treaty Negotiations

The same year it authorized homesteading of Indian lands in the Oregon Land Donation Act, Congress passed a statute authorizing negotiations with the Indians of the Northwest, under which Indian lands would be purchased and the natives removed to lands not wanted by white settlers. Between 1851 and 1853, Anson Dart negotiated a number of treaties with tribes in Oregon's Willamette Valley, but the results were unsatisfactory to the natives because they required removal to small reservations with other bands and tribes with whom they may not have been friendly and because their hunting, fishing, and gathering places were not on the new reservations. Moreover, whites failed to wait for Congress to ratify the treaties before moving onto Indian lands, and white commissioners decided treaty disputes unfavorably to the natives. The Office of Indian Affairs refused to recommend that Congress ratify the treaties, because they allowed the natives to retain sovereignty over a portion of their lands, rather than being completely removed from white settlement areas. The Office viewed this as being inconsistent with the existing Indian policy of removal, established in the relocation of the tribes in the Southeast to Oklahoma in the previous decade. As a result, Congress failed to ratify the treaties, and violence broke out in southern Oregon and northern California.[6]

Against this grim backdrop, the newly appointed governor of the Washington Territory, Isaac Ingalls Stevens, who was also the territory's superintendent of Indian affairs and a surveyor of a potential transcontinental railroad to the Northwest, began to negotiate treaties to "pacify" Indians along the proposed route and open up lands for settlement and gold mining. In a remarkably short period of time — about seven months — Stevens and Oregon territorial governor Joel Palmer signed nine treaties with representatives of over 17,000 Indians that terminated Indian title to some 64 million acres that now comprises much of the states of Idaho, Montana, Oregon, and Washington for just $1.2 million. The tribes retained less than six million acres, two-thirds of which was later lost when the U.S. government adopted an "allotment policy" in the late 19th century under which much reservation land was divided into small parcels and awarded to individual Indians, while "surplus lands" were made available for white homesteading.[7]

Stevens and Palmer, like Dart before them, found that the Indians were willing to part with much of their land, but they opposed being removed to centralized reservations. As a result, Stevens was unable to achieve the degree of concentration he hoped for because the treaties called for much more removal than the Indians wanted.

Under this compromise, numerous small reservations were established in western Washington; east of the Cascades the reservations were larger.[8]

The record of the treaty negotiations reveals that both sides made good-faith pronouncements, as indicated in the following exchange between Governor Stevens and Chief Sealth (Seattle) at the Treaty of Point Elliott:

Governor Stevens:

> All this rejoices my heart, my heart is right and I am glad yours is. Our hearts are all the same. The Great Father wishes you to send him back a paper showing your desires and wishes. The Great Father thinks you ought to have homes as I before told you. The Great Father knows that you are Christians, looking to a future state, and that you have wives and children and he wants you to have a school where your children can learn to read and can be made farmers and be taught trades. He is willing that you should catch fish in these waters and get roots and berries back in the mountains. He wishes you all to be virtuous and industrious and to become a happy and prosperous community. Is this good and do you want this? If not we will talk further (All answer, we do).

> My children. I have simply told you the heart of the Great Father and what are his wishes and desires. But the lands are yours and we swear to pay you for them. We thank you that you have been so kind to all the white children of the Great Father who have come here from the east. Those white children have always told you that you would be paid for your lands, and we are now here to buy them.

> The whites are children of the Great Father, but no more his children than you are, have come here, some to build mills, some to till the land

and others to build and sail ships. My children, I believe that I have got your hearts, you have my heart. We will put our hearts down on paper, and then we will sign our names. . . .

Chief Seattle:

I look upon you as my father. I and the rest regard you as such. All of the Indians have the same good feeling towards you, and will send it on paper to the Great Father. All of them, men old men, women and children rejoice that he has sent you to take care of them. My mind is like yours. I don't want to say more — My heart is very good towards Dr. Maynard (a physician who was present) I want always to get medicine from him.[9]

The Makah tribe symbolized its trust by presenting Stevens with white flags at the Treaty of Neah Bay. One of the Makah leaders explained, "Look at this flag, see if there are any spots on it. There are none, and there are none in our hearts."[10]

Each side recognized that the treaties aimed to benefit both the natives and the white settlers. The settlers were to receive clear title to most of the region's land, while the tribes would receive money, missionaries, schools, and federal protection of their reserved properties. Governor Stevens explained to the Chinooks and Cowlitz along the Lower Columbia that the Great Father not only wanted to pay them for the lands the white settlers had seized but would also provide them with homes "where no white man will go without your wish." He also told the tribes east of the Cascades that if they agreed to move on to reservations, "we can better protect you from bad white men there."[11]

Although both sides exhibited good faith, the treaty negotiations can hardly be characterized as the product of equal bargaining. Governor Stevens was a young and ambitious politician, and he was determined to facilitate rapid white settlement. With the aid of lawyer and ethnologist George Gibbs, he organized small bands of natives into larger tribes, effectively creating new political entities, for the purpose of negotiating the treaties. The "chiefs" that Stevens appointed were naturally those who had some sort of friendly contact with whites, although most were men of importance in their communities. Various "bands," or fragments of tribes, were arbitrarily assigned a subordinate status to other "tribes," which would thereafter represent the subordinate groups.[12]

All "chiefs" had to have some familiarity with Chinook jargon, a simple dialect of about 300 words, derived from several native languages as well as from French and English. Many of the natives could not understand Chinook jargon, but Stevens' interpreter could, although there is some question as to his facility with native languages. The treaty language itself was written in English and was drafted before any formal "negotiation" meetings. In the federal government's view, those who signed the treaties had the authority to sell land, although there was no native precedent for signing legal documents, nor any culturally-sanctioned method of alienating land.[13]

The natives recognized they had to part with much of their land, but they not only resisted relocation to distant, centralized reservations, they zealously sought to preserve their historic fishing practices, due to their economic, cultural, and religious dependence on salmon. For example, one native chief at Neah Bay explained to Governor Stevens that he was willing to sell his land, but he wanted to retain the right to fish; another said he only needed a small piece of land where he would live as a friend to the whites, and they would fish together; another stated that while he did not wish to leave his land, he would give the whites half, retaining for himself "the place where the stream comes in." One native expressed the overriding sentiment of all the natives when he asked not to be forced to leave his fishing places, stating, "I want to fish in common with the whites."[14]

Stevens understood the critical importance the natives attached to maintaining their fisheries, whose economic importance increased with the advent of white settlement.

In a September 1854 letter Stevens wrote to the Commissioner of Indian Affairs, he stated:

> The subject of the right of fisheries is one upon which legislation is demanded. It never could have been the intention of Congress that Indians should be excluded from their ancient fisheries, but, as no condition to this effect was inserted in the donation act, the question has been raised whether persons taking claims, including such fisheries, do not possess the right of monopolizing. It is therefore desirable that this question should be set at rest by law.

In December 1854, another territorial officer wrote the Commissioner of Indian Affairs that "[t]he Indians on Puget Sound . . . form a very considerable portion of the trade of the Sound. . . . They catch most of our fish, supplying not only our people with clams and oysters, but salmon to those who cure and export it."[15]

Protection of native fishing was clearly a prerequisite to the signing of the treaties. At the Neah Bay negotiations, an Indian known as Kalchote Neah Bay thought he ought to have the right to fish, take whales, and get food where he liked. He was afraid that if he could not take halibut where he wanted, he would become poor. Governor Stevens informed him that, far from wishing to stop native fishing, he wished to send oil kettles and fishing apparatus to allow them to continue to fish. During the Treaty of Point No Point negotiations, a native chief expressed similar concerns:

> I wish to speak my mind as to selling the land — Great Chief. What shall we eat if we do so? Our only food is berries, deer and salmon. Where then shall we find these? I don't want to sign away all my land. Take half of it and let us keep the rest. I am afraid that I shall become destitute and perish for want of food.[16]

Governor Stevens clearly heard and understood these concerns. He repeatedly assured the natives that signing the treaties would guarantee the right to continue to fish as they always had. At the same Point No Point treaty negotiations, he said:

> Are you not my children and also children of the Great Father? What will I not do for my children and what will you not for yours? Would you not die for them? This paper is such as a man would give to his children and I will tell you why. This paper gives you a home. Does not a father give his children a home? This paper gives you a school. Does not a father send his children to school? It gives you mechanics and a doctor to teach and cure you. Is not that fatherly? *This paper secures your fish.* Does not a father give food to his children? Besides fish you can hunt, gather roots and berries. . . .

Stevens' assurances led to the signing of treaties which extinguished native claims to some 64 million acres but which also reserved to the tribes: 1) the exclusive right to harvest fish on their land reservations, and 2) "the right of taking fish" at all their customary fishing locations "in common with" the white settlers. It was clear at the time of negotiations that the natives bargained for this language in the belief that it would assure them access to their traditional fishing grounds, especially those outside of the newly-created reservations. The tribes were particularly concerned that the relatively small reserves did not contain a sufficient number of fishing sites to supply them with an adequate food supply. As Stevens noted in transmitting the treaties to Washington for Senate ratification, "the provisions as to reserves and as to the taking of fish . . . had strict reference to their condition . . . to their actual wants and to the part they play and ought to play in the labor and prosperity of the territory."

To this day, all of the Stevens and Palmer Treaty tribes celebrate their treaty signing in annual festivities and trace their political identity to the treaties of the 1850s. The right of taking fish was not merely the bedrock of what was one of the largest real estate transactions in history, but also the origin of modern sovereignty for many Northwest tribes.[17]

The Aftermath of the Treaties

Although the goal of the treaties was to promote peaceful white settlement, peace did not come immediately. Stevens had promised the tribes two years in which to move to their new reservations, but he broke that promise by opening up Yakama[*] lands to white settlement only twelve days after concluding negotiations. As a result, war broke out and quickly spread west over the Cascades to Puget Sound. The Northwest Indian War was a brief one, as the natives in western Washington were quickly routed, and their leader, Chief Leschi, hanged. East of the Cascades, however, the tribes were not "pacified" for some three years, until 1858. As a result, Congress delayed ratification of some of the treaties until 1859.[18]

After hostilities subsided, there were few disputes over native fishing for some two or three decades. This quiescence was due largely to the fact that salmon were abundant, white settlers relatively few, and most of the fish were harvested and sold by natives. For a while Stevens' prediction of the natives playing an integral part of the frontier economy through their fish harvests proved to be an accurate one.[19]

By the 1880s, however, a number of technological developments created increasing conflicts between native fishing and the proliferating white settlers. Perfection of the canning process and the advent of transcontinental rail transport combined to increase significantly the export market for salmon in the East and overseas by the 1880s. The first cannery was built on the Columbia in 1866; by 1883 some 40 canneries packed 600,000 cases of salmon, two-thirds of the West Coast harvest. With demand for the resource mushrooming, a non-native commercial fishery began to out-compete native fishing by introducing fishing techniques, such as beach seining with horses, large fish

---

[*] The Yakama Indian Nation changed the spelling of its name in 1993 to reflect its historic spelling.

traps, and fish wheels. The whites' new technologies out-performed the Indians' dip nets, seine nets, hooks and lines, and harpoons.[20]

The whites also effectively preempted upriver native fishers by seizing advantageous locations lower in watersheds. Their use of gasoline-powered engines enabled them to introduce white troll fisheries in the ocean and in Puget Sound which further reduced the Indian harvest. Puget Sound canneries mushroomed from three in 1894 to twenty-four in 1905, as numerous investment syndicates formed companies to construct canneries and operate fish traps. On the Columbia, canneries came even more quickly and in greater numbers, growing from one in 1866 to thirty-seven in 1884.[21]

The technological preemption of tribal fisheries was a part of massive changes that the landscape of the Pacific Northwest was undergoing in the late 19th century, which combined to create salmon shortages. Political preemption of tribal fisheries then followed as a response to those shortages. Both were products of a fundamentally different economy that white settlement brought to the region.

The political process also worked to disenfranchise the tribes by regulating harvests to favor non-Indians. Especially after Washington achieved statehood in 1889, the state legislature acted to control tribal fishing in the name of "conservation." Not only were restrictions imposed on traditional tribal harvest practices, but the freshwater fisheries bore the brunt of fishing closures, while the ocean and Puget Sound fisheries generally were not restricted. "Salmon preserves," where fishing was proscribed by regulation, invariably displaced native fishing grounds.[22]

Thus, within roughly three decades of the signing of the Stevens and Palmer treaties, the federal government's plan to integrate the tribes into the regional economy through commercial salmon harvesting had failed. The development of an export market for salmon prompted development of a non-Indian commercial fishery with the economic and political power to effectively preempt the tribal fishery. The tribes were left with the remnants of the salmon runs, particularly in the Columbia Basin where they were at a geographic disadvantage.

The Gift Economy vs. the Market Economy

The economy of the pre-white settlement Northwest has been described by Jim Lichatowich as a "gift economy," which had evolved over 1,500 years. In this economy, one attained social position not by accumulation of wealth but through the size of one's gifts. Gifts were the basic source of exchange and commerce. Natural resources, like salmon harvests and fishing sites, were gifts from nature, not for individual ownership and exclusive possession, but to be shared with others and passed on to succeeding generations. Salmon, which had a conscious spirit, would remain abundant if treated with respect. The natural world was filled with such spirits, which humans needed to cultivate to ensure a continuous food supply and other necessities.[23]

The new market economy introduced by white settlers was fundamentally different. Salmon and other natural resources were commodities to be captured and sold for profit. Unlike the gift economy, in which cultural and religious taboos supplied an inherent check on excessive harvests, the market economy contained no such checks. As white settlers began to arrive in numbers — the non-native population of the state of Oregon grew from just over 50,000 in 1860, to over 90,000 in 1870, to over 175,000 in 1880, to over 300,000 in 1890, to over 400,000 in 1900 — they overwhelmed the natives and their gift economy. By the turn of the century 1.1 million people lived in the states of Oregon, Washington, and Idaho. Fewer than 20,000 were natives, who had experienced a 95 percent decline in their numbers since the onset of white settlement, mostly due to disease.[24]

The market economy the white settlers established had no internal checks of legends and taboos to moderate resource use. Natural resources were not kindred spirits but commodities essential to maximizing profits. Profits were often a function of the demands of distant markets, not local subsistence. Short-term wealth became more important than long-term sustainable use.[25]

The new market economy did more than just displace tribal fishers: it had devastating effects on the salmon resource. There were two reasons for this result: changed fishing techniques and loss of salmon habitat. Even if the white-dominated fishery of the 19th century did not harvest more aggregate fish from the Columbia than the native harvests — and recent estimates place peak harvests of both just over 40 million pounds — the manner of harvest was materially different, concentrated in the lower river and compressed into a four-month season (the tribes generally fished nine months of the year), in order to concentrate efforts on the most prized salmon species. New harvest technologies, including fish wheels, captured higher percentages of particular runs. Waste at canneries was widespread, something not condoned in the pre-existing gift economy.[26]

The second consequence of the introduction of the market economy was habitat loss. As beavers were trapped, streams mined, farms irrigated, livestock grazed, trees logged, mills operated, and cities settled, salmon habitat shrunk. Joseph Taylor concisely summarized the situation:

> Oregon country Indians had harvested massive quantities of salmon for many centuries before whites arrived, but their impact on the rest of the landscape was relatively benign. Salmon encountered a far different world in the second half of the nineteenth century. . . . Trappers, farmers, miners, irrigators, loggers, and boosters transformed nature in ways that made it less hospitable to aquatic life. The clear, cool, unimpeded streams of precontact times had become dirtier, warmer, and more often obstructed. By 1900, Euro-American settlement had already reduced significantly the spawning ranges of salmon in the Columbia and other basins. This was the ecological context of the industrial fishery during the late nineteenth century.[27]

The new economy thus not only preempted tribal harvests, it damaged the salmon runs themselves. Harvests declined 50 percent between 1884 and 1889, rebounded briefly as harvesters switched from chinook to coho and sockeye, then fell again. Thirty-nine canneries in 1887 became twenty-one by 1889. By the turn of the century, harvests in both Alaska and British Columbia exceeded Columbia River harvests. This "free-for-all" was over within just thirty years. Never again would Columbia Basin salmon be thought of as a limitless resource. Throughout the 20th century, there would always be more harvest capacity than available salmon; the chief issue would become not who possessed the better harvest technology but who had the better harvest rights. Allocating an increasingly scarce resource would become a vexing problem for scientists, regulators, and reviewing courts.[28]

4 — JUDICIAL INTERPRETATION OF THE TREATIES

With no realistic possibility of safeguarding treaty fishing through the political process, the tribes, assisted by federal Justice Department officials, turned to the federal courts. Unlike state judges, who usually are elected for terms, federal judges are appointed for life and thus are somewhat removed from the political process. They therefore may be more sensitive to minority rights. Beginning in 1887 and continuing over the next century, the federal courts, including the Supreme Court, repeatedly confirmed that the treaties of the 1850s reserved to the tribes a "right of taking fish" that could not be denied by property law concepts, fish wheels, license fees, or discriminatory regulations. Despite these rulings, state officials responsible for regulating salmon harvests used their discretion to deprive the tribes of a fair share of the resource. Not until the 1970s did the federal courts rule that the treaties required the states to guarantee the tribes one-half of the salmon harvests. By specifying a precise harvest share, the courts substantially reduced the discretion of state officials and ushered in the modern era of salmon management.[1]

First Judicial Treaty Interpretations

The first decision to interpret the meaning of the treaty fishing right was an 1887 case involving the Yakama tribe's access to their Tumwater fishery on the Columbia River at Wishram. O.D. and Frank Taylor had secured homestead patents to the shorelands and proceeded to construct a fence that blocked native access to the usual fishing sites. The Yakama, like other Northwest tribes were, as one reservation agent put it, "great sticklers for their rights," of which they were "well posted." Tribal members complained to the reservation agent, who convinced the federal government to file suit in territorial court in 1887.[2]

The district court at North Yakima upheld the Taylors, but on appeal the Washington Territorial Supreme Court reversed, ruling that the federal government's grant of homestead patents to the Taylors did not extinguish the preexisting tribal fishing right. Judge Hoyt employed a U.S. Supreme Court rule that treaty rights must be "liberally construed in favor of the Indians" to "best subserve the object which the Indians at the time of the treaty would have been most likely to have desired and understood." This rule led him to conclude that in the treaty the tribe *reserved* preexisting fishing rights; the treaty was not a grant of rights from the government to the tribe. Consequently, the court rejected the Taylors' argument that the treaty guaranteed the tribe only the same rights to fish as white citizens. Instead, in light of what the court characterized as "common knowledge that these Indians were always tenacious in adhering to past customs and traditions," Judge Hoyt concluded that the treaty preserved tribal access to traditional fishing places like the Tumwater fishery. Thus, according to the court, homesteaders like the Taylors took title to land subject to the treaty-guaranteed easement that ensured tribal access to their historic fishing grounds. In short, the court recognized that the treaty created a property right in the tribe: an easement to reach their historic fishing places.[3]

Despite this court victory, the Yakamas' access to their Tumwater fisheries was hardly secure. The tribe complained that the Taylors were uncooperative the year following the 1887 decision, and by 1891 white fences and fish wheels again excluded native fishers from Tumwater. The local Indian agent reported that tribal members were "bitter if not hostile" at the lack of justice.[4]

The Warm Springs tribe had similar difficulties accessing their traditional fishing ground of Celilo Falls, on the Lower Columbia near The Dalles. And in Puget Sound the Alaska Packing Company excluded the Lummi tribe from its traditional fishing sites on the reefs of Point Robert by using a Washington state law that gave fishermen a specified territory around each net in all directions, which effectively allowed them to claim the entirety of the tribe's fishing grounds. The federal district court upheld the Alaska Packing Company's claim in 1897. But the Washington Supreme Court surprisingly sided with the Tulalip tribe in a dispute with white fishermen over tribal access to tidelands within the boundaries of their reservation in a 1903 decision. The court ruled that those lands could not be sold by the state consistent with the state's act of admission and its constitution, which disclaimed state jurisdiction over tribal and federal lands.[5]

It was at Celilo Falls that the most bitter and longstanding conflict occurred. For nearly forty years after the treaty of 1855, whites attempted to monopolize the fishery, while Indians complained to federal authorities, and special agents conducted investigations on the conflict. One investigator termed the tribal exclusion from Celilo Falls "a great injustice;" another suggested that land be purchased for a permanent tribal fishery there. Finally, in 1895, after the Winans Brothers Packing Company and other local canneries constructed fences excluding the natives, the Office of Indian Affairs pressured the Department of Justice to take legal action, and the local U.S. Attorney, William Bricker, filed suit against Winans Brothers as a test case to reestablish treaty fishing rights throughout the region.[6]

The Winans Doctrine

In the mid-1890s, Lineas and Audubon Winans operated four fish wheels at Celilo Falls under license from the state of Washington. They also possessed federal homestead patents to shorelands adjacent to the falls on the Washington side of the river. Invoking these authorizations, the Winans brothers fenced their lands and destroyed huts that native fishers had built for curing salmon. While the case was pending, the local district court decided that tribal members should be allowed access to their traditional sites, giving the natives a temporary victory. But because Judge C.H. Hanford limited his ruling to unfenced areas, the Winans brothers were able to quickly exclude tribal fishers by erecting new fences. Ultimately, in 1896, Judge Hanford — the same judge who would allow the Alaska Packing Company to exclude the Lummi tribe at Point Robert the next year — ruled for the Winans brothers, determining that the treaty gave the natives only a guarantee of equal treatment with whites; it recognized no special proprietary rights.[7]

Nine years later, in 1905, the U.S. Supreme Court reversed, in a landmark decision that remains the bedrock of Indian treaty fishing rights. The opinion by Justice Joseph McKenna concluded that the treaty recognized tribal property rights in off-reservation fishing grounds, notwithstanding the issuance of state licenses or federal homestead patents. The Court rejected the argument that the treaty right entitled the tribes merely to equality of treatment, suggesting that such a result would be an "impotent outcome to negotiations and a convention that seemed to promise more and give the word of the Nation for more." In eloquent prose that survives the passage of the years, Justice McKenna drew a clear distinction between preexisting rights reserved by the natives in the treaty and rights granted to the natives by the federal government:

> The right to resort to the fishing places in controversy was a part of larger rights possessed by the Indians, upon the exercise of which there was not a shadow of impediment, and which were not much less necessary to the existence of the Indians than the atmosphere they breathed. New conditions came into existence, to which those rights had to be accommodated. Only a limitation of them, however, was necessary and intended, not a taking away. In other words, the treaty was not a grant of rights to the Indians, but a grant of rights from them — a reservation of those rights not granted.[8]

These reserved rights included access to historic fishing places, the Court concluded, impressing a "servitude," or "right in land," that burdened the federal government and its grantees like the Winans brothers. This servitude was a property right burdening "every piece of land as though described therein," giving the Indians the right to occupy and make use of lands despite "the contingency of future ownership." Thus, the Court made clear that the treaty servitude took precedence over private land titles. Moreover, Justice McKenna determined that this servitude also was enforceable against subsequently established states like the state of Washington, so state laws had to respect treaty rights, even though the state was not a party to the treaty. The Court did suggest, however, that the exercise of treaty fishing rights could be subjected to state regulation — language that proved to be the source of enduring controversy over the next 75 years.[9]

Despite the Court's unfortunate statement concerning state regulation, the *Winans* decision was a landmark case. Its articulation of treaty promises as reserved rights, its use of rules of treaty construction favorable to the tribes, its application of treaty fishing rights to private land titles, and its rejection of the argument that statehood divested treaty rights articulated fundamental principles of Indian law. *Winans* was also the harbinger of another landmark decision authored by Justice McKenna three years later: *Winters v. U.S.*, where the court applied the reserved rights doctrine to water diversions. And while the *Winans* court held only that the treaty right created a tribal property right guaranteeing physical access to historic native fishing grounds, subsequent cases would expand upon the *Winans* principles to help ensure that the treaty promise of "the right of taking fish" was a meaningful one.[10]

The Winans Progeny

The *Winans* case may have established enduring principles, but it did not conclusively settle fishing rights at Celilo Falls. The Seufert Brothers Packing Company interpreted *Winans* to forbid fencing out native fishers only on the Washington side of the falls, so the company excluded native fishers from the Oregon side. Seufert's position was that since the boundary of the lands the Yakama Indian Nation ceded to the United States in its 1855 treaty was the north side of the Columbia River, the treaty right to take fish did not extend beyond the mid-point of the river. The Supreme Court did not agree, noting that the treaty had to be interpreted as the tribes would have understood it, and that native fishers from all tribes used both sides of the falls before and after the treaty. Responding to the Seufert brothers' complaint that this result would impose an unwarranted "servitude on Oregon soil," the Court pointed out that there was sufficient notice of the existence of this property right not only from the treaty itself but also from the "habitual and customary use of the premises, which must have been so open and notorious . . . that any person, not negligently or willfully blind to the conditions of the property he was purchasing, must have known of them."[11]

This judicial recognition that the treaty fishing right burdened unceded lands was significant for two reasons. First, it meant that the treaty promise protected all customary fishing places regardless of boundary lines established by the treaty. Second, courts would not employ ordinary common law rules in interpreting the treaty fishing right. Instead, they would construe the treaty as the tribes, "an unlettered people," would have understood them.

A quarter century later, in 1942, the Supreme Court returned to the Yakama treaty, reviewing a Washington State Supreme Court decision which affirmed a 1939 criminal conviction against Sampson Tulee, a Yakama tribal member who caught and sold salmon without a $5.00 state dipnet license. No licenses were required for hook and line fishermen, effectively exempting non-Indian recreational fishermen. Again employing the rule that the treaty was to be interpreted as the tribes would understand, the Court, in an opinion by Justice Black, reversed the conviction. The Court determined that the state license requirement served both to raise money to support state government and to regulate the harvest for conservation purposes and concluded that the state's legitimate conservation concerns could be accomplished without charging tribal members license fees. Because the state was unable to show that the fees were "indispensable" to the effectiveness of the state's conservation concerns, Justice Black decided that the fees could not be "reconciled with a fair construction of the treaty."[12]

The Supreme Court rejected Washington's argument that, while the treaty fishing right guaranteed the tribes access to their customary places, state sovereignty allowed the state to charge the same license fees as it did to white fishermen. By rejecting the state sovereignty argument, the Court confirmed that the treaty recognized an unusual servitude in favor of the tribes, one the Washington Supreme Court correctly identified as a *profit à prendre*: it guaranteed the tribes not only an easement to the fishing places, but also prohibited the state from imposing even apparently nondiscriminatory fees on the tribes' fishing rights. Thus, financial barriers, like physical barriers, that interfered with the tribes' right to freely exercise their treaty fishing rights, were also prohibited by the treaty.[13]

The Washington Supreme Court's upholding of Tulee's conviction was rather typical of the state court's hostility to treaty rights. For example, a decade after the *Winans* case, that court erroneously suggested, in patronizing, racist language, that natives had no lawful right to fish outside reservations except as permitted by state law:

> The premise of Indian sovereignty we reject. The treaty is not to be interpreted in that light. At no time did our ancestors, in getting title to this continent, ever regard the aborigines as other than mere occupants, and incompetent occupants, of the soil. Any title that could come from them was always disdained. . . . Only that title was esteemed which came from white men. . . .
>
> The Indian was a child, and a dangerous child, of nature, to be both protected and restrained. In his nomadic life he was to be left so long as civilization did not demand his region. When it did demand that region, he was to be allotted a more confined area with permanent subsistence. . . .
>
> These arrangements were but the announcement of our benevolence, which, notwithstanding our frequent frailties, has been continuously displayed. Neither Rome nor sagacious Britain ever dealt more liberally with their subject races than we with these savage tribes, whom it was generally tempting and always easy to destroy and whom we have so often permitted to squander vast areas of fertile land before our eyes.[14]

Hostility to native fishing was not limited to the state judiciary. In 1927, two years after the Washington legislature declared that steelhead were "game" fish, outlawing net harvesting, it eliminated an exception for streams on or bordering Indian reservations, effectively banning native steelhead harvest and eliminating an important source of winter food for the tribes. In 1933, a successful initiative sponsored by sport fishers established a new Washington Game Department, funded primarily by license fees, to serve sports fishing interests and which soon became a virulent opponent of native fishing rights. Two years later, in 1935, another successful initiative banned use of all fixed harvest gear, such as traps, which had the effect of reallocating harvests in favor of ocean trollers, gillnetters, and purse seiners, and displacing native fisheries.

Quite apart from discriminating against tribal harvests, banning fixed harvest gear made no biological sense, since it redirected effort downriver and to the ocean where salmon would be overharvested in mixed stock fisheries. It was this law banning fixed harvest gear of which Sampson Tulee was convicted in 1939.[15]

A decade later, in 1950, the coastal Makah Tribe sued Washington's Director of Fisheries over the state's ban on native net fisheries. Although the federal district court upheld the state, the court of appeals reversed, ruling that the state failed to demonstrate that the ban was necessary for conservation. Across the river, Oregon also attempted to use its authority to regulate for conservation in order to disenfranchise the tribes. In 1958, the state banned fishing on all Columbia and Snake River tributaries, while allowing in-river harvests by non-Indians. A federal appeals court determined that the state's regulation was not a "necessary" conservation measure because the ban was designed to protect non-Indian sport and commercial harvests. In both cases, measures to protect the salmon could have been adopted without banning the native harvests; therefore, the bans were not "necessary" because the state failed to show that they were, in the words of the Supreme Court in the *Tulee* case, "indispensable" to conservation. The court also indicated that this standard required the state to show that the conservation objective was not achievable by regulating the non-native fishery alone. Thus, the court imposed a significant burden on states: to show that conservation measures affecting natives were both necessary and indispensable. The appeals court recognized that "conservation" was often a guise for allocation: "conserving" fish for non-Indian commercial and recreational fisheries.[16]

Had the appeals court's use of *Tulee's* indispensability language survived, that test might have obviated a great deal of subsequent litigation. Unfortunately, the U.S. Supreme Court discarded the indispensability test in the first of three cases the Court decided in the space of nine years concerning state regulation of tribal harvests on Washington's Puyallup River, discussed below. These state conservation measures not only reveal the states' attempts to legally preempt tribal harvests, they also illustrate the states' reaction to dwindling salmon runs. Instead of concerning themselves with the habitat destruction at the root of the decline, the states concentrated on using their regulatory authority to reserve harvests for white fishers and attempted to compensate for habitat loss by expanding hatchery production. Preoccupation with disadvantaging tribal harvests thus helped to divert attention from the real causes of declining salmon runs.

The Puyallup Trilogy

The conflict on the Puyallup River began in 1963, when the Washington Department of Game filed suit seeking to enforce the state's ban against net fishing of steelhead at the Puyallup tribe's fishing grounds. The state Supreme Court ruled the ban was permissible if the state could show that it was a necessary conservation measure, and the court remanded the case to the trial court to determine whether the ban was in fact necessary to conserve Puyallup River steelhead. Surprisingly, the U.S. Supreme Court took the case and issued a confused opinion by Justice William O. Douglas. Although the Court indicated that the treaty right "may, of course, not be qualified by the state," it indicated that "the manner of fishing, the size of the take, the restriction of commercial fishing, and the like may be regulated in the interest of conservation, provided the regulation . . . does not discriminate against the Indians." The Court restricted *Tulee's* indispensability requirement, which imposed a heavy burden on the state, to license fees. By doing so, it seemingly approved widely-ranging state regulation of the treaty right if the state merely showed that the regulation was a "reasonable and necessary" conservation measure, an issue left to the state courts to decide. Professor Ralph Johnson wrote a sharp critique of the Court's decision, warning that under the rubric of "reasonable conservation measures" the state had and would continue to "conserve" fish for the non-native harvesters whose license fees were an important source of state revenue.[17]

When the state courts upheld the ban on net fishing of steelhead harvests on the Puyallup River, the issue quickly returned to the Supreme Court. In a second opinion by Justice Douglas, the Court had an apparent change of heart, unanimously striking down the ban as discriminatory. Justice Douglas concluded that "[t]here is discrimination here because all Indian net fishing is barred and only hook-and-line fishing, entirely pre-empted by non-Indians, is allowed." He called for "a fair apportionment" of harvest rights, warning, however, that "the Treaty does not give the Indians a federal right to pursue the last living steelhead until it enters their nets."[18]

The Supreme Court was not able to extricate itself from the *Puyallup* controversy without a third decision because in 1974, after the first two decisions, a federal court of appeals determined that the Puyallup reservation had not been extinguished, meaning that most of the tribal harvest actually took place on-reservation, where the tribe had exclusive harvest rights and where the state had no regulatory jurisdiction. But in its third *Puyallup* decision the Supreme Court was unwilling to concede that twelve years of litigation had proceeded on an erroneous premise. Over two dissents, the Court, in an opinion by Justice Stevens (Justice Douglas having retired), feared that the claim to exclusive harvest rights on the lowest seven miles of the river would allow the tribe to "interdict completely the migrating fish run and 'pursue the last living steelhead,'" in violation of Justice Douglas' dictum. The Court therefore approved a state court's allocation of 45 percent of steelhead harvests to the tribe, regardless of whether the harvests were on- or off-reservation. The court declined to rule on whether the state could exclude hatchery fish from the apportionment formula, however.[19]

The *Puyallup* decisions reflected a judicial willingness not only to protect the exercise of treaty fishing rights against physical obstructions, like fences, but also against discriminatory regulatory obstructions. Because the states had a long history of using state regulations to restrict tribal harvests, this evolution of the treaty fishing right was a significant development.

The Belloni Decision

Protecting the treaty fishing right against physical and fiscal obstructions and discriminatory regulations through limits imposed on the state by the federal courts was, while important legally, an inefficient and uncertain way to manage a complex fishery.

Neither the state nor the tribes could be certain that the state's "conservation" regulations would pass judicial muster, and every season was vulnerable to court injunction. What was needed was an affirmative right to a share of the harvest: the "fair apportionment" Justice Douglas called for in the second *Puyallup* case.[20]

While the long-running *Puyallup* controversy played itself out, federal district judges in Oregon and Washington heard cases that eventually would produce the kind of judicial allocation of salmon harvest rights that Justice Douglas suggested was necessary. In the mid-1960s, members of the Yakama Indian Nation, soon joined by the federal government, challenged longstanding Oregon regulations that limited Columbia River harvests above The Dalles Dam to hook-and-line fisheries, effectively closing that part of the river to net fishing traditionally used by the tribes. Like Washington, Oregon interpreted the treaty fishing right to give the tribes only the same rights as other citizens. Federal district judge Robert Belloni, in *Sohappy v. Smith*, replied that "[s]uch a reading would not seem unreasonable if all history, anthropology, biology, prior case law, and the intention of the parties to the treaty were to be ignored."[21]

Oregon argued in *Sohappy* that the upriver closure of net fishing was the kind of necessary conservation measure the Supreme Court had approved a year earlier in the first *Puyallup* case. But Judge Belloni was able to see — as the Supreme Court later would — that Oregon's "conservation" regulations were meant not only to ensure the perpetuation of the species, but also to allocate salmon among competing harvesters. And in so doing, the upriver closure foisted the entire conservation burden on the tribes, while allowing non-native sport and commercial harvests to continue unabated.

Judge Belloni concluded that the native fishers were entitled to a "fair share" of the harvests, and he ordered the state to adopt an objective of conserving salmon for native fishery as a "regulatory policy coequal with the conservation of fish for other users." He later established detailed substantive standards and procedural measures that the state had to follow in achieving "coequal" status for the native fishery. These standards included 1) allowing the tribes to "participate meaningfully" in the development of harvest regulations, and 2) ensuring that such regulations were "the least restrictive which can be imposed [on the tribes] consistent with assuring the necessary escapement of fish for conservation purposes," meaning that non-Indian commercial and recreational fishers had to bear conservation burdens before the tribes' harvest could be restricted. The Belloni Decision, as it came to be called, revolutionized salmon management on the Columbia River, although it would take nearly a decade for the revolution to be codified into a comprehensive management plan.[22]

The Boldt Decision

Although no one appealed the Belloni Decision, numerous members of tribes in Washington continued to be arrested for violating that state's harvest regulations. Consequently, in 1970, the year after Judge Belloni handed down his decision, the federal government, on behalf of numerous Washington tribes with treaty rights, filed suit claiming that the "fair share" to which Judge Belloni referred meant that the tribes were entitled to harvest half the salmon destined for their traditional fishing grounds. The government and the tribes also claimed that hatchery-produced salmon should be included in the tribes' harvest share, and that the treaties implicitly protected the habitat on which the salmon depended.

After nearly four years of proceedings, Judge George Boldt handed down an historic decision which concluded that Washington's regulatory scheme systematically discriminated against native fishing. State regulation had, the court concluded, totally closed many historic tribal fishing sites to net fishing "while permitting commercial net fishing for salmon elsewhere on the same runs of fish." Trial evidence showed tribal harvests to be only about five percent of the total harvest. Judge Boldt noted that "notwithstanding three years of exhaustive trial preparation," the state failed to produce "any credible evidence showing any instance, remote or recent, when a definitely identified member of any plaintiff tribe has exercised his off reservation treaty rights by any conduct or means detrimental to the perpetuation of any species of anadromous fish."[23]

Because Judge Boldt determined that salmon harvests in the state were not sufficient to meet all demands, and that regulation of both the native and non-native harvest was necessary to ensure perpetuation of the salmon runs, he concluded that salmon must be fairly allocated between natives and non-natives. Judge Boldt arrived at a formula for allocation based on his interpretation of the treaty language "in common with." That language meant, according to the judge, "by dictionary definition and as intended and used in the Indian treaties . . . sharing equally the opportunity to take fish" destined for historic tribal fishing grounds. Thus, he instructed the state to restrict the non-native fishery to 50 percent of the harvest of those fish. Judge Boldt excluded from the equal sharing formula fish harvested by tribes on reservations as well as fish not destined to pass the tribe's historic fishing sites and fish caught outside Washington waters, even if they were destined for the tribe's fishing grounds. By 1977, this formula allowed the tribes to harvest 43 percent of Puget Sound harvests, although, due to exclusions such as those mentioned above, this amounted to only 18 percent of the total harvest of Washington salmon. Judge Boldt deferred deciding the tribes' claims for including hatchery fish in the allocation formula and for protection of salmon habitat until he decided the allocation issue.[24]

Like southern whites fighting desegregation two decades earlier, the state of Washington and its citizens resisted the Boldt Decision vigorously, despite the fact that the federal court of appeals quickly affirmed, and the Supreme Court declined to review the case. Widespread noncompliance with the state's grudging efforts to implement the court's orders occurred during 1975-77; shooting threats were even reported. Then, in 1977, in response to a suit brought by non-native fishers, the Washington State Supreme Court ruled that the state lacked authority to implement Judge Boldt's sharing formula, claiming it was contrary to both state statutes and the federal Constitution. As a result, Judge Boldt was forced to enter a series of orders that had the effect of directly managing the fishery. Although these orders were widely decried as usurping the state's role in managing the fishery and establishing the court as a "fishmaster," the orders were upheld again by the appeals court, which noted that:

The state's extraordinary machinations in resisting [Judge Boldt's] decree have forced the district court to take over a large share of the management of the state's fishery in order to enforce its decrees. Except for some desegregation cases . . . the district court has faced the most concerted official and private efforts to frustrate a decree of a federal court witnessed in this century. The challenged orders in this appeal must be reviewed by this court in the context of events forced by the litigants who offered the court no reasonable alternative.[25]

This conflict between federal and state courts at last induced the Supreme Court to review the case. In 1979, the Court, in a 6-3 decision by Justice Stevens, largely upheld Judge Boldt. Ratifying the 50/50 sharing formula, the Court noted that the treaty right prevented the state from "crowding out" the tribal fishery and that neither party could destroy the other's share of the resource. The Court concluded that:

the central principle here must be that Indian treaty fishing rights to a natural resource that was once so thoroughly and exclusively exploited by the Indians secures so much as, but not more than, is necessary to provide the Indians with a livelihood — that is to say, a moderate living.

According to Justice Stevens, under this "moderate living" standard, the tribes' share could be reduced below fifty percent where a tribe dwindles "to just a few members" or finds "other sources of support that lead it to abandon its fisheries." In the two decades since the Court's decision, there has been no evidence of either of these two conditions.[26]

The Court did modestly reduce the tribe's share in two ways: by including on-reservation harvests as well as ceremonial and subsistence harvests in the tribal share, and by including only fish caught by Washington citizens in state or federal waters in the non-native share. The latter exclusion would contribute to an international stalemate with Canada over allocating salmon harvests between the two countries by essentially exempting harvests in Alaskan waters from the equal sharing formula.[27]

The Aftermath of the Belloni and Boldt Decisions

The Belloni and Boldt Decisions marked the advent of modern salmon law. Both decisions confirmed the *Puyallup* cases' revelation that the treaty right was more than an access right or an insulation from license fees. But, unlike the *Puyallup* litigation, the Belloni and Boldt Decisions reached beyond a particular regulation on a particular river to impose systematic restrictions on state regulation. Judge Belloni forbade the state from using its regulatory authority to create a conservation problem once the salmon reached the native fishing grounds by allocating virtually all of the harvest to non-natives downriver and in the ocean. Judge Boldt's sharing formula removed most of the ambiguities involved in satisfying the treaty "right of taking fish" while ensuring conservation of the salmon resource. Judge Belloni soon applied the Boldt formula to the Columbia.[28]

Perhaps the most discernable result of the two decisions was a kind of re-tribalization among Northwest Indian tribes, which now had an economically important resource to allocate among their members. It became important to be a tribal member eligible to invoke the tribe's harvest rights. Salmon harvests offered the prospect of once again sustaining economic livelihoods for tribal members.[29]

A second consequence of the Belloni and Boldt Decisions was the fact that, as Judge Boldt recognized and an appeals court confirmed, the tribes not only have property rights to harvest at their traditional fishing sites (allowing them to cross the land of others and to be free of state license fees and discriminatory state regulations), they also have governmental regulatory authority. The judge recognized tribes as fish managers, not merely harvesters, a ruling subsequently affirmed by the Ninth Circuit. This recognition required the tribes to develop the scientific and technical expertise necessary to manage harvests while preserving the resource. To develop and employ this expertise the tribes founded inter-tribal coordinating bodies: the Columbia River Inter-Tribal Fish Commission (in the Belloni case area; see map 7), and the Northwest Indian Fisheries Commission (in the Boldt case area), staffed with biologists, hydrologists, and lawyers.

Map 7 — Stevens Treaty Tribes in the Columbia Basin

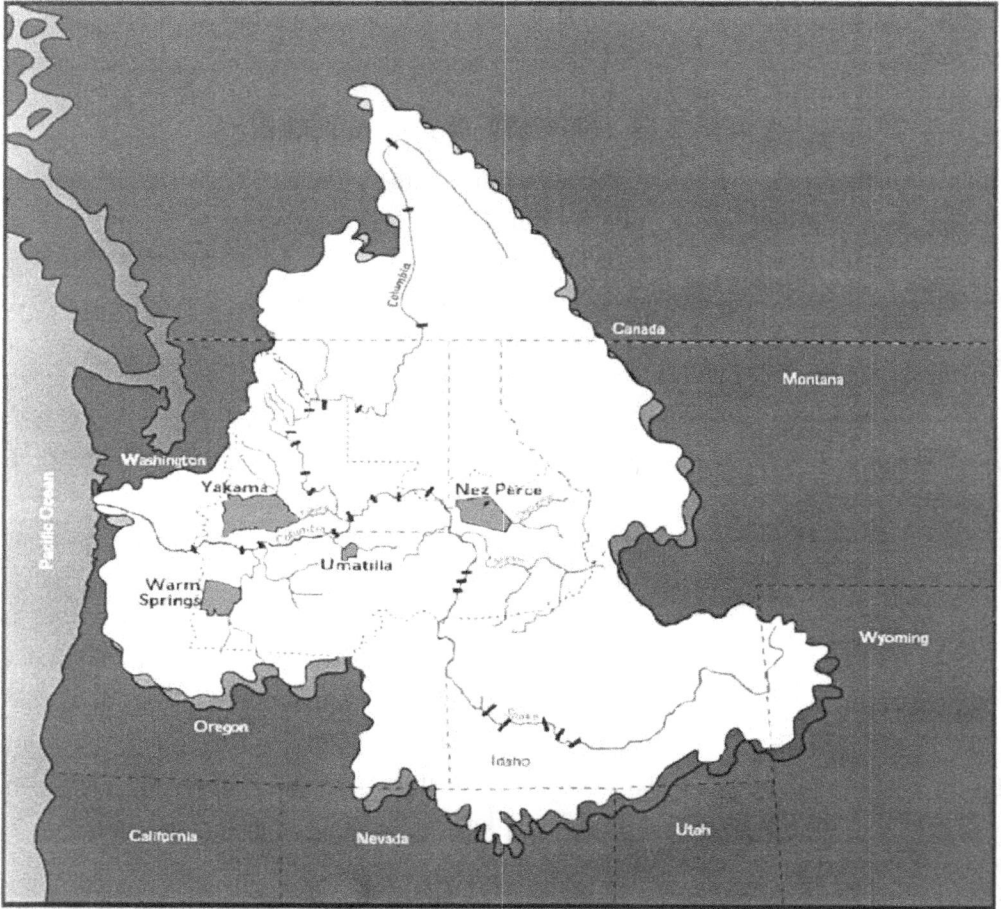

© Columbia River Inter-Tribal Fish Commission 1996

☐ Columbia River basin
▨ Present-day reservation boundaries.
▨ Lands ceded to U.S. by four tribes in 1855 treaties.
— Dams on Columbia & Snake rivers.

Courtesy of the Columbia River Inter-Tribal Fish Commission

These commissions enabled the tribes to become effective co-managers of salmon harvests with the states.[30]

The evolution of tribes as harvest co-managers redounded to the benefit of the salmon. State biologists now had to coordinate with tribal biologists, and both needed more information about the salmon's life cycle to manage the resource effectively. By sharing information and undertaking cooperative research, the state of the art of salmon biology advanced.

Through the harvest co-management process, the state fishery agencies and the tribes, long mortal enemies, began to see that they had much in common, at least with respect to hydropower developments adversely affecting salmon habitat. By the late 1970s the state agencies and the tribes forged a "fishery coalition" that successfully lobbied for congressional action to establish a program to rebuild the Columbia River salmon runs that had been decimated by the world's largest hydroelectric system. Later, this coalition would submit comprehensive recommendations that became the bedrock of the rebuilding program. The coalition would also prove instrumental in the successful negotiation of an international treaty to govern salmon harvests in the Pacific Ocean. Only a decade after shots had been fired in the "Northwest fish war," the state fishery agencies and the tribes had become allies on many issues that did not involve harvest allocation, especially those involving the environmental degradation at the root of the salmon's decline.

As a consequence of the formation of their coalition with the state (and federal) fish agencies, the tribes began to concentrate more on legislative and regulatory issues than on litigation in the years following the Belloni and Boldt Decisions. Litigation was still necessary to encourage a comprehensive management plan to allocate harvests on the Columbia, and to ensure that ocean harvests did not violate the 50/50 sharing formula. The former, embodied in the Columbia River Management Plan first agreed to in 1977 and extended in 1988, governed harvests in-river until the late 1990s, when Endangered Species Act procedures were imposed on Columbia River harvest allocation, as discussed in chapter 9. The latter restricted ocean harvests off the coasts of Oregon and

Washington. But harvests in the Alaskan offshore have yet to be subjected to treaty rights limits, although the threat of doing so led to the Pacific Salmon Treaty in 1985, as discussed in chapter 8. In the 1980s, the tribes primarily focused on regulatory processes that promised to restore salmon runs. After those processes failed to produce the promised restoration in the mid-1990s, the tribes began to consider reviving their long-held assertion that the treaty right to take fish not only entitled them to access to traditional fishing sites, insulation from state license fees, and a 50 percent share of the harvest, but also provided the salmon with protection against environmental degradation. In early 2001, twenty tribes filed suit against the state of Washington, alleging that faulty construction of culverts that block salmon from 3,000 miles of streams violate their treaty rights. This part of the story is taken up in chapter 12.[31]

5 – DAMMING THE COLUMBIA BASIN

The Columbia River is the defining natural resource of the Pacific Northwest. Rising in central British Columbia and emptying into the Pacific Ocean at the border between Oregon and Washington over 1,200 miles downstream, the river drains more than a quarter of a million square miles, an area larger than France. The Columbia's principal tributary, the Snake, rises in northwest Wyoming, flows through Idaho, marks the boundary between Idaho and Oregon, and meets the Columbia in south-central Washington. The Columbia is the West's biggest river system, with the force to pierce the Cascades. The Columbia has seven times the flow of the Colorado, two hundred times that of the Rio Grande. Its salmon runs were the lifeblood of native peoples for more than 10,000 years.[1]

The sheer size of the Columbia was not mightier than the human imagination, however. In roughly forty years of the twentieth century — from the 1930s to the mid-1970s — the Columbia was tamed in the name of flood control, navigation, irrigation, and hydropower. Today, there are eleven large dams on the mainstem of the Columbia, seven more on the Lower Snake. Some 150 dams exist throughout the Columbia Basin, producing over 40 percent of the nation's hydropower.[2]

William Dietrich has aptly called the Columbia the quintessential 20th century river — in contrast to the Mississippi, which remains in the American mind a 19th century river of "Tom and Huck, of sternwheeler and flatboat, of the siege of Vicksburg and the Battle of New Orleans." On the other hand, according to Dietrich, dams of the Columbia

represent the optimistic faith in technology of the century's beginning, and the restless misgivings about large-scale engineering at the century's end. It is the river of the turbine, the dynamo, the reactor, and the airplane. It is the river of Tom Swift, Franklin D. Roosevelt, *Popular Mechanics*, and Nagasaki. In the first three decades after World War II, major dams were completed in the Columbia Basin at a pace faster than one per year. It is a river not so much transformed as seemingly invented. If you want to see how America dreamed at the height of the American Century, come to the Columbia.[3]

This invented river of the turbine and the dynamo today produces an average of 18,500 megawatts of electricity, providing the Northwest with the cheapest electric rates in the nation and supporting a large aluminum industry which subsists off cheap hydropower. The dammed river also yields a deepwater port at Lewiston, Idaho, 465 miles from the sea, from which barges now supply cheap transportation for wheat and other grains as well as crops irrigated with water from Columbia Basin reservoirs, such as potatoes, sugar beets, and alfalfa. Approximately six percent of Columbia Basin streamflows are diverted to irrigate some 7.8 million acres of land. 3.8 million acres, nearly half of that total, are irrigated by some 73 percent of Snake River flows above Milner Dam; there are altogether 13.5 million acre-feet of storage in the Snake Basin.[4]

Taming the Columbia came at great cost, however. Chinook salmon and steelhead are now extinct in over 50 percent of their historic Columbia Basin range east of the Cascades, and only two percent of the basin's watersheds have strong salmon runs. Although it is true that salmon habitat has been damaged by logging, grazing, and mining activities, the predominant cause of the decline of most Columbia Basin salmon runs is the development and operation of the largest interconnected hydroelectric system in the world. This chapter explains how hydropower came to dominate the Columbia Basin and its salmon.[5]

Beginnings: The Progressive Impulse[6]

The seeds of the damming of the Columbia were planted by the Progressive conservation movement. Progressives were disturbed by the overcrowding, poverty, and crime that accompanied a seven-fold increase in the nation's urban population between 1860 and 1910. They saw government-sponsored natural resources projects, especially water developments, as a means to preserve the rural, small town, individualistic life that post-Civil War industrialism threatened with big corporations, big cities, and big political machines. Progressives were especially concerned with the growing monopolization of the emerging electric power industry because monopolies produced high rates and poor service. To combat electric monopolization and ensure widespread distribution of electricity at low rates, Progressives advocated an active role for the federal government as planner, regulator, and developer of hydroelectric projects.[7]

Hydropower was a key element of the Progressive Conservationist agenda because unlike electricity generated from coal, waterways were considered public resources. Progressives like Theodore Roosevelt and Gifford Pinchot insisted that private developments on public waterways should be government-regulated, subjected to limited license terms, and required to pay annual charges. Roosevelt appointed the Inland Waterways Commission, which in 1908 declared water to be a public resource and recommended basin-wide federal water development planning to serve multiple purposes, including navigation, flood control, water power, irrigation, and pollution control. The Commission advocated creation of a centralized, national water planning agency that would employ scientific principles, not congressional politics, as the chief litmus test for water project development. However, many in Congress opposed a centralized water agency, as did the U.S. Army Corps of Engineers which since 1824 had been (and remains today) the nation's chief navigation agency. The Corps and its allies in Congress blocked passage of authorizing legislation until 1917, and then succeeded in terminating the Commission as part of a compromise by which the Federal Water Power Act was passed in 1920.

The 1920 statute, discussed in detail in chapter 11, was the Progressive Conservationists' last hurrah. The legislation substituted federal regulation of nonfederal water projects for the Progressive dream of a centralized water planning agency, but failed to incorporate important items on the Progressive agenda by authorizing only relatively low federal charges on hydropower projects (which were not, in any event, earmarked for federal multiple-purpose purposes). However, the 1920 Act did reflect Progressive thinking in its provision for limited-term licenses, which reserved ultimate ownership in the public, and its preference for water projects which were publicly-owned.

Progressive principles fell out of favor in the 1920s "normalcy" years, as the businessman, rather than the scientific bureaucrat, became the national paradigm. The Federal Power Commission, created by the 1920 Act to regulate private hydropower development, but hampered by limited staff and funding, functioned as little more than a clearinghouse. With few regulatory requirements and nominal federal charges, private hydropower boomed. Concerns over electric monopolies declined. In 1926 alone, there were more than 1,000 private utility mergers. Mergers would become an issue again in the 1930s, fueling interest in public power.

But completely harnessing the Columbia River's flows proved to be beyond the financial resources of private utilities. Moreover, dams on the Columbia could generate far more electric power than the Northwest needed. For example, a 1912 study estimated that a dam at The Dalles would generate enough electricity to power a city thirteen times as large as 1912 Portland. Thus, the ascendancy of private power in the 1920s, coupled with limited public financial resources and inadequate demand for electricity, impeded the Progressive dream of comprehensive water development of the Columbia Basin. The dream was not abandoned, however. In fact, it was adopted by local economic boosters like Rufus Woods, publisher of the *Wenatchee World*, who began advocating a large reclamation and hydropower project at Grand Coulee in 1918 and continued to trumpet the project throughout the next decade-and-a-half.[8]

In the mid-1920s, Congress encouraged the efforts of the dam boosters when it directed the Corps of Engineers to survey river basins for likely water project locations. The resulting "308 reports" helped the Corps become a convert to multiple purpose project development. In the Columbia Basin, encouraged by Washington Senator Wesley Jones, the Corps produced a detailed study in 1932 that envisioned a grandiose program of ten dams on the Columbia, all managed as a single system. However, the report did not advocate federal financing of what would be the largest development of any river basin in the world; instead, the report saw the federal role as being limited to coordination and regulation. Such a role would not realize the dreams of the boosters.[9]

The New Deal: The Dream Comes True[10]

Although the philosophical underpinnings of Columbia Basin water project development lay in the Progressive impulse, the economic realities of the Great Depression transformed that philosophy into action. The Corps' 308 report on the Columbia supplied New Dealers with a handy blueprint to implement their belief that the federal government could stimulate economic recovery through public works projects. Federal water project development was also a response to the high prices and inadequate distribution of electric power provided by public utilities. Federal projects could electrify rural areas that private utilities deemed uneconomic to serve and could also produce public power that would serve as a "yardstick" by which to measure the reasonableness of private power rates.

When New York Governor Franklin D. Roosevelt, who had established a public power agency in his state, brought his presidential campaign to the Northwest in the fall of 1932, he told a cheering crowd of public power partisans in Portland that the federal government would never part with its sovereign control of water power, and he promised that the next federal hydropower project would be on the Columbia River. Actually, as Roosevelt spoke, the first dam on the Columbia, the utility-owned Rock Island Dam, built by the holding company controlling Puget Sound Power and Light, was nearing completion on the Mid-Columbia south of Wenatchee. That project, although only 40-feet high (only about one-ninth of the height of the proposed 350-foot Grand Coulee Dam), generated twice the amount of electric power then used in the region. But the lack of market demand neither deterred public power crusaders, nor gave pause to advocates of federal public works designed to relieve unemployment and stimulate economic development. Roosevelt's election ensured that a federal dam on the Columbia would become a reality.[11]

The precise location for a federal dam on the Columbia was hardly clear, however. Boosters in Washington, like Senator Clarence Dill, lobbied for the Grand Coulee site, while boosters in Oregon, like Governor Charles Martin and Senator Charles McNary, advocated a site on the Lower Columbia closer to Portland. Roosevelt, the master of compromise, gave each state what they wanted, and in 1933 construction began both at Grand Coulee and at a site near the Cascades on the Lower Columbia that would become Bonneville Dam. These two projects would eventually employ up to 10,000 workers and, when finished, would begin the transformation of both the river and the Pacific Northwest economy.[12]

The Bonneville Project Act

With construction proceeding both at Bonneville and Grand Coulee, the Supreme Court threw an unexpected monkey wrench in 1935, when it ruled that the projects had not been authorized by Congress. But the dams quickly received congressional authorization, and construction proceeded. Resolving how to distribute the electricity produced by the projects would prove considerably more time consuming.[13]

Neither project was authorized primarily for hydropower generation; their authorizing legislation made hydropower secondary to navigation (in the case of Bonneville) and flood control, downstream flow control, and irrigation (in the case of Grand Coulee). But allocating the "surplus power" from the projects invoked old tensions between urban and rural areas, between public and private power, and between advocates of central planning and market forces. Public power and rural partisans favored an entity like the Tennessee Valley Authority, which would have comprehensive authority to generate and market power, giving preference to public bodies at uniform, "postage stamp" rates, and constructing transmission lines to serve rural areas. Private utilities sought a more limited federal role, favoring both project operation and federal sales by existing federal agencies (the Corps of Engineers in the case of Bonneville Dam; the Bureau of Reclamation in the case of Grand Coulee) at the point of generation to private marketers. They also opposed uniform, "postage stamp" rates, favoring rates that reflected the cost of transmission, and they wanted limited federal transmission line construction. The Portland Chamber of Commerce feared that postage stamp rates and federal transmission line construction would lead to increased electric rates in Portland and undermine its locational advantage close to Bonneville Dam.[14]

Beginning in 1935 thirty-eight bills were introduced in Congress to govern power marketing from Bonneville Dam, but old conflicts over power allocation prevented passage of legislation until the Bonneville project was nearly completed in 1937. Then, influenced by the recommendations of the Pacific Northwest Regional Planning Board, a public-private advisory committee, Congress passed a compromise bill that rejected a comprehensive planning authority and left the Corps as project operator, but established a new agency to market power and construct transmission lines. The bill also gave preference to public bodies, although it did not prohibit sales to private utilities or industries. By creating a regional power marketing agency but denying that agency authority to initiate new projects, the legislation planted the seeds of regionalism without comprehensive planning authority. The result was the beginning of a complex mosaic of institutional jurisdictional boundaries that would eventually inhibit development of a truly comprehensive response to the decline of the Columbia's salmon runs.[15]

And What of the Salmon?[16]

The effects of the Bonneville and Grand Coulee Dams on the Columbia's salmon runs were not entirely ignored in the rush to market the projects' power. Four months before enactment of the 1937 Bonneville Project Act, the Senate adopted a resolution directing the Commissioner of Fisheries to study the effect of the dam on the salmon and to recommend steps "to attain the full conservation of [the salmon] and the preservation of the fishing industry." The ensuing report concluded that it would be years before the full ramifications of the dam would be known. But the report anticipated many of the problems that salmon would confront in attempting to coexist with water project development in the Columbia Basin. Bypass problems for juvenile fish at the dams, unscreened irrigation diversions, unsophisticated hatchery technology, and mixed-stock ocean harvests were all noted as potential problems in the Commissioner's report. These problems would continue to contribute to the decline of the salmon runs over the next half century.

The Grand Coulee project, which damaged salmon far more than the Bonneville project — because it sealed off more than 1,000 miles of spawning grounds — also prompted unprecedented mitigation efforts. As discussed in chapter 6, the Coulee project induced a massive effort to relocate upper basin salmon to tributaries below the dam. This sort of transplantation effort was not unusual in Columbia Basin hatchery operations, but transplantation generally produced poor results, and the extensive loss of habitat due to Grand Coulee was irreplaceable.[17]

The 1937 report on the Bonneville Project Act also emphasized funding scientific research into salmon migrations and the effects of dams on fish runs. Because of the vast areas traveled by salmon during their life cycle, considerable scientific uncertainty has always surrounded salmon migration. Despite over a half century of studies, these uncertainties persist. However, these scientific uncertainties never stopped hydroelectric developments pending their resolution. Even the federal Commissioner of Fisheries assumed water development must proceed, despite his unsettling conclusion that "the protection of individual runs menaced by virtual extinction must at the present be left to chance."[18]

The 1937 report led Congress to enact the Mitchell Act a year later. The Mitchell Act, discussed further in chapter 6, authorized funding of measures to preserve and protect Columbia Basin salmon, including hatcheries, fish ladders, irrigations screens, and habitat protection and restoration projects, as well as scientific studies. The Act also contained a broad directive to the Secretary of Interior to "perform all other activities necessary to the conservation" of Columbia Basin salmon. Despite this grant of expansive authority, the Secretary never interpreted it to include attempting to change the operation of Columbia Basin dams to improve salmon migration.[19]

Over the years, scientific uncertainty has been turned into a "heads I win, tails you lose" proposition for Columbia Basin salmon. Not only would dam building continue while scientific studies were undertaken, but federal power marketing and dam operating agencies increasingly took the position that no changes in river operations to benefit salmon could take place unless they were grounded on scientific proof, an attitude that would become pervasive concerning all activities with adverse effects on salmon. Thus, although Congress never expressly indicated that Columbia Basin salmon should be sacrificed in pursuit of navigation, irrigation, or hydropower, the federal agencies managing the dams ensured the decline of the salmon runs by employing optimistic assumptions about the adverse effects of the dams and by calling for more scientific study before making operational changes. Although these agencies funded the work of numerous biologists studying various aspects of the salmon life cycle, the demand for scientific certainty inhibited meaningful protection and restoration efforts.

One activity that did proceed despite scientific uncertainty was the construction of hatcheries funded under the Mitchell Act. Most of these hatcheries were situated in the Lower Columbia Basin below the dams, so that the salmon they produced would not be confronted with dam passage problems. This produced unfortunate distributional consequences, as upper basin fishers, including Indian tribes and Idahoans, bore the brunt of the dam-related losses with little or no compensation for many years.

Even worse, there is now widespread recognition that heavy reliance on hatchery fish damages wild fish productivity through competition for limited food and habitat, transmission of disease, and loss of genetic integrity through inbreeding. Hatchery fish also perform poorly in the wild: one study found wild salmon to be eight times more productive in terms of returning adults than hatchery salmon. Many biologists now consider hatcheries to be a narcotic, serving only to mask the magnitude of the problems that dam-induced alterations in streamflow regimes present for salmon. There are growing doubts about whether hatchery fish can even assist in rebuilding self-sustaining fish runs that spawn naturally. Virtually no biologists now believe that hatcheries can substitute for river conditions which facilitate fish spawning and migration.[20]

World War II and Its Aftermath[21]

Bonneville Dam began generating electricity in 1938; Grand Coulee came on line three years later, just eight months before Pearl Harbor. The defense build-up that began in 1940 provided the demand that obviated concerns over excess electricity. Lured by the prospect of abundant, cheap hydropower, Alcoa began building the first aluminum plant west of the Mississippi River in December 1939. Five more plants soon followed, and by 1942, aluminum plants consumed three-quarters of the electricity produced at Bonneville and Grand Coulee. During the war, the Northwest produced over 40 percent of the nation's aluminum, supplying essential components for aircraft, ships, and other war-related construction. Today, the Northwest still produces over 40 percent of U.S.-produced aluminum.[22]

Thus, the war turned what had been an overabundance of electricity into a lure for an electricity-intensive industry that would establish manufacturing as an important part of the Northwest economy, a region that had long been subjected to the boom-and-bust cycles associated with farming, fishing, and forestry. As the war drew to an end, regional planners sought to preserve the wartime economic boom with additional water projects. Driven by a fear of a post-war depression, Congress authorized an unprecedented number of water projects in the 1944 Flood Control Act and the 1945 Rivers and Harbors Act.[23]

In the Columbia Basin, the foundation for these congressional authorizations was laid in 1938 when the Corps of Engineers reviewed and amended its plan for water project development. Whereas the Corps' original 1932 plan called for ten dams on the Columbia, the focus of the 1938 plan shifted attention to the Lower Snake River, even though the Lower Snake had limited hydropower potential. The change was due to uncertainty as to whether the market for electricity could absorb more hydropower (later answered by the wartime boom and federal transmission line development that expanded markets) and the attractiveness of creating a slack-water navigation channel linking Lewiston, Idaho with the ocean. Even though such a navigation channel was hardly justified economically — the Corps estimated its benefits at only 15 percent of its costs

— local shipping and agricultural interests convinced the Corps to leave the issue "to the wisdom of Congress."

Seven years later, in the 1945 Rivers and Harbors Act, with no specific mention of any project or location, "the wisdom of Congress" authorized "such dams as are necessary" to produce the navigation channel, allow irrigation, and provide "surplus power." In this rather cavalier fashion Congress authorized four dams on the Lower Snake, the last of which was completed thirty years after its authorization, in 1975. These dams transformed the Lower Snake from a free-flowing river into a series of lakes and led to a precipitous decline in Snake River salmon which culminated in Endangered Species Act listings in the 1990s.

Congress did not, however, intend dam building on the Lower Snake to extinguish the river's salmon runs. In the same 1945 statute authorizing the Snake projects, Congress authorized construction of McNary Dam, situated just below the confluence of the Columbia and Snake, pledging that "adequate provision shall be made for the protection of anadromous fishes by affording them free access to their natural spawning grounds." By promising access to natural spawning grounds, Congress might have been interpreted to have established federal policies of ensuring that dam operations provide maximum fish passage and of favoring wild fish protection over hatchery production. But those who managed the dams and the salmon never interpreted the statute in this way. Instead, the operative assumption was that dam-related losses could be offset through hatchery production. This reliance on one technology to minimize the adverse effects of another proved disastrous.[24]

In the wake of catastrophic flooding in the spring of 1948, Congress directed the Corps to revise its Columbia Basin plan again. The ensuing report relied heavily on flood control as a rationale for recommending projects, notably recommending construction of two more dams on the Lower Columbia: The Dalles and John Day Dams. These dams, along with the already-authorized Lower Snake Dams, would complete the navigation channel to Lewiston, although the Corps anticipated navigation only ten months per year due to ice blockages.

The Corps' 1948 report gave considerable attention to salmon protection, outlining a $20 million plan of fish ladders, irrigation screens, habitat improvement, and hatchery construction that focused on the Lower Columbia. The plan envisioned mitigating upriver runs by "developing the salmon runs in the lower tributaries to the highest level of productivity." This commitment, coupled with a 1948 interagency agreement calling for federal-state coordination in implementing the Mitchell Act (discussed more fully in chapter 6) began the Lower Columbia River Fishery Development Program. The program aimed to maintain salmon harvests by using federal money to construct hatcheries situated almost exclusively in the lower basin. This federal money funded fish biologists to study hatchery technology, disease prevention, and nutrition.

As a result of increased hatchery production, fishery managers designed harvest seasons that would prevent too many hatchery fish returning to the hatcheries. Little thought was given to the effects of these high harvest levels on wild salmon, or to the effects of hatchery fish in terms of the carrying capacity of the rivers or ocean feeding grounds. Consequently, the federal money for the lower river fishery program proved to be, at best, a Faustian bargain. The program also disregarded treaty rights of tribes, whose fishing grounds were upriver from the program's focus.

Among the more notable broken promises of the Lower Columbia River Development Program was its commitment to avoid damming lower basin tributary streams like the Deschutes, Lewis, and Cowlitz Rivers. Although the federal government built no dams on these tributaries, utilities made no such commitment. Aided by expansive court interpretations of the Federal Power Act, utilities succeeded in obtaining hydroelectric licenses on those rivers in the 1950s, over the vigorous opposition of state fish agencies. In addition, four new non-federal dams joined the Rock Island Dam on the mainstem Mid-Columbia, leaving only the Hanford Reach (adjacent to the federal nuclear weapons reserve) undammed. On the Middle Snake, three non-federal dams built by the Idaho Power Company near Hells Canyon extinguished Southern Idaho and Eastern Oregon salmon runs and sealed off the Snake River's principal fall chinook spawning grounds. The expansion of private hydroelectric development in the 1950s made coordinating the power system more complex and organizing salmon restoration efforts more difficult.[25]

The Columbia River Treaty[26]

By the 1960s, nearly all of the sites for large hydroelectric projects in the U.S. Pacific Northwest had been developed or were under construction. Even so, the 30 percent of Columbia River flows that originated in Canada remained uncontrolled until they crossed the border. As a result, in years of high runoff, much of the Columbia's spring freshet had to be spilled around lower basin dams, producing no power. Although worthless for power production, the unharnessed freshet was vital to the efficient transportation of young salmon on their journey to the ocean each spring.

Damming the Columbia near its headwaters in Canada, where large storage sites existed, had been the subject of treaty negotiations since 1944. No agreement could be reached because Canadian storage would increase the power generating and flood control capability of every downstream dam in the U.S., and Canada wanted a share of those downstream benefits. The U.S. would not agree, and the ensuing deadlock lasted nearly two decades. Canada finally broke the logjam in the late 1950s by threatening to proceed with an alternative, unilateral development plan on the Peace River. Consequently, the U.S. reluctantly agreed to share downstream benefits on an equal basis. This agreement led to the 1961 signing of the Columbia River Treaty.[27]

The treaty called for the construction of four storage projects, three in Canada and another inundating Canadian lands. However, a dispute between the British Columbia provincial government and the Canadian federal government over who was to pay for construction costs, and where the power would be marketed, prevented ratification of the treaty until 1964. The four projects authorized by the treaty added over 20 million acre-feet of storage, doubling the storage capacity in the Columbia Basin and largely harnessing the Columbia's freshet, producing large-scale, unintended adverse effects on salmon runs.

Ratification of the Columbia River Treaty signaled the beginning of a mature Columbia Basin hydroelectric system. Not only did the treaty projects double the basin's storage capacity, the treaty induced downstream project operators to install additional generators to capture the river's increased power capacity. These modifications increased the ability of dam operators to meet peak electric demands. Unfortunately, seasonal peak loads in the Northwest do not occur during the spring and early summer high flows but instead during the winter, when electricity is used for space heating (an inefficient use of the electric resource). Consequently, hydroelectric operators seek to store the spring/summer freshet for release later in the year. But young salmon are dependent on high river flows in the spring and early summer for transport to the sea. The treaty gave system operators the means to change the hydrograph of the Columbia River from a river with large spring/summer flows to one in which much of the spring/summer freshet is stored for release in the fall and winter to meet power demands (see chart 2). This changed hydrograph is a reflection of hydropower's status as the *de facto* dominant use of the river.

Chart 2 — The Changed Hydrograph

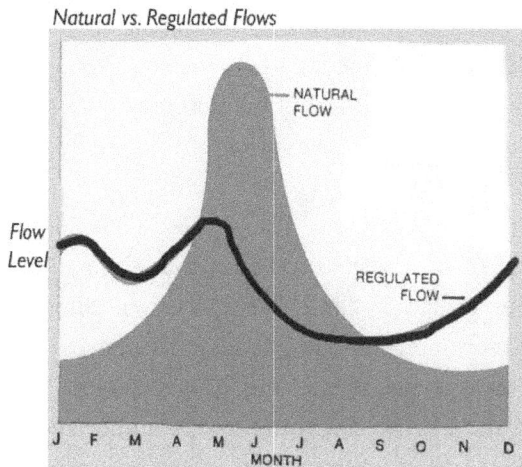

Courtesy of the Northwest Power Planning Council

The loss of the natural hydrograph is a major reason for depleted Columbia Basin salmon runs. Nothing in the Columbia River Treaty expressly elevated hydropower to the status of dominant use, however. No provision of the treaty purported to change any of the purposes for which dams below the treaty projects were authorized; hydropower remains a secondary purpose of these projects. Further, the treaty contains a provision which appears to allow a reduction in Canadian power benefits when water bypasses power generators and is not used for power production. Yet system operators often cited the treaty as justification for hydropower's dominance of Columbia Basin system operations, and there is no question that the planning processes spawned by the treaty largely ignored the needs of salmon.[28]

The most important planning process ushered in by the treaty was formalizing coordination of the new treaty projects among federal and nonfederal project operators downstream. Although project operators had been coordinating voluntarily for some time, the treaty's principle of sharing downstream benefits was premised on a fully integrated system. This integration was ensured by the signing of the 1964 Pacific Northwest Coordination Agreement. In the agreement the Bonneville Power Administration (BPA), the Corps of Engineers, and a number of public and private utilities agreed to detailed operating criteria, power exchange principles, and a formula for allocating downstream benefits. Through this long-term contract, the region's project operators agreed to fully integrate system operations, often referred to as the "one utility" concept.

At least until the Endangered Species Act began to affect system operations in the 1990s, annual planning under the Coordination Agreement gave little or no consideration to environmental impacts or public involvement. The operative assumption was that the dominant use of Columbia Basin dams was hydropower. Yet the Coordination Agreement expressly disclaimed any intent to elevate hydropower over "nonpower uses," such as salmon flows, and promised to "preserv[e] priority to such nonpower uses." Unfortunately for salmon, the system operators never interpreted the agreement to provide meaningful protection for migrating salmon, and the planning process it set in motion was aimed almost exclusively at maximizing hydropower benefits.[29]

Perhaps the most significant result of the Columbia River Treaty and the Coordination Agreement was confirmation of BPA's central role in system operations. For example, BPA purchased the Canadian portion of the downstream benefits for a 30-year term, which the Canadians earlier had sold to a consortium of U.S. utilities. Thus, through 1998, BPA had complete control over the Canadian entitlement, but this control was not used to prevent the decline of Columbia River salmon.

Another example of how the treaty cemented BPA's central role in Columbia Basin system operations concerned the construction of BPA's transmission line that electrically connects Northwest dams with California markets. Congress authorized construction of this "intertie" shortly after the treaty was ratified in 1964 to ensure that there would be markets for the additional power generated as a result of the treaty projects. However, the prospect of an intertie alarmed the aluminum industry, which feared the new California markets would jeopardize its access to the cheap hydropower which initially drew the industry to the Northwest. As a result of these concerns, Congress also enacted the Northwest Preference Act, signed into law only three weeks after it approved intertie construction funding. The Preference Act limited Northwest Power exports to power "surplus" after the needs of the Northwest, including the aluminum loads, had been satisfied.[30]

Thus, the legacies of the Columbia River Treaty were many and varied. The treaty prompted full integration of system operations, produced enhanced hydroelectric peaking capacity, began California power sales, and confirmed BPA's role as the region's principal hydropower agency. But by harnessing the spring freshet on which Columbia River salmon depended, the treaty and its aftermath helped to throw salmon runs into a decline from which they have yet to recover.

The Rise and Fall of BPA's Hydro-Thermal Program[31]

The Bonneville Power Administration (BPA) began the 1960s with a surplus of power due to an economic recession and new electric marketplace competition from a proliferation of nonfederal power projects built in the 1950s, like those on the Mid-Columbia and Middle Snake. As a result, BPA revenues fell, and the agency experienced a series of budget deficits that jeopardized its ability to repay the U.S. Treasury for the cost of the hydropower share of the federal dams. Instead of raising rates to increase revenues, however, the BPA Administrator decided to double industrial power sales. This strategy kept Northwest electric rates low, but it increased demand on the system and, within a few years, made power shortages appear imminent.

By the late 1960s, regional electric forecasts were predicting large-scale shortages. This rather rapid swing from surplus to shortage was due not just to increased industrial power sales, but also to an expanded planning horizon and forecasts of steady increases in electric consumption. The upshot was an expected tripling of anticipated power demand. In response, BPA and a consortium of over a hundred public and private utilities formed the Joint Power Planning Council to develop a plan for expanding the Northwest electric power system. The plan was to construct a series of coal and nuclear plants, adding new generators to Columbia Basin dams to meet peak load demands, and expanding transmission lines. This "Hydro-Thermal Power Program" was an integrated public/private partnership designed to expand the Northwest electric system beyond its hydroelectric capacity, which would largely reach its limit with the completion of the Columbia River Treaty projects. (See map 8.) The program envisioned coal and nuclear plants serving base loads, while hydroelectric power, with its great flexibility, would meet peak loads. River flows, in short, would be manipulated to coincide with high electric demands, on both a daily and a seasonal basis. Unfortunately, salmon need dependable daily flows and high flows during migration peaks in the spring and summer, whereas electric demand in the Northwest peaks during the morning and early evening and in the winter. The Hydro-Thermal Program gave no consideration to the needs of the salmon in fashioning hydropower's role in meeting peak power demands.

As initially conceived, the centerpiece of the Hydro-Thermal Program was a creative financing scheme under which BPA would purchase in advance the output of a thermal plant constructed by a utility customer of BPA. BPA would pay for these "electricity futures" by issuing credits to the utility — up to 85 percent of the utility's BPA bill for wholesale power and transmission line services. Known as "net billing," this financing scheme was an inventive way around BPA's lack of congressional authority to construct projects. The scheme allowed a coalition of public utilities with little

Map 8 — Major Dams on the Lower Columbia and Snake Rivers

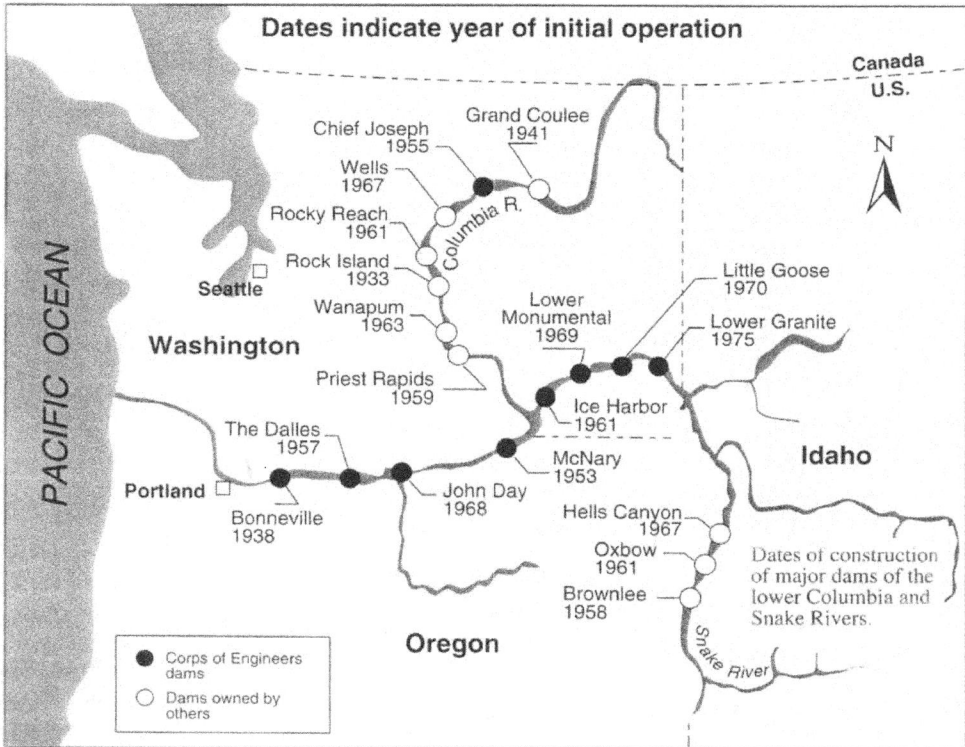

Dates indicate year of initial operation

Canada
U.S.

Chief Joseph 1955
Grand Coulee 1941
Wells 1967
Rocky Reach 1961
Rock Island 1933
Seattle
Wanapum 1963
Washington
Priest Rapids 1959
Columbia R.
Lower Monumental 1969
Little Goose 1970
Lower Granite 1975
Ice Harbor 1961
Idaho
The Dalles 1957
McNary 1953
Portland
John Day 1968
Bonneville 1938
Hells Canyon 1967
Oxbow 1961
Brownlee 1958
Oregon
Snake River

PACIFIC OCEAN

N

Dates of construction of major dams of the lower Columbia and Snake Rivers.

● Corps of Engineers dams
○ Dams owned by others

Courtesy of the U.S. Army Corps of Engineers

capital, known as the Washington Public Power Supply System (WPPSS), to begin construction of three nuclear power plants. In effect, these three WPPSS plants, along with part of the Trojan nuclear power plant built by Portland General Electric, were regionally insured, as BPA effectively assumed the risk of plant failures. Assumption of this risk would eventually cost BPA roughly $7 billion, and four of the WPPSS nuclear plants were stillborn.

Five years after its 1968 initiation, the Hydro-Thermal Program came to an abrupt halt. First, skyrocketing construction costs exceeded BPA's capacity to "net bill," as the cost overruns outstripped the amounts the participating utilities owed BPA. Second, the Internal Revenue Service revoked the tax exemption for bonds financing net-billed plants. When BPA terminated net billing in 1973, several nuclear plants were under construction, but the region was left with projected electric shortages and no plan to address them.

As a result, BPA and its customers quickly agreed to a new version of the Hydro-Thermal Power Program, christened "Phase 2." Phase 2 sought construction of seven more thermal plants but was dependent on BPA's negotiating experience instead of its deep pockets. Rather than purchase the future output of the proposed plants, under Phase 2 BPA would negotiate agreements between the utilities constructing the projects and BPA's customers. This would guarantee the utilities a market for their power, but the utilities, not BPA, would bear the risk of plant delays or failures.

A central element of the Phase 2 program was renegotiating power contracts with BPA's industrial customers to allow greater interruptability of industrial loads. In this way, BPA's industrial customers would supply residential and farm electric consumers with a form of insurance against power shortages as a result of plant delays or unforeseen electric load growth. But in 1975, when BPA attempted to issue its first new industrial contract to a new aluminum plant, environmentalists succeeded in obtaining a federal court injunction to prevent contract issuance until BPA satisfied the environmental assessment and public disclosure requirements of the National Environmental Policy Act (NEPA). Shortly thereafter, a federal court enjoined the entire Hydro-Thermal Program on NEPA grounds, for it also had been formulated with no consideration of environmental implications and no public involvement.[32]

Thus, BPA could not proceed with plans to expand the electric system until it produced an environmental impact statement on its Hydro-Thermal Program. Unfamiliar with NEPA's requirements, it took BPA nearly five years, until 1980, to produce the required documentation. In the interim, BPA notified its preference customers that it could no longer guarantee to meet increases in their power demands after 1983. The agency also informed its industrial customers that their contracts would be unlikely to be renewed when they expired in the 1980s.[33]

The demise of the Hydro-Thermal Program thrust the Pacific Northwest into an electric power crisis. Not only was the region facing apparent power shortages, rate inequities between consumers served by BPA's preference customers (public utilities) and those served by private utilities (which had been largely cut off from BPA's low-cost power in 1973) became apparent. Since most of the private utilities were in Oregon, while most of the public utilities were in Washington, the region seemed ready to embark on an interstate war over hydropower entitlements. Prospects for this war heightened when the Oregon Legislature enacted a law authorizing a public authority that would become a BPA preference customer for all domestic and rural consumers in the state. The city of Portland also filed suit seeking a judicial declaration that its residents were entitled to preference rights to BPA power.[34]

The impending shortages and growing rate inequities prompted a search for a congressional solution. Beginning in 1977, many bills were introduced in Congress to revise BPA authority. It was not until 1980, however, that Congress overhauled BPA's marching orders, as discussed in chapter 7.[35]

Salmon vs. Hydropower

Forty years of dam building transformed the Columbia into what Richard White has called "the organic machine." But although the dams have imposed obstacles to salmon migration and hold back the spring freshet that salmon need for transport to the sea, no federal statute authorizes hydropower dominance over salmon. In fact, the McNary Dam authorization of 1945 arguably required maximum passage for wild fish, but the hydroelectric system's operators never interpreted the statute this way. Similarly, the Secretary of Interior construed his apparent plenary authority to conserve salmon under the 1938 Mitchell Act narrowly, largely limited to funding hatcheries to compensate for dam-created losses.[36]

On the other hand, hydropower authorities were broadly interpreted. The Columbia River Treaty was often cited as authorization for hydropower dominance, despite the absence of any clear directive in this regard. Perhaps the epitome of this willingness to stretch existing authorities was BPA's invention of the "net billing" concept which allowed the agency to invest in nuclear plants without apparent legislative authority. BPA was able to find implied authority to use net billing to invest $7 billion in nuclear plants, yet the agency claimed it had no authority to take into account the needs of migrating salmon in the formulation and implementation of its Hydro-Thermal Program.

The $7 billion nuclear power debt reverberated throughout the region for years. Among other things, it meant that a significant percentage of BPA revenues went to serving the nuclear plant debt. Especially as market rates for electricity declined in the 1990s, this debt became a key factor in BPA's resistance to changes in system operations that would benefit salmon but reduce power revenues. In the mid-1990s, the agency brokered a "salmon cost cap" that was perhaps the most dramatic example of how the nuclear debt pitted the need to generate power resources against the costs of salmon restoration. As a federal judge wrote in another context, BPA's nuclear debt caused salmon restoration efforts to "proceed in a deficit situation."[37]

It did not have to be this way. The public nature of waterways articulated by Progressives and recognized by New Dealers could have been interpreted to include both hydropower generation and salmon migration. But even when system operators appeared to recognize that salmon were among the multiple users for which Columbia Basin dams should be operated, as in the Corps of Engineers' 1948 report, the operators quickly ignored their promises. Instead of taking seriously statements that salmon were to be protected by the "best possible means" of fish passage, and that the dams were to produce "minimum interference" with salmon habitat, the Corps pursued what Ed Chaney has called a "shadow policy" of pretending that the operation of the dams to maximize hydropower would not significantly damage salmon runs, or assuming that whatever damage occurred could be offset by the smallest investments possible, particularly by building hatcheries. This "shadow policy" allowed the Corps and BPA to elevate hydropower as the dominant purpose of Columbia Basin streamflows. However, this hydropower dominance was without legislative authority, ignored the warnings sounded as early as the 1937 report of the Commissioner of Fisheries, and severely crippled the signature natural resource of the Columbia Basin. Consequently, by the late 1970s, federal fish and wildlife agencies were considering the propriety of listing Columbia Basin salmon under the Endangered Species Act.[38]

6 — SECOND PROMISE: THE FALSE HOPE OF SALMON HATCHERIES

Attempts to enhance Columbia Basin salmon runs artificially through hatcheries began a century and a quarter ago when the first hatchery was situated on the Clackamas River in 1877. The initial impetus for hatcheries was overfishing — 19th century cannery owners saw hatcheries as a means of maintaining commercial salmon harvests in the face of a massive increase in fishing. In the 20th century, hatcheries became "mitigation" to offset the effects of development and operation of Columbia Basin dams: a means by which the region could have both hydropower and salmon. As a result, for nearly a half-century, hydroelectric dams and salmon hatcheries were inseparable elements of Columbia Basin water resource development. Then, when the dam-building era ended in the 1970s, more hatcheries were touted as the way to increase run sizes so that court-ordered allocations to treaty Indians could be satisfied while maintaining non-Indian harvests.[1]

In the last decade, listings under the Endangered Species Act have caused scientists to begin to question the efficacy of hatcheries. The century in which artificial production was the salmon mitigation measure of choice apparently had ended, due to widespread recognition of the costs that hatchery fish impose on naturally spawning fish, including disease, competition for food and habitat, and loss of genetic diversity. Scientists began to refer to hatcheries as an ill-advised technology aimed at fixing the damages caused by another technology, the dams. Some even claimed that hatcheries were the equivalent of a narcotic that masked the damage done to the salmon's ecosystem by hydropower and other habitat-damaging activities. Astonishingly, in 1999, 122 years after the first hatchery, the Northwest Power Planning Council claimed that hatchery production "must still be considered an experimental program," since it had yet to demonstrate its value.[2]

Early History

The first salmon hatchery on the West Coast was founded by Livingston Stone on the McCloud River, a tributary of the Sacramento River, in 1872. The thinking was that a Pacific coast hatchery would allow chinook salmon to be transplanted to denuded Eastern streams. Stone shipped the live eggs from the McCloud hatchery across the U.S. in refrigerated railroad cars for placement in Eastern rivers. About 20 percent of the 30,000 eggs survived the journey, but few adult salmon were produced, largely due to the fact that the transplantation was done in complete ignorance of the fact that salmon are divided into individual stocks with different genetic traits. In fact, Stone did not recognize the stock concept, believing that salmon returned to streams in a random, haphazard manner. Still, by 1877 Stone was shipping salmon eggs all over the world, to places like Prussia, Germany, the Netherlands, England, France, Canada, and Australia.[3]

In 1877, Stone journeyed to the Columbia Basin to build a salmon hatchery on the Clackamas River in Oregon for cannery owners on the Columbia River. But according to Stone, the Clackamas hatchery suffered from "unfavorable conditions," such as timber harvesting, mill operations, dams, and being "too near civilization." As a result, the operation proved to be a disappointment, and it was shut down in 1881, although it was later reopened as a federal hatchery in 1888. The McCloud hatchery also closed in the mid-1880s, although its resumption in 1887 encouraged the construction of canneries and the shipping of fresh salmon to markets in San Francisco and elsewhere. By the turn of the century, there were some fifteen hatcheries operating on the West Coast.[4]

After the turn of the century, salmon culturalists began experimenting with ponding and feeding salmon fry to increase survival rates, as some 50 million juvenile salmon were being released into the Columbia River to no apparent effect. The Oregon legislature began to fund salmon hatcheries, prompting construction on the Columbia, Willamette, McKenzie, and North Santiam Rivers. By 1917, returns to hatcheries had improved. Fish culturists claimed the improved returns validated new feeding practices, and subsequently these practices were adopted by the federal government. However, by the 1920s some federal scientists, like Stanford zoologist Willis Rich, claimed that there was no discernible scientific evidence showing that hatcheries improved run sizes. But culturalists continued to transfer salmon eggs cavalierly out of the basin which produced them, ignoring the evolving "home stream" theory which was challenging Stone's "random chance" theory of salmon migration. British Columbia scientists had presciently grasped the "home stream" theory as early as 1880, when A.C. Anderson, the province's Inspector of Fisheries, introduced the notions that salmon were organized into separate stocks, that the supply of salmon varied from river to river, and that there was a relationship between parent spawners and the health of the fish runs. That wisdom was not widely understood south of the Canadian border until the 1930s, however.[5]

The early experience with hatcheries reflected an overarching assumption that human intervention could improve upon and successfully manipulate nature. As early as 1857, George Perkins Marsh recognized the damaging effects of development on fish habitat, but concluded that habitat restoration in New England was "impractical." Thus, although fishery managers were aware of the adverse effects of habitat destruction in the 19th century, they either chose not to attempt to avoid habitat loss or presumed they could not control it. Instead, they focused on enhancing salmon production despite the habitat loss. This single focus on increasing production continued throughout most of the 20th century. The implicit assumption was that hatchery technology could overcome the adverse effects of damaging technologies like dams, mills, and timber harvests. Hatcheries offered the apparent promise of developing aquatic resources without considering the effects on salmon, yet maintaining salmon harvests. Another assumption underlying the proliferation of hatcheries was that the limiting factor in a species' overall productivity was spawning and rearing habitat, either because of habitat damage or because human intervention could improve on natural spawning. Although there was an undeniable attractiveness to assuming that hatcheries would compensate for all habitat loss, this promise proved to be unfounded.[6]

Dam Mitigation

The dam building era, which began in earnest in the 1930s, saw hatcheries take on a new significance. Hatcheries became the means by which Columbia Basin dam proponents could claim that the hydropower, flood control, and irrigation benefits of dams could be had without significant losses to salmon runs. In fact, as early as 1910, the policy of the states of Oregon and Washington was to allow dam builders to construct hatcheries instead of fishways for salmon passage. Given the fact that the efficacy of hatcheries was assumed and, at any rate, would take a long time to disprove, dam proponents could employ the promise of hatchery production to suggest that salmon runs would be unaffected by the dam construction and operation. Failure to impose a burden of proof on hatchery effectiveness allowed development to proceed unabated.[7]

In 1937, the year Congress enacted the Bonneville Project Act, the U.S. Commissioner of Fisheries reported to the U.S. Senate on the expected effects of Bonneville and Grand Coulee Dams on Columbia River salmon. The commissioner described "a dearth of information" about the effects of the dams and suggested what would become known in a later generation as an "adaptive management" approach to salmon conservation: modifying policies as new information became available. The report called for a new federal commitment to salmon research and described an "extensive program of transplantation of millions of fry" involving collection and reprogramming of upper basin salmon that would be blocked by Grand Coulee. The commissioner observed that "large investments are soon to be made in fish-cultural apparatus and property and millions of fry will be produced to compensate for the runs obstructed by Grand Coulee Dam." Consequently, he called for research on fish nutrition, hatchery-related diseases, and the effects of commercial harvests on individual runs. Although the commissioner called for increasing the federal fish research budget by three- or four-fold, the imperative of taking prompt action to attempt to compensate for dam-induced losses led him to conclude that protection of individual salmon runs "must at the present time be left to chance."[8]

The Mitchell Act, the Lower Columbia Fishery Development Program, and the Lower Snake Compensation Plan

Congress responded a year later by enacting the 1938 Mitchell Act, which authorized funding of a wide variety of remedial salmon measures in the Columbia Basin, including hatcheries, fish ladders, irrigation screens, habitat restoration projects, and scientific studies. Although the Mitchell Act was designed as an emergency measure to compensate for salmon losses due to Bonneville and Grand Coulee, the statute's cap of just $500,000 annually prevented hatchery construction and limited fishery managers' activities to a census and survey of most of the Columbia River tributaries. The statute also authorized the Secretary of the Interior to "perform all other activities necessary for the conservation of fishery resources of the Columbia River Basin," but that provision was never interpreted broadly by the secretary to enable him to change the operation of dams to facilitate salmon migration. The operative assumption was still that fishery concerns could not alter development.[9]

As World War II drew to a close, Congress authorized more dam building in the Rivers and Harbors Act of 1945. The act authorized "such dams as are necessary" on the Lower Snake River for navigation and irrigation. These dams became the four Lower Snake Dams. Also authorized was McNary Dam on the Columbia just below the confluence with the Snake. But Congress also expressly called for safe passage for salmon and "free access to their natural spawning grounds." This provision could have been interpreted as a federal policy favoring spawning fish over hatchery production, but none of the federal agencies interpreted it in this manner.[10]

The next year, in 1946, Congress amended the Mitchell Act, removing the $500,000 limit and authorizing agreements between federal and state fishery agencies to implement the statute. Two years later, in 1948, the states and the federal government used this authority to formulate what was called the "Lower Columbia Fishery Development Program." This program charted an ambitious plan of hatchery construction as mitigation for dam construction. The federal Fish and Wildlife Service and the Bureau of Indian Affairs had recommended halting dam construction until salmon problems were overcome, but the 1948 agreement assumed that attempting to halt dam construction would be futile. Although the program called for removing obstructions to fish passage, abating water pollution, screening water diversions, constructing fishways, transplanting of upriver runs to the lower river, and establishing fish refuges, most of its attention was focused on hatchery construction. Between the late 1940s and the early 1960s, Congress used Mitchell Act authority to fund construction of twenty-four hatcheries called for in the plan, twenty-three in Oregon and Washington but just one in Idaho, reflecting the lower basin bias of the program. This bias may have made sense in terms of minimizing the effects of the dams on hatchery-produced salmon, but it deprived upriver fishers — notably, treaty Indians and Idahoans — of replacement salmon.[11]

Also in 1948, the Corps of Engineers revised its plan for developing the Columbia River and its tributaries, which endorsed the Lower Columbia Fishery Development Program as the best means of maintaining the basin's salmon runs while continuing to construct dams. The Corps' revised plan also called for 1) "conservation of salmon and other migratory fish to the maximum practical extent," 2) "minimum interference . . . with existing fish and wildlife habitat," and 3) "the best possible means of passing salmon upstream and downstream at the dam sites." However, these promises were never taken seriously by the Corps or other dam operators, which apparently believed that fish protection was some other entity's problem: they were empty promises, forgotten in the rush to produce every possible kilowatt of hydropower from the Columbia River and its tributaries. The fate of the Columbia Basin salmon runs was to be left to the hatcheries called for by the Lower Columbia program and funded by the Mitchell Act. By the mid-1980s, Mitchell Act hatcheries were releasing approximately 100 million hatchery salmon annually in the Columbia River and its tributaries, roughly half of all hatchery fish produced in the basin.[12]

Congress finally reacted to the Lower Columbia Fishery Development Program's bias in favor of the lower basin by authorizing the Lower Snake Compensation Plan in 1976. This initiative was designed to mitigate the effects of the four federal dams on the Lower Snake. But those dams had been authorized 30 years before, in the 1945 Rivers and Harbors Act. No hatchery fish were produced under the Lower Snake plan until 1981, fully 35 years later and some two decades after the first of the Lower Snake Dams were finished. Thus, even if hatcheries could effectively compensate for habitat lost due to the dams, the Snake Basin incurred years of uncompensated losses. The plan called for releases of 27 million hatchery fish from nine hatcheries and eleven rearing facilities in the Snake Basin, but it emphasized sports fish, like spring chinook and steelhead, and made little attempt to replace fall chinook (the tribal mainstay), sockeye, or chum.[13]

Adverse Effects of Hatcheries on Wild Salmon[14]

Arguably, the Columbia Basin's dependence on hatchery salmon has maintained aggregate salmon numbers while reducing genetic diversity. However, genetic diversity is the key to healthy reproductive populations because natural genetic variability, the product of natural selection, is a reflection of the population's fitness to its habitat. Diversity is a consequence of years of reproductive isolation, which in turn is due to physical isolation and homing instincts. Hatchery-produced fish are the product of artificial selection, not natural selection. That means that their offspring are less likely to have genetic traits favorable to survival in the wild.

Under the artificial selection of the hatchery, salmon are selected on the basis of desired traits like large smolt size, early spawning capability, and early return time. Unfortunately, these traits often have little or nothing to do with successful reproduction in the wild, especially when artificial selection is accompanied by inbreeding resulting from mates sharing the same genetic characteristics. Artificial selection also factors in teaching hatchery fish to adapt to the hatchery environment by becoming tolerant of overcrowded conditions, responding to mechanized feeding, and learning to out-compete other fish for pellet food. Fish who succeed in this environment obviously have no special advantages once released into the wild.

Hatcheries also increase the probability of genetic drift, the likelihood that mating patterns will by chance produce decreased variability in genetic material, due to low numbers of "founding" salmon. Thus, hatcheries' greatest threat to genetic diversity is due to the hybridization of hatchery salmon and wild salmon. Hybrid offspring have lower survival rates in the wild than wild fish and lower survival rates than pure hatchery fish in hatcheries, reflecting the low fitness level of hybrid fish. The problem is that interbreeding of wild and hatchery fish prevents the traits of wild fish from becoming established while diluting wild fish survival characteristics.

Hatchery salmon also adversely affect wild salmon through competition for food and habitat, and the introduction of diseases. Since hatchery salmon are typically more abundant and often older and larger, they frequently swamp wild juvenile salmon in the competition for food and rearing habitat. Hatchery fish also carry and transmit diseases harmful to wild populations. Hatchery overcrowding, poor water quality, and other stressful conditions are fertile incubators of diseases like bacterial kidney disease, infectious hematopoietic necrosis, furunculosis, and whirling disease. Hatcheries have had both direct and indirect effects on habitat: the former occurring when hatchery fish exceed stream carrying capacity through mass production of a few selected species and effluent releases of polluted water; the latter due to the fact that hatcheries became the mitigation technique of choice, helping to justify habitat-damaging activities like logging and dam building.

Perhaps the most significant indirect adverse effect of hatcheries on wild salmon stocks concerns mixed stock harvests. In the ocean, where stocks are intermingled, harvest managers historically set harvest rates based on total abundance of salmon. This allowed maintenance of traditional harvest rates but also produced overharvests of weak wild stocks. Thus, the adverse effects of hatcheries on wild salmon include not merely a loss of genetic diversity, increased competition and diseases, and habitat damage but also pernicious harvest management regimes.

Supplementation

Supplementation involves changing hatchery practices by using native, wild broodstock, matching the broodstock to the local environment, and rearing fish in conditions as natural as possible in order to boost productivity of weak stocks or to seed barren streams. Supplementation, as the name implies, seeks to supplement, not supplant, wild salmon stocks. Advocates of supplementation hope that it will produce spawning runs as close as possible to the genetic composition of native runs. The ultimate goal is to create healthy runs which will no longer require hatcheries. Critics fear that supplementation will incur the same genetic problems as traditional hatcheries and claim that it represents yet another technological fix that encourages fishery managers to avoid confronting the root causes of salmon declines, like habitat destruction and overfishing.[15]

Supplementation efforts have a long history, beginning with Stone's program in the 1870s at the McCloud and Clackamas hatcheries, from which he shipped salmon eggs all over the world. One notable transplantation program was the effort in the 1940s to mitigate the effects of the Grand Coulee Dam's destruction of over 1,000 miles of salmon spawning habitat. Fishery managers collected salmon trying to surmount the dam, trucked them to a hatchery, spawned them artificially, reared the offspring for a year in the hatchery, and turned them loose in tributaries below the dam. This effort to reprogram the upper basin stocks to the Mid-Columbia was first regarded as a success, but a quarter-century later was criticized for salvaging nothing. However, a 1999 assessment concluded that the program at least managed to avoid adversely affecting the genetic diversity of salmon stocks in the Mid-Columbia, since it apparently left little genetic legacy.[16]

Despite the apparent contemporary perception that the Grand Coulee transplanting program was a success, fish managers did not pursue supplementation on a large scale for two reasons. First, successful supplementation requires available habitat, and the aggressive dam building that occurred in the Columbia Basin after World War II eliminated most of the prime habitat. Second, the apparent success of hatcheries in producing enormous numbers of fish for harvest induced fish managers to abandon efforts to reestablish naturally spawning stocks. As hatcheries became the prime production tools, managers concentrated on building new rearing ponds, developing better fish food pellets, and discovering new drugs instead of preserving natural habitat.[17]

In the 1980s, fish managers rediscovered supplementation. This renewed interest was a consequence of the serious adverse consequences stemming from reliance on hatcheries to maintain harvests, although it reflected the same mechanistic world view. The ESA listings of the early 1990s confirmed that the existing system was badly broken. The listings served as a wake-up call to regional fishery officials who, through the Columbia Basin Fish and Wildlife Authority (CBFWA), an interagency organization comprised of federal, state, and tribal fishery agencies, released an integrated basinwide plan in June of 1991 which included supplementation as a primary means of promoting salmon recovery.[18]

The CBFWA plan helped initiate a regional debate on the merits of supplementation to help restore spawning salmon stocks, which continues to this day. Wild fish proponents oppose supplementation, claiming that it will further exacerbate risks of genetic harm to wild stocks. They also maintain that a reemphasis on supplementation would be just another short-sighted attempt to increase harvests that disregards the real causes of salmon decline. The basin's Indian tribes, on the other hand, whose upriver locations meant they were served worst from the historic emphasis on hatchery production in the lower basin, believe that the risks are negligible and are outweighed by the potential benefits. The tribes point to many tributaries where spawning salmon have been largely extirpated and urge that supplementation, if carried out with a concern for maintaining genetic diversity, can be a valuable recovery mechanism in coordination with other conservation and restoration measures. Perhaps the most successful example of supplementation is in the Hanford Reach, where the basin's most productive spawners, the Hanford Reach fall chinook, are supplemented by Priest Rapids hatchery fish. But the efficacy of supplementation, like hatcheries in general, remains unproven.[19]

Assessments of Hatchery Efficacy

Over the last decade, there have been several evaluations of the effectiveness of Columbia Basin salmon hatcheries. All of the studies expressed serious doubts about the capability of traditional hatchery operations to maintain run sizes without producing substantial adverse effects on naturally spawning salmon. One study did recommend maintaining hatchery production in an effort to produce a balance between continuing ocean and lower river harvest levels and minimizing adverse effects on spawning salmon. But most of the studies evinced considerable skepticism about the ability of existing operations to avoid harm to wild salmon. The studies included two findings of jeopardy to listed salmon from current hatchery programs and numerous calls for protecting and restoring habitat and observing ecological principles in the design of all artificial production efforts. Following is a discussion of those studies.

National Fish Hatchery Review Panel (1994). In response to a request from the Director of the U.S. Fish and Wildlife Service, the National Fish and Wildlife Foundation convened a panel of scientists to review the Fish and Wildlife Service's hatchery program and to suggest ways in which the program could foster ecosystem management objectives. The resulting 1994 report called for a fundamental redirection of the program, accusing it of lacking definite goals, objectives, and implementation and evaluation strategies.

The report identified habitat alteration or destruction as the primary cause of fish population decline and concluded that hatcheries were not a suitable substitute for lost habitat. For example, the report found that mitigation based solely on hatchery production failed to halt population declines. Instead, it recognized habitat protection and restoration as the keys to native fish stock survival. The report called for a new role for hatcheries, which would be governed by ecosystem management plans, including 1) genetic and ecological evaluations of native stocks, 2) risk assessments, 3) limiting hatchery production to stocks similar to native stocks known to inhabit the same type of habitat, and 4) eliminating the stocking of non-native species.[20]

The CBFWA Draft Program EIS (1996). In 1996, the CBFWA prepared a draft program environmental impact statement (EIS) on hatcheries for three federal agencies which operate or fund hatcheries: the National Marine Fisheries Service, the U.S. Fish and Wildlife Service, and the Bonneville Power Administration. The draft EIS, which has yet to be put in final form, evaluated the effects of Columbia Basin hatcheries in recognition that changes in hatchery operations "to meet historic and new fishery management challenges" were necessary. The draft considered a variety of basinwide policy alternatives but no specific hatchery or supplementation programs or local carrying capacities.

The draft EIS explained many of the negative effects of hatcheries on wild fish discussed above, but it also emphasized the competition that occurs between hatchery and wild fish in reservoirs and in estuaries and predation, which is exacerbated by predators attracted by the numerous hatchery fish. The draft EIS also suggested that hybridization of hatchery and wild fish might be minimized by improvements in streamflows, increased acclimation, upstream release sites, and use of older smolts.

The preferred alternative selected by the draft EIS was to continue to provide hatchery fish in the lower basin to support harvest, while increasing natural production to about a 35 percent seeding level within twenty-five years, mostly by increasing supplementation in the Snake and Upper Columbia subbasins. In short, the draft attempted to change policy from producing hatchery salmon almost exclusively for harvest to producing fish for both harvest and natural stock recovery. Among the alternatives rejected was one that would have shifted emphasis away from supporting harvests to enhancing natural production from supplementation in order to achieve a 75 percent natural seeding level within twenty-five years, and another that would have virtually eliminated all hatchery production and instead focused on preserving genetic diversity. Apparently, CBFWA rejected these alternatives because of the disruption to harvest they would produce. The draft EIS concluded, "[p]roperly operated and monitored, modern hatcheries should be able to minimize any risks of adversely impacting the long-term biological reproductive capability of naturally spawning populations." Native fish advocates would not agree. Neither did several ensuing scientific reports.[21]

Return to the River (1996). Also in 1996, the independent scientific group advising the Northwest Power Planning Council issued its report, *Return to the River,* which considered, among other issues, the role of hatcheries in salmon restoration. The scientists were much more skeptical of the value of hatchery production than was the CBFWA report discussed above, noting that 80 percent of Columbia Basin salmon are of hatchery origin, that fully 40 percent of the expenditures on salmon restoration during the 1980s was spent on hatcheries, and half of the Council's expected increase in salmon production was to come from hatcheries. The report was critical of this continued reliance on hatcheries, observing that since 1960 hatchery production has increased substantially while returning salmon have not. Moreover, the scientists claimed that there was substantial evidence that hatchery fish not only do not compensate for habitat destruction, they adversely affect wild fish due to spread of disease, increased competition with wild fish for food and habitat, overharvests in mixed fisheries, and genetic interactions reducing fitness and genetic variability.[22]

The scientists suggested that the role of hatcheries in the Columbia Basin ought to be redefined, limited, and integrated into a comprehensive restoration strategy focused on habitat protection and restoration. The report acknowledged that hatcheries could have a useful temporary role during the time it takes to reduce the causes of natural mortality or to rebuild depressed populations through supplementation. But the report carefully limited its endorsement of supplementation by describing supplementation as an experimental approach requiring careful design and rigorous evaluation. The scientists recommended undertaking a comprehensive evaluation of Columbia Basin hatcheries to determine whether the costs of hatcheries are worth their benefits, whether particular hatcheries are achieving their original purposes, and whether they are adding to or substituting for wild fish.[23]

Upstream (1996). A third 1996 report that considered the role of hatcheries in salmon restoration was the National Research Council's study, *Upstream: Salmon and*

Society in the Pacific Northwest. The report's perspective on hatcheries was quite similar to that of *Return to the River.* The report considered hatcheries, despite their 120-year history, to be an unproven technology that has damaged wild runs, and which is unlikely to compensate for habitat loss over the long run. The report did see a short-term role for hatcheries as a temporary aid in rehabilitating natural salmon populations. But *Upstream* cautioned that the purpose of hatcheries had to change, from being a mechanism to maintain harvests or compensate for losses of juvenile fish due to hydropower-related habitat loss to being a component of a comprehensive restoration plan in which hatcheries will be employed only where they will not harm wild fish.[24]

The report concluded that current hatchery operations fail to operate within a coherent strategy based on the genetic structure of salmon populations. Most hatcheries have no protocols to ensure that they will operate consistently with other hatcheries or with a genetic conservation policy. The report recommended that hatcheries be tested for their effects on wild fish, dismantled or reprogrammed if they interfere with strategies aimed at rebuilding naturally spawning salmon, and confined to areas where freshwater habitats are limited both in the short and long terms. *Upstream* counseled that hatcheries should be considered merely as an experiment, used only as part of a program of adaptive management, and excluded altogether from areas where the prognosis of freshwater habitat rehabilitation is good. The report concluded by advocating a goal of conserving genetic diversity among and within both hatchery and naturally spawning populations, meaning that all hatchery practices contributing to genetic interaction between wild and hatchery-produced salmon would be carefully monitored and controlled.[25]

Regional Reviews: RASP and IHOT.[26] Two other notable hatchery reviews were the reports of Regional Assessment of Supplementation Project (RASP) and the Integrated Hatchery Operations Team (IHOT). The 1992 RASP reviewed supplementation efforts, developed a model estimating the risks and benefits of supplementation, and established guidelines to eliminate negative genetic and ecological interactions between wild and hatchery fish. The report called for establishing qualitative measurements of supplementation efforts, such as harvest distribution, stock selection, and run timing; identifying limiting factors in fish populations; and subjecting all supplementation projects to risk analysis and close monitoring and evaluation.

The IHOT grew out of the Northwest Power Planning Council's 1992 program amendments and called for improvements in the coordination and operation of hatchery facilities. The IHOT report is a kind of hatchery operations manual, including performance standards and guidelines on fish health, ecological interactions, and genetics. The report established a goal of producing hatchery fish with minimal effects on wild stocks, while contributing to harvest opportunities and spawning populations. But while the report called for hatchery programs to minimize adverse effects on aquatic ecosystem productivity and to maintain adequate genetic variation and fitness in populations, it did not address the adequacy of monitoring and assessment programs to achieve these policies.

The NMFS BiOps.[27] In 1995, NMFS evaluated the effect of 71 federal and non-federal hatcheries operated by five federal agencies and three states in terms of their effect on ESA-listed Snake River salmon. NMFS also consulted internally on the operation of 25 hatcheries that it operates under Mitchell Act authority. In combination, the hatcheries annually release over 200 million hatchery fish into basin streams.

Unlike the optimism expressed in the CBWFA draft EIS, NMFS concluded that continued hatchery operations would in fact jeopardize the continued existence of Snake River salmon because the operations were inconsistent with its proposed recovery plan. NMFS expressed particular concern that hatchery production was exceeding the Snake Basin's carrying capacity. While its biological opinion (BiOp) found no specific hatchery operation likely to jeopardize a listed species, NMFS did freeze hatchery releases at 1994 levels: 20.2 million in the Snake Basin and 197.4 million throughout the Columbia Basin. NMFS also recommended that in order to avoid jeopardy to listed species, hatchery operators should eliminate all non-endemic stocks and adopt measures to prevent straying which can produce hybridization and its associated adverse effects.[28]

In 1999, NMFS issued a new BiOp that, as discussed in chapter 9, determined that hatchery operations would jeopardize the continued existence of listed Lower Columbia and Snake River steelhead. Jeopardy was a consequence of non-endemic hatchery stocks threatening the listed species with genetic introgression. The BiOp consequently imposed a number of conditions on operations at several Columbia Basin hatcheries, the first time such operational changes were required by the ESA.[29]

The Spirit of the Salmon (1995). In 1995, the main proponent of supplementation, the four Columbia Basin tribes with Stevens Treaty fishing rights — the tribes of the Umatilla, Yakama, and Warm Springs reservations and the Nez Perce tribe — through the Columbia River Inter-Tribal Fish Commission (CRITFC), released their comprehensive salmon plan, *Wy-Kan-Ush-Mi Wa-Kish-Wit*, or *The Spirit of the Salmon*. A centerpiece of the tribal plan was its advocacy of supplementation to recover fish "populations that are fragmented and declining, and where other remedial actions cannot be implemented quickly enough or on a scale that is large enough to halt further population losses." The plan stated that hatcheries should simulate natural conditions to ensure that natural and hatchery fish groups are managed as a single gene pool. The goal was to reestablish naturally spawning salmon runs, instead of continuing hatchery operations which employ rearing and release methods.[30]

The Spirit of the Salmon would use supplementation both to increase diminished runs and to create salmon populations where they do not exist. The tribes maintained the genetic risks associated with supplementation could be minimized, and they challenged the notion that the best way to restore salmon runs is to concentrate exclusively on conserving the genetic integrity of severely depleted runs through conservation efforts. The tribes claimed that the fallacy of this approach is reflected in the fact that even runs benefitting from strict preservation measures have suffered increasing loss of genetic diversity. In short, since exclusive reliance on habitat preservation will not rebuild salmon runs to produce economically viable harvests, the tribal plan concluded that supplementation must be an indispensable part of any restoration effort and asserted that "the increasing likelihood of species extirpation is in fact the far greater genetic risk."[31]

The Northwest Power Planning Council's Review of Hatchery Production (1997). In 1997, Congress asked the Northwest Power Planning Council and its Independent Scientific Advisory Board to review all federally funded hatchery programs in the Columbia Basin and recommend a coordinated policy to spend limited federal dollars in a cost-effective fashion that also maximized benefits to the fish. In November 1999, the Council released a report which, remarkably, noted that even after nearly a century and a quarter of experience with hatcheries, artificial production's success at providing harvest opportunities remains questionable, especially in terms of providing long-term, sustainable harvests. Yet the report noted that hatchery fish comprise roughly 50 percent of Columbia Basin adult fall chinook, 70-80 percent of Columbia Basin spring/summer chinook, and 95 percent of Columbia Basin coho.[32]

The Council observed that questions about the efficacy of hatcheries have grown in recent years because the issue of efficacy is no longer judged solely on hatcheries' ability to produce fish for harvests but also includes 1) broadening harvest opportunities to more areas; 2) improving the survival of hatchery fish by using techniques that mimic natural spawning, rearing, and migration patterns; 3) avoiding harm to naturally spawning fish; and 4) actually assisting in preserving and rebuilding naturally spawning fish runs. The report suggested that, given the uncertainties and complexities surrounding hatcheries, the key issues to be resolved by policymakers is how much risk to accept, and how to manage that risk.[33]

The Council's report adopted several policies to guide the use of artificial production. These included a policy of considering hatcheries only in the context of the environment in which they will be used, thus allowing artificial production to proceed only if consistent with an ecological, science-based foundation for fish and wildlife recovery. Because the ability of artificial production remains unproven over the entire salmon life cycle, the report concluded that hatcheries must still be considered to be an experimental program which should be implemented with an experimental design, including an "aggressive program to evaluate benefits and address scientific uncertainties." The report also asserted that, in light of recent scientific studies, effective Columbia Basin salmon restoration will depend "far more on protecting and restoring biological diversity than simply increasing abundance." Consequently, a central consideration in all hatchery program designs must be to minimize effects on biological diversity and use artificial production, where possible, to help reverse declines in biological diversity. This may be accomplished, the report suggested, by using locally adapted or compatible broodstocks and reducing stock transfers and use of non-endemic stocks. While it sounds revolutionary, this suggestion merely repeated the advice given by Canadian biologist Russell Foerster a half century before.[34]

Although the Council's report acknowledged that production for harvest remains a legitimate management objective, that goal was secondary to maintaining naturally spawning populations. Perhaps most significantly, the report stated that entities operating hatcheries must explicitly 1) identify the purpose of the facility, 2) explain the underlying biological problem the hatchery attempts to remedy, and 3) determine how long the hatchery operation will persist. The latter requirement seemed to imply that hatcheries were a temporary expediency, an assumption not widely accepted among hatchery operators.[35]

Initially, these policies caused the Council's independent scientific review panel to recommend not funding numerous CBFWA hatchery projects in 1999, including several belonging to tribes. The panel subsequently recommended funding most after a second review, and the Council ended up conditionally funding many of the projects. But the experience reinforced the necessity of independent scientific review of all projects, including supplementation programs. The upshot seemed to be to impose a new burden of proof that hatchery proponents, including the tribes' supplementation projects, must sustain.[36]

The Future of Hatcheries

Hatcheries have been called a "halfway technology" that is doomed to fail. It seems abundantly clear that hatcheries cannot solve the Columbia Basin salmon crisis. In fact, the evidence suggests that, however well intentioned, traditional hatchery management is a major factor in the decline of Columbia Basin salmon, causing loss of genetic diversity, overuse of and adverse effects on habitat, disease proliferation, and overharvesting of wild salmon in mixed stock fisheries. Hatcheries are also expensive to operate and dependent upon the willingness of politicians to continue to appropriate taxpayer dollars to operate them. For all these reasons, the future of hatcheries as the mainstay of Columbia Basin salmon harvests, particularly in light of the Northwest Power Planning Council's apparent determination to make hatcheries justify their operation as a prerequisite for funding, is open to serious question.[37]

The tribes' supplementation plans are perhaps more meritorious, although they too must now shoulder the burden of proof to obtain federal funding. That may be frustrating to the tribes, who were neglected by Columbia Basin hatchery policy for virtually all of the 20th century. But supplementation probably ought to bear the burden of proof, given that it remains largely an unproven, although intriguing, technology. For example, one study of supplementation projects found that success is rare: of 316 projects studied, just 25 successfully supplemented existing naturally spawning runs.[38]

Moreover, adverse effects on wild stocks have occurred. But if hatchery stock is closely related to natural spawning stocks, the chances for success improve. And supplementation programs seeking to reestablish naturally spawning runs in areas where salmon have been extirpated have demonstrated some success, as have supplementation programs involving stocks with short freshwater life cycles. Supplementation of chinook, however, has usually failed. And supplementation projects that mimic traditional hatchery practices produce the same problems in terms of flooding ecosystems with artificially introduced fish, along with accompanying low survival rates and neglect of habitat problems.[39]

The tribes' approach to supplementation, as reflected in their *The Spirit of the Salmon* plan, may survive close scientific scrutiny. First, the tribes' reliance on supplementation is not a single-focused effort at recovery: the plan also advocates habitat improvement, including drawdown of several mainstem reservoirs. Second, the tribes propose to use supplementation only under the most favorable of circumstances: mostly (not entirely) in streams without spawning salmon, with local broodstock and species that have short freshwater life cycles. Given the desperate state of most of the salmon runs the tribes depend upon for their livelihood, their religion, and their culture, it does not seem unreasonable to allow the tribes to experiment with supplementation, especially since the region continues its longstanding, although unsuccessful, experiment with traditional hatchery technology throughout most of the basin.

7 — THIRD PROMISE: THE NORTHWEST POWER ACT

The forecasted power shortages, rate inequities, and court injunctions described in chapter 5 that caused the Northwest electric power crisis of the late 1970s coincided with a status review examining whether Columbia Basin salmon runs had declined to such an extent that they warranted listing under the Endangered Species Act. The search for a response to both crises led Congress to draft legislation designed both to restructure the Northwest electric power industry and to rebuild depleted Columbia Basin salmon runs. That remarkable law, the Northwest Power Act, signed into law by President Carter in late 1980, established a number of pathbreaking fish and wildlife principles. These principles included the concept that Northwest electric ratepayers should pay the full cost of restoring fish and wildlife damaged by the construction and operation of the hydroelectric system. The goal was to make fish and wildlife restoration a "co-equal partner" with hydropower generation, to produce parity between the two resources. After two decades of implementation, this parity goal remains elusive, as hydroelectric operators continue to resist restructuring system operations. Eventually, the inability to create the "co-equal partnership" envisioned by the Act's drafters led to the Endangered Species Act listings of the 1990s.[1]

The "co-equal partnership" the Northwest Power Act sought to create was actually the product of a false premise: that Columbia Basin salmon could be restored through altering hydroelectric operations alone. The Act emphasized improved fish passage at dams and improved river flows from upstream reservoirs which, the statute claimed, were substantially obtainable from the existing hydroelectric system. The assumption was the standard appeal of technological fixes: the region could restore salmon with relatively small changes to the operation of the hydroelectric system while retaining other benefits of the dams, like irrigation and navigation. Twenty years later, it seems clear that incremental, technical changes to the hydroelectric system will not be sufficient to restore the Columbia Basin's salmon runs because those changes do not address protection and restoration of critical spawning and rearing areas. As chapter 13 argues, restoring the endangered Snake River runs will probably require breaching the economically marginal federal dams on the Lower Snake.[2]

Even if the basic premise and optimism of the Northwest Power Act was flawed, and even if its processes were eclipsed by the Endangered Species Act in the 1990s, the 1980 Act and its implementation are still worthy of study. For one thing, hydroelectric dams remain the major source of human-induced salmon mortalities. For another, the regional focus of the Northwest Power Act is more attuned to an ecosystem approach than the single-species focus of the Endangered Species Act. Finally, however misguided its basic premise, the Northwest Power Act was unable to achieve even its limited objectives. That failure is instructive for other, more ambitious restoration efforts, because it reveals how easily economic interests wishing to preserve the status quo can resist changes which would threaten their hegemony.[3]

Origins

In September 1977, the Bonneville Power Administration (BPA) and its customers drafted legislation introduced by Senator Henry Jackson of Washington designed to resolve the region's electricity problems. Neither that bill, nor a less complex successor introduced a year later, progressed very far by the time the 95th Congress adjourned in late 1978. Some thought all that was needed was a one-sentence bill authorizing BPA to acquire new power sources to serve increased demands. However, many of BPA's customers were suspicious of granting the agency more authority, and they wanted assurances that their access to low-cost hydropower would continue.[4]

In the 96th Congress, BPA's customers coalesced behind a bill that would allow BPA to acquire new power sources. But the bill subjected acquisition authority for large resources to oversight by a new interstate entity, the Northwest Power Planning Council. The Council would also have the responsibility to forecast future electric demands. Other provisions established a complex rate-setting process, guaranteeing continued preference to BPA power for public utilities but diminishing rate disparities between public and private utilities. The bill also authorized long-term industrial contracts, which were included in the bill that passed the Senate in August 1979. The Senate bill contained only a vague provision regarding fish and wildlife. But aided by a General Accounting Office report which concluded that Columbia Basin dams were the chief cause of the decline of the salmon, fish and wildlife concerns became a major issue in the House of Representatives, delaying the bill for over a year.[5]

House Commerce Committee Chairman John Dingell of Michigan, who had fished for steelhead in the Northwest, made it clear that unless the Senate bill became a vehicle for fish and wildlife restoration, the bill would not pass his committee. Under Dingell's leadership, the House bill included a number of unprecedented fish and wildlife provisions. By the time the House passed the bill in November 1980, the election of Ronald Reagan had occurred, many members of Congress had not been reelected, and the Senate had time only to accept or reject the House bill. Two days after its passage in the House, the Senate agreed to the House version of the bill, and President Carter signed the Northwest Power Act into law on December 5, 1980.[6]

The New Mandate[7]

Since 1937, Congress had authorized BPA to market power at the "lowest possible rates" according to "sound business principles" to encourage "widespread electric use." Although the Northwest Power Act did not repeal these provisions, it fundamentally modified each of them. First, the Act changed the widespread use directive by giving priority to conservation and efficient use of electric power, a reflection of the fact that conservation programs are often the cheapest means of meeting increased electric demand. By considering conservation to be a priority resource, the Act aimed to reduce the number of large, expensive central generating plants — especially coal and nuclear plants — the construction of which had caused rates to rise so precipitously in the 1970s. The Act was remarkably successful in ushering in an era of meeting demands without constructing large new plants: in the 1980s, the statute's encouragement of conservation and its assignment of forecasting to the new interstate

Council helped the region avoid continuing to make commitments to expensive (and risky) coal and nuclear plants. In the 1990s, technological developments, electric deregulation, and market forces made gas turbines the resource of choice to meet increased demand.[8]

Second, by creating the new interstate Council and also calling for involvement of the states, local governments, and the public in regional electric power planning, the 1980 statute recognized that "sound business principles" is not a technical question left to the engineers and accountants at BPA. Instead, the Act required BPA to seek out and involve the public to ensure that "sound business principles" result from a pluralistic process and systematic consideration of divergent perspectives. Closely related to this commitment to open process was the statute's concept of shared powers, best reflected in the creation of the interstate regional Council. An eight-member agency comprised of two gubernatorial appointees from each of the four Northwest states, the Council was created to impose a check on BPA, ensuring against unwise investments through its authority to veto large BPA power acquisitions and promulgate a regional electric power plan to forecast electric demand. The Council is an unusual entity, since it is not a federal agency, yet derives its authority from a federal statute that vested the new interstate agency with an uncertain amount of oversight over federal agencies like BPA and the Corps of Engineers. In short, the Act sought to reduce the risk of errors, like those BPA made in the 1970s in its nuclear program, by establishing a new system based on open and pluralistic administrative processes, shared decision making powers, and the availability of judicial review.[9]

Third, and perhaps most important, the 1980 statute modified the mandate of "lowest possible rates" by promising that electric users would pay all the costs of developing and transmitting electricity, including environmental costs. In fact, the Act not only required future actions to internalize environmental costs, it also made a significant commitment to compensate for past losses sustained by Columbia Basin fish and wildlife caused by the hydroelectric system. The Northwest Power Act thus embraced a theory of enterprise liability which recognized that electricity prices should include all the costs of production, including fish and wildlife and environmental costs.[10]

Statutory Innovations[11]

The Northwest Power Act directed the Northwest Power Planning Council to create a program "to protect, mitigate, and enhance" the Columbia Basin's fish and wildlife "to the extent affected by the development and operation" of the basin's hydroelectric system. The Act specifically ordered improved river flows and bypass systems at mainstem dams for better salmon migration. The statute's legislative history admitted "past mistakes" and envisioned that the Council's plan would make fish and wildlife "co-equal partner[s]" with hydropower production, "on a par" with other project purposes. The congressional architects recognized that this co-equal partnership would necessitate power losses, but they were confident that "imaginative and effective measures" could avoid "unreasonable" power losses because power interests had testified that they were "anxious to accommodate fish and wildlife needs."[12]

To achieve these objectives, the Act included a number of innovative provisions that place it in the vanguard of federal fish and wildlife law. First, the statute called for a systemwide remedial program for the entire Columbia Basin. Second, the Act revolutionized the philosophy of wildlife mitigation by emphasizing changes in dam operations instead of merely creating substitute resources. Third, where operational changes could not compensate for losses — that is, where losses were irretrievable — the statute authorized "offsite enhancement," in order to focus restoration efforts on areas where habitat remained. Fourth, Congress lowered the burden of proof for undertaking remedial action by requiring that the program 1) be based on only the "best available scientific knowledge," not scientific certainty; 2) favor biological outcomes over economic ones; and 3) defer to the recommendations of agencies and Indian tribes with fish and wildlife expertise. Fifth, the Act ordered the Council to treat the river on a systemwide basis, not as a collection of discrete parts, a directive that only recently produced an integrated approach to salmon restoration. Sixth, the legislation tapped the revenue stream generated by hydroelectric sales as the principal source of financing for the restoration program it required. This avoided some of the uncertainties and inequities of relying on future congressional appropriations.[13]

Finally, the Northwest Power Act substantially revised a number of institutional relationships. Most notable was the creation of the interstate Council as a voice for regionalism. Less obvious, but perhaps of greater long-term significance, was the statute's persistent recognition of Indian tribes as the equal of state fish and wildlife agencies in the development and implementation of the Council's program. Historically, state fish and wildlife agencies and Northwest Indian tribes fought epic battles over the allocation of salmon, to the detriment of the resource itself. The 1980 Act continued the transformation — begun by the 1974 Boldt Decision — of these foes into allies. The state agencies and tribes subsequently forged a regional coalition that proved to be an effective voice for fishery restoration measures. A prominent example of the success of this coalition was the negotiations which culminated in the ratification of the Pacific Salmon Treaty in 1985.[14]

A less successful institutional innovation was the Northwest Power Act's attempt to give the nonfederal Council some control over the federal water projects and operators — namely BPA, the Corps of Engineers, the Bureau of Reclamation, and the Federal Energy Regulatory Commission — charged with implementing the Council's program. Unfortunately, the statute's ambiguously drafted enforcement provisions and the Council's unwillingness to involve itself in implementation issues allowed a number of important program provisions to be essentially ignored. In addition, the deference that Congress expected the Council to give to the fish and wildlife agencies and tribes on biological issues was achieved only inconsistently; it was especially lacking concerning mainstem river flows. Despite the statute's deferential instructions and an admonition in the legislative history that the Council not become a "super" fish and wildlife agency, the interstate agency sometimes ignored the biological judgment of the agencies and tribes on some of the most controversial and longstanding issues it faced, such as river flows and spills of water at dams to facilitate fish passage. Many of the problems of the

Columbia Basin Fish and Wildlife Program, described below, were the product of the Council's biological hubris and its lack of interest in enforcement.[15]

A different criticism of the implementation of the Northwest Power Act came from the Northwest Power Planning Council's own independent scientific group in 1996. The scientists faulted the Council's fish and wildlife program for lacking a coherent conceptual foundation. They claimed that a decade-and-a-half after its promulgation, the program was merely a collection of poorly connected measures, most of which were the product of individual recommendations from fishery agencies and tribes. This produced a fragmented program, one not focused on the Columbia Basin ecosystem and how to repair it. This view held that the Council's relatively weak scientific expertise put it in a poor position to create an integrated, ecologically-based vision of the future.[16]

The Council could be too deferential to the fishery agencies and tribes, leading to a program that resembled a hodgepodge of disconnected measures, yet at the same time exhibit biological hubris concerning hydroelectric operations, because of the interest group politics that dominated the development and implementation of its Columbia Basin Fish and Wildlife Program. The fishery agency and tribal recommendations concerning hydropower met stiff opposition by what the Ninth Circuit termed as "entrenched river users:" the federal agencies which have operated the federal dams largely to maximize hydropower production and the utilities and industries which benefit from cheap power and transportation. This opposition prevented the Council from calling for significant changes in the way Columbia Basin dams operated; at times the Council even articulated its opposition to material changes in the status quo in scientific terms. On the other hand, there was no governmental opposition to, for example, fishery agency recommendations for continuing to fund the region's large-scale commitment to hatcheries as the mitigation program of choice. Thus, the Council could be overly deferential to the fishery agencies and tribes on hatcheries, while simultaneously ignoring their recommendations concerning hydropower operations. In fact, by sanctioning only small changes in hydropower operations, the Council had every incentive to acquiesce to the fishery agencies on hatcheries, since that at least gave the fishery agencies half of what they were seeking. In both contexts, the Council responded to interest group pressure in predictable fashion.[17]

The Columbia Basin Fish and Wildlife Program[18]

Because Congress realized that the newly formed Northwest Power Planning Council would have no fish and wildlife expertise, it created a unique process to develop the program. Rather than have the Council fashion the program out of whole cloth, Congress directed the Council to request recommendations from the region's fish and wildlife agencies and Indian tribes as well as from power interests and the public. In April 1981, five months after the statute was signed into law, a coalition of federal and state fish and wildlife agencies (fishery coalition) submitted over 700 pages of recommendations to the Council. These recommendations included increased river flows, improved fish bypass at dams, habitat protection and restoration measures, and hatchery facilities. The fishery coalition maintained that there was a strong correlation between river flows and fish survival; therefore, its recommendations set forth detailed, month-by-month minimum flows at several Columbia Basin dams. The coalition also recommended a series of actions aimed at achieving "coequal partnership" in system operations, including studying how BPA's power marketing and its implementation of the Columbia River Treaty and the Pacific Northwest Coordination Agreement could accommodate the recommended river flows. In addition, the coalition made detailed suggestions for increasing interaction between fish and wildlife experts and federal water managers, including mandatory consultation with fish and wildlife agencies and the tribes. The coalition presented the most comprehensive set of recommendations the Council received; hence, their suggestions formed the basis of much of the program the Council adopted in 1982.[19]

The adopted program differed in two important respects from the fishery coalition's recommendations, however. First, the program emphasized that hatcheries would be used only where they would not jeopardize the genetic integrity of wild salmon. Second, the Council rejected the detailed series of fixed minimum flows advocated by the coalition, instead adopting a dedicated volume of water — known as the "water budget" — to facilitate downstream salmon migration. This budget could be "spent" at the discretion of representatives of the fish and wildlife agencies and tribes. The water budget concept had two advantages over the recommended fixed flows: it would cost less in terms of foregone hydropower revenues, and it would involve fishery representatives in day-to-day system operations. It therefore seemed to be precisely the kind of "innovative and imaginative" approach that Congress sought when it enacted the Northwest Power Act.[20]

Although it became the centerpiece of the Council's fish and wildlife program, the water budget suffered from at least three shortcomings that ultimately undermined its effectiveness. First, the budget failed to provide a sufficient volume of water to meet the fishery coalition's recommended flows on the Snake. Second, the budget was supposed to be in addition to specified "firm power flows," which turned out not to be provided by the hydroelectric system's managers. Instead, in low flow years they essentially ignored the Council's directives to give budget flows priority over secondary power sales and reservoir refill. Thus, the budget was regularly unmet. For example, in 1985, budget requests were satisfied on only six of twenty-six days during the critical migration season. Third, the budget period from mid-April to mid-June had no real biological justification, since the peak migration of many runs extends beyond mid-June.

Although the water budget was its centerpiece, the Council's fish and wildlife program contained other provisions designed to provide salmon a safer journey on the Columbia and Snake Rivers. In addition to improved flows, the Northwest Power Act ordered the Council to improve salmon passage at mainstem dams. Mainstem passage survival for downstream migrating juvenile salmon can be improved in three ways: 1) by installing mechanical bypass systems to keep young salmon out of the dam's power turbines, 2) by providing spills of water around the dams so the salmon avoid going through the dam entirely, and 3) by removing the salmon from the river and trucking or barging them downstream below the dams and the reservoirs.[21]

The Council's program emphasized installing mechanical bypass systems at the dams, in part because such systems cost less in terms of foregone hydropower revenues than spills (because spilled water cannot be run through power turbines). The Council called upon the Federal Energy Regulatory Commission, which has jurisdiction over non-federal hydroelectric projects, to require mechanical bypass at five Mid-Columbia public utility district dams by 1987, and to prescribe spill programs in the interim comparable to the best available bypass system. The Council called for similar measures at federal dams operated by the Corps, although it set no deadlines for bypass installation, perhaps in recognition of the fact that funding for these measures was a function of the congressional appropriations process. Moreover, the Council was not specific about the level of interim spills — an issue which haunted the program for years.

With the water budget unable to provide the river flows that the fishery coalition recommended, and with little assurance that biologically-based spills would be supplied, transportation of juvenile salmon by truck or barge became a vital part of salmon protection measures. The Corps of Engineers favored truck and barge transportation as an alternative to in-river measures like increased flows and spills because it reduced hydropower losses. The Corps' opposition to substantial changes in river management helped to make fish transportation a *fait accompli*. Fish and wildlife agencies acquiesced in truck and barge transportation during low flow conditions, especially on the Snake where the flows are the lowest and the runs are the weakest. They never accepted artificial transportation as a substitute for improved river conditions, however, as the benefits of transportation have never been clearly demonstrated. This is perhaps because transported fish suffer from stress due to collection and handling that adversely affects them after their release in the lower river. Moreover, because substantial numbers of salmon cannot be collected and transported, these fish must confront river conditions in any event. By the mid-1990s the Corps' transportation program had become one of the most controversial aspects of salmon restoration efforts.

An important aspect of the program, which the Council approved in 1982, was a preference for measures aimed at restoring wild salmon stocks. Here, the Council deviated from the recommendations of the fishery agencies, which emphasized reliance on hatcheries as well as habitat improvements to restore run sizes. But the Council continued to approve funding of hatcheries despite its wild-stock preference. Another significant achievement of the Council's program was its inclusion of conditions to protect fish and wildlife in new hydroelectric projects in the Columbia Basin, as well as a promise to designate streams where no new hydroelectric development should occur. In addition, it included measures aimed at 1) improving the effectiveness of adult fish ladders, 2) pressuring ocean harvest managers to set harvests to ensure that an adequate number of salmon return to the river (the Council has no direct authority over ocean harvests), and 3) giving special attention to restoring salmon runs in Central Washington's Yakima Basin. The Council also instructed BPA to pursue "the most expeditious means" of funding program measures. BPA's inability to fund program measures in an expeditious manner would soon cause the Council to amend its program.[22]

Finally, the program devoted attention to enforcement of its provisions. The Northwest Power Act paid little attention to enforcement, merely stating that BPA should act in "a manner consistent" with the program. The Act also instructed all federal water managers (BPA, the Corps, the Bureau of Reclamation, and the Federal Energy Regulatory Commission), in tortuous language, to "take [the program] into account at every relevant stage of their decisionmaking to the fullest extent practicable." The Council interpreted these directives to mean that the federal water managers had to implement the program or explain in writing why implementation was "physically, legally, or otherwise impracticable, including all possible allowances to permit implementation."[23]

Over the next two decades, the Council amended the program several times in response to new scientific information and legal developments, including ESA listings. The program gradually got more specific and imposed more deadlines and performance standards. But not until the 1994 amendments, when the Council called for seasonal reservoir drawdowns to facilitate downstream salmon migration, did the Council attempt to assume a leadership role. Unfortunately, immediately thereafter, the membership of the Council changed, resulting in a deadlock under which the Council became unable either to change the program or muster the will to implement it.

1984 Amendments[24]

The Council's original program, approved in November 1982, ran into implementation difficulties almost immediately. As a result, after only two years of implementation, the Council substantially revised the program in 1984. Most of the amendments aimed to increase the specificity of program measures because ambiguities had allowed federal water managers to disagree with fishery agencies and the tribes over the pace of funding, the scientific basis for taking action, and the anticipated biological consequences. The primary innovation of the 1984 amendments was a five-year action plan that established deadlines for implementing numerous program provisions. Also, because BPA proved unable to adequately supervise studies that would allow the Council to establish program goals, the amendments established interim goals of 1) increasing the quality and quantity of Columbia Basin salmon through effective use of the water budget, 2) establishing protections against new hydroelectric development, and 3) increasing systemwide production capacity.

The most significant of the new deadlines established by the 1984 amendments were those for installing mechanical bypass systems at several Corps dams, thus correcting an oversight in the 1982 program. However, while focusing on installment of new bypass facilities, the Council failed to take action to improve fish passage at the dams in the interim. It rejected recommendations to base spill levels on bypass efficiency; that is, to base spills on the percentage of fish avoiding the power turbines. Instead, the Council continued with spills based on a 90 percent survival rate at each dam, a less stringent measure because not all young salmon perish in the turbines, and one that is considerably more difficult to monitor and control. According to the fishery agencies and tribes the 90 percent survival standard was inadequate, providing no protection in excess of a "no spill" alternative. If 90 percent of juvenile survive each dam, only 43 percent of Upper Snake River runs (which must pass eight dams) would survive to below the dams, only 35 percent of Upper Columbia River runs (which must pass nine dams).

Although the fishery agencies and tribes convinced the Council to reconsider the 90 percent survival standard in 1986, the Council rejected its own staff's recommendations to increase the survival standard. The Council members claimed that a more stringent standard lacked "significant biological benefit," due to computer models which showed high salmon mortality rates in reservoirs. The Council also refused to require the Corps of Engineers and the fishery agencies and tribes to agree on a spill program. These actions encouraged the Corps to ignore the agencies and tribes' spill requests. The spill decisions revealed a Council reluctant to defer to the biological expertise of the fishery agencies and tribes, as the Northwest Power Act required. The Council had apparently anointed itself as a "super" fish and wildlife agency, in direct opposition to the instructions in the Act's legislative history. Moreover, by not producing a significant improvement in fish passage at mainstream dams, the Council's program was inconsistent with an express statutory directive.[25]

1987 Amendments

In 1987, the Council amended its program to establish an interim goal of doubling existing Columbia Basin salmon runs, to approximately 5 million returning adults. This goal was based on a rather remarkable Council study which estimated that the hydroelectric system was responsible for 5 to 10 million of the estimated 7 to 14 million salmon lost annually, a result of a habitat loss due to water projects and other developments throughout the Columbia Basin. This historical study was unprecedented, since it essentially established the scope of the remedial program Congress charged the Council with formulating. Although it fixed hydropower's responsibility at approximately 8 million salmon annually, the Council opted for the lesser goal of doubling run sizes, due to current socioeconomic and biological conditions. The Council deferred setting a date for reaching the interim goal until completion of a systemic program of subbasin planning, also established by the 1987 amendments. The subbasin planning program acknowledged that each of the 31 major watersheds in the Columbia Basin is home to fish populations likely to be genetically distinct.[26]

The 1987 amendments did nothing to improve fish flows, despite the fact that it was now evident that an unintended effect of the water budget's boosting of spring flows was a reduction of flows in the summer, when many salmon runs were still migrating. Worse, often the promised water budget flows were not provided, as the Corps regularly ignored budget requests and instead shaped flows for power sale, flood control, and reservoir refill purposes. The fishery agencies and tribes asked the Council to amend its program to establish a dispute resolution process concerning use of the water budget, but the Council refused. The Council also refused a request to account for water budget use on an average daily basis. Instead, the Council decided to employ an average weekly basis, claiming that average weekly flows were less costly and just as biologically effective as average daily flows. As in its approach to fish spills the year before, the Council seemed to ignore the biological expertise of the fishery agencies and tribes and assumed the role of a "super" fish and wildlife agency.

The 1987 amendments also refused to increase spill level and rejected a fishery agency and tribal proposal that would have required the Corps to agree jointly with them on an annual fish passage plan. However, the Council also rejected a Corps proposal to maximize artificial transportation of juvenile fish under all flow conditions. The Corps has consistently favored maximizing transportation because that option requires the fewest changes in hydroelectric system operations. But the fishery agencies and tribes oppose transportation except at low flows when river conditions are particularly lethal to juvenile salmon. They believe that transportation can never substitute for better in-river conditions because not all juvenile salmon can be collected and transported. Further, fish that survive transportation do not return as adults as often as in-river fish which survive the dams. Most likely this is because of the stress associated with being collected, loaded, and transported in trucks and barges. The Council rejected the Corps' proposal because it would have effectively removed the fishery agencies and tribes from decision making about transportation, inconsistent with both the program and the Act, a belated recognition by the Council of the biological expertise of the fishery agencies and tribes.

1988 Amendments

In 1988, the Council amended the program to designate approximately 44,000 stream miles as "protected areas," where new hydropower developments would be restricted because they would cause unacceptable harm to fish and wildlife habitat. Protected area status has no effect on the operation of existing projects and does not entirely foreclose hydropower development. It does make federal licensing more difficult within the Columbia Basin, however, and also prevents the Bonneville Power Administration from purchasing the output of any new project in a protected area. These designations represented an important regional commitment to discourage new hydroelectric development, a signal of widespread agreement that the region's rivers were overdeveloped. The designations, to which the Federal Energy Regulatory Commission and BPA have deferred, also showed that protecting against future development is considerably more popular politically than attempting to restructure existing hydroelectric operations which damage fish and wildlife habitat.[27]

In late 1988, as a result of lawsuits challenging BPA's attempt to upgrade its transmission lines to California without considering the effects on salmon migration, BPA agreed to a ten-year program of spills at mainstem dams, supplying the kind of fish passage that the fishery agencies and tribes unsuccessfully sought from the Council earlier. The new agreement provided fish passage protection outside of the water budget period (April 15 to June 15) for the first time. The Council quickly adopted the agreement as part of its program in February 1989, ending the longstanding dispute over the magnitude and timing of spills to facilitate salmon passage at mainstem dams. The resolution came, however, not through Council leadership, but as a result of a lawsuit brought by the state of Idaho, environmentalists, and tribes, which gave the fishery agencies and tribes the leverage they needed to negotiate for improved spills. Thus, by the late 1980s the Council contented itself with ratifying deals negotiated by others. That is perhaps not surprising from a four-state body comprised of political appointees, but was inconsistent with the congressional intent that the Council become a regional leader in devising innovative and imaginative solutions to the Columbia Basin salmon problem.[28]

The Fish Flow Issue

By 1990, a decade after it was authorized by Congress, the Columbia Basin Fish and Wildlife Program had a decidedly mixed record. It had designated stream reaches protected from most new hydroelectric developments, established a program of setting production goals on a watershed by watershed basis, and announced a policy of maintaining genetic diversity while doubling the basin's salmon runs. The Council also showed itself to be an effective advocate for obtaining congressional funding for mechanical bypass systems at mainstem dams, no small feat in an era of immense federal budget deficits. But the interstate agency proved unable to restructure hydroelectric operations to accommodate the biological needs of salmon. The only reason that spills improved at the dams was a negotiated settlement of a lawsuit, and spring flows under the water budget increased only marginally, arguably at the expense of summer flows. The result reflected the continued inequity between salmon and other river interests.

Fish flows are a difficult issue for several reasons. First, although they do not reduce the hydroelectric system's capability to produce power, they change the timing of power generation, from fall and winter to spring and summer. The price of hydropower in the marketplace, however, is largely a function of timing: there is little market for additional power in the Northwest in the spring and summer, although there are markets in southern California and the Southwest, especially in the summer. Second, the agencies which control the operation of the hydroelectric system lack any real incentive to consider seriously material changes in operations, since the Northwest Power Act was ambiguous concerning the Council's ability to require operational changes, and the Council made few significant demands on the operators in any event. Instead, the Council seemed more intent on overruling the fishery agencies and tribes on biological grounds, even though the statute seemed to require the Council to defer to the biological expertise of the fishery agencies and tribes.

Third, the Council — comprised of eight gubernatorial appointees who generally had no prior experience in dealing with complex biological issues — was not a good institutional choice to impose significant changes in system operations. Faced with the staunch opposition of entrenched agencies like the Corps and BPA, and with its members serving limited terms, the Council proved reticent in requesting changes to old ways of doing business. Even when it did ask for modest changes, it lacked interest in enforcing the changes. In retrospect, if Congress wanted to make material changes in system operations, it should have given the authority to prescribe biologically-based fish flows to the region's fishery agencies and tribes, instead of giving the chore to a new interstate agency comprised of political appointees with no biological expertise. It also should have imposed a statutory deadline for achieving the prescribed flows.

The 1991 Amendments

In 1991, the Council was again induced to amend the program, this time in response to impending salmon listings under the Endangered Species Act (described in chapter 9). Although this attempt to ward off such listings was in vain, the 1991 amendments nevertheless had positive effects. The amendments made the first improvement in Snake River flows since the program was first promulgated in 1982 by calling for 1) lowering of the four Corps reservoirs on the Lower Columbia to "near minimum operating pools," 2) releasing 900,000 acre-feet of water from Dworshak Dam to provide fish flows in low water years, 3) shifting flood control storage space from Snake River reservoirs to Columbia River reservoirs, 4) tapping uncontracted storage in Bureau of Reclamation and Idaho Power projects, and 5) using innovative water practices, such as leasing water rights and funding efficiency improvements. All told, these measures were expected to produce about 1.4 million acre-feet of water for fish flows. But the Council's program still only prescribed spring monthly flow averages of 85,000 cubic feet per second, which were the same flows the program had been calling for since 1982 (and just 60 percent of the flows that the fishery agencies and tribes recommended in 1981). However, the new amendments promised summer flows for the first time and made it much more likely that the spring flow targets would be achieved.

Because Snake River flows remained far below what the fishery agencies and tribes considered to be biologically necessary, the 1991 amendments continued a heavy reliance on barge and truck transport of juvenile fish. Controversial since its inception two decades earlier, artificial transport of juvenile salmon is supported by most fishery agencies only in extremely low flows, when in-river migration is particularly lethal. Most fishery agencies did not view artificial transportation as a substitute for improved river flows, but the Council's modest flow targets meant barge and truck transport was to be the norm.

The 1991 amendments did offer some hope for improved river conditions in the future. They called for proceeding with a drawdown of one of the reservoirs in the Lower Snake River during the peak juvenile salmon migration in the spring by 1995 "unless shown to be structurally, or economically infeasible, biologically imprudent, or inconsistent with . . . the Northwest Power Act." The Council also established some biological goals; for example, calling for a 23 percent improvement in survival of fish passing mainstem dams and an average of 300 or more spawning fall chinook during 1992-1995, reaching the 500 annual spawners necessary to preserve the genetic integrity of the species by 2000, and eventually producing one thousand spawners by 2004-2009. Finally, the amendments established a committee to study how to obtain an additional one million acre-feet of water for fish migration in the Snake River.[29]

Still, except for fall chinook, the program prepared to enter its second decade without any detailed biological objectives, apparently content with calling for incremental improvements in hydropower/salmon tradeoffs before establishing the goals those improvements aim to achieve. Although the Council recognized that its amended program would not be sufficient to restore the Columbia's salmon, it mostly opted for more study before more action. Many critics thought that the nearly 10-year-old program had ample opportunity for study and charged that the Council remained too sensitive to the alleged economic costs that river users, like navigators and utilities, would suffer.[30]

Judicial Intervention

Although the 1991 amendments promised the first improvement in river flows in nearly a decade, even Council Chairman Ted Hallock conceded that they were "not enough for the fish." Dissatisfied with a decade of deference to a status quo favoring hydropower, a coalition of environmentalists and the Yakama Indian Nation filed suit, claiming that the 1991 amendments offered too little fish protection. In response, the industries served by low BPA rates (mostly aluminum companies) filed suit, claiming that the amendments were too fish protective.[31]

On September 9, 1994, a three-judge panel of the federal Ninth Circuit Court of Appeals unanimously agreed with the environmentalists and the tribe. The court described the case as a "classic struggle" between salmon and hydropower, "the two great natural resources of the Columbia River Basin . . . [a]t odds for most of this century." The court observed that Columbia Basin salmon had declined from 10-16 million adult fish to 2.5 million, and that hydropower was responsible for 80 percent of the decline. The court lauded the Northwest Power Act as "mark[ing] an important shift in federal policy," aimed at "making fish and wildlife a 'coequal partner' with the hydropower industry." Judge Thomas Tang noted that the 1980 statute contained several legislative innovations, including its basinwide perspective, its redefinition of fish and wildlife mitigation to emphasize changes in dam operations, its lowering of the burden of proof for undertaking remedial action, and its tapping of hydroelectric revenues for funding fish and wildlife restoration efforts. But despite these legislative innovations, the court concluded that the program — which the Council once touted as "possibly, the most ambitious effort in the world to save a biological resource" — failed to satisfy the mandates of the statute.[32]

The court's ruling was surprising, since the 1991 amendments to the program increased salmon protection and because the program had gone unchallenged for nearly ten years. The court faulted the amendments for 1) failing to establish biological objectives, and 2) failing to explain in the program the statutory basis for rejecting recommendations for restoration measures the Council received, particularly those it received from the region's fishery agencies and Indian tribes. According to the court, the Council owed those recommendations "a high degree of deference." Ruling that the statute required the Council to "heavily rely" on the recommendations of the fishery agencies and tribes, the court held that the Council failed this duty when it rejected the recommended flow regime and continued to rely heavily on an artificial transportation program that most fishery agencies and tribes opposed.[33]

The Ninth Circuit also rejected aluminum industry arguments that the measures in the program had to satisfy a cost-benefit test, noting that "a fish and wildlife measure cannot be rejected solely because it will result in power losses and economic costs . . ." because the Northwest Power Act "prevents cost considerations from precluding sound restoration of anadromous fish in the Columbia River Basin . . . so long as an adequate, efficient, economical and reliable power supply is assured." Requiring program measures to meet a cost-benefit test would have bogged the program down in endless economic studies and delayed program implementation. Presumably, this is precisely what the industry sought.[34]

The court's decision served to institutionalize the program recommendations of the region's fish and wildlife agencies; the Council could no longer fashion its program outside the statutorily prescribed receiving and considering of recommendations. A key ruling of the court was its establishment of the deference principle. The Council owed deference, according to the court, not only to the scientific opinions of the fishery agencies and tribes, including allowing for "reasonable inferences and predictions," but also to their interpretations of the Northwest Power Act. This rather remarkable conclusion is a reflection of the fact that the court assumed that the key implementation entities of the statute, in terms of fish and wildlife restoration, are the fishery agencies and tribes, not the Council. The court concluded by criticizing the Council for adopting the premise "that only small steps are possible, in light of entrenched river user claims of economic hardship. Rather than asserting its role as a regional leader, the Council has assumed the role of consensus builder, sometimes sacrificing the Act's fish and wildlife goals for what is, in essence, the lowest common denominator acceptable to power interests and [industry]." The court clearly seemed to be saying that the Council's pursuit of incremental improvements, while salmon populations continued to nosedive, was no longer acceptable.

The 1994 Amendments[35]

In December 1994, the Council approved program amendments that in part responded to the court's opinion. For the first time, the Council applied adaptive management principles to the issue of whether river conditions should be improved to accommodate juvenile salmon migration or whether to continue the truck and barge transportation program. The amendments called for a comparison in fish survival between transported fish and fish migrating under improved river conditions. The improvements were the result of setting new monthly Snake River flow "targets" of 85,000 cubic feet per second (cfs) to 140,000 cfs in the spring and 50,000 cfs in the summer. On the Lower Columbia, the Council called for flows of 220,000 cfs to 300,000 cfs. The peak flows of 140,000 cfs on the Snake and 300,000 cfs on the Lower Columbia were the same as the state fishery agencies made in the 1991 flow proposal, except the fishery agencies expressed their recommendations in terms of instantaneous flows and daily averages, which are much more dependable than the average monthly "targets" established by the Council's program. In fact, the National Academy of Sciences' National Research Council criticized the use of monthly targets because they gave too much discretion to dam operations and recommended that flow measures be imposed as "operating constraints" that would take precedence over power production.[36]

The chief means to meet these increased flows was the purchase of an additional one million acre-feet of water from willing sellers in the Snake River Basin. This water was in addition to the 427,000 acre-feet authorized in the Council's 1991 amendments. The Council also endorsed the mainstem passage experiment under which salmon survival would be carefully monitored, and the results of the increased flows would be compared to the results of the transportation program. Under this experiment, roughly the same number of juvenile salmon would be transported as left to migrate in-river, which would mean that fewer fish would be transported than previously.

To achieve the new flow targets the amendments authorized water purchases and called for a phased approach to seasonal reservoir drawdowns, a measure which had been championed by outgoing Idaho Governor Cecil Andrus. The 1994 amendments called for a two-month, 25-foot drawdown of Lower Granite reservoir in 1995, and a 45-foot drawdown in 1999. Little Goose reservoir would be drawn down in 1999 to spillway crest level (making the reservoir level with the dam's spillway) for two months during the spring. In 2002, the amendments called for the Council to decide whether to draw down the other two Lower Snake reservoirs to either spillway or natural river levels.

On the Lower Columbia, the Council called for John Day reservoir to be operated at near minimum operating pool on a permanent basis beginning in 1996. However, the amendments made this reservoir drawdown contingent upon "full, prior mitigation" of adverse impacts on irrigators and other reservoir users. The Council was frank that efficacy of reservoir drawdowns was unproven, but maintained that the best way to analyze their effectiveness was to conduct them and monitor their effectiveness. In other words, the Council sought to practice adaptive management, which it had long employed in other aspects of its program but never previously applied to the mainstem passage issue.

The 1994 amendments also called for restricting barging and trucking of juvenile salmon to "extremely adverse conditions," as determined by the fishery agencies and tribes, except for fish transported for purposes of the mainstem experiment. In addition, the Council adopted a fundamentally different policy toward hatchery production than that which dominated salmon management throughout the 20th century. Under this new policy, continuation of BPA funding for existing hatcheries would be conditioned on consistency with the basin's carrying capacity, conserving genetic diversity, and not interfering with naturally spawning salmon populations. The Council also promised to scrutinize supplementation projects, including those proposed by the tribes, to assess their biological risk. Moreover, the Council said that BPA money would not support new hatchery production unless it was demonstrated that the need for fish could not be met with existing facilities.

The 1994 amendments represented a bold attempt by the Council to change river operations to improve salmon survival. Their controversial nature was reflected in the fact that they were approved only by a vote of 6-2, with both Montana members voting against the amendments. Shortly after the amendments were approved, the membership of the Council changed considerably. Idaho's Democratic Governor, Cecil Andrus, was replaced by a Republican. The newly appointed Republican Council members from Idaho opposed seasonal drawdowns and strenuously resisted any attempt to purchase water rights to improve river flows, so the Council was deadlocked: unable to amend the program it approved, yet unwilling to attempt to implement it. The upshot was that the 1994 amendments' attempt to undertake a mainstem passage experiment was never carried out. The amendments' shift of the burden of proof on hatchery programs receiving ratepayer money to demonstrate their effectiveness eventually produced substantial changes in hatchery operations, but whether juvenile salmon were trucked or barged or left in the river — and the river conditions to which they would be subjected — were left to the federal consultation process under the Endangered Species Act, as discussed in chapter 9.

The Search For Better Science

In 1994, in the wake of the Columbia Basin salmon listings under the Endangered Species Act, the Council formed its Independent Scientific Group (ISG) and charged it with reviewing the science underlying its salmon restoration program and developing a scientific conceptual foundation for the program — on which it would be based and against which it would be measured. The ISG played an extremely important role in the wake of the Council's 1994 amendments. The new Idaho members charged that the amendments were based on faulty science and demanded independent scientific review. The ISG supplied this review which largely (not entirely) vindicated the amendments. So, while a deadlocked Council could not manage the will to implement its 1994 amendments, the ISG's scientific review ensured that there would be no weakening amendments to the program in the short term.

Two years after it was formed, in September 1996, the ISG issued a report, entitled *Return to the River*, which charged the Council's program with a lack of adequate conceptual foundation and claimed that, unless salmon restoration changed direction,

Columbia Basin wild salmon face extinction in the next half century. The report proposed an ecologically-based framework which would seek to reestablish healthy salmon runs through what the report referred to as "normative" river conditions, or conditions that provide functional norms essential to productive salmon runs.[37]

The report emphasized that changed hydroelectric operations alone could not restore Columbia Basin salmon; it noted that upland management, estuarine protection, and favorable oceanic conditions were also necessary. The scientists claimed that the Council's program was merely a collection of individual measures proposed by diverse interest groups, based on the "fundamentally flawed" assumption that fish populations can be managed in isolation from other components of their ecosystem. The program's emphasis on technological fixes — like hatcheries and truck and barge transport — as a substitute for lost ecosystem functions had failed, in the judgment of the scientists. As a result, the report urged fundamental change: to move from a view of the Columbia River as a vehicle for economic development to a view which accommodated both economic activities and a functional salmon-producing ecosystem.[38]

The most significant revelation of *Return to the River* was its finding that the big historic producers of salmon were the mainstem of the Columbia and lower portions of major tributary rivers. These alluvial reaches were biologically rich areas that had supported "metapopulations" of salmon: populations large enough to colonize adjacent areas. This recognition of the importance of the mainstem as a spawning area led to the report's most arresting recommendation: to restore mainstem spawning habitat by permanently drawing down reservoirs like those created by the John Day and McNary Dams. By reestablishing the ecological conditions that historically allowed these mainstem areas to support salmon metapopulations, the report suggested that Columbia Basin salmon populations could be revitalized.[39]

Perhaps just as significant as the scientists' recommendation to restore mainstem alluvial reaches was its position that more scientific proof must be required of technological fixes designed to cure the biological problems of the salmon. The report noted that technologies like hatcheries and barging and trucking had been adopted with little or no scientific study, and the scientists suggested radical change. According to the report, "[t]echnology that attempts to circumvent the normative river (*e.g.*, hatcheries and transportation) should only be implemented on a large scale basis after intensive evaluation." Had these technologies been forced to shoulder the burden of proof, there is little doubt that they would not dominate Columbia Basin salmon recovery efforts today.[40]

The Gorton Rider

Just after the publication of *Return to the River*, Senator Slade Gorton of Washington, who earlier attempted to impose a legislative cost cap on salmon restoration efforts, included a rider in the 1997 energy and water development appropriations bill designed to require scientific evaluation of the Council's program measures. This provision proved to be largely redundant, since the Council had already taken steps to ensure independent scientific review of its efforts. However, the Gorton rider established a process by which an independent scientific panel analyzes projects submitted to the Council for BPA funding and requires the Council to "fully consider" the panel's recommendations and explain in writing its reasons if it rejects them. Since the Council must only "fully consider" the scientific panel's recommendations, the Gorton rider did not necessarily conflict with the Ninth Circuit's ruling that the Council owes "a high degree of deference" to program recommendations submitted by the fishery agencies' and tribes. In fact, the rider did not even amend the provision which the court interpreted.[41]

The Gorton rider also required the Council to consider the effect of ocean conditions, to conduct a review of hatchery programs, and to determine whether restoration projects are cost effective. The latter provision seemed redundant of the statute it amended. The hatchery review led to a 1999 report and the imposition of a new burden of proof on hatchery operations, as discussed in chapter 6. The ocean provision required express consideration of ocean conditions — about which there is overwhelming uncertainty, and little prospect of overcoming it in the foreseeable future.[42]

Prior to the passage of the Gorton rider, the Council and NMFS had agreed to establish an Independent Scientific Advisory Board (ISAB) to advise both agencies concerning salmon restoration issues. In 1999, the ISAB responded to congressional requests for advice on funding structural improvements associated with salmon recovery efforts, such as bypass systems and surface skimmers at the dams, and on the efficacy of hatchery programs. The ISAB recommended that Congress fund only those structural improvements which satisfied a biological effectiveness test showing that the improvements would foster conditions essential to the salmon's life history. The scientists also noted that many of the strategies that are working best are those that were not the product of design but the result of trial and error, like many ice and trash sluiceways and the surface bypass system at Wells Dam. A 1999 Council report on the Corps of Engineers' fish passage program attempted to carry out some of these scientific recommendations by suggesting that two paradigms should guide all fish passage investments: 1) protecting biodiversity, and 2) favoring passage solutions which fit natural behavior patterns.[43]

Equitable Treatment and the Non-Treaty Storage Suit

The Northwest Power Planning Council's Columbia Basin Fish and Wildlife Program is not the only fish and wildlife protection supplied by the Northwest Power Act. Congress also required federal water managers — BPA, the Corps of Engineers, the Bureau of Reclamation, and the Federal Energy Regulatory Commission — to produce "equitable treatment" to fish and wildlife along with serving the other purposes of the Columbia River dams and hydroelectric system. This obligation, the courts ruled, was a duty independent of the Council's program and a substantive one, meaning that it aimed to produce results, not just process. But until 1997, the courts had never evaluated whether a particular federal water management action actually produced equitable treatment.[44]

The case that resulted in the first full evaluation of this provision began in 1990 when BPA contracted with British Columbia Hydro to obtain rights to use water stored in Columbia River Treaty projects in Canada that was beyond the amount of water called for by the treaty. Use of this "non-treaty storage" was under the unilateral control of Canada until BPA entered into a series of agreements beginning in 1983, in part to increase BPA revenues to offset the cost of complying with the Council's water budget. The 1983 agreement was followed by a ten-year agreement in 1984, which in turn was superceded by a 1990 agreement that gave BPA control until 2003 and expanded the amount of water subject to the agreement from 2 million acre-feet to 4.5 million acre-feet. As part of a two-year review process of public comments and meetings, BPA entered into agreement with fish and wildlife agencies, promising that its use of non-treaty storage would not adversely affect salmon; how it would implement this promise was not specified. The agency also dedicated some non-treaty storage water to power production in a contract with Mid-Columbia public utility districts. But BPA made no promises to use the storage water to increase flows to aid salmon migration.[45]

A coalition of environmental groups sued BPA, and in 1997 — some seven years after the agreements went into effect — the Ninth Circuit upheld BPA in a curious decision. The court ruled that, although BPA owed equitable treatment to fish and wildlife, it did not have to dedicate a portion of the Canadian storage water over which it had gained control because the non-treaty storage agreement left most of the storage capacity unallocated (although the agency did in fact dedicate some water to power production in the Mid-Columbia utility contact), and "BPA may well decide that its responsibilities to provide equitable treatment require it to use a reasonable portion of this water for the benefit of fish." On the basis of such speculation, the court decided it was "premature" to order BPA to share any of its acquired storage with fish. Instead, the court upheld BPA's position that its statutory duty to produce equitable treatment did not have to be satisfied in "every discrete power marketing action" but instead could be satisfied on a system-wide basis. The court did not make clear — and it remains unclear today — how BPA must fulfill this system-wide equitable treatment requirement, although the court quite clearly stated that the agency had to demonstrate equitable treatment for fish and wildlife "[o]nce BPA allocates the non-Treaty storage."[46]

In many respects this decision serves as a metaphor for the Northwest Power Act and its implementation over two decades. The act contains many innovative provisions, like the commitment to give equitable treatment to fish and wildlife, but implementation of those provisions never achieved their promise. Sometimes the inequity occurred due to a judicial unwillingness to make agencies like BPA show they were fulfilling the statute's directives. More often it was due to the implementing agencies' failure to provide the parity between hydropower and fish and wildlife which the statute envisioned. In either case, the Northwest Power Act became another in a long list of unexecuted promises to protect and restore Columbia Basin salmon.

The Multi-Species Approach

In the wake of the ISG criticism of the lack of a coherent conceptual foundation in the Council's program, and the scientists' urging that any viable foundation must focus on the ecosystems through which salmon travel during their life cycle, the Council helped convene what it called the Multi-Species Framework Project. The project is a joint effort of state, federal, and tribal governments to achieve a common vision for conserving the Columbia Basin and associated ecosystems. The motivation was the ISG's insight that the salmon inhabiting the basin require both healthy and connected habitats in freshwater, estuaries, and the ocean as well as a variety of other organisms in those habitats. The goal was to agree upon a specific set of ecological theories, assumptions, and principles that would guide decisionmakers, especially federal agencies and the Council.[47]

The ambitions of the multi-species approach may exceed its grasp. The project must shape social, economic, political, and ecological considerations into a long-term governing framework for species protection throughout the basin. The nature of this challenge is reflected in the fact that agreeing on basic goals proved elusive during the first year of meetings. There is probably value in having opposing forces articulate competing perspectives of the future, even if no consensus is achieved. As one commentator has observed, "even if the project does not lead the contending parties to a single vision, it will have begun to shift the parties' thinking toward a broader ecosystem whose parts connect." But the process of achieving this modest shift in thinking is expensive, both in terms of time and resources. Perhaps there is no cheaper way.[48]

The 2000 Amendments

Deadlocked for some six years, the Council initiated a program amendment process in early 2000. After receiving 55 different amendment proposals and issuing a draft program, the Council approved "Phase I" program amendments in October 2000. These amendments, the first since the 1996 *Return to the River* report criticized the program for lacking a coherent conceptual foundation, featured interim program goals, basinwide objectives, and scientific justifications. "Phase II" amendments, to be approved in 2001, will establish mainstem and subbasin plans.

The 2000 program amendments established several interim program goals: 1) to halt the decline of salmon runs above Bonneville Dam by 2005; 2) to restore the "widest possible set of healthy, naturally producing populations" of salmon by 2012; and 3) to increase total salmon runs above Bonneville Dam to an average of 5 million adult fish by 2025. The vehicle for reaching these goals is a mainstem plan and a subbasin planning process throughout the 53 subbasins of Columbia Basin. The program echoed the stress that *Return to the River* placed on the importance of habitat:

> This is a habitat-based program rebuilding healthy naturally producing fish and wildlife populations by protecting and restoring habitats and biological systems within them, including anadromous fish corridors. Artificial production and other non-natural interventions should be consistent with the central effort to protect and restore habitat and avoid adverse impacts to native fish and wildlife.

The amendments endorsed *Return to The River*'s emphasis on replicating natural processes, but they deleted the term "normative" river, apparently because the phrase had become a subject of derision among the program's critics.[49]

The details of the amended program won't be known until the Council approves the "Phase II" amendments in 2001, although the Council did approve BPA funding increases both for the program itself and for the mainstem and subbasin planning efforts, and also for a habitat acquisition fund and for high priority projects. Priority will be given to buying habitat, including water rights that will benefit ESA-listed species. However, the relationship between the Council's subbasin plans and NMFS's call for the Council to assume responsibility for the offsite mitigation effort prescribed in its 2001-05 BiOp on hydroelectric operations (discussed in chapter 9) remains unclear. There are also unresolved questions about how to apportion the cost of implementing the ESA BiOp between regional ratepayers (through BPA expenditures) and national taxpayers (through congressional appropriations).[50]

The 2000 amendments adopted a vision for the program that, within the context of recent Council gridlock and twenty years of sidestepping the causes of declining salmon runs, seemed noteworthy:

> The vision for this program is a Columbia Basin ecosystem that sustains an abundant, productive, and diverse community of fish and wildlife, mitigating across the basin for the adverse effects to fish and wildlife caused by the development and operation of the hydrosystem and providing the benefits from fish and wildlife valued by the people of the region. This ecosystem provides abundant opportunities for tribal trust and treaty harvest and for non-tribal harvest and the conditions that allow for recovery of fish and wildlife affected by the operation of hydrosystem and listed under the Endangered Species Act.
>
> Wherever feasible, this program will be accomplished by protecting and restoring the natural ecological functions, habitats, and biological diversity of the Columbia River Basin.[51]

If this vision leads the Council to adopt specific provisions in its mainstem and subbasin plans, and if federal agencies actually implement those provisions, perhaps Columbia Basin salmon verge on a new era. However, the experience of the last two decades suggests that rhetoric is not easily translated into meaningful action.

The Future

Despite the 2000 amendments' adoption of *Return to the River*'s concepts of preserving and restoring ecological function, two decades of Northwest Power Act implementation efforts — which might charitably be described as inconsistent — counsel that the 2000 amendments are unlikely to produce meaningful changes in the operation of Columbia Basin dams. For example, the Council was ineffective at enforcing its water budget in the 1980s and was unwilling to push implementation of its seasonal reservoir drawdowns in the 1990s. Innovative statutory provisions like equitable treatment became casualties of agency evasion and judicial obfuscation. So while it may be true that the statute rather simplistically proposed that restructuring the hydropower/salmon balance would be sufficient to restore salmon runs, the Council proved unable to alter even that balance significantly.

A vivid reminder of hydropower's continued dominance was supplied in January 2001 when BPA declared a "power emergency," which allowed the agency to release storage water from federal dams to generate hydropower in violations of rules for salmon protection set under the Endangered Species Act. The emergency was a consequence of the second-lowest runoff in the historical record and the California electricity crisis, which drove up power costs throughout the West and made it difficult for BPA to purchase power for Northwest needs. The releases of storage water for power greatly reduced the chance of the hydroelectric system being able to supply sufficient salmon flows and spills during the impending spring and summer migration season. The result was testament to the fact that, two decades after the Northwest Power Act sought to give equal footing to hydropower and salmon, short-term power needs continue to outweigh long-term salmon requirements.[52]*

---

* As a result of storage releases to generate power in the winter of 2001, only about 10 percent of the amount of water called for by the operative salmon plan was available for spills to improve fish passage at the dams in the spring and summer. Consequently, juvenile salmon survival plummeted to among the lowest rates ever recorded. How this result produced equitable treatment for salmon is far from clear.

This track record makes it quite questionable whether a redesigned Columbia Basin Fish and Wildlife Program — one emphasizing ecological function and habitat restoration instead of concentrating on mainstem fish passage — can successfully establish comprehensive, integrated, water-focused planning as the centerpiece of restoring harvestable Columbia Basin salmon runs. Perhaps the chief lesson of the Northwest Power Act experience is that high-minded principles and innovative provisions are no match for entrenched river interests and institutional inertia favoring the status quo.

8 — FOURTH PROMISE: REDUCING SALMON INTERCEPTIONS UNDER THE PACIFIC SALMON TREATY

Columbia Basin salmon usually migrate northward once they reach the ocean, spending several years in marine waters (the amount of time varies depending on the species). Once in the marine environment, their immense migratory range poses management problems because salmon ignore international boundaries, migrating northward to Canadian waters and often back into U.S. waters in southeast Alaska before retracing their path (see map 9). These border-hopping migrants are prime candidates for harvest by jurisdictions other than their country of origin because the intercepting jurisdiction reaps all of the rewards and none of the costs associated with protecting spawning and rearing grounds or operating hatcheries. This skewed cost-benefit ratio creates a classic "tragedy of the commons," where all the incentives are to harvest rather than conserve the species.[1]

For most of the 20th century, the North Pacific has been the scene of continued friction between Canada and the U.S. over salmon interceptions. The early conflicts concerned Canada's Fraser River sockeye runs, which migrate through U.S. waters in the Strait of Juan de Fuca and northern Puget Sound into large net fisheries. In 1913-14, crews blasting a railroad right-of-way through the Fraser River canyon triggered slides that obstructed the river in several places, the worst being at a narrows called Hell's Gate. With access to many salmon spawning grounds cut off, the Fraser River salmon runs dropped off precipitously, as did both Canadian and U.S. harvests.[2]

A decade-and-a-half after the slides, protracted negotiations between the U.S. and Canada produced the Fraser River Convention of 1930. The Convention established the International Pacific Salmon Fisheries Commission and charged it

Map 9 — Major Chinook Salmon Management Regions Under the Pacific Salmon Treaty

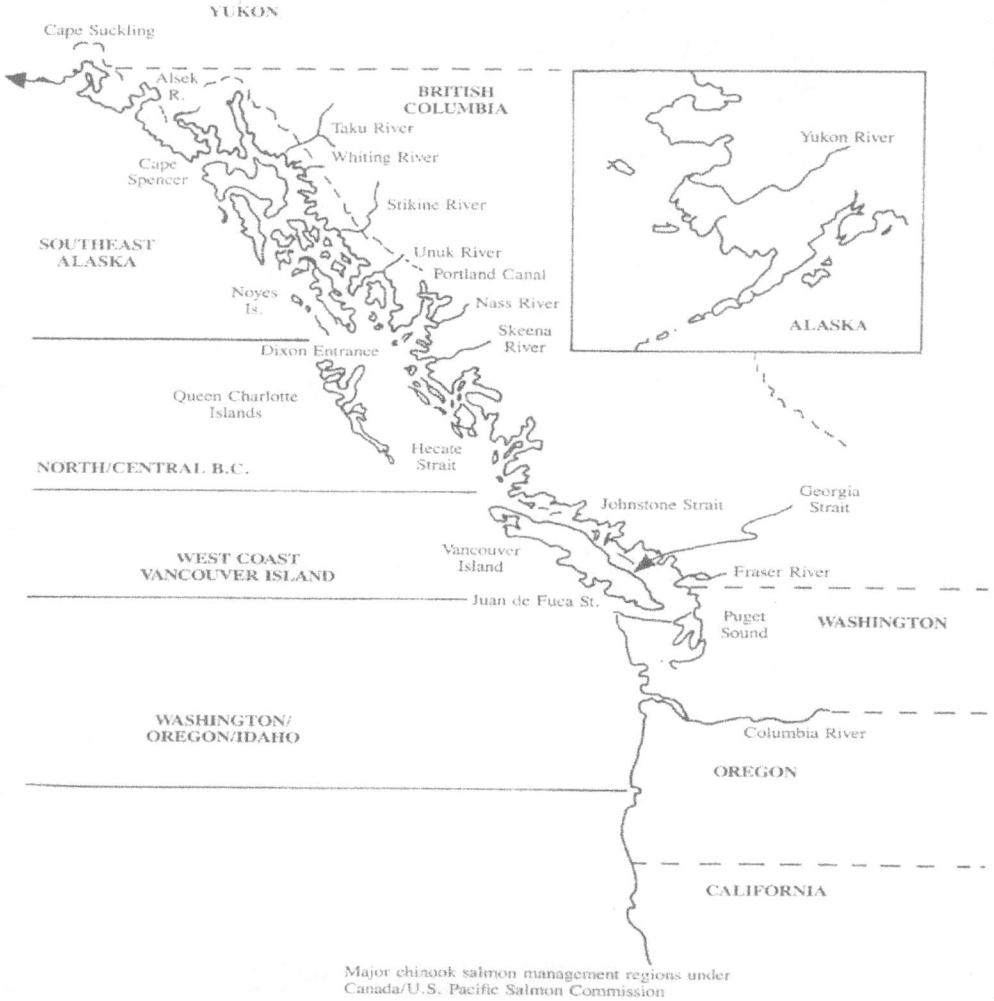

Major chinook salmon management regions under
Canada/U.S. Pacific Salmon Commission

Courtesy of the Pacific Salmon Commission

with rebuilding the Fraser River sockeye runs. The costs of restoration were to be paid by the U.S. In return, the Convention guaranteed that U.S. fishers could harvest 50 percent of Fraser River sockeye. In 1957, the two countries extended the Convention's provisions to include Fraser River pink salmon as well.[3] In the 1960s and 1970s, both Canada and the United States expanded their jurisdictional claims to offshore fisheries from between three and twelve miles to 200 miles in response to increased fishing by mobile fleets from the Soviet Union, Japan, West Germany, Poland, and other countries. The expanded jurisdictional claim of the U.S. was embodied in the Magnuson Fishery Conservation and Management Act of 1976. In United Nations Law of the Sea Treaty negotiations, both the U.S. and Canada championed the notion that salmon could be harvested only by the countries in whose rivers they had spawned. This principle, known as the "state-of-origin" doctrine, was flatly inconsistent with the Fraser River Convention's ratification of substantial U.S. interceptions of Canadian spawned fish. As a result, the two countries entered negotiations to reduce their interception fisheries on both coasts. The Pacific salmon fishery was to prove the most intractable interception fishery to the negotiators.[4]

One reason for the difficulties in the U.S.-Canada Pacific salmon negotiations was the peculiar tension within the U.S. between Alaskan and Lower 48 salmon harvesters. Alaskans harvested salmon in mixed stock fisheries offshore of southeast Alaska, including salmon which spawned both in Canadian rivers and in rivers in the Lower 48, like the Columbia. To compensate for Alaskan interceptions of Canadian-spawned salmon, Canadians harvested salmon originating in Lower 48 rivers, especially the Columbia, in mixed stock fisheries off the coast of Vancouver Island. So Columbia Basin salmon were subject to harvest by both Alaskan and Canadian fisheries. Consequently, the Alaskans had a very different perspective on whether there should be a treaty, and what its terms should be, than fishers in Oregon and Washington.

Negotiating the Treaty

Canada and the U.S. began negotiations on a treaty to govern salmon harvests in the North Pacific in 1971. At that time there were no real conservation concerns, as harvests were relatively stable, and the goal appeared to be to limit interceptions to then-prevailing levels. But the 1974 Boldt Decision, which recognized that treaty tribes had harvest rights to half of the salmon runs, complicated matters considerably. This ruling led the state of Washington to commit to an ambitious expansion in hatchery production, as the state grappled with how to satisfy the treaty share without unduly disrupting existing harvests. The Columbia Basin was also increasing hatchery production as mitigation for dam building. As a result, fall and spring chinook hatchery releases nearly quadrupled between 1960 and 1977.[5]

At the same time, Canada committed itself to a major program aimed at doubling Fraser River sockeye production by creating new spawning habitat. Both U.S. and Canadian enhancement efforts promised to increase the numbers of salmon crossing international borders, and both countries wanted to ensure that the fruits of their investments were not harvested by the other country. Thus, by the late 1970s, there were strong incentives to reach an agreement.

An agreement would not be easily forthcoming, however. U.S. fishermen benefitting from interception fisheries in northern Puget Sound resisted suggestions to reduce interceptions, as did those in the southeast Alaska, where more than half of the harvested chinook originated outside the state of Alaska. Similarly, Canadian fishermen off the west coast of Vancouver Island opposed attempts to reduce interceptions because there they were harvesting fully 40 percent of the total coastwide take of Columbia River chinook. This opposition prevented an agreement and interceptions increased in the late 1970s and early 1980s.[6]

In the early 1980s, a new problem emerged: a startling decline in West Coast chinook. Scientists suggested that the high numbers of interceptions were threatening spawning levels necessary to perpetuate several salmon runs. As the total numbers of salmon declined, the percentage of the catch harvested by the relatively unregulated interception fisheries increased. The Columbia Basin treaty tribes successfully used their treaty rights under the Boldt Decision, affirmed by the U.S. Supreme Court in 1979, to restrict ocean harvests to ensure that they would receive half of the harvest beginning that year. Then, in 1981, the tribes sought to break the stalemate in U.S.-Canada negotiations by charging that Alaskan interceptions were violating their treaty rights, just as ocean harvests offshore of Oregon and Washington had. The lawsuit provided impetus for a draft treaty in 1982. But opposition from the Alaskan congressional delegation bottled up the draft treaty in the State Department for some two years.

Finally, a number of factors converged and led to an agreement in December 1994. These factors included persistent lobbying by a broad-based coalition of fishing and environmental groups and Indian tribes in favor of a treaty; the election and appointment of key political leaders familiar with the treaty negotiations, such as Senator (and former Northwest Power Planning Council Chair) Dan Evans, U.S. negotiator Ted Kronmiller, and White House aide Bruce Chapman; the threat of the tribes' suit against Alaska; and the Reagan Administration's desire to improve relations with Canada in the wake of its refusal to take action on another transboundary issue of great concern to Canada, acid rain. The treaty was ratified and entered into force in March 1985, removing the threat of the tribes having the courts apply the Boldt Decision to Alaska.[7]

The 1985 Treaty

The two basic precepts of the Pacific Salmon Treaty were 1) equitable harvest allocation and 2) conservation. During its first fourteen years, the treaty was disappointing on both counts, prompting amendments agreed to in 1999. Under the first principle, each country was to receive "benefits equivalent to the production of salmon originating in its waters." Under the second, the countries pledged to avoid overfishing. The treaty established a new body, the Pacific Salmon Commission, comprised of four members from each country, to carry out these provisions. Commission action requires the assent of both four-member sections from each country. To supply technical and regulatory advice to the Commission, the treaty created three bilateral oversight panels:

1) one for salmon stocks originating north of Cape Caution, British Columbia (roughly the northern tip of Vancouver Island); 2) one for stocks from south of Cape Caution; and 3) one concerning Fraser River sockeye and pink salmon The new commission replaced the old Fraser River Commission.[8]

The treaty imposed a number of interim harvest ceilings for various fisheries, which in the case of chinook and coho extended only until 1987 and, in the case of Fraser River sockeye and pink salmon, extended until 1993. These ceilings represented significant harvest reductions in chinook and coho — about a 25 percent cutback from 1984 harvest levels. However, the ceilings were established without regard to how many salmon were actually available for harvest — a number which varies from year to year — so the ceilings could not assure conservation of the fisheries.

Implementation of the treaty in the U.S. required both legislation and a court order. The Pacific Salmon Treaty Act of 1985 gave primary implementation responsibility to the states and Indian tribes, while limiting the federal role to an advisory capacity, although the U.S. may intervene if there is jeopardy of failing to fulfill treaty obligations. For example, the Act assigned membership in the four-person U.S. Section of the Commission as follows: one to an Alaskan resident appointed by the president from a list supplied by the Alaskan governor, one to an Oregon or Washington resident appointed from a list supplied by the Oregon and Washington governors, one to a person appointed from a list supplied by the tribes, and one to a federal official. Only the state and tribal members vote; the federal member is advisory only. The statute required the six-member U.S. section of the Southern Panel, which has responsibility for Columbia River stocks in treaty waters, to be comprised of two representatives of treaty tribes, one each representing the states of Oregon and Washington, a representative of the federal government, and a representative of the fishing industry. The 1985 Act thus exemplified a prime recognition of the co-management status of the Northwest Indian tribes.[9]

As part of the political price to secure Alaska's assent to the treaty, the tribes agreed to a settlement of their suit against the state. The settlement, approved by the court, provided that decisions of the U.S. Section of the Pacific Salmon Commission under the treaty would satisfy the tribe's treaty rights, but required the Section's decisions to be unanimous, effectively giving the tribes a veto.[10]

Implementation Problems

The chief problems with the treaty concerned its failure to define what it meant by "equitable" harvests and its pledge to maintain existing fisheries. The U.S. and Canada adopted different meanings of equity: Canada maintained that equity benefits are quantifiable, and that it should be entitled to harvest or obtain compensation for all the fish originating in its waters. In contrast, the United States believed that equity had to include more than mere numbers or pounds of intercepted fish because of the other treaty principles of optimizing production and avoiding overfishing. So rather than quantify specific harvest amounts, as Canada advocated, the U.S. promoted a "mutual benefits" approach, in which each country would present its own wish-list of conservation and production goals, and the Commission would resolve any conflicts between the two. These interpretive differences over the meaning of equity became a key factor in the treaty's failure. The treaty's attempt to protect existing fisheries while reducing interceptions produced a second source of conflict. Since many existing fisheries were also interception fisheries, both promises could not be kept. And they were not. For nearly a decade, the countries lingered in a virtual stalemate concerning treaty implementation.[11]

The first year of treaty implementation, 1986, involved start-up activities, including selecting chairs for the Commission and the panels, adopting bylaws, and other administrative and organizational activities. The Commission did make some minor changes in the management regimes, but did little else substantively. By 1987, however, the parties began renegotiating the terms of five of the six fishery regimes. Each party sought to regain the harvest allocations they had lost in signing the treaty, leading to gridlock. After ten days of failed negotiations, the Commission adjourned in frustration, and instead of setting new harvest allocations, simply retained the 1985 allocations. The

Commission failed to reach agreement on transboundary rivers (that is, rivers originating in Canada and flowing through Alaska), but it did make some progress by setting parameters for "overages and underages" (the amount of chinook or coho caught over or under the prescribed harvest levels). It also decided that future fishing regimes would include consideration of "associated fishing mortalities," or the amount of fish inadvertently harvested while targeting another species. Despite these small gains, the failed negotiations of 1987 set the stage for future disputes.[12]

The 1988 negotiations signaled a moderate rebound from the previous year's strife. For one thing, no harvest regimes were open for renegotiation, so the countries avoided repeated debates over equitable allocation. Also, the Commission finally agreed on a transboundary rivers regime and established a five-year joint sockeye enhancement regime. The rebound did not last, however, because by 1989, Canada began to insist that the Commission address the equity issue.

For several years, the Commission struggled with the meaning of equity. Canada believed, and the interception data seemed to indicate, that the treaty harvest regimes favored the United States. In 1989, the parties exchanged interception estimates, but the estimates differed substantially, and the underlying data proved unreliable. Then in 1991, the U.S. and Canada began to present their respective views as to how to value interceptions. Canada stressed that each country should receive the economic value of each salmon spawned in its rivers, measured by its value if it returned to the country of origin. The U.S. thought that this approach unrealistically simplified the equity issue and maintained that valuation must factor in the treaty obligations to prevent overfishing and provide for optimum production as well. Because the two countries could not agree on how to value interception harvests, they adopted different definitions of equity. Thus, in 1992, when Canada presented a "yardstick" in which it quantified the debt it believed the U.S. owed it, the U.S. disagreed, claiming it owed Canada nothing at all. As a result, during 1992-93 negotiations, the countries stalemated.[13]

The two countries' struggle to arrive at a definition of equity continued in subsequent years, despite persistent negotiations. When the interim harvest allocations established by the treaty annexes expired in 1993, there still was no consensus on equity, and no agreement in sight. In 1994, after Canada refused to continue to negotiate, the two countries agreed to submit their dispute to non-binding mediation, with all materials and the mediator's report remaining confidential. After seven months of attempted mediation, the mediator announced that the parties remained at an impasse. The documents and mediator's report remain sealed.[14]

In 1997, the two countries pursued an alternative negotiating strategy. Rather than engage in country-to-country negotiations, they attempted to negotiate a deal among "stakeholders," including salmon harvesters and those with an economic interest in harvests. Not surprisingly, given the diverse interests represented, the stakeholder negotiations produced more deadlock.

Meanwhile, tensions on the waters escalated. British Columbia fishermen, suffering from harvest cutbacks and depleted Columbia Basin salmon runs, pointed to Alaskan harvests of Canadian-origin chinook as a violation of the treaty's equity principle. In 1997, they blockaded an Alaskan ferry and held it hostage for several days in protest. When the blockade ended, the British Columbia government sued the U.S. in U.S. federal court for violating the treaty. The court dismissed the suit on the ground that the issue was a political question which had to be decided diplomatically. But the suit reflected the Canadian frustrations with the stalled negotiations.[15]

The 1999 Amendments

In early 1998, the two countries achieved a limited compromise that imposed new harvest limits on salmon originating in Oregon, Washington, and southern British Columbia, but could not reach an agreement concerning northern-originating salmon. Finally, on June 3, 1999, the two countries culminated seven years of negotiations with an agreement to amend the treaty. This agreement included provisions concerning allowable harvests, international cooperation, and habitat protection.[16]

The 1999 amendments established mechanisms that will govern harvests for ten years, and in the case of Fraser River salmon, for twelve years. The most significant provisions concern a change from the 1985 treaty's fixed-catch harvest ceilings to an "abundance-based" harvest management, under which harvests will vary based on current fish populations. One of the chief problems of the 1985 treaty's fixed ceilings was that they were based on abundance figures from 1979-83, which failed to reflect subsequent run size declines. Consequently, the fixed ceilings produced overharvests. In contrast, the new abundance-based approach is based on annual population variations, and harvests are limited to a fixed percentage of overall fish mortality. The latter is an important change from the previous regime, which based harvests on marketable catch. Targeting fish in that way did not account for the fact that in catch-and-release and gillnet fisheries around 20 percent of the released fish die.

The abundance-based harvest regimes represented a conservation improvement over the fixed harvest ceilings, but they still risked overharvesting weak salmon runs by aggregating strong and weak stocks in the ocean to determine the allowable harvest in a mixed stock fishery. Thus, an abundance of one stock might allow overharvest of other weaker stocks. The 1999 agreement contained "weak stock" provisions, under which harvests are set by individual stock populations, but these provisions apply only in marine waters close to rivers of origin.[17]

The 1999 amendments promised that the U.S. harvest of Fraser River salmon would decline, decreasing to 16.5 percent over three years for sockeye and capping U.S. pink salmon harvests at 25.7 percent. To facilitate these cutbacks, the amendments required the state of Washington to implement a buy-back program to reduce the number of harvesters licensed to take Fraser River salmon. Since these provisions apply only to non-Indian harvesters, the tribal share of Fraser River salmon will increase to more than two-thirds of the U.S. allotment.[18]

The 1999 amendments also required substantial harvest cutbacks from Alaskan fishers on salmon from transboundary rivers flowing through the Alaska panhandle and in sockeye and pink fisheries in Southeast Alaska and Northern British Columbia. Canada agreed to reduce harvests of certain chinook stocks by 36.5 percent, while the United States agreed to reduce harvests by 40 percent. The 1999 agreement established only a framework for coho harvests: until a harvest regime can be developed, harvest levels in southern British Columbia and Washington will remain at 1998 levels. For chum, recently added to the U.S. Endangered Species Act list, Canada agreed to release summer chum, and both countries promised to collect better data on chum stocks.[19]

In addition to the new harvest regimes, the 1999 amendments established two funds to support restoration and enhancement work in the northern and southern areas covered by the treaty. Although the total amount of the funds is $140 million over ten years, obtaining the money is uncertain, dependent upon annual appropriation decisions. The new agreement also established a Committee on Scientific Cooperation to improve scientific data collection and analysis and resolve scientific disputes. Finally, the amendments included a provision concerning the importance of habitat protection and restoration, requiring the two countries to use their best efforts to protect and restore habitat and provide safe passage for salmon. The Commission must report annually on those salmon stocks for which harvest management controls are insufficient to ensure their viability, suggest options for restoring those stocks, and explain implementation efforts.[20]

Outlook For the Future

The 1999 amendments to the Pacific Salmon Treaty represented a breakthrough in a stalemate that lasted for most of the 1990s. The commitment to abundance-based management is no doubt a therapeutic development. Whether the "weak-stock" provisions of the agreement will be sufficient to prevent the slide of weak stocks toward extinction is not clear. The promise of better science to inform policymakers is welcome, of course, but scientists do not make policy, and the results of scientific research have often been manipulated by non-scientists. The funds for enhancement and restoration measures are also welcome, although the money is not guaranteed. The habitat provisions are long overdue, but do not appear to be specific enough to ensure that protective actions will in fact be undertaken. Once again, concern over harvest allocation preoccupied treaty negotiators, producing only vague statements of good intentions about habitat.

Although the 1999 amendments are an improvement from the status quo, the friction created during the last decade among the parties is unlikely to dissipate quickly. The British Columbia government, kept out of the negotiations by the Canadian federal government, quickly charged that Alaskan harvests under the amendments remain too high to provide sufficient protection for Canadian-origin salmon. The head of the Alaska Trollers Association, on the other hand, claimed that Alaska harvesters are bearing an unfair burden of protecting southern-originating salmon stocks, since Alaskans have already incurred significant harvest cutbacks. He claimed that the focus needs to shift to habitat restoration instead of reduced harvests. These attitudes will make implementation of the 1999 reforms challenging.[21]

The decades-long experience of negotiating and implementing the Pacific Salmon Treaty provides a case study in the difficulties of allocating salmon harvests by consensus. The need for the two countries to agree produced a long stalemate over treaty implementation — hardly a surprising development, since the U.S. was itself deadlocked over the issue of Alaskan harvests. And concern over short-term allocation issues persistently overwhelmed any long-term conservation efforts. The 1999 amendments may herald a new era, but the past 15 years of implementation disagreements counsels warns against optimism.[22]

9 — FIFTH PROMISE: ENDANGERED SPECIES ACT PROTECTION

Despite its billing as the most ambitious biological restoration project in world history, by 1990 it was obvious to many that the Northwest Power Act's Columbia Basin Fish and Wildlife Program was not going to achieve its goal of doubling the basin's salmon runs in a genetically sensitive manner. Although spending considerable sums of money, the program suffered from imperfect design, poor enforcement, and lack of authority over harvest management, hatchery operations, and habitat-damaging activities. Its failure to fundamentally restructure river flows led the Columbia Basin Fish and Wildlife Authority, a coalition of federal and state fish and wildlife agencies and Indian tribes, to propose in 1990 a completely revised flow regime, one that would significantly boost flows in the spring and summer. This flow regime was actually quite similar to one the fishery agencies and tribes originally proposed to the Northwest Power Planning Council in 1981, which the Council rejected in favor of its flawed water budget. Nearly a decade later, little progress had been made in restructuring the flows in the mainstem Columbia and Snake Rivers to reflect the biological needs of salmon.[1]

The situation was actually considerably bleaker than a mere inability to change the status quo of hydropower's dominance of the river. The salmon runs were experiencing a steep decline. In fact, in 1991, the American Fisheries Society's Endangered Species Committee reported a Pacific Coast-wide salmon crisis: 101 naturally spawning salmon species faced "a high risk of extinction;" another 58 had a "moderate risk of extinction;" and 54 more were judged to be of "special concern." About one-third of those fish runs were in the Columbia Basin. This report helped to launch the Endangered Species Act (ESA) era of Columbia Basin salmon management.[2]

But nearly a decade after the first Columbia Basin salmon listings under the ESA, it was evident that the ESA was no panacea for the basin's imperiled salmon runs.

Implementation of the statute in the Columbia Basin belied its reputation as a draconian, economically insensitive straightjacket. In fact, as this chapter reveals, in several instances ESA-ordered measures were actually less stringent than measures imposed by other legal requirements. In practice, the ESA proved to be quite sensitive to its economic effects, which might come as a surprise both to the statute's detractors in Congress and to those who hoped it would be the vehicle to restore Columbia Basin salmon.

The Salmon Summit and the Drawdown Proposal

In March 1990, the Shoshone-Bannock tribe filed a petition to list Snake River sockeye under the ESA. Two months later, in May 1990, a coalition of environmental groups petitioned to list Snake River chinook and coho runs. In response to these petitions, Oregon Senator Mark Hatfield convened a series of meetings with major river users in an effort to seek a way to avoid listings. Dubbed the "Salmon Summit" by the press, the meetings failed to produce a plan to avert the listings, but they succeeded in generating a noteworthy contribution to salmon restoration efforts: a proposal, championed by Idaho Governor Cecil Andrus, to draw down Lower Snake River reservoirs during the spring by 25 feet or more, in order to increase water flow velocity to speed salmon migration. Idaho favored this approach to salmon restoration because by reducing the cross-sectional area of a reservoir, a drawdown would allow flow velocity increases with less water released from Idaho reservoirs upstream. Reservoir drawdowns would become a prominent issue in subsequent restoration proposals.[3]

Another response to the ESA petitions was Senator Hatfield's request that the Oregon Department of Fish and Wildlife and the National Marine Fisheries Service (NMFS) produce a status report on the petitioned salmon runs. The figures in the ensuing report were so alarming — for example, spring chinook were only six percent of their 1961 quantity in the Salmon River, the Snake's principal tributary — that there was little doubt that the ESA listings were imminent.[4]

The Listings

In November 1991, NMFS responded to the Shoshone-Bannock petition by listing Snake River sockeye as an endangered species. The listing cited hydropower development and water withdrawals for irrigation and storage among the principal reasons for the desperate condition of the species. In the year they were listed only four Snake River sockeye returned to their last remaining spawning ground, Redfish Lake.[5]

Five months later, in April 1992, NMFS responded to the environmentalists' petition by listing two species of Snake River chinook under the Act. Snake River spring/summer chinook, which once accounted for more than 40 percent of all the chinook in the Columbia Basin, had declined to less than ten percent of their historic strength by the 1990s, and just one percent of their former 1.5 million adult fish returned in 1991. Snake River fall chinook fared no better. For the first half of the twentieth century, despite the 1901 construction of Swan Falls Dam on the Snake in south central Idaho — which cut off fall chinook from over 100 miles of their spawning grounds — the population stabilized at around 70,000 fish. But the construction and operation of four federal and three Idaho Power Company dams on Lower Snake between 1955 and 1975 devastated the fall chinook. In 1990, only 78 salmon surmounted Lower Granite Dam, the last passable dam on the Snake River. The reasons for the chinook decline were similar to those for sockeye. They included hydropower development, water storage, water withdrawals for irrigation, siltation, and water pollution.[6]

These listings in late 1991 and early 1992 ushered in the Endangered Species Act era of Columbia Basin salmon. After the listings, neither the interpretation of the statute, nor the species would be the same. Unfortunately, the former changed considerably more than the condition of the latter.

The Evolutionarily Significant Unit Concept

The ESA offers protection for species, subspecies, and "distinct population segments." To define a distinct population segment eligible for listing in the context of Pacific salmon, NMFS developed the concept of an "evolutionarily significant unit" (ESU). To be considered an ESU, a population must be "substantially isolated" from other populations and represent an "important component in the evolutionary legacy of the species." The policy's emphasis on reproductive isolation seems misguided, since salmon experience a certain amount of natural straying and interbreeding that is important for the colonizing of new habitats by healthy spawning stocks. Hatchery and wild stocks also interbreed, so a wild stock might not qualify as an ESU separate from its hatchery counterpart. Thus, plentiful hatchery fish could foreclose the listing of scarce wild fish, despite their differences in terms of genetics and ecological value.

According to NMFS, the evolutionary legacy of a species is "the genetic variability that is the product of past evolutionary events and which represents the reservoir upon which future evolutionary potential depends." In other words, if a particular population became extinct, would its loss represent a significant loss to the ecological or genetic integrity of the species? While this seems to be a sensible criterion, reproductive isolation is still required. Thus, the ESU policy apparently elevates reproductive isolation of the species over other statutory policies, like protecting ecosystem health, conserving imperiled domestic populations even when a species is relatively abundant elsewhere in the world, and providing management flexibility in the face of scientific uncertainty. The ESU policy is therefore likely to cause unanticipated difficulties for NMFS in salmon listing decisions.[7*]

---

* While this book was in press, Judge Michael Hogan struck down NMFS's listing of Oregon coho because NMFS included both wild and hatchery stock in the ESU, but limited its management prescriptions to wild coho. The court ruled that once NMFS identifies an ESU, it may not list part of the population and exclude another part. *Alsea Valley Alliance v. Evans*, 2001 WL 11005100 (D. Or. Sept. 10, 2000). Within weeks, irrigators used the decision to file delisting petitions for numerous other salmon ESUs. Apparently, all but one salmon ESU (Southern California steelhead) includes hatchery fish. The court ruling thus casts a cloud over the future of the ESA on salmon management, a cloud that NMFS could remove by eliminating the preoccupation the current ESU policy has with reproductive isolation.

One result of NMFS's application of the ESU concept was its rejection of several populations of salmon for listing, including its initial rejection of Lower Columbia River coho and Illinois River winter steelhead. NMFS and the U.S. Fish and Wildlife Service also removed Umpqua River cutthroat trout from the ESA list by combining the Umpqua ESU with an ESU comprised of cutthroat trout from rivers in southwest Washington.[8]

The Importance of Citizen Petitions

The citizen petition process has been absolutely critical in the era of the ESA in salmon restoration efforts. Under the ESA citizens may petition to list a species, and the pertinent Secretary (Interior in the case of terrestrial species, Commerce in the case of marine species including salmon) must respond by determining whether the petition presents substantial information indicating that a listing may be warranted. If so, the Secretary must perform a status review of the species within twelve months of the filing of the petition. This review is to determine whether the species is in danger of extinction throughout all or a significant portion of its range (an "endangered species"), or is likely to become an endangered species within the foreseeable future (a "threatened species").[9]

The great virtue of the citizen petition process is that it triggers the ESA's science-based decision making, since the agency must make its decisions on scientific grounds. Hence, biological information, not economic concerns, is the driving force behind ESA listing decisions. All of the initial Columbia Basin salmon listings, and many of the later ones, were triggered by the citizen petition process. Without this "action-forcing" provision of the ESA, it is quite doubtful that the federal government would have decided to list Columbia Basin salmon populations on its own motion, given the widespread changes in land and water use decision making that were likely to result.

The Enlarged Mandate

Listing of Columbia Basin salmon under the ESA subjected many activities to systematic biological scrutiny for the first time. Prior to the first listings in 1991-92, only hydroelectric operations were scrutinized for their adverse effects on salmon under the provisions of the Northwest Power Act. The listings led to a more comprehensive approach to salmon restoration by expanding the focus of attention beyond hydroelectric operations to include inquiry into hatchery, harvest, and habitat activities that were largely beyond the scope of the Northwest Power Act. The ESA therefore offered the prospect of designing a restoration program that covered most human-induced forms of salmon mortality.[10]

The ESA proscribes the "taking" of species listed as endangered. The statute's regulations broadly define taking to include significant habitat modification where the result injures the species by significantly impairing essential behavior patterns like breeding, feeding, or sheltering. Federal agencies also must not jeopardize the continued existence of species or adversely modify designated critical habitat. The key to implementing the ESA's enlarged mandate in the Columbia Basin was the statute's federal consultation procedure, established by section 7 of the Act. This procedure requires federal agencies to consult with NMFS in order to evaluate the effect of their proposals on listed salmon. The effect of the consultation process is to remove significant decision making authority from the agencies proposing the action and to give it to NMFS, which issues biological opinions (BiOps) on proposals that may adversely affect listed species. In these BiOps, NMFS, using "best available" science, specifies the expected effects of proposals on listed species and their habitat and suggests alternatives designed to avoid jeopardizing the species or adversely affecting its critical habitat. According to the Supreme Court, BiOps are "virtually binding" on agencies proposing actions. BiOps are thus the means by which the ESA's directives of avoiding species jeopardy or adverse habitat modification are carried out.[11]

There are limits to the scope of BiOps, however. They apply only to federal activities, although that includes federal permitting and licensing of private activities. But land use decisions on private lands are not typically subject to federal control, nor are most decisions on water withdrawals. Those activities can run afoul of the statute's ban on "takes," but proving that a take has occurred is not usually easy. Where a take is certain to occur, it may be authorized when a non-federal entity prepares a suitable "habitat conservation plan," as discussed below. With respect to species listed as threatened, section 4(d) of the ESA authorizes regulations which set conditions under which activities may take place without violating the statute. As discussed in chapter 14, the states have formulated plans which they hope will be approved under section 4(d) to control developments affecting salmon habitat. However, the key decision making process for Columbia Basin salmon has been a series of BiOps.[12]

The Initial Hydropower BiOps

NMFS issued its first BiOp on Columbia Basin hydroelectric operations shortly after listing Snake River sockeye and chinook. The agency determined that proposed 1992 operations would not jeopardize the continued existence of the listed salmon because the 1991 amendments to the Columbia Basin Fish and Wildlife Program under the Northwest Power Act promised to improve salmon survival over previous years. Even though this standard was controversial — since improvements over the status quo would not necessarily reverse the decline of the species — the 1992 BiOp was not challenged in court.[13]

NMFS's jeopardy standard was not to go unchallenged for long, however. In 1993, NMFS refined the standard to include a two-step analysis, requiring 1) improved survival over a designated "base period," and 2) hydroelectric operations that, in combination with all other human effects on salmon, were reasonably likely to reduce mortalities to stabilize salmon populations in the long run. Since it determined that proposed 1993 operations met both criteria, NMFS again issued a "no jeopardy" opinion, including the rather modest goal of merely stopping the decline of salmon populations within four salmon life cycles, about fifteen years. However, the states of Idaho and Oregon promptly filed suit, claiming that the 1993 BiOp violated the ESA.[14]

Idaho Dept. of Fish and Game v. NMFS: Judicial Intervention

In March 1994, U.S. District Judge Malcolm Marsh agreed with the states that both elements of NMFS's two-part jeopardy test were flawed. First, he concluded that NMFS's explanation of why it chose the years 1986-90 for the baseline period, years of drought and low salmon runs — allegedly to promote "consistent management practices" — was neither factually accurate nor biologically sound. NMFS had employed longer baselines in its 1992 BiOp, and Judge Marsh decided that the agency's concern over maintaining consistent management practices was biologically suspect because it focused more on the hydroelectric system's capability than upon the needs of the salmon. Choosing a baseline comprised of years of poor salmon returns made it relatively easy for NMFS to produce a "no jeopardy" opinion by claiming that 1993 operations would improve the status quo. Judge Marsh determined that this focus on the status quo, instead of the stabilization of the species, represented arbitrary decision making.[15]

Second, NMFS's "no jeopardy" opinion was flawed because it relied on life-cycle modeling that discounted pessimistic assumptions and disregarded worst-case consequences. This approach allowed NMFS to inflate the confidence levels of its optimistic projections and to ignore completely the risks associated with small populations, where inbreeding and environmental catastrophes can produce extinctions. The judge concluded that NMFS's failure to consider the full range of risk assumptions was arbitrary.[16]

To remedy its flawed methodology and arbitrary decision making, Judge Marsh suggested that NMFS modify its analysis in two ways: 1) consider alternative baseline periods, and 2) satisfy the ESA's directive to employ "best available" scientific information by considering the views of state and tribal fishery biologists. The latter ruling suggested a pluralistic approach to interpreting the meaning of "best available" science. Judge Marsh concluded his opinion by advising that, given the state of Columbia Basin salmon runs, small, incremental changes would not satisfy the ESA:

[T]he process is seriously, 'significantly,' flawed because it is too heavily geared towards a status quo that has allowed all forms of river activity to proceed in a deficit situation — that is, relatively small steps, minor improvements and adjustments — when the situation literally cries out for a major overhaul. Instead of looking for what *can* be done to protect the species from jeopardy, NMFS and the other action agencies have narrowly focused their attention on what the establishment is capable of handling with minimal disruption.[17]

No major overhaul in system operations would be forthcoming, however, in part because the fishery agencies and tribes could not agree what the overhaul should involve, and in part because, in the face of this disagreement, the courts were unwilling to overturn NMFS's risk assessment decisions.

The 1995-99 BiOp[18]

Following the litigation over NMFS's 1993 BiOp, NMFS issued a five-year BiOp designed to govern hydroelectric operations during 1994-98. Environmentalists challenged this BiOp as well, even though it called for an additional 500,000 acre-feet of water stored in federal reservoirs in the Snake basin to be released for fish flows. They claimed that the new multi-year BiOp violated the ESA by erroneously relying on truck and barge transport to conclude that there would be no jeopardy. However, the court delayed hearing the suit, giving NMFS a chance to bring the new BiOp into compliance with its decision in the *Idaho Dept. of Fish and Game* case.

In early 1995, NMFS began circulating a series of draft BiOps which eventually became the new 1995-99 BiOp. The first draft stated that "the evidence suggests . . . that transportation alone is not likely the solution to rebuilding listed salmon populations." Instead, it called for an additional 3.5 million acre-feet of storage water to be released for fish flows in the Columbia and an additional one million acre-feet to boost Snake River flows. The draft also called for a detailed schedule of minimum flows, including biweekly average minimum flows of 85,000 to 100,000 cubic feet per second in the Snake in the spring, and 50,000 to 55,000 in the Snake in the summer. The Lower Snake

River reservoirs were to be drawn down to near minimum operating pool, with immediate planning for a drawdown to natural river levels. John Day reservoir, on the Lower Columbia, was also to be drawn down to minimum operating pool.

Subsequent drafts of the multi-year BiOp, however, began to water down salmon protection. The final BiOp, released in March 1995, contained the same flow schedule as the earlier draft but reduced the flows to a "goal" that operating agencies should "take into account." Moreover, the flow objective was reduced from a bi-weekly average to a seasonal average, giving the operating agencies considerably more flexibility but depriving the salmon of dependable flows. The earlier requirements to obtain 3.5 million acre-feet of Canadian storage to boost flows in the Columbia and one million acre-feet to boost flows in the Snake disappeared, replaced by vague exhortations to release water for fish enhancement. The John Day drawdown was now conditioned on funding to supply "economic mitigation," such as moving irrigation pumps and boat docks. A 24-year period for judging whether jeopardy was likely to occur disappeared. The final BiOp also adopted a dual probability standard for jeopardy: proposed actions had to demonstrate a "high likelihood" of species survival, but only a "moderate likelihood" (50 percent probability) of species recovery, making it considerably easier to avoid jeopardy conclusions.[19]

The final BiOp made no attempt to justify any of these changes on biological grounds; NMFS explained them as reasonable accommodations with cost concerns and other system uses. None of the new compromised measures was subjected to biological modeling, so NMFS could not be assured that its selected alternative would in fact avoid species jeopardy, an apparent statutory violation. All of the eleventh-hour changes were concessions to the status quo against which Judge Marsh had warned earlier. None favored salmon.

The revised BiOp continued to rely heavily on a twenty-year old program of transporting juvenile salmon downstream by truck and barge instead of improving river conditions. NMFS estimated that about 74 percent of Snake River spring/summer chinook arriving at Lower Granite Dam (the uppermost of the four Corps dams on the Lower Snake) would be transported at normal river flows. The BiOp promised that NMFS would revisit the transportation issue when the BiOp expired in 1999. At that point NMFS would make a long-term decision as to whether truck and barge transportation could be a main ingredient in Columbia Basin salmon recovery. The time frame for making this decision was subsequently delayed until late 2000.[20]

American Rivers v. NMFS: Judicial Acquiescence

A coalition of environmental groups challenged the revised BiOp, claiming that it violated the ESA by authorizing mortalities of up to 86 percent of juvenile Snake River sockeye and spring/summer chinook and up to 99 percent of juvenile Snake River fall chinook. The environmentalists also challenged the dual standards for jeopardy, ignoring critical habitat, and failing to implement key provisions like the John Day drawdown. Although Judge Marsh had struck down the 1993 BiOp three years earlier, he upheld the 1995-99 BiOp, even though he noted that "[a]s a long-time observer and examiner" of salmon restoration efforts, he could not help but "question the soundness of [NMFS's] selected level of risk tolerance." Despite these reservations, he concluded that the ESA "says nothing about risk tolerance, and the limits of judicial review dictate that I not interfere with a federal agencies' [sic] exercise of professional judgment or their reasoned evaluations."[21]

The court was influenced by NMFS's claim that it was implementing an "ecosystem management" approach to salmon recovery by establishing a systematic comparison of the ability of transported fish to return to spawn as compared to fish left in the river. In addition, NMFS noted that other species, like bull trout (a freshwater salmonid) and sturgeon, might suffer from the higher river flows that the environmentalists sought. Finally, unlike the case three years earlier, Idaho flip-flopped its position, now supporting NMFS, and the Columbia Basin tribes split over the BiOp: the upper basin Colville and Spokane tribes sought to protect reservoir levels in Lake Roosevelt, the reservoir formed by Grand Coulee Dam — which would be lowered to achieve the flows that the lower basin tribes advocated. Thus, just three years after he called for a "major overhaul" in system operations, Judge Marsh upheld the revised BiOp as not being irrational, but he did so on the basis of assurance from the NMFS Regional Director that "a 'long-term system configuration' will achieve sufficient improvements in salmon survival to ensure perpetuation of the species." This decision essentially allowed NMFS to proceed with its experiment comparing the survival levels of transported versus in-river salmon until 2000. The court noted, however, that promised improvements in salmon survival were essential:

> whether the salmon may be saved in time to benefit from such long term system improvements is the risk that NMFS and the action agencies have assumed within this process. Given the dwindling numbers, time is clearly running out.

The court of appeals affirmed Judge Marsh in early 1999.[22]

The Search For Better Science: The PATH Process

Judge Marsh struck down the 1993 BiOp in large part because it ignored the biological advice of the states and the tribes. In response, one of the innovations of the 1995-99 BiOp was to create an independent working group of scientists to assist NMFS in gathering and evaluating the best available scientific information. This group, known as the Plan for Analyzing and Testing Hypotheses (PATH), was comprised of about 25 federal, state, tribal, and independent scientists who operated under accepted scientific procedures and whose work was peer-reviewed. This multi-agency process applied life cycle models to estimate historical trends in salmon reproduction and survival, generated hypotheses about sources of salmon mortality, and projected the effects of future management actions on salmon populations.[23]

The PATH results indicated that breaching the Lower Snake Dams would be much more likely to meet survival and recovery standards for listed Snake River fall and spring/summer chinook than hydroelectric operations under the 1995-99 BiOp. Under its life cycle modeling fall chinook had an average 82 percent likelihood of meeting recovery criteria over a 48-year time horizon, while non-breaching alternatives had only a 47 to 50 percent chance, which failed to satisfy NMFS's recovery criteria. For spring/summer chinook, the models also showed that dam breaching was the superior alternative, showing a 100 percent probability of recovery under many scenarios. Dam breaching would increase spawning habitat for the mainstem spawning fall chinook by 70-80 percent (although there are questions about quality of the habitat) and eliminate high mortality rates in Little Goose reservoir. PATH did not analyze listed sockeye and steelhead, but NMFS agreed that the likely results from breaching could be inferred from the spring/summer chinook analysis, except that there are significantly higher mainstem harvest rates for steelhead, meaning that there might be alternative paths to recovery for that species.[24]

The Cumulative Risk Initiative

Perhaps because it did not like the answers it was getting from the PATH scientists, or perhaps (as NMFS claimed) to complement the PATH process and examine factors which PATH did not consider, in 1999 NMFS established its own "cumulative risk initiative" (CRI) to help the agency decide on a new 5-year BiOp on hydroelectric operations. The CRI team, comprised of about 25 NMFS scientists, did not limit itself to improvements in the hydroelectric system but also considered opportunities to promote salmon recovery through the salmon life cycle, including changes in hatchery operations, harvest controls, and habitat improvements. The holistic CRI approach is in keeping with the ecosystem management concepts, discussed in chapter 14, but its comprehensiveness may divert attention from the hydroelectric system, the chief cause of human-induced mortalities.

The CRI analysis, which is detailed in chapter 13's discussion of dam breaching, concluded that some spring/summer species have "considerable" risks of extinction within ten years. For example, for two Snake River "index stocks" (Marsh Creek and Sulpher Creek) the extinction risks were 15 percent and 10 percent, respectively. All index stocks for spring/summer chinook, fall chinook, and steelhead had "substantial" chances (50 percent or more) of extinction over the next 100 years. Despite these grave risks, and despite concluding that dam breaching would likely be sufficient to recover fall chinook and steelhead, the CRI did not endorse dam breaching because it concluded that 1) breaching by itself would not likely recover spring/summer chinook, and 2) the attractiveness of dam breaching would lessen if fish transported in barges and trucks do not in fact suffer significant delayed mortalities after their release in the lower river. With respect to the latter issue, the CRI analysis noted that recent studies suggested that transported fish suffer from lower mortality rates than the PATH studies assumed; therefore, according to the CRI, dam breaching might not provide as significant a boost in survival as the PATH studies showed. Moreover, CRI noted that breaching the Lower Snake Dams would assist only the Snake River species, not other listed species with declining growth rates, like Upper Columbia spring chinook and steelhead and Middle Columbia and Upper Willamette steelhead.[25]

The 2001-05 BiOp and the Basinwide Recovery Strategy

In December 2000, NMFS released a new five-year BiOp on Columbia Basin hydroelectric operations, including fourteen dams in the lower basin, 31 upper basin projects operated by the Bureau of Reclamation, and the juvenile salmon transportation program. Accompanying the BiOp was a basinwide salmon recovery strategy produced by several federal agencies, collectively known as the Federal Caucus, which aimed to prevent salmon extinctions and fostering recovery throughout the salmon life cycle. Like the CRI analysis, the basinwide recovery strategy focused not only on hydropower operations, but also habitat, hatchery, and harvest measures.[26]

The BiOp concluded the proposed hydroelectric operations would likely jeopardize the continued existence of all eight listed salmon species which spawn above Bonneville Dam, including all listed Snake River species, Upper Columbia spring/summer chinook and steelhead, Middle Columbia steelhead, and Columbia River chum. To avoid jeopardy, NMFS developed a series of mitigating measures which, when combined with the recovery measures outlined in the accompanying recovery strategy, allowed NMFS to conclude that the listed salmon would not only survive but recover over the long-term. Basically, the BiOp's approach was to assume that the Lower Snake Dams would not be breached, then attempt to craft an aggressive restoration program around the continued existence of the dams. This approach drew the BiOp's focus away from the hydroelectric system, the cause of most man-induced salmon mortalities, and instead emphasized what the BiOp referred to as "offsite mitigation," mostly habitat protection and restoration.[27]

The centerpiece of the BiOp was a series of performance standards needed to avoid jeopardy. Hydroelectric systems measures, described as "the best the hydrosystem can do without breaching," included systemwide survival rates of 50 percent for Snake River juvenile steelhead, 57 percent juvenile Snake River spring/summer chinook, and 66 percent for juvenile Upper Columbia spring/summer chinook. The BiOp established hydrosystem survival rates for both adult and juvenile species at each dam as well as systemwide. These standards must be met on an average basis over ten years, although NMFS promised to review and evaluate the results after five and eight years. In those reviews, NMFS "will rely on estimates of life stage survival increases and productivity," referred to as lambda. A lambda of 1.1 each year over eight years will produce a population doubling; on the other hand, a lambda of 0.95 on an annual basis will produce halving of the population. NMFS stated that with lambda values below 0.95 by 2008 the species "would be considered at risk of extinction," and the BiOp "will be considered to have failed." Lambda values between 0.95 and 1.1 will require a new BiOp.[28]

To improve the prospects of satisfying the requisite lambda, NMFS continued to endorse artificial transportation, in fact directing an increase in transportation during the summer. On the other hand, NMFS rejected transportation from McNary Dam in the spring, due to poor results. It also directed a change in transport of Snake River stocks, increasing barge transport while decreasing truck transport.[29]

The BiOp included several water management measures, mostly continuing various water releases from storage to meet streamflow objectives and establishing reservoir levels to facilitate salmon migration. It continued seasonal flow objectives at

Lower Granite Dam on the Snake River at 85,000-100,000 cubic feet per second (cfs) in the spring and 50,000-55,000 cfs in the summer; at McNary Dam on the Lower Columbia, the objectives remained at 220,000-260,000 cfs in the spring, and 200,000 cfs in summer; and the BiOp continued to call for 135,000 cfs at Priest Rapids Dam on the Mid-Columbia. The BiOp also established detailed operational criteria for various federal and non-federal projects, including continuing an earlier directive to the Bureau of Reclamation to provide 427,000 acre-feet of storage water from Upper Snake River reservoirs; boosting river flows through water conservation, eliminating illegal water use, and purchasing water rights; and increasing fall and winter flows to promote spawning below Bonneville Dam.[30]

The BiOp contained numerous other measures covering juvenile passage through reservoirs, adult fish passage, and water quality. But perhaps more notable were the BiOp's references to habitat, harvest, and hatchery measures promised in the accompanying basinwide recovery plan. Only through improvements in these areas was the BiOp able to conclude that there was a 50 percent chance of salmon recovery. To implement the BiOp, NMFS required various federal agencies to develop a series of one and five-year implementation plans, which are to evaluate the status of species, recent data and research results, the feasibility and timing measures, and their probabilities of success. Regular reporting of new information and progress toward meeting performance standards was also required. In this manner, the BiOp was able to enlist anticipated improvements in non-hydroelectric actions as a reason to suggest that proposed hydroelectric operations could avoid jeopardy to listed salmon without breaching the Lower Snake Dams.[31]

The NMFS BiOp did not entirely rule out the possibility of breaching the Lower Snake Dams, which it referred to as the most risk-adverse alternative, an alternative providing "more certainty of long-term survival and recovery than would other measures." This risk assessment originally caused NMFS to call for breaching the dams unless dramatic improvements in survival were attained over a 5-year period in a draft BiOp. However, when agencies like the Corps of Engineers and the Bonneville Power

Administration protested that they had no authority to proceed with breaching, NMFS changed the BiOp to suggest that it would recommend breaching only if it determined that 1) the measures in the BiOp failed to avoid jeopardy (a lambda below 0.95) during the promised 5- and 8-year reviews of the BiOp, and 2) some of the uncertainties concerning the efficacy of breaching (especially uncertainties concerning delayed mortalities after transportation) were reduced.[32]

In this fashion the NMFS BiOp deferred the breaching issue, while endorsing a life-cycle approach to recovery which emphasized not only improvements in the hydroelectric systems but also endorsed what the BiOp referred to as "offsite mitigation:" improved hatchery practices, harvest management, and habitat restoration. Critics of the draft BiOp charged that it relied on overly optimistic assumptions about possible increases in survival due to offsite mitigation and a failure of the CRI process to consult with state and tribal biologists, which seemed crucial to the BiOp's conclusions. These arguments were quite similar to those that convinced the district court to strike down the 1993 BiOp. Critics of NMFS's failure to endorse dam breaching could also point to a statement of the director of the U.S. Fish and Wildlife Service, who observed at a press conference that it was a "no brainer" that a free flowing river was an improvement for salmon and other wildlife. The debate over the dam breaching issue is explored further in chapter 13.[33]

Whether the BiOp's reliance on off-site mitigation to avoid jeopardy satisfies the ESA is a fair question. First, most of the offsite mitigation measures are contained in the accompanying non-binding basinwide recovery plan. It is hardly clear that NMFS may conclude that species jeopardy can be avoided through a document containing no enforceable promises and directed at agencies other than those proposing the actions that triggered ESA consultation. Second, the effect of relying on off-site mitigation, mostly habitat protection and restoration, effectively shifts restoration responsibilities from the federal government, as operator of the basin's federal dams, to state and local governments, which control most land and water use practices. One wonders whether the federal government may legitimately shift the conservation burden to other governments in this manner. Third, the BiOp's designation of 1980 as the baseline by which to measure improvements is also questionable, given that Judge Marsh struck down the earlier baseline of 1986-90 as unreasonable. Salmon advocates might justifiably think that the baseline year from which to measure improvements should have been 2000, the year of the BiOp, since presumably 1980 conditions had nothing to do with the reasons that proposed 2001-05 hydroelectric operations would jeopardize salmon populations absent (mostly off-site) mitigation. These issues will surely be raised in court proceedings challenging the 2001-05 BiOp on hydroelectric operations.

The 1995 Hatchery BiOp

As discussed in chapter 5, a patchwork of federal and state statutes authorizes hatchery programs in the Columbia Basin to support salmon harvests and to try to compensate for the effects of habitat loss from hydroelectric development. Although each hatchery is subject to the standards of its authorizing statute, NMFS's decisions to list salmon under the ESA provided a framework for considering the combined effect of all hatchery programs on an ecosystem-wide scale.

In 1995, NMFS considered the effects of 71 federal and non-federal hatchery programs during 1995-1998 on listed Snake River salmon. These programs are operated by five federal agencies and three states. In its BiOp, NMFS analyzed the numerous hatchery programs in light of the goals proposed in its 1995 recovery plan. NMFS concluded that the hatchery operations would jeopardize the continued existence of listed Snake River salmon because the operations were inconsistent with the recovery plan. NMFS expressed concern that the hatchery operations would exceed the basin's carrying capacity for Snake River salmon and would allow levels of genetic introgression (introduction of a gene from one gene complex to another), competition, and predation beyond that tolerated in the proposed recovery plan. As a result, the agency imposed a cap on hatchery fish releases at 1994 levels (20.2 million hatchery releases in the Snake Basin and 197.4 million throughout the Columbia Basin) and other measures designed to address differences between the hatchery program and NMFS's proposed recovery plan. This use of the proposed recovery plan gave life to the 1995 document, and NMFS would employ the proposed recovery plan in other situations, even though it remains in proposed form as of this writing.[34]

Supplementation: The Nez Perce Hatchery BiOp

Also in 1995, the Columbia River Inter-Tribal Fish Commission, a technical and policy-coordinating body representing the four Lower Columbia Basin tribes with treaty fishing rights, released its own plan for Columbia Basin salmon restoration. Like NMFS's proposed recovery plan, the tribal plan (discussed in more detail in chapters 6 and 14) recognized a role for hatchery production to restore salmon runs. Unlike the NMFS plan, the tribal plan relied on supplementation (explained in chapter 6), a form of hatchery production that is less intrusive to wild salmon populations than traditional hatchery production, but which nevertheless has its critics, including NMFS.[35]

Despite its misgivings about supplementation, in 1997, NMFS issued a BiOp on a hatchery proposed in the Northwest Power Planning Council's program for the Nez Perce reservation involving supplementation. The proposal was subject to ESA consultation because it was to be funded by the Bonneville Power Administration and the Bureau of Indian Affairs. The Nez Perce Tribe proposed a supplementation program for the Clearwater River in the Snake Basin, aiming to produce more than 700,000 spring chinook smolt and 2.8 million fall chinook smolt fish within 10 years. Using techniques characteristic of supplementation, the Nez Perce hatchery would outplant sufficient fish into Clearwater tributaries to establish healthy and harvestable salmon runs within twenty years. This proposal, conditioned on an innovative ecosystem monitoring and evaluation program, was subsequently scaled back to about half the proposed size by the Northwest Power Planning Council, after its Independent Science Review Panel suggested it was out of scale with the rest of the Council's program. Early returns of a test of supplementation of Snake River fall chinook showed promise, however.[36]

NMFS concluded that the Nez Perce proposal was not likely to jeopardize the continued existence of listed salmon, even though it determined that "[a]ny further degradation of [the listed species' biological requirements] would have a significant impact" on those species. As it did with the 1995-98 hatchery BiOp, NMFS evaluated the proposal in light of its proposed recovery plan. For most listed salmon, the greatest risk from the Nez Perce program would be the potential co-occurrence of hatchery fish with wild fish in either the Clearwater or Columbia Rivers. The Nez Perce sought to minimize these risks by keeping the number of fish released below the cap called for in NMFS's proposed recovery plan and to limit the amount of genetic introgression into wild populations consistent with the plan. Consequently, NMFS determined that the program would not produce species jeopardy.[37]

NMFS's evaluation of hatchery programs in these two hatchery program BiOps is part of a trend of considering hatchery programs on an ecosystem level. NMFS's use of its proposed recovery plan as a baseline for judging the programs is an example of this trend. Another example is Congress's directive to the Northwest Power Planning Council to review all federally funded hatchery programs in the Columbia Basin and to recommend a coordinated hatchery policy (discussed in chapter 6). The ensuing report called for integrating natural salmon production with hatchery production at the sub-basin level, based on scientific principles.[38]

The 1999 Hatchery BiOp

In 1999, NMFS updated its 1995-98 BiOp on hatchery operations, noting that hatchery fish made up 95 percent of coho, 70-80 percent of spring/summer chinook, 50 percent of fall chinook, and 70 percent of the steelhead in the Columbia Basin. The BiOp considered the effect of hatchery programs that produce unlisted salmon throughout the basin on listed salmon and concluded that most hatchery operations would not jeopardize listed species. With respect to the Nez Perce hatchery, the BiOp assumed that the supplementation program will have a net benefit on fall chinook because adults killed in hatchery operations would be offset by increased natural fall chinook abundance produced by the tribal program. The BiOp admitted that the assumption of net benefit had "not been rigorously tested," however.[39]

The NMFS BiOp did find jeopardy to listed Lower Columbia and Snake River steelhead because release of hatchery steelhead would increase competition with listed steelhead juvenile fish. The biggest potential threat would be due to use of non-endemic stocks which might adversely affect listed salmon through genetic introgression. As a result, the BiOp imposed a number of conditions on hatcheries along the Grande Ronde, Tucannon, Lower Salmon, Salmon Creek, Lower Clackamas, and Snake Rivers.[40]

Harvest BiOps

Overexploitation of the region's salmon encouraged the siting of numerous hatcheries which are now the foundation of both ocean and in-river harvests. Once nearly unregulated, harvesting salmon has evolved into a complex management system for allocating the resource among commercial, recreational, and tribal harvesters. Recent harvests pose considerably less of a threat to salmon survival and recovery than hydropower operations, hatchery practices, and habitat loss because managers have restricted harvests to account for these other sources of mortality. Still, any harvest of listed salmon directly affects the population by reducing the number of spawning adults returning to natal streams.[41]

Although listed salmon are not the object of harvests, they do suffer incidental takes in both ocean and in-river harvests aimed at non-listed salmon. To minimize incidental takes, harvest decisions are subject to a number of management plans derived from a maze of treaty rights obligations, court orders, and administrative actions. Despite this apparently coordinated harvest management, however, salmon numbers continue to decline. With the listings of salmon under the ESA, NMFS became a key decision maker in the area of harvest management because without its approval of harvest decisions through the ESA biological consultation process, individual harvests would be required to obtain an incidental take permit. This is a time-consuming and expensive process that would include preparation of a habitat conservation plan. Thus, the NMFS BiOps on harvest management plans effectively authorize individual takes of listed species.[42]

The 1996 Ocean Harvest BiOp. Harvest management of Pacific salmon has both international and domestic components. Internationally, the Pacific Salmon Treaty and its amendments govern the allocation of salmon between the U.S. and Canada, as discussed in chapter 8. Within the U.S., commercial and recreational harvests off the coasts of California, Oregon, and Washington are governed by the Pacific Fishery Management Council (PFMC) under the terms of the Magnuson-Stevens Fishery Conservation and Management Act. Alaskan harvests are governed by the North Pacific Fishery Management Council (NPFMC) under the same statute. The PFMC and NPFMC prepare fishery management plans subject to approval by the Secretary of Commerce, through NMFS. Because that approval is a federal action subject to ESA consultation, NMFS must consult internally as to whether a plan is likely to jeopardize listed salmon.[43]

In 1996, NMFS issued a BiOp on the PFMC's plan that for the first time considered the plan's consistency with NMFS's proposed recovery plan. Evaluating the plan in terms of its effects on all the listed Snake River species, NMFS determined that PFMC's plan would affect only fall chinook, since ocean harvests take few, if any, sockeye and only a small number of spring/summer chinook. However, a lack of data and uncertainty in estimated mortality from the ocean harvest made it impossible for NMFS to quantify the actual loss of fall chinook. But by modeling harvest rates over a five-year period, NMFS estimated that all harvests combined took 43 percent of listed fall chinook. The PFMC-controlled harvest accounted for 26 percent of that total; Alaskan and Canadian harvests accounted for the remaining 74 percent.[44]

As in the case of the hatchery BiOps, NMFS compared the ocean harvest rate for Snake River fall chinook against its proposed recovery plan. The recovery plan adopted the management strategies of the Pacific Salmon Commission under the Pacific Salmon Treaty, which set rebuilding goals for naturally spawning chinook, as a baseline for determining whether the PFMC plan was likely to jeopardize listed species. But the treaty harvests failed to meet the established rebuilding goals between 1993 and the 1996 BiOp, and the treaty controlled over two-thirds of the ocean harvest. Consequently, NMFS determined that it could no longer rely on the international treaty to protect Snake

River fall chinook and that additional conservation measures were necessary: a 50 percent reduction in harvests in the absence of a new agreement with Canada (achieved in mid-1999), or a 30 percent reduction with an agreement. The ocean BiOp therefore made two significant accomplishments: it required the PFMC to implement NMFS's proposed recovery plan, and it required harvest reductions, although promising smaller reductions upon the successful outcome of U.S.-Canada negotiations.[45]

1998 Steelhead BiOp. Managing in-river harvests also plays a crucial role in determining the fate of listed Columbia Basin salmon. The 1918 Columbia River Compact between Oregon and Washington created an interstate agency which allocates in-river harvests between the two states. Not until the tribes sued the states in the late 1960s did the courts order the states to ensure the tribes received a fair share of the harvests. As explained in chapter 4, that share is half of the harvest. Since the late 1960s, the federal district court in Oregon has resolved disputes between the states and the tribes and also induced the parties to negotiate the Columbia River Comprehensive Fish Management Plan to govern in-river harvests.[46]

A well-publicized dispute erupted in 1998 over tribal commercial harvests of fall chinook. The conflict began when NMFS's regional administrator suggested limiting tribal harvests of listed steelhead from 20 percent to 5-7 percent of the available harvest in response to the fact that the wild Upper Columbia steelhead run had declined to around 900, only about 20 percent of NMFS's goal of 4500. This harvest reduction would have the effect of significantly limiting the tribes' harvest of fall chinook, the tribes' only remaining commercial fishery, because steelhead are caught incidental to the fall chinook harvest. The tribes therefore objected to the restrictions, pointing out that their incidental harvests were small in comparison to mortalities caused by the hydroelectric system. Eventually, NMFS and the tribes reached an agreement that reduced the tribal incidental harvest of steelhead to 15-20 percent, a considerable reduction from the 32 percent figure in the court-approved comprehensive plan. But when NMFS sought approval of the reduction from Judge Malcolm Marsh, the states objected on the grounds that NMFS had failed to subject the agreement to ESA consultation.[47]

This dispute was significant for two reasons. First, it had the potential to put the tribes' treaty rights at odds with the ESA. The states were arguing for ESA procedures, while the tribes contended that the ESA did not apply to the exercise of their treaty rights. Judge Marsh never directly addressed this issue because he decided the case on a second issue: whether the ESA required NMFS to perform a BiOp on the agreement because it produced a significant change to the comprehensive management plan for the Columbia River. NMFS claimed that there was no federal action, since the plan was actually the product of the settlement of a litigation and implemented through court order, and therefore ESA consultation procedures did not apply. However, Judge Marsh focused on the fact that an interagency technical advisory committee, which included federal members, had written an assessment of the agreement. He reasoned that this was sufficient federal involvement to trigger federal consultation requirements under the statute's broad definition of federal "action."[48]

On September 10, 1998, just a week after the court's decision, NMFS issued a BiOp on the effect of the agreement on listed species. The BiOp concluded that the most vulnerable species was the Snake River B-run steelhead, a late migrating species, on which the agreement anticipated a 20 percent incidental tribal harvest. This amount, NMFS determined, would produce species jeopardy. As a result, NMFS imposed a requirement of reducing the incidental harvest to 15 percent or less. In reaching this decision, NMFS conceded that it did not know the degree to which the B-run steelhead numbers had to increase to avoid jeopardy. However, the BiOp noted that survival would be primarily a function of actions other than harvest restrictions on the tribal fishery, observing that the tribal fishery had now been cut back by 38 percent over its ten-year average. NMFS therefore allowed tribal harvests to continue, subject to the 15 percent ceiling, while deferring to the tribes' discretion as to how to achieve the reductions.[49]

The in-river harvest conflict highlighted NMFS's role as both a salmon protector and manager of harvests among competing fishers. The competing concerns of maintaining the tribes' fall chinook harvests, their last commercial fishery (the tribes ended their harvests of summer chinook in 1964 and spring chinook in 1977), while preserving the wild B-run steelhead, threatened to destabilize decision making under the Columbia River harvest management plan. The court's decision essentially made NMFS the key decision maker, although Judge Marsh required the agency to make its decisions through the BiOp process, not through direct negotiations with the tribes. Whether NMFS's restriction of tribal harvests, while simultaneously sanctioning high levels of salmon mortalities inflicted by other sources like the hydroelectric system, fulfills its federal trust obligations to the tribes is unclear. A recent Secretarial Order which requires federal agency actions curbing tribal rights to be the "least restrictive alternative" available, suggests that the 1998 BiOp did not.[50]

Habitat BiOps

Protecting salmon habitat has been a neglected issue of salmon restoration efforts, overshadowed by the perceived need to obtain immediate changes in hydroelectric operations and hatchery practices. Habitat protection cannot promise short-term improvements in run sizes. In fact, it is hardly clear what the loss of a particular spawning and rearing habitat may mean in terms of run size declines. The uncertainties in correlating habitat protection to run sizes have made habitat BiOps an overlooked area of salmon restoration.

Another reason for the relative obscurity of habitat BiOps is that NMFS has taken steps to reduce their prominence. In August 1995, NMFS signed a memorandum of agreement (MOA) with the U.S. Forest Service, the U.S. Fish and Wildlife Service, and the Bureau of Land Management. The agreement established an interagency process to "streamline" project-specific ESA consultations. This MOA was revised by the federal agencies in February 1997, is now employed throughout Idaho, Oregon, and Washington, and may well become national policy. Under the MOA, which represented NMFS's response to congressional concerns that ESA consultation was impeding timber sales, NMFS and the federal agency proposing the action will establish interagency teams. This interagency collaboration will help the agency produce better biological assessments, a precursor document to a BiOp, by attempting to reach consensus on whether there is adequate data on listed species and the effects of the proposed action on listed species.

The upshot is that about 75 percent of consultations under the MOA now culminate in a biological assessment and NMFS concurrence that an action is not likely to cause species jeopardy or affect critical habitat. This determination takes place without a BiOp, which in effect substitutes informal ESA consultation for formal consultation procedures and cuts typical consultation time in half. Unfortunately, it also substitutes off-the-record negotiations for written biological opinions and deprives the public and reviewing courts of a full biological record.[51]

Pacific Rivers Council v. Thomas: BiOps on Existing Federal Land Management Plans. After the listing of Snake River chinook as threatened in April 1992, the ESA required federal land managers like the U.S. Forest Service and the Bureau of Land Management to evaluate whether a host of federal land management activities — principally timber, grazing, and road projects — might affect the listed salmon. Although the land managers agreed to submit ongoing and proposed activities to biological consultation under the ESA, they did not agree to subject previously approved land management plans to consultation. The federal agencies contended that the ESA did not apply to plans approved before the listings because land management plans were not "ongoing" activities subject to ESA consultation but instead were merely "programmatic" documents that did not authorize any specific actions.

Environmental groups, led by the Pacific Rivers Council, sued to challenge the Forest Service's failure to submit the land management plans of the Umatilla and Wallowa-Whitman National Forests in Eastern Oregon and Washington to consultation. The federal district court agreed with the environmentalists that the ESA contained no exemption from consultation for previously approved land management plans. However, although the court enjoined the Forest Service from conducting any new timber sales pending compliance with the ESA, it refused to enjoin ongoing or announced projects.[52]

Both the Forest Service and the environmentalists appealed, and the Ninth Circuit upheld the environmentalists' position in a 1994 decision. The court ruled that land management plans, which it described as "comprehensive management plans governing a multitude of individual projects," had "an ongoing and long-lasting effect even after adoption," and therefore represented ongoing federal actions requiring ESA consultation. The court noted that one of the forest plans under review allocated 60,000 acres of public lands surrounding Snake River chinook spawning grounds by establishing guidelines for logging, grazing, and road-building. The plan also set allowable sale quantities of timber and established schedules for forage, road-building, and other economic activities. Given their importance "in establishing resource and land use policies for the forests," the Ninth Circuit concluded that the ESA required previously approved plans to undergo biological consultation. The court also reversed the district court's ruling that timber sales which had already undergone consultation could continue, ordering the timber harvests enjoined until the forest plans governing the sales had undergone consultation as well. This decision was subsequently applied to enjoin ongoing timber sales in six national forests in Idaho.[53]

These decisions brought ESA consultation to public land management plans throughout the portion of the Columbia Basin still accessible to salmon. Land managers could no longer authorize individual activities consistent with a land management plan without considering the plan's effect on listed salmon and their habitat. This principle of requiring plan consultation is especially important given NMFS's policy of using the consultation process to enforce provisions in pre-existing areawide plans, as evidenced in the hatchery and harvest contexts. The obligation to consider salmon habitat in public land decision making encouraged new approaches to federal land management. For example, the Interior Columbia Basin Ecosystem Management Project, a massive land planning process covering some 75 million acres east of the Cascades, offers the promise of significantly changing the concept of multiple use in public land management, although the project faces an uncertain political future. An agreement between the U.S. Forest Service and the Bureau of Land Management provides interim protection, known as PACFISH, pending approval of the Interior Columbia Basin Project. But PACFISH applies only to federal lands, which NMFS has indicated provides insufficient salmon protection. Moreover, the Columbia River Inter-Tribal Fish Commission maintains that implementation of PACFISH protections fails to protect salmon habitat even where it applies.[54]

Umpqua Timber Sales: Failing To Implement Ecosystem Management. Land management changes induced by aquatic protection concerns will occur only if the aquatic protections are actually enforced. Initial enforcement efforts were hardly encouraging, as reflected in the events leading to a district court decision in a case brought by the Pacific Coast Federation of Fishermen's Associations against NMFS. The case involved the intersection between ESA consultation and another broad ecosystem management program, the Northwest Forest Plan, which was created in response to the listing of the northern spotted owl in 1990 and which includes lands both within and outside the Columbia Basin. The plan not only attempted to preserve owl habitat in old-growth forests but also to establish a system of watershed analysis and riparian reserves aimed at protecting aquatic species. In 1994, a federal district court upheld the Northwest Forest Plan as satisfying the ESA and other statutes, although the court cautioned that the plan's legality rested largely on its successful implementation.[55]

In August 1996, a little over two years after the Northwest Forest Plan's approval, NMFS listed as endangered the Umpqua River cutthroat trout, a salmonid species just outside the Columbia Basin. The listing, which cited habitat degradation from logging as a principal threat to the species' continued existence, prompted NMFS to issue a BiOp on the effect of the Northwest Forest Plan and the activities authorized by it on the listed cutthroat and several other species proposed for listing. The BiOp concluded that meeting the aquatic conservation strategy of the forest plan would avoid jeopardy and satisfy the ESA, but the BiOp did not specifically consider the plummeting populations of cutthroat and the poor habitat conditions in the Umpqua Basin. Moreover, the BiOp did not complete consultation on particular habitat-degrading activities like clearcutting and roadbuilding, although it did establish a matrix and checklist to help a team of biologists determine whether additional BiOps on individual activities would be required to satisfy the ESA. Government biologists had recommended eliminating the clearcuts, but the Forest Service and the Bureau of Land Management did not do so, although they did cancel new road construction. NMFS subsequently approved dozens of timber sales in individual consultations completed in 1997, even though it conducted no systematic analysis of the cumulative effects of continuing to clearcut in already-degraded watersheds.[56]

A coalition of fishing and environmental organizations challenged the NMFS BiOp, and a district court enjoined the sales, while upholding the consultation on the federal land management plans themselves. The decision seemed to indicate that the plan consultation required by the Ninth Circuit in the *Pacific Rivers Council* case would not receive close judicial scrutiny, due to the level of generality employed in land management plans. But courts will not allow specific projects to proceed on the basis of NMFS's assumption that the protections promised in the land management plans will be implemented. Instead, NMFS must demonstrate at the project stage that the proposed actions will actually comply with the aquatic protection strategy contained in the Northwest Forest Plan. If adopted by other courts, this decision may mean that the ESA's biological consultation process could become a vehicle to ensure that the broad promises made in ecosystem management plans are in fact carried out. Moreover, the court quite clearly considered compliance with the Northwest Forest Plan irrelevant to compliance with the ESA: the plan and the statute imposed discrete duties.[57]

If the ESA consultation process is to become a mechanism to achieve ecosystem management promises, the courts will apparently have to continue to oversee NMFS. In December 1998, NMFS employed its new concept of "streamlining" the consultation process to approve nine BLM Umpqua Basin timber sales that had been enjoined earlier by the court, with virtually no changes from the proposals contained in BLM's biological assessments. NMFS concurred in these timber harvests without performing a BiOp, despite admitting that the sale areas were "dominated by conditions rated largely as 'not properly functioning' or 'at risk'," and acknowledging that the environmental baseline "does not currently meet all of the biological requirements for the survival and recovery of the listed species within the action area." Nevertheless, NMFS reasoned that there would be no jeopardy to the species because the sale would involve only "minor short-term adverse effects" like increased sediment loadings, due to mitigation measures such as those contained in the Northwest Forest Plan. NMFS reached this conclusion even though some of the sales were within riparian reserves established by the forest plan and without considering separately the effect of the sales on designated critical habitat.[58]

NMFS's attempt to ratify 23 timber sales in the Umpqua Basin, including the nine mentioned above and three others also involved in the earlier litigation, in four new BiOps issued in late 1998 was also struck down by the federal court. Judge Barbara Rothstein of the Western District of Washington reiterated that the Northwest Forest Plan required timber sales to comply with the plan's aquatic conservation strategy at the individual timber sale level; compliance with the strategy at the watershed level was not enough. Since there was considerable evidence in the record indicating that the proposed sales would produce adverse aquatic effects in terms of increased sediment loadings, altered flows, decreased pool quality, and reduced large woody debris, the court determined that NMFS's BiOps were not consistent with the requirements of the Northwest Forest Plan. Judge Rothstein also ruled that the plan required NMFS to consider the short-term effects of the timber harvests, not merely their effects after ten years. In addition, the court held that NMFS violated the plan's riparian reserve requirements by authorizing timber harvests within reserves without evidence of any aquatic benefit from the harvests. The results of the second Umpqua case seemed to indicate that, despite its reputation as a "preservation at all costs" statute, the ESA — at least as interpreted by NMFS — is less protective of aquatic habitat than the Northwest Forest Plan.[59]*

Inland Land BiOp: Taking Seriously Cumulative Impacts and the Environmental Baseline. Standing in sharp contrast to the Umpqua timber sales is the Inland Land BiOp, where NMFS took a contextual approach in concluding that a proposed withdrawal of Columbia River water would jeopardize listed salmon, due largely to the biologically unsatisfactory nature of the Columbia River's existing environment. NMFS determined

---

  * The effect of Judge Hogan's invalidation of the Oregon coho listing (discussed above in footnote 7*), coupled with NMFS's delisting of Umpqua cutthroat (discussed above in text with note 8), may mean that the contested timber sales can proceed, since there do not seem to be any remaining listed species affected by the sales.

that the proposed diversion, in the context of existing water withdrawals and likely future withdrawals, would make an already inadequate streamflow regime worse.

The Inland Land proposal was to build a pumping facility capable of withdrawing some 300 cubic feet per second from John Day reservoir in the Columbia River, in order to irrigate land near Boardman, Oregon. Because the proposal concerned a project in a navigable waterway, the project needed a permit from the U.S. Army Corps of Engineers, triggering ESA consultation requirements. As a result, the Corps wrote a biological assessment which concluded that the proposal would have no adverse effects on listed salmon. In an illustrative example of the contested nature of current salmon science, NMFS determined that the Corps' assessment was inadequate. The Corps then revised its assessment, again concluding that the proposal would produce no adverse effects because the pumping operation's effect on salmon migration would be "nearly immeasurable." NMFS again emphatically disagreed, concluding in its BiOp that the facility would jeopardize listed salmon.[60]

NMFS's reasoning in the Inland Land BiOp was grounded largely on the biologically unsatisfactory state of Columbia and Snake River flows. The agency concluded that the proposed project — in concert with existing and reasonably foreseeable future withdrawals — would make an already unsatisfactory situation worse. NMFS estimated that some 30 million acre-feet of water is withdrawn for irrigation from Columbia Basin streams each year. That amounts to roughly 40 percent of the average annual natural river flow at McNary Dam in low flow years. NMFS determined that these irrigation withdrawals were "the principal reason" that the flow objectives established in its 1995 BiOp on hydroelectric operations went unmet. In fact, NMFS asserted that "[b]ut for irrigation withdrawals, summer flow objectives [for the Snake River at Lower Granite Dam] would be met every year . . . whereas with withdrawals, summer flow objectives are met less than fifteen percent of the time." The situation was similar on the Lower Columbia, where summer flow objectives would be met 74 percent of the time without irrigation withdrawals, but are met only 26 percent of the time with current withdrawals.[61]

Because NMFS "concluded that flow reductions in the Snake and Columbia Rivers are a cause of decline of listed Snake River salmon," the agency determined that the existing environmental baseline was inadequate to meet the listed species' biological requirements. If it were to allow the proposed withdrawal to proceed, NMFS noted that it might have to allow similar withdrawals in the future. Because many water withdrawals are not subject to NMFS scrutiny under ESA consultation procedures due to a lack of federal agency action, NMFS decided that the Inland Land proposal, in combination with the cumulative impacts produced by existing and likely future withdrawals, would produce species jeopardy. This jeopardy could be avoided, NMFS concluded, only if the project were conditioned upon "no net loss" of streamflows during the spring salmon migration season and several other measures designed to ensure that NMFS's flow objectives would likely be met on a weekly basis. These conditions essentially made the project infeasible from Inland Land's perspective.[62]

The Inland Land BiOp produced allegations from some in Congress that the ESA was unlawfully abrogating state water rights, since Inland Land had a pending water right from the state of Oregon for the pumping facility. NMFS responded that its usual position is to "meet ESA water needs consistent with state law," but that courts have required state water right holders to act consistent with ESA requirements. The cases that have considered the intersection between ESA requirements and state water rights have ruled that 1) the Corps of Engineers could require a federal permit from a Colorado water right holder because of ESA concerns in Nebraska; 2) a California water right holder had to exercise its right in a manner that did not violate ESA requirements; and 3) Texas groundwater pumpers had to observe ESA-imposed restrictions to preserve habitat in an aquifer. NMFS's restrictions on the Oregon water right holder hardly seemed different than these cases. Even so, while blocking the Inland Land withdrawal, NMFS has yet to subject continued water deliveries to irrigators under Bureau of Reclamation contracts to ESA consultation, despite Ninth Circuit rulings that existing water contracts are not immune from regulatory requirements, including ESA requirements.[63]

The contrast between NMFS's position in the 1997 Umpqua timber sale BiOp and its Inland Land BiOp, also written in 1997, is remarkable. In the former, NMFS approved new timber sales in an area that already had biologically unsatisfactory habitat due to past timber practices; in the latter, NMFS refused to allow a water withdrawal that the Corps had concluded would have a "nearly immeasurable" effect on listed salmon because the proposal would exacerbate the biologically unsatisfactory state of river flows. The contradictory results may reflect NMFS's inconsistent implementation of the ESA. Or the difference may be due to the fact that in the Umpqua situation NMFS claimed that the timber sales were consistent with the requirements of the Northwest Forest Plan, an ecosystem management plan promising both sustainable species and timber harvests (a claim that the court did not accept). On the other hand, in the Inland Land BiOp, the only relevant ecosystem plan was NMFS's own BiOp on hydroelectric operations, which called for specific flows for salmon migration, and those requirements had not been met. The fact that the ecosystem plan for the river contained specifics that the forest plan did not may explain why NMFS's decision making on the individual projects was materially different.

Escaping ESA Consultation: FERC-Licensed Dam Operations and Bureau of Reclamation Water Deliveries

Despite the broad scope of activities now subject to ESA consultation, not every federal activity having significant adverse effects on listed salmon has or is undergoing biological consultation. Two glaring exceptions are dam operations licensed by the Federal Energy Regulatory Commission (FERC) and Bureau of Reclamation water management activities.

There is no question that a decision by FERC to relicense a dam is a federal action triggering ESA consultation. Thus far, however, operation of federally licensed dams has managed to escape consultation, largely on the basis of two curious judicial interpretations of the Federal Power Act's provision authorizing judicial review of FERC actions. First, a district court ruled that environmental plaintiffs could not challenge FERC's failure to consult on the ongoing effects of a licensed dam because section 313 of the Federal Power Act reserved exclusive jurisdiction over FERC decisionmaking to the circuit courts of appeal. Second, the Ninth Circuit refused to allow another group of environmentalists to challenge FERC's failure to consult on ongoing license operations because it construed section 313 to require a FERC order to trigger judicial review, and FERC refused to act on the environmentalists' request. The latter result seems inconsistent with a D.C. Circuit decision ruling that FERC could not, consistent with the Federal Power Act, fail to consider protective fish and wildlife conditions in annual operating licenses while a relicensing proceeding was underway. If FERC may exempt itself from ESA procedures by choosing not to act, it will effectively enable federally licensed dams to escape the consultation requirements imposed on federally owned dams.[64]

The Bureau of Reclamation is another agency that has thus far managed to escape ESA consultation on its Columbia Basin operations. The Bureau operates a series of dams in Idaho, Oregon, and Wyoming, collectively storing 6.5 million acre-feet of water. Neither the Bureau's operation of these dams nor its water deliveries to irrigators, some of whom are not authorized to receive such federally stored water, has been subjected to comprehensive analysis in a BiOp. In 1997, NMFS wrote a draft BiOp on the Bureau's Snake River operations, but that analysis considered only efforts to obtain the 427,000 acre-feet of water for fish flows called for in NMFS's existing BiOp; it did not evaluate the effects of Bureau project operations on listed salmon. Moreover, in 1996 the Bureau signed an agreement with Idaho Power Company, the FERC licensee operating the Hells Canyon dams, in which the Bureau agreed to limit flows in a way that ensures that salmon flow targets downstream on the Snake River usually will not be met. Neither that agreement nor its implementation has ever been subject to consultation, and environmentalists are considering an ESA suit.[65]

This evasion of ESA consultation by FERC and the Bureau shows that, while the ESA has subjected most salmon-damaging activities of the federal government to consultation, the statute is not yet truly comprehensive in subjecting federally controlled salmon-damaging activities to biological scrutiny. Since the ESA does not authorize

NMFS to make recalcitrant agencies consult, the burden to ensure compliance is apparently left to non-governmental implementation through the ESA's citizen suit provision.[66]

Incidental Take Permits, Habitat Conservation Plans, and the "No Surprises" Policy

Section 9 of the ESA prohibits "taking" of listing species by anyone. The statute defines a take broadly to include harming or harassing species, and the implementing regulations include habitat modification which adversely affects listed species' essential behaviors, like breeding and nesting. The regulations were upheld by the Supreme Court in 1995, so the taking prohibition now provides significant habitat protection on private lands, since unlike the consultation process, the take prohibition is not limited to federal activities or lands.[67]

The ESA provides two ways to authorize takes of listed species: 1) through the federal consultation process, and 2) through an "incidental take permit." Private activities requiring federal approval subject to ESA consultation may be approved in the consultation process by what is known as an "incidental take statement." An authorized taking cannot jeopardize the species' continued existence, and the federal agency must ensure that adverse effects of the take are minimized. The other way to authorize a nonfederal take of a listed species is through an "incidental take permit" issued by the agency responsible for the species. This permit requires preparation of a habitat conservation plan (HCP), which must minimize adverse effects of the take and demonstrate that it will "not appreciably reduce the likelihood of the survival and recovery of the species in the wild." Typically, HCPs require the permittee to set aside some land or other habitat to protect the species or to refrain from certain activities in exchange for the right to take listed species as incidental effects of their otherwise lawful activities.[68]

One benefit of obtaining an incidental take permit is a federal regulatory policy of promising to impose no new land use restrictions or additional financial compensation for the period of the permit. This assurance of "no surprises" insulates the permittee from new requirements for the life of the permit, even if unforeseen circumstances indicate that more measures are required to save the species. The government may order those additional measures, but it must pay for them. The "no surprises" policy has caused widespread concern that, given the long terms of incidental take permits (fifty years and more) and the numerous uncertainties concerning the full range of threats to species viability, the policy is a recipe for extinctions or unanticipated government spending. As a result, the policy is now under court challenge.[69]

The Proposed Mid-Columbia HCPs

In 1993, operators of public utility district dams on the mainstem Mid-Columbia began negotiations with federal and state fishery agencies, tribes, and environmentalists to produce a conservation plan which would govern salmon restoration from Chief Joseph Dam to the confluence of the Yakima and Columbia Rivers. That plan evolved into separate HCPs for the three dams, Rocky Reach, Rock Island, and Chelan, which have been submitted to NMFS. NMFS is now analyzing the plans and preparing an environmental impact statement on them. A decision on the HCPs is not expected until sometime in 2001.[70]

The proposed HCPs are for fifty years, and their goal is to achieve 100 percent "no net impact" for each salmon species affected by the three dams. That means that each species will complete its life cycle in the same numbers as would exist if the dam did not obstruct its migration. The proposed HCPs seek to accomplish this goal by ensuring 91 percent survival in the area of the project, including 95 percent juvenile salmon survival passing the dams. The nine percent mortality rate is to be compensated by a hatchery program (seven percent) and a tributary improvement program (two percent). How to achieve these species survival goals will be left largely to the discretion of the dam operators and to hatchery and tributary committees who will develop implementation plans. NMFS touted this approach as promoting salmon recovery while allowing permittee flexibility. Former Vice President Al Gore praised the proposed

HCPs as the toughest standards ever to protect Columbia Basin salmon while demonstrating the value of collaboration and flexibility.[71]

Not everyone is as enthusiastic about the proposed HCPs. The Columbia River Inter-Tribal Fish Commission complained that the proposed tributary improvement program did not even require the dam operators to monitor whether the tributary improvement program actually compensates for a two percent mortality rate. Moreover, the HCPs assume that a two percent increase in habitat will correlate to a two percent increase in returning adult salmon, but there is no scientific support for that proposition. It is also questionable whether there is sufficient scientific support for NMFS to make the two statutorily required findings which are prerequisite to issuance of an incidental take permit: 1) that the HCP will "minimize and mitigate the impacts" of the dams; and 2) that the continued operation of the dams "will not appreciably reduce the likelihood of survival and recovery of the listed salmon in the wild." NMFS has, as yet, done no quantitative analysis of biological data on the Mid-Columbia salmon runs, which would seem necessary to make these findings.[72]

Beyond the scientific questions, there is the legal question of whether federally licensed activities under the Federal Power Act qualify for an incidental take permit. Both the ESA and NMFS's HCP handbook appear to limit the activities which may qualify for an incidental take permit to non-federal actions. Incidental takes may be issued to federally licensed activities, like the Mid-Columbia dams, but only through the federal consultation process, to which the "no surprises" policy does not apply. That would mean that non-federal dam operators could not receive assurance that nothing more would be required of them during the term of their HCP.[73]

The length of the proposed HCPs is their most troublesome aspect. Their 50-year length exceeds the projects' existing Federal Power Act licenses by roughly forty-five years. The HCPs stipulate that any party may withdraw from the HCP if the federal licensing agency, the Federal Energy Regulatory Commission, fails to include the entirety of the HCP in its relicense of the dam, or adds terms and conditions "inconsistent" with the HCP. The proposed HCPs also seek to prohibit the parties from invoking or relying on any reopener clauses in the project's license to obtain additional salmon protection. If approved in their proposed form, the HCPs will therefore shield the dam operators from any unforeseen problems with restoring salmon runs affected by their dams. Whether the certainty thus provided to the operators is worth the risks to the species — particularly in view of the fact that a significant portion of the "no net impact" pledge is based on hatchery production — is open to question. In the last ten or fifteen years, hatchery compensation has gone from the preferred method of compensating for the costs of developments that damage salmon habitat to a mitigation measure that is now considered one of the causes of salmon decline. A commitment to hatchery production for another half century as mitigation for dam-related losses seems imprudent.

The 4(d) Salmon Rule: Encouraging State and Local ESA Programs

Activities resulting in takes of listed species may be authorized through the federal consultation process, through incidental take permits, or through 4(d) rules. Section 4(d) of the ESA requires NMFS to adopt rules for the conservation of species listed as "threatened." Before the salmon listings, NMFS and its sister agency, the U.S. Fish and Wildlife Service, generally used 4(d) rules simply to make the same take prohibitions that apply to endangered species also applicable to threatened species. However, influenced by Oregon Governor John Kitzhaber's unsuccessful efforts to avoid salmon listings by developing a state conservation plan (discussed in chapter 14), NMFS promulgated a 4(d) salmon rule in July 2000 which described how state and local governments may gain blanket exemptions from the take prohibition for activities affecting fourteen populations of salmon listed as threatened.[74]

The 4(d) salmon rule could revolutionize federal-state relations concerning ESA implementation because it encourages states and localities to assume a proactive role in protecting listed salmon. NMFS claimed that by encouraging state and local governments to develop approvable programs, salmon will benefit more than they would from a blanket taking prohibition (which would have been previously applied) because of "the program itself and by demonstrating to similarly situated entities that practical and realistic salmonid protection measures exist." One advantage that 4(d) programs may offer in terms of salmon protection is that, unlike federal consultation procedures or habitat conservation plans, the goal of 4(d) conservation is species recovery, not merely avoiding species jeopardy.

Despite its recovery goal, the vagueness of the 4(d) rule will make it difficult for state and local governments to predict whether their programs will satisfy the rule. Although the rule did specifically approve a few conservation programs, such as Washington's forest practices rules and Oregon's road maintenance program, the rule is replete with generalities. For example, concerning local land development ordinances, the rule simply says they must 1) "avoid" development in inappropriate areas like unstable slopes, wetlands, high habitat value areas and stream crossings by roads and utilities; 2) "adequately" avoid stormwater discharges, protect riparian areas, and preserve the hydrologic capacity of streams to pass peak floods; and 3) provide "necessary" enforcement, funding, reporting, implementation mechanisms, and plan evaluations at least once every five years. Moreover, the rule only requires NMFS to take into account such factors — there are twelve in all, including maintaining "properly functioning" ecological conditions — but NMFS need not assure that a program fulfills all twelve conditions. NMFS also promised to "periodically" evaluate approved programs and identify program changes necessary to provide "desired" habitat functions to support population productivity levels needed to conserve listed salmonids. If those changes are not made, "in the shortest time feasible," but no longer than one year, NMFS will revoke program approval, meaning that compliance with the program will no longer insulate developments from the statute's take prohibition.[75]

If the promised revolution in federal-state relations in ESA implementation is to occur, the 4(d) rule must survive litigation. Both environmentalists and developers have filed suit. The environmentalists, along with commercial fishing groups, claimed that approval of the Washington forest practice rules and the local land use program rules will not conserve salmon, as required by section 4(d) of the ESA, but instead will harm salmon by authorizing habitat destruction. They asked a federal district court to require NMFS to prepare an environmental impact statement which would evaluate alternatives to the rule and assess their cumulative effects on salmon habitat. On the other hand, the developers claimed the 4(d) salmon rule was unnecessary and an unconstitutional invasion of state land use authority. The developers asserted that if NMFS had not excluded hatchery fish from the definition of species, had taken effective action against bird and sea lion predators, and had reduced salmon harvests more than it has, the 4(d) rule would have been unnecessary. Neither the environmentalist nor the developer challenge to the rules had been resolved as of this writing.[76]

The ESA and Tribal Salmon Harvests

One troublesome issue of ESA implementation concerns the effect of the statute on tribal salmon harvests protected by the Stevens Treaties. As discussed in chapter 4, the tribes' 50 percent harvest share under the treaties is 50 percent of the salmon available for harvest *after* conservation needs are met. The ESA in effect redefines conservation, so it may be a mistake to depict a conflict between the ESA and tribal harvests. Conservation of the species always takes precedence over harvests, even tribal harvests.[77]

How to allocate harvest cutbacks due to the ESA is hardly clear, however. One might infer from several federal court decisions that the cutbacks would be allocated 50 percent to the tribal fishery and 50 percent to the non-tribal fisheries. But, as discussed in chapter 4, in his 1969 landmark decision in *Sohappy v. Smith*, Judge Belloni stated that restrictions on tribal harvests must be the "least restrictive" consistent with conservation necessity. Moreover, a 1997 secretarial order on the ESA, treaty rights, and federal trust responsibilities, described more fully in chapter 12, requires that any restrictions on treaty rights under the ESA be imposed only after a determination that necessary conservation cannot be achieved by reasonable regulation of non-Indian activities alone. Under this order, all of the additional conservation burden imposed by the ESA could be allocated to non-Indian fishers, which is how NMFS interpreted the order in 2000. The tribes would like to see the order applied not only to non-Indian harvests by fishers, but also to non-Indian harvests by dams — a far greater source of salmon mortality. The states believe the conservation burden should be allocated on a 50/50 percent basis. This issue will almost certainly require resolution by the federal courts.[78]

A related issue that already seems to have been decided by the courts concerns the process for determining the level of harvest necessary to satisfy the ESA. Under the ongoing *United States v. Oregon* case, the court sets an allowable harvest level based on recommendations of an interagency technical advisory committee, whose first goal is to ensure that there is sufficient spawning fish for propagation. In 1998, Judge Marsh ruled that the recommendations of the advisory committee were federal actions subject to ESA consultation. This is an odd ruling, since the recommendations are not actually final decisions but merely advice to the court. And it is hardly clear that a judicial decision is an action subject to federal consultation under the ESA. Yet that is apparently the current state of the law.[79]

The Salmon's ESA Legacy[80]

The advent of the ESA era in salmon restoration has forever changed both the implementation of the statute and land and water use decision making in the Northwest. Whether the new era has actually produced changes that will benefit salmon runs is far less certain.

The salmon's legacies to ESA implementation are numerous. First, in an example of how the law shapes and constrains science, NMFS invented the ESU concept in order to manage the listing process. This concept limits the salmon populations eligible for listing to those considered evolutionarily significant, but the ESU concept emphasizes reproductive isolation at the expense of ecological considerations. Since hatchery fish are not reproductively isolated from wild fish, it is not clear that NMFS has the authority under this policy to list only wild fish under the ESA or to manage only for their restoration. Moreover, the reproductive isolation criterion seems misguided, since the restoration goal is not to produce reproductively isolated salmon stocks but to have healthy, self-sustaining stocks colonize quality habitat. NMFS would be wise to adopt a definition of ESU that is more consistent with the ecosystem preservation purpose of the ESA.

A second change to the implementation of the ESA as a result of the salmon listings was NMFS's adoption of "streamlining" to speed up the process of consultation. The result of "streamlining," which is unlikely to be confined to Northwest salmon, was that about three-quarters of the ESA consultations subject to streamlining culminated not with a NMFS BiOp, but instead with a NMFS summary concurrence approving mitigation measures contained in an action agency's biological assessment. Certainly there is a benefit to expedited procedures, but the net effect of streamlining may be to emphasize NMFS's off-the-record negotiations with action agencies in improving their assessments, instead of its biological expertise as reflected in written BiOps. This reduction in publicly accessible records offers insufficient assurance that biological considerations will predominate in ESA consultation.

A third salmon legacy to ESA implementation concerns the use of multi-year BiOps, first initiated in the context of Columbia Basin hydroelectric operations. The institution of these long-term plans raised the stakes in federal consultations by adding a significant temporal dimension for ongoing activities. The resulting attention devoted to the multi-year BiOp on hydroelectric operations encouraged NMFS to make numerous compromises protecting economic concerns at the expense of salmon. Although these compromises arguably were inconsistent with the intent of the ESA, courts have refused to reverse the compromises that NMFS struck.

A fourth legacy of the salmon listings to ESA implementation involved the use of the consultation process to enforce pre-existing ecosystem management plans like the Northwest Forest Plan. These plans can include multi-year BiOps, as evident in the Inland Land BiOp. Perhaps more significantly, NMFS appears to have employed consultation to implement measures contained in its proposed (but not yet completed) Columbia Basin salmon recovery plan. If implementing ecosystem plans through federal consultation becomes commonplace, it is important that the plans themselves be subject to consultation, as required by the Ninth Circuit in the *Pacific Rivers Council* decision. It is even more important that they be specific enough to serve as a guide for subsequent actions.

A fifth contribution to ESA implementation from salmon restoration concerns the definition of "best available" science. Judge Marsh refused to accept NMFS's interpretation of that statutory mandate where the agency had ignored the views of state and tribal biologists. This refusal indicated that the ESA demands a pluralistic process of intergovernmental consultation in arriving at best available science, a tacit recognition of the contested nature of current salmon science. NMFS appeared to agree, establishing a process for independent scientific review of its actions. Although NMFS was unwilling to accept the recommendations of independent scientists on whether to breach the Lower Snake River dams (see chapter 13), the process of obtaining independent scientific review now seems well established.

A sixth contribution of the salmon to the ESA is an innovative use of section 4(d) of the statute. NMFS's 4(d) rules for salmon do not simply make the Act's taking prohibition applicable to "threatened" species (as had been the case before the salmon listings), they instead encourage states and localities to develop conservation programs. If approved by NMFS, these programs will authorize "takes" of salmon while, according to NMFS, contributing to the survival of the species. Whether the 4(d) rules will actually contribute to the salmon's survival is unknown but, if emulated for other species, the rules could produce significant defederalization in ESA implementation.

The ESA's Salmon Legacy

If the salmon's effects on the ESA have been many and varied, the ESA's contribution to salmon restoration is far less certain. There is no question that the ESA listings have produced a massive amount of process, albeit some of it now "streamlined." Even more process may be on the way, with suggestions that NMFS may undertake a "mega-BiOp" in which Columbia Basin hydroelectric operations, hatchery operations, harvest, and habitat management all would be considered in the same document. However, all this process has yet to produce significant improvements in Columbia Basin salmon runs. Although there are some indications that the juvenile salmon survival rate is increasing, there is as yet no increase in adult spawners, the key to salmon recovery.

Part of the problem with the lack of substantive results is that despite all the process, some damaging activities have escaped biological review. For example, hydroelectric operations under existing FERC licenses would seem to be an ongoing federal action requiring ESA consultation, as would Bureau of Reclamation water deliveries under existing contracts. Yet neither type of activity has been subjected to consultation, and it may be necessary once again that citizens ask courts to order the agencies to fulfill their ESA duties.

The most significant ESA decision was NMFS's 2000 decision to continue artificially transporting juvenile salmon by truck and barge instead of recommending breaching the four Lower Snake River dams to let the fish migrate in the river. This determination was perhaps the best indication that what the ESA mostly offers listed salmon is elaborate process and economically sensitive decisionmaking. Despite strong evidence that dam breaching is both the best means to recover listed Columbia Basin salmon and economically affordable, NMFS sought to avoid the political controversy that would surround dam breaching by supporting continued barging and trucking. Equipped with judicial approval of its previous BiOp on hydroelectric operations — a plan that promised just a fifty percent chance of recovering listed salmon — and with a potential "mega BiOp" in the wings that could shift some of the focus away from hydropower to other sources of salmon mortality, NMFS may have sufficient discretion to continue artificially transporting salmon downstream indefinitely. If so, NMFS is unlikely to materially change the way the Columbia and Snake Rivers flow, despite the failure of the trucking and barging program to produce discernible improvements in salmon returns over more than two decades.

Perhaps the chief lesson is that the ESA affords NMFS sufficient authority to resolve scientific uncertainties in a way that allows the pursuit of the politically palatable, instead of the biologically necessary. This state of affairs is hardly breaking news, as historians have shown that science has been frequently employed, interpreted, or ignored by policymakers depending on what best served their immediate purposes. But the ESA/salmon saga does give lie to the widespread notion that the ESA is a draconian, economically insensitive statute whose implementation focuses on species preservation to the exclusion of all competing social values.[81]

10 — SIXTH PROMISE: THE CLEAN WATER ACT

The Clean Water Act substantially assumed its current form in 1972, when Congress amended what was then called the Federal Water Pollution Control Act. The 1972 amendments made it national policy to "restore and maintain the chemical, physical, and biological integrity of the Nation's waters." They emphasized control of point source discharges; that is, activities employing pipes, ditches, or other "discernible, defined, and discrete conveyance[s]" to discharge pollutants into the waters of the United States, defined to include both navigable and nonnavigable waters. Under the amendments, all such dischargers require federal or state-issued permits, which must incorporate national discharge standards and water quality-based controls. Violators are subject to civil and criminal penalties, which may be sought by federal or state agencies or members of the public in citizen suits.[1]

The Clean Water Act is not limited to control of point sources, however. It also attempts to regulate polluted runoff; that is, everything that is not point source discharges, generally referred to as nonpoint source pollution. Typical nonpoint sources include agricultural, timber, grazing, mining, and land development activities such as roads, parking lots, and lawns, where the runoff is not channelized. But the Act does not demand that nonpoint sources obtain a permit, and it leaves their regulation almost entirely to the states. As a result, the nonpoint share of water pollution has grown over the last quarter century and now amounts to more than half of the nation's pollutant loadings.[2]

The Clean Water Act also requires states or the Environmental Protection Agency (EPA) to set ambient standards for waterways called water quality standards. Actually, the water quality standards requirement antedated the Act's 1972 amendments, originating in the 1965 Water Quality Act. Congress left the water quality standards provision intact when it overhauled the law in 1972, when it added the requirement of obtaining point source permits and directed those sources to meet water quality standards. The statute provided no ready mechanism to ensure that most nonpoint sources satisfied water quality standards, however.[3]

Until recently, achieving water quality standards took a back seat to the technology-based controls imposed on point sources, but that is changing. A deluge of citizen suits has prompted EPA to get much more serious about making states set what are called "total maximum daily loads" (TMDLs) for stream segments that fail to meet water quality standards. Setting and enforcing TMDLs promises to shift the focus of the Clean Water Act from just technology-based point source controls to water quality-based controls on all sources of water pollution. And since nonpoint sources are in theory subject to TMDL limits, many nonpoint sources may be subjected to serious scrutiny in terms of their water quality effects for the first time. This new era may have significant effects on Columbia Basin salmon.[4]

Exempting Dams From Permit Requirements

Large hydroelectric dams, such as those in the Columbia Basin, produce significant adverse water quality effects. They release water low in dissolved oxygen and high in dissolved metals, temperature, and supersaturated gases (creating gas bubble disease in fish). They also trap sediments and alter fundamental biological processes downriver in the Columbia River estuary. One way to ameliorate these effects would be to require Clean Water Act point source permits for dam operation. The permits could specify operating practices aimed at achieving applicable dissolved oxygen, nitrogen supersaturation, and temperature water quality standards. Violating permit terms would subject dam operators to Clean Water Act sanctions, which no doubt would prompt remedial action.

More than twenty years ago, the National Wildlife Federation petitioned EPA to subject dams to the Act's permit program, but EPA declined, mostly on grounds of administrative convenience. EPA decided it did not want to assume the chore of regulating dam operators, including other federal agencies like the Corps of Engineers or the Bureau of Reclamation, let alone oversee the regulation of those operators by states with approved permit programs.[5]

As a result, EPA denied the environmentalists' petition, and the issue went to court. EPA's position was that dams did not "discharge" pollutants into waters because they added nothing to the waters, merely providing a medium through which water passes. Without a discharge, there is no requirement to obtain a permit. In 1982, the District Court for the District of Columbia disagreed with EPA, relying partly on the ambitious purpose of the statute (to restore and maintain the integrity of the nation's waters), partly on the fact that the permit program was Congress's preferred method for achieving that goal, and partly on the court's determination that the goal could not be attained without regulating dam-caused pollutants. But on appeal the D.C. Circuit reversed the lower court and upheld EPA's interpretation of the statute because it was not unreasonable. The appeals court did not emphasize the goals of the Clean Water Act, nor how to achieve them without regulating dams. The upshot was that the water quality problems caused by dams were left largely to ineffectual state nonpoint source programs and to uncertain water quality-based regulation, which would not materialize for nearly two decades.[6]

A second court challenge concerned the alleged discharge of dead fish from a hydroelectric dam into Lake Michigan, an arguable pollutant under the Clean Water Act. The National Wildlife Federation argued that this situation was different from EPA's generic failure to demand permits of all dams because dead fish fell within the statute's definition of pollutants, which includes biological materials. Therefore environmentalists contended that the dam was in fact discharging pollutants, triggering the permit requirement. In 1987, a district court agreed with the environmentalists, holding that dead fish amounted to an addition of a pollutant for which the Clean Water Act required a permit. The Sixth Circuit reversed the lower court the next year, however, agreeing with EPA that the dam merely changed the form of the fish (from live fish to dead fish), adding nothing to the water that had not been there before. Therefore, the critical trigger of adding a pollutant was absent, so no permit was required.[7]

Thus, through EPA's opposition and judicial acquiescence to that opposition, dams were effectively removed from Clean Water Act permit requirements. That certainly did not mean that the water quality problems that dams cause went away. It simply meant that EPA successfully relieved itself of the administrative chore of requiring permits for all dams causing water quality problems by adopting a rather technical interpretation of the Clean Water Act, one that the courts could not say was unreasonable, despite the statute's express goal of maintaining and restoring the chemical, physical, and biological integrity of the nation's waters. The issue thus shifted to water quality standards, the statute's means of ensuring that both point and nonpoint sources of pollution protect water quality.[8]

Water Quality Standards

The Clean Water Act requires states to set water quality standards "to protect the public health and welfare, enhance the quality of water, and serve the purposes" of the Clean Water Act. These standards must be approved or disapproved by EPA, which must promulgate federal water quality standards if it determines that the state standards are not sufficient to protect existing uses or meet other requirements of the Act. States must review and hold hearings on water quality standards every three years. Permits for point source discharges must achieve water quality standards, as must federal activities if they result in either the discharge or runoff of pollutants. Activities requiring federal licenses or permits must obtain certification from the state that they will comply with water quality standards.[9]

Water quality standards consist of 1) designated uses for which the water body must be protected, 2) water quality criteria to protect those uses, and 3) antidegradation provisions designed to prevent significant deterioration of water quality. They also prohibit eliminating uses that existed in 1975, whether designated or not. Water quality criteria may be expressed in narrative form — such as no unreasonable effects on designated uses — or in numeric form — such as specified concentrations of pollutants. Numeric criteria are more readily enforceable, but the Supreme Court has made clear that states have broad authority to take action to protect designated uses, enforce narrative criteria, and implement their antidegradation policies. In 1994, in *PUD No. 1 of Jefferson County v. Washington Dept. of Ecology,* the Court ruled that a state could, as part of its water quality certification, require a federally licensed hydropower project to meet minimum flow conditions in order to protect a stream's designated uses or to satisfy either narrative criteria or the antidegradation policy.[10]

Where waterbodies do not meet state water quality standards, the Clean Water Act requires EPA or the states to identify the noncomplying streams (called water quality-limited segments), rank them in order of priority, and set TMDLs to bring the waterbody into compliance with water quality standards. After the states ignored their TMDL obligations for the better part of two decades, EPA is now under numerous court orders to develop them. This TMDL litigation offers the prospect of finally making nonpoint sources subject to state water quality standards. Setting TMDLs may become an important part of salmon restoration efforts, as the vast majority of Columbia Basin streams have temperatures too high for successful salmon spawning, rearing, and migration. But setting a TMDL will not necessarily require any point or nonpoint source to do anything; that requires allocating pollution rights consistent with the TMDL, and the statute is extremely vague as to how that task is to be accomplished. However, the Act requires federal activities, including nonpoint sources like dams, to comply with state water quality standards independent of the setting of TMDLs. This obligation is at the center of the suit involving the Lower Snake Dams, discussed in a succeeding section.[11]

Water Quality-Limited Streams in the Columbia Basin

Throughout the Columbia Basin, water quality remains in poor condition, largely due to ineffective regulation of nonpoint sources. In Washington, for example, some 636 stream segments failed to meet water quality standards in 1998. This represents more than half of the stream segments tested for water quality, and it no doubt understates the severity of the problem because of the state's restrictive listing criteria. More than one-half of the noncomplying segments failed due to high temperatures. The main causes of high temperatures are nonpoint sources, such as timber harvesting, overgrazing, irrigation and other water diversions, and land developments that involve shade removal and produce excessive sedimentation. The second largest reason for water quality standards violations was fecal coliform bacteria: 289 segments failed to meet the standard in 1998, mostly due to sewage disposal, animal wastes, and failing septic systems. Other sources of water quality standards violations included reduced dissolved oxygen levels from road building, construction, and agriculture, all producing high levels of sediment. In Puget Sound, federal studies have shown that even short, three-week stays in urban estuaries have significant sublethal effects on salmon, including causing immune deficiency disorders and failure to migrate normally.[12]

In Oregon, there were 1,067 stream segments failing to meet water quality standards in 1998, involving 13,687 stream miles. Most of these segments failed to meet temperature standards: 862 streams, involving 12,146 miles. The second most violated standard in terms of stream miles was dissolved oxygen, with 1,130 miles in violation, involving 61 noncomplying streams and four lakes. Third was the hydrogen ion concentration (pH) standard (measuring acidity), with 1,117 stream miles in violation, although involving many more streams than the dissolved oxygen standard.[13]

The situation is actually much bleaker than depicted above, since water quality data is available for fewer than half of Oregon streams. Worse, as discussed below, NMFS has recently called into question the capability of current standards to meet the biological requirements for survival and recovery of listed salmon species, even in streams where the standards are being met.[14]

In Idaho, the situation is not materially better. The water quality standard most often violated is the state's sediment standard. A total of 573 stream segments, totaling 6,483 miles, were in violation in late 1999. The second biggest problem was temperature, with 145 streams and 1,769 miles in violation. High temperatures decrease dissolved oxygen levels and are often an indication of excessive sediments, poor width/depth ratio, and loss of instream flows and riparian vegetation.[15]

High temperatures produce numerous adverse physiological and behavioral effects on salmon, both from persistent and intermittent exposures, although cumulative exposures may be a key element. Adverse effects due to high temperatures include increased spawning mortalities, reduced juvenile growth, diminished ability to compete for food and habitat with non-salmonids, decreased resistance to and increased virulence of disease, and delay or prevention of smoltification. Low levels of dissolved oxygen can increase the time necessary to hatch and decrease growth and survival rates. Low oxygen levels also inhibit the ability to migrate, forage, and avoid predators. They also increase the toxicity of metals and ammonia, a particular problem for eggs in redds (nests).[16]

The pH standard reflects the acid-based equilibrium achieved by various dissolved solids and gases: low levels are acidic; high levels alkaline. Low pH levels are toxic to fish, due to dissolved metals in the water column and sediments, especially aluminum. At higher pH levels, ammonia is a problem. Lower pH levels occur mostly west of the Cascades; pH levels rise in the eastern Columbia Basin, mostly due to geology and climate, but also due to acid drainage from mines, releases of water stored in reservoirs, agricultural runoff, and nutrients from fertilizers and animal wastes.

Not many states have sediment standards, as Idaho does. Sediment can inundate gravel spawning grounds. In streams with elevated sediment levels, salmon suffer from reduced survival and size when they emerge from the gravel, particularly in streams with low dissolved oxygen levels.[17]

TMDL Litigation in the Pacific Northwest

Where waterbodies fail to meet applicable water quality standards, the Clean Water Act requires states to identify infractions, establish a priority ranking, and set a "total maximum daily load" (TMDL) for each pollutant that violates the standards. Although the TMDL requirement has existed for nearly thirty years, for most of its life EPA and the states ignored the requirement. It took citizen suits, beginning in the 1980s, to require EPA and the states to begin to set TMDLs. In the Columbia Basin, the TMDL effort began in Oregon in 1986, when EPA agreed to a settlement of a suit brought by the

Northwest Environmental Defense Center, which charged that although the state had identified noncomplying waterbodies, it had failed to set TMDLs. The settlement called for Oregon to establish TMDLs for the identified waters within five years. Two more lawsuits ensued, alleging that EPA had failed to ensure that the state identified all of the noncomplying waters for which TMDLs must be developed. Another settlement produced a memorandum of agreement between EPA and the state which promised that the state would develop a complete list of TMDLs, along with implementation plans, within ten years.[18]

In Washington, litigation was also necessary to make the state implement its TMDL duty. Environmental groups led by Northwest Environmental Advocates filed suit in 1991, leading to a settlement under which the state promised to develop TMDLs. When the state failed to meet the terms of that settlement, a new settlement was reached in 1998 under which the state agreed to not only develop TMDLs on a fifteen-year schedule, but also to accompany them with implementation plans. Unfortunately, the Washington legislature did not fund implementation of the settlement until 1999. In addition, EPA reached an agreement with the timber industry that will postpone development of TMDLs associated with logging for ten years. That settlement is now under court challenge. This federal and state recalcitrance will discourage future TMDL settlements and encourage environmentalists to seek court-ordered implementation schedules.[19]

In Idaho, environmentalists brought two suits that effectively activated TMDLs in that state. In the first, the court ordered EPA to develop a schedule for identifying water quality-impaired waters and to cooperate with the state in establishing a schedule for developing TMDLs. In the second, the court upheld an EPA decision that the state's existing water quality standards were deficient and ordered EPA to promulgate new ones. The upshot of the litigation and an ensuing settlement agreement is that some 962 stream segments in Idaho will have new water quality standards and TMDLs over an eight-year period. The prospect of attaining fishable waters in Idaho finally may be on the horizon.[20]

The Lower Snake Dams Suit

The movement to enforce water quality standards in the Columbia Basin is not limited to attempting to require the states to set and implement TMDLs. It also concerns making federal activities, like dam operators, comply with water quality standards. The paradigmatic example is the suit over the Lower Snake River dams.

In 1999, a coalition of environmental organizations led by the National Wildlife Federation filed suit against the Corps of Engineers, operator of the four federal dams on the Snake River below the Hells Canyon Complex. The environmentalists charged that these dams operate in violation of the state of Washington's numerical water quality standards for temperature and dissolved gas. They also claimed that the operations violated the state's narrative criteria concerning the impairment of reproduction of salmon, an existing use of the Snake River, a violation of the state's antidegradation policy. Unlike most nonpoint sources, the Clean Water Act expressly requires federal nonpoint sources, such as federal dams, to comply with state water quality standards. In fact, the Forest Service has had several timber sales enjoined for failing to demonstrate compliance with those state standards. The Corps of Engineers would seem to be no in different a position than the Forest Service.[21]

Washington's water quality standards for the Snake River require that the temperature must not exceed 20 degrees Celsius due to human activities. The standards also stipulate that dissolved gas cannot exceed 110% of saturation. Since Washington designated the Snake River as a "class A" river, it must also meet or exceed the needs of salmon migration, spawning, and rearing. And the state's antidegradation policy requires that "existing beneficial uses shall be maintained and protected and no further degradation which would interfere with beneficial uses shall be allowed."[22]

The state has listed the Snake River as failing to meet its water quality standards since 1994, identifying the likely cause for failure to meet the temperature standard as "stratification behind impoundments." In 1998, the result was more than 80 days of temperature violations. In its BiOp on hydroelectric operations, NMFS determined that both high temperatures and dissolved gas supersaturation posed serious problems for listed Snake River salmon. Although the state has waived the dissolved gas standard to facilitate salmon passage at the dams, dissolved gas standards regularly exceed the amounts specified in the state's waiver.

In December 1999, the Corps of Engineers released a draft environmental impact statement (EIS) on breaching the Lower Snake Dams. The draft EIS considered alternatives to breaching, none of which would cure the existing water quality standards, and failed to recommend a preferred course of action. This drew sharp criticism from the EPA, which claimed that the EIS failed to adequately address water quality issues and lacked a plan for meeting applicable water quality standards. The Corps responded that water quality standards "were not within the scope of the EIS," a claim that seems in error given EIS regulations requiring action agencies to consider the relationship between their proposals and applicable legal standards. EPA responded by stating that the operation of the Corps' Snake River dams violates the Clean Water Act. The Corps denied it was in violation of the statute, pointing to upriver water management practices and runoff patterns. The Corps suggested that if the two agencies could not resolve their disagreements over the applicability of water quality stands, the matter could be resolved by the Council on Environmental Quality. Alternatively, the Lower Snake Dams suit could resolve the issue.[23]

Unlike the ESA, the Clean Water Act contains no consultation procedure by which EPA may sanction on-going activities or operations. So the court could order the Corps to develop a plan for achieving compliance with the water quality standards. In March 2000, the federal district of Oregon agreed with environmentalists that the Corps was not exempt from complying with water quality standards in operating its dams, and that the dams were a substantial cause of water quality standards violations. The court has yet to order the Corps to take action to comply with standards, however. One option for improving water quality in the Lower Snake would be to breach the four Lower Snake Dams, as discussed in chapter 13.[24]

Water Quality Standards and ESA Consultation

The Lower Snake Dams case is premised on enforcing existing state water quality standards. But many state standards do not provide sufficient protection for salmon listed under the ESA. A potentially significant event for salmon restoration was the 1999 BiOp on EPA's approval of the state of Oregon's water quality standards. EPA's approval of state standards is clearly a federal action subject to ESA consultation, but this was the first time in the region that NMFS subjected federal approval of a state's water quality standards to scrutiny under ESA procedures. Although the results produced only one rejection of a state standard — Oregon's 68 degree Fahrenheit temperature standard for the Willamette River — the long-term consequences could be quite significant.

The BiOp began by discussing the current state of Oregon water quality in terms of its fitness to meet the needs of listed salmonids. It determined that because "not all of the biological requirements of the listed and proposed species for freshwater habitat in general, and for water quality in particular, are being met under the environmental baseline in many streams and watersheds," there had to be "significant improvement . . . to meet the biological requirements for survival and recovery of these species." The BiOp reached the unsettling conclusion that "[a]ny further degradation in these conditions would significantly reduce the likelihood of survival and recovery of these species due to the amount of risk that salmon face under the current environmental baseline."[25]

NMFS scrutinized EPA's proposed approval of standards for dissolved oxygen, temperature, and hydrogen ion concentration (pH), as part of EPA's triennial review of the state's water quality. However, due to several problems, such as the fact that the temperature standards were not being enforced by the state, and the fact that many of the standards themselves were not protective of listed species, EPA attached several conditions to its approval. Among these conditions was a "regional temperature criteria project," which is to develop and recommend over a two-year period "more ecologically relevant temperature criteria protective of all salmonid life history stages." In the ensuing BiOp, NMFS determined that there were problems not only with the state's temperature standards, but also with its dissolved oxygen standards.[26]

One problem is that Oregon's water quality standards vary temporally and spatially, depending on the state's estimate of when and where salmon spawn, emerge from gravel, and migrate. For example, in eight of nine river basins considered, NMFS concluded that the state's estimated period of salmon spawning to emergence of fry from gravel was too short, providing inadequate protection for early and late spawners. As a result, Oregon has inadequate dissolved oxygen standards, allowing poor water quality that has adversely affected numerous salmonid runs, including Snake River chinook and steelhead, Southern Oregon coastal chinook, Upper Willamette River chinook and steelhead, Middle and Lower Columbia River steelhead, Columbia River cutthroat, and Umpqua cutthroat. Moreover, NMFS also concluded that the state must undertake more stringent monitoring of intergravel dissolved oxygen levels in order to protect salmonid eggs after spawning. Among the conservation measures the state accepted was a federal-state study to identify the geographic areas and time periods in which salmon spawning actually occurs in three pilot river basins to be selected by NMFS.[27]

NMFS also concluded that both the state's cold and cool water dissolved oxygen standards were inadequate to protect a host of salmon species, including Lower Columbia chinook, coho, steelhead, and cutthroat; Oregon Coast chinook and steelhead; Upper Willamette chinook and steelhead; Middle Columbia steelhead; and Lower Snake chinook and steelhead. Part of the problem is that many state standards are expressed in terms of daily or weekly averages, while NMFS concluded that a daily minimum of dissolved oxygen was the key criterion in terms of fish health.[28]

The BiOp also scrutinized the state's temperature standards. Oregon's temperature standard for streams where salmon rearing is a designated use is 64 degrees, except in the Lower Columbia and Willamette Rivers, where it is 68 degrees. A 1995 study by a state technical advisory committee concluded that temperatures above 60 degrees posed a risk to young salmon. Where native salmon spawn, the standard during the period from spawning to emergence is 55 degrees. For native bull trout streams, the standard is 50 degrees. All standards are expressed as a seven-day moving average of daily maximum temperatures, which means that higher temperatures on some days can be offset by lower temperatures on others and still satisfy the standard. During the summer the highest daily temperature is usually 1 to 3.5 degrees higher than the seven-day average.[29]

EPA proposed conditional approval of most of the state's standards, although it deferred a decision on the Lower Willamette standard. The agency decided to issue a conditional approval despite finding that a wide variety of salmon runs were "likely to be adversely affect[ed]" by the standards, "pos[ing] a risk to their viability." NMFS in turn determined that a 64 degree rearing standard was "likely to cause lethal and sublethal adverse effects" on adult salmon, salmon eggs, and young salmon in the Snake, Upper Willamette, Lower and Middle Columbia, and Umpqua basins, and along the Oregon Coast. But NMFS also observed that attainment of the standard would produce a "substantial improvement over the current environmental baseline in many watersheds." Even so, according to the agency, meeting the standard "likely will not meet the biological requirements" of listed salmon species. This seems to be the equivalent of claiming that the new standard is an improvement because the fish will die more slowly.[30]

The spawning temperature standard of 55 degrees was problematic as well, since NMFS disagreed with most of the state's spawning dates. As a result, NMFS concluded that the standard would likely have adverse effects on early spawning spring/summer chinook in the Snake, Upper Willamette, Lower Columbia, and Oregon Coast. Similarly, late spawning Snake River fall chinook would be adversely affected by the state's designated spawning dates.[31]

NMFS did not find that any of the standards would jeopardize the continued existence any listed salmon species, but it did suggest that EPA cooperate with it on studies concerning 1) historic water temperatures in representative ecoregions of the state; 2) models of stream temperatures that could be attained based on changes to vegetation, flows, and restoration of hydrologic connections to groundwater and flood plains in representative ecoregions; and 3) fish studies of how temperatures at sublethal levels affect salmon distribution and reproduction. NMFS also recommended that EPA cooperate with the state on any fish kill investigation in waters meeting the states' standards and to ensure that NMFS obtained the results. In addition, NMFS promised to evaluate every six months the implementation of conservation measures that EPA and the state agreed to undertake, including EPA's temperature criteria development project and a variety of state measures including 1) identifying geographic areas and time periods for salmon spawning and proposing revised standards in light of this information in three pilot basins; 2) developing a plan for implementing the state's anti-degradation policy; and 3) expanding water temperature monitoring into the spring and fall.

The upshot of the ESA consultation on Oregon's water quality is that NMFS signaled it will no longer rubber-stamp EPA's approval of state water quality standards. Instead, NMFS has essentially issued a gentle prod to EPA and the state that more will be expected in the future. This is certainly a welcome development in terms of salmon restoration efforts, but it does not assure that more protective standards will be required in the future and, in any case, is a tacit admission that today's standards are insufficient to meet the biological requirements of salmon, let alone improve their condition to where they might be no longer listed under the ESA. Thus, NMFS's endorsement of EPA's approval of the Oregon standards seems to be a violation of the ESA, as claimed in a notice of intent to sue by environmentalists.[32]

The results of NMFS's consultation on Oregon water quality standards are unlikely to be confined to Oregon. If similar results occur in the other Columbia Basin states, it may be that the ESA will become the engine to revitalize water quality standards and propel the Clean Water Act into the forefront of ESA restoration efforts. It would seem only logical that the statute should assume this position, since one of its goals is the attainment and preservation of fishable levels of water quality. Ironically, if the ESA's application to water quality standards produces standards which are aimed at facilitating salmon spawning, there may be less administrative discretion in approving activities which threaten water quality standards, since there is no procedure in the Clean Water Act similar to the ESA's biological opinions which can sanction damaging activities.[33]

11 — RELICENSING NONFEDERAL DAMS: A HIDDEN PROMISE

Dams not authorized by Congress are subject to the licensing requirements of the Federal Power Act (FPA). The FPA requires licenses of all large nonfederal dams producing hydroelectric power. The statute is legally complex, vesting the Federal Energy Regulatory Commission (FERC) with licensing authority but also including important roles for state water quality agencies, federal land managers, and federal fishery agencies. Unlike federal dams, whose authorizations have no fixed lifespans, dams subject to the FPA are periodically subject to relicensing requirements. Relicensing allows for review of the project and its environmental effects and may produce substantial changes to project operations. In a few cases, it has even led to dam removal. Since there are many FERC-licensed dams throughout the Pacific Northwest, and since those dams are often the key determinant of flows and access to habitat throughout an entire watershed, FPA licensing is frequently a critical variable in salmon restoration. In fact, a good case can be made that an FPA settlement agreement controlling streamflows on the Mid-Columbia is chiefly responsible for the health of the Hanford Reach fall chinook, the last viable spawning population of salmon above Bonneville Dam.[1]

Among the watersheds significantly affected by the operation of FERC-licensed dams in the Columbia Basin are the Lower Snake, affected by Idaho Power Company's Hells Canyon Complex; the Mid-Columbia, affected by five dams licensed to public utility districts; the Deschutes, affected by Portland General Electric's Pelton Dam Complex; the MacKenzie, affected by several dams licensed to Eugene Water and Electric Board; the Lewis and Cowlitz, affected by the city of Tacoma's Mossyrock and Mayfield projects; and the White Salmon, affected by PacifiCorp's Condit Dam. While Columbia Basin-wide salmon restoration cannot be accomplished by FERC licensing alone, neither can it effectively proceed by ignoring the opportunities the relicensing process presents. In many sub-basins, effective FERC relicensing will be indispensable to restoration efforts. But because of the complexity of the FPA, and because FERC has a long history of shortchanging fish and wildlife concerns in the licensing process, it is quite important for the public and other federal and state agencies to have a clear understanding of the critical roles they can play in the dam relicensing process.

Licensing Authority

Section 4(e) of the FPA authorizes FERC to issue licenses for power purposes, requiring the agency to give "equal consideration" to energy conservation, "the protection, mitigation of damages to, and enhancement of fish and wildlife (including related spawning grounds and habitat)," recreation, and environmental quality. Under section 10(a) of the statute, FERC must determine that its license decisions are "best adapted" to a comprehensive waterway plan accounting for a variety of uses, including water power, fish and wildlife, irrigation, flood control, water supply, and recreation. FERC prepares no such plans, however, since it interprets section 10(a) merely to require a fully developed administrative record showing its licensing decisions are in the public interest. In so doing, FERC must consider plans governing waterway uses which are prepared by others, such as the Northwest Power Planning Council's Columbia Basin Fish and Wildlife Program, although FERC is not bound by such plans.[2]

According to the Supreme Court, FERC may issue licenses that are inconsistent with state laws, but states may effectively veto FERC licenses through the Clean Water Act's water quality certification process. Licenses on federal land reservations must satisfy conditions prescribed by federal land management agencies. Similarly, FERC licensees must meet "fishway" conditions promulgated by the federal fishery agencies. All FERC license decisions must "adequately and equitably protect, mitigate damages to, and enhance" fish and wildlife and their habitat. FERC's fish and wildlife conditions must be based on recommendations of fish and wildlife agencies, although FERC may reject such recommendations by making certain findings.[3]

The FPA authorizes FERC to issue licenses for up to fifty years, but FERC generally issues relicenses for thirty or forty years. There is no entitlement to a relicense. In fact, relicensing is based on a new look at the project, its effect on the environment, and a contemporary vision of the public interest. However, as discussed below, the appropriate environmental "baseline" by which to judge a dam's effects at relicensing, is apparently the river with the dam in place. The federal government has the authority to take over licensed projects at the end of their terms by paying the licensee's "net investment value" in the project, plus severance damages. FERC may also decide to issue a non-power license.[4]

Fish and Wildlife Conditions and Recommendations

Section 10(j) of the FPA, added by amendments in 1986, requires FERC to include in licenses conditions that will "adequately and equitably protect, mitigate damages to, and enhance" fish and wildlife and their habitat affected by licensed projects. Section 10(j) conditions must be based on recommendations of federal and state fish and wildlife agencies, but those recommendations cannot veto a project. Moreover, if FERC believes that section 10(j) recommendations are inconsistent with the "purposes and requirements" of the FPA or other statutes, FERC must attempt to resolve the inconsistency, giving "due weight" to the recommendations, expertise, and statutory responsibilities of the fishery agency. If FERC decides not to adopt the recommendations, it must publish findings explaining 1) why the recommendations are inconsistent with applicable law, and 2) how FERC's conditions will adequately and equitably protect, mitigate damage to, and enhance fish, wildlife, and habitat. The legislative history of section 10(j) indicated that Congress intended to impose a non-degradation standard, stating that the "equitable" language in the statute "seeks to ensure that non-power values are, to the greatest extent possible, as healthy and abundant after licensing and development as before." It is not at all clear that FERC has accepted this interpretation.[5]

Section 10(j) recommendations are restricted to federal and state fish and wildlife agencies. The statute does not mention Indian tribes, and FERC does not consider recommendations submitted by tribes to be section 10(j) recommendations. The effect is to relieve FERC from making the statutorily required findings in the event it does not adopt the tribal recommendations. Tribes in effect must have their recommendations endorsed by federal land managers or fishery agencies. To be considered as a section 10(j) recommendation under FERC's regulations, agencies must submit the recommendation within 60 days of the time that FERC publishes notice that a license application is ready for environmental analysis. FERC requires 10(j) recommendations to be supported by "substantial evidence" and will not consider as 10(j) recommendations those that it considers to be unsupported by substantial evidence. FERC may evaluate these recommendations under its general licensing authority but will not employ section 10(j) procedures or findings.[6]

FERC has rejected numerous 10(j) recommendations. Moreover, it has rejected other recommendations for consideration under section 10(j), such as requests not to construct or operate a project, requests for post-licensing studies, proposed funds for ecosystem restoration, and recommendations which would give authority over project operations or the final design of fish and wildlife enhancement to agencies other than FERC. This authority to "reclassify" section 10(j) recommendations as falling under other provisions of the FPA, which relieves FERC of making specific findings, was challenged in *American Rivers v. NMFS*. In that case, the Ninth Circuit upheld FERC's interpretation on the rather weakly reasoned ground that section 10(j) vests ultimate decision making authority with FERC and does not allow other agencies to veto projects. If other courts adopt the Ninth Circuit's logic, FERC will be able to continue to avoid making the statutorily required findings by reclassifying recommendations as falling under provisions other than section 10(j). This ability to reclassify in order to avoid making statutorily required findings is the most problematic aspect of section 10(j) implementation.[7]

Federal Land Reservation Conditions

The FPA prohibits licenses in national parks or monuments, but section 4(e) of the statute allows licenses in other federal reserves, like national forests and Indian reservations, if a two-part test is satisfied: 1) FERC must determine that the project will not interfere with or be inconsistent with the purposes of the reservation; and 2) the license includes conditions deemed necessary by the federal land management agency. The latter proviso, the conditioning authority of land management agencies, reflects the fact that Congress did not intend FERC to have absolute decision making authority over all hydroelectric licensing decisions. FERC was slow to understand this, however, and that produced an important Supreme Court opinion.[8]

In 1984, in *Escondido Mutual Water Co. v. LaJolla Band of Mission Indians,* the Supreme Court rejected FERC's longstanding position that section 4(e) conditions were merely advisory. A unanimous Court concluded that the plain meaning of the statute required FERC to impose the conditions required by the federal land managers, even if FERC disagreed with them. The Court ruled that section 4(e) conditions could not veto a project, and they must be reasonably related to the reservation's purpose. But the determination of the reasonableness of a condition is a matter for the courts, not FERC, to determine. The Court also confined the geographic scope of 4(e) conditions to the boundaries of the reservation; FERC licenses that adversely affect downstream reservations are not subject to 4(e) conditions. Finally, the Court interpreted the FPA to allow FERC to license projects on Indian reservations, even over tribal objections.[9]

According to FERC's regulations, like 10(j) recommendations, 4(e) conditions must be submitted within 60 days of FERC's notice that the license application is available for environmental review. The regulations also attempt to require land managers to "specifically identify and explain the mandatory terms or prescriptions and their evidentiary and legal basis." This requirement is open to some question in the wake of the Ninth Circuit's interpretation of section 18 conditions, discussed below.

The D.C. Circuit has ruled that land managers may base their 4(e) conditions on the purposes for which the reservation is managed as well as the reservation's original conditions. Although FERC has repeatedly acknowledged that the Supreme Court's *Escondido* decision requires that it either impose the 4(e) conditions or deny the license, FERC has maintained that it may determine which conditions qualify as 4(e) conditions, and it has rejected provisions that would give land management agencies authority over project operations. This position is also suspect under the Ninth Circuit's decision discussed below.[10]

Fishway Conditions

Section 18 of the FPA authorizes federal fishery agencies (not state fishery agencies) to prescribe fishway conditions. This authority is quite similar to the federal land management conditioning authority to prescribe land reservation conditions under section 4(e). Section 18's fishway requirement was first enacted in 1920 and assumed its current form in 1935, but only recently has it received substantial attention. Since the 4(e) conditioning authority is limited to federal reserved lands, the section 18 authority is arguably the most important conditioning authority under the FPA. In fact, section 18 may lead to dam removal, especially dams which are of marginal economic utility.[11]

FERC has taken a characteristically narrow interpretation of section 18. Its 1991 regulations originally defined fishways to include only facilities used for the upstream passage of fish. When that definition generated a furor of protest, FERC quickly amended it to include both upstream and downstream fish passage facilities. FERC then attempted to convince Congress to amend section 18 to make the fishway prescriptions advisory, but Congress refused. Instead, it overturned FERC's revised fishway definition and required any new regulatory definition to have the concurrence of both federal fishery agencies. Congress also defined fishways to be mechanisms that provide "for the safe and timely upstream and downstream passage of fish . . . limited to physical structures, facilities, or devices necessary to maintain all life stages of such fish, and project operations and measures" necessary to ensure the effectiveness of fishways.[12]

As in the case of section 10(j) recommendations and section 4(e) conditions, FERC's regulations give fishery agencies 60 days from the time FERC issues notice that the license application is ready for environmental review to specify fishway conditions. The regulations also require the fishery agencies to "specifically identify and explain the mandatory terms or prescriptions and their evidentiary and legal basis." This regulation is now of questionable validity in light of a recent Ninth Circuit interpretation of section 18. As in the case of section 4(e) conditions, FERC has asserted authority to "reclassify" section 18 conditions that fail to meet the standard it has created for section 18 conditions. Using this asserted authority, FERC has rejected monitoring and inspection requirements, consultation requirements, design testing, fish mortality standards, requirements dependent on future conditions or new information, modifications to project structures, and changes in project operations that have the effect of regulating river flows. All of these positions are questionable in light of the case discussed next.[13]

In *American Rivers v. FERC,* the U.S. Department of the Interior, the Oregon Department of Fish and Wildlife, and environmentalists challenged FERC's relicensing of the Leaburg-Walterville project on the McKenzie River in Oregon. Of particular concern was FERC's authority to reclassify some proffered section 18 conditions and reject others. Relying heavily on the Supreme Court's interpretation of section 4(e) conditioning authority in *Escondido,* the Ninth Circuit rejected FERC's argument that it had the authority to define the term fishways. The court borrowed a phrase from the D.C. Circuit and described FERC as merely a "neutral forum," responsible for compiling a record concerning section 18 conditions for the courts of appeals. According to the Ninth Circuit, FERC

> may not modify, reject, or reclassify any prescriptions submitted by the [federal fishery agencies] under color of section 18. Where [FERC] disagrees with the scope of a fishway prescription, it may withhold or voice its concerns in the court of appeals, but at the administrative stages, 'it is not [FERC's] role to judge the validity of [the federal fishery agencies'] position — substantively or procedurally.'

This language calls into question not only FERC's rejection of the section 18 conditions mentioned above, but also its regulations requiring section 18 conditions to be based on substantial evidence and imposing the burden of proof on federal fishery agencies to explain the basis of their conditions. In fact, the court's language indicates that even FERC's attempt to impose a 60-day time limit in the regulations may be inconsistent with the statute's assignment of section 18 authority to the fishery agencies, not FERC. Moreover, given the court's equation of section 18 conditioning authority to section 4(e) conditioning authority, FERC may not be able to impose any substantive or procedural limitations on land management agencies either.[14]

Water Quality Certification

Not all of the conditioning provisions affecting the FPA licensing process are contained in the FPA itself. Section 401 of the Clean Water Act requires FERC license applicants to obtain state certification that their projects will meet the state's water quality standards. Thus, although the FPA preempts most state laws, such as laws establishing minimum streamflows, states may use the water quality certification process to effectively veto FERC-licensed projects which would violate water quality standards or "any other appropriate requirement of state law." In short, the Clean Water Act gives states authority to affect FERC licensing decisions that would otherwise not be available under the FPA. The Act allows state certifying agencies one year in which to act on water quality requests; failure to act is a waiver of section 401 requirements. FERC's regulations require water quality certification for amendments to FERC applications only if they produce a material adverse effect on water quality.[15]

The Supreme Court gave a sweeping endorsement to the role of water quality standards in FERC licensing in its 1994 decision, *PUD No. 1 of Jefferson County v. Washington Dept. of Ecology* (*Dosewallips*), involving the proposed Elkhorn project, which would have diverted water from the Dosewallips River in Washington and run it through a pipeline equipped with power turbines before returning the water to the river. In order to satisfy applicable state water quality standards that made salmon spawning a "designated use" of that portion of the river, the state imposed conditions protecting fish flows. The project applicant challenged the state's conditions, and the case eventually reached the Supreme Court.

The Court, in an opinion by Justice O'Connor, ruled 7-2 that the flow conditions imposed by the state were permissible conditions in a 401 certification because they aimed to protect salmon habitat, the designated water quality standard use for the stream. Even though the state had established no quantitative flow standards for the Dosewallips River in its water quality standards, the Court upheld the state's authority to set flow conditions for the project under general narrative criteria aimed at protecting salmon spawning and rearing. Alternatively, the Court suggested that the antidegradation provision in the state's water quality standard could be the basis of minimum flows. Perhaps most importantly, the Court endorsed the imposition of water quality standards on the project as a whole. Specifically, the Court approved conditions on a withdrawal of water from the stream, not merely on the discharge point of the project. The Court's opinion gave states the ability to substantially affect project operations of FERC-licensed projects. One place where the states' ability to condition FERC dams on water quality standards may loom large is at Hells Canyon, where Idaho Power Company is attempting to relicense its three-dam complex, and where downstream water quality problems produce a lethal environment for salmon. Interestingly, relicensing the Hells Canyon complex will require water quality certification from both Idaho and Oregon.[16]

Another important court opinion concerning section 401 was another *American Rivers v. FERC* decision, a 1997 ruling of the Second Circuit which rejected FERC's position that a state may not impose conditions which reserve to the state the discretion to reopen the certification whenever it deems appropriate. Quite like the Ninth Circuit concerning section 18 conditions, the court ruled that while states may impose conditions affecting water quality, the authority to decide which conditions are reasonably related to water quality resides with the courts, not with FERC. The court interpreted the Supreme Court's *Escondido* decision to mean that FERC lacks the authority to second-guess conditions "imposed by an independent government entity with special expertise," even where those conditions involve assertions of authority over project operating conditions. The court noted that if FERC decides that a state's conditions conflict with its interpretation of the FPA, FERC's only administrative option is to deny the project a license. Although the licensee could appeal the denial in the courts, the licensee would have to shoulder the burden of demonstrating that the decision to deny the license was not based on "substantial evidence."[17]

The combination of the Supreme Court's *Escondido* and *Dosewallips* decisions, and the *American Rivers* decisions of the Second and Ninth Circuits, gives federal land management, federal fisheries, and state water quality agencies substantial authority over the licensing and relicensing of FERC projects. Where such conditions apply to existing projects of marginal economic utility, the net effect of these conditions may be the removal of the projects when they come up for relicensing.

ESA Consultation

As discussed in chapter 9, FERC licensees seem somehow to have escaped ESA consultation once their projects have been licensed. The decisions sanctioning this exemption — one not granted by any statute — have been based on procedural grounds. One case held that federal district courts had no jurisdiction over alleged ESA violations because the FPA gave exclusive jurisdiction to federal appeals courts; the other construed the FPA to grant judicial review only where FERC actually issued an order: its failure to act to implement the ESA was, according to this reasoning, not subject to review. As a result of these cases, FERC has been able to ignore the implications of the Ninth Circuit's decision in *Pacific Rivers Council v. Thomas*, also discussed in chapter 9, which ruled that previously approved federal land management plans were subject to ESA consultation. If previously approved land management plans are subject to ESA consultation, it is hard to see why existing FERC licenses are not. Nevertheless, FERC for some time has taken no apparent notice of a petition seeking to subject Idaho Power Company's Hells Canyon projects to ESA consultation.[18]

These results fly in the face of the ESA's all-encompassing attempt to reach all actions "authorized, funded, or carried out" by any federal agency. The ESA regulations indicate the statutory intent is to subject any discretionary federal action to ESA consultation. FERC-licensed projects with clauses allowing FERC to change operating conditions based on changed circumstances — and virtually all Columbia Basin FERC projects include such provisions — would seem to fall within the EPA's expansive definition of federal actions subject to ESA consultation. Yet FERC-licensed projects seem to have evaded ESA review as of this writing.[19]

Relicensing and Environmental Review

FERC requires its applicants to engage in what it calls pre-filing consultation with environmental and fish and wildlife agencies. This consultation is supposed to be the basis of fish-protective operating conditions imposed both by FERC and other agencies. Of course, there is now some question as to whether FERC may impose procedural requirements on agencies promulgating conditions under sections 4(e) and 18 of the FPA and section 401 of the Clean Water Act, due to the Ninth Circuit's 1999 *American Rivers v. FERC* decision. License applicants must also file an "Exhibit E" report with FERC that details both the project's anticipated environmental impacts and the results of the required consultation with the resource agencies.[20]

In 1997, FERC changed its regulations to offer a "collaborative option" to its existing licensing procedures. The new rules allowed for the establishment of alternative procedures that will be governed by a "communications protocol" agreed to by consensus among the license applicant, the resource agencies, Indian tribes, and citizen groups. All requests for studies and preliminary fish and wildlife recommendations, mandatory conditions, and comments are due during the pre-filing period. However, due to the Ninth Circuit's *American Rivers* decision, it is no longer clear that FERC can impose procedural requirements like these on mandatory conditions promulgated under sections 4(e) and 18 of the FPA and section 401 of the Clean Water Act.[21]

In a 1984 decision of the Ninth Circuit involving the relicensing of the Rock Island Dam on the Mid-Columbia, the court ruled that FERC must treat environmental issues involved in relicensings in the same way as initial licensings. As a result, environmentalists claimed that the appropriate baseline for considering the adverse effects of previously licensed projects was pre-project conditions. FERC, on the other hand, maintained that the appropriate baseline for considering a project's effect was the conditions existing at the time the project sought a new license. The environmentalists contended that FERC's interpretation would skew the evaluation of alternatives required by the National Environmental Policy Act. For example, under FERC's interpretation, the mandatory "no action" alternative would simply be a continuation of the status quo, instead of a decision not to relicense the project. Moreover, any improvements to the status quo would then be considered to be "enhancement" measures instead of mitigation for the environmental damage caused by the project.[22]

In *American Rivers v. FERC,* the Ninth Circuit sided with FERC, concluding that a current conditions definition of the environmental baseline was a reasonable interpretation of the FPA. The court thought a pre-project baseline "defies common sense and notions of pragmatism [because it would] require [FERC] to 'gather information to recreate a 50-year old environmental base upon which to make present day development decisions.'" The court did observe that adopting a present-day baseline would not preclude consideration of conditions "that enhance fish and wildlife resources and reduce negative impacts attributable to a project since its construction." But if present-day conditions are the standard from which to measure a project's effects on the environment, it seems obvious that much less protection and restoration of fish and wildlife is likely to result from relicensing decisions.[23]

Another contentious issue in the relicensing of FERC projects is the treatment of cumulative impacts of multiple relicensings in the same river basin. Licensees want FERC to consider only the impacts of individual projects; environmentalists want FERC to defer all long-term license decisions until all the projects in a river basin can be considered simultaneously. FERC has chosen a middle path in its policy on cumulative impacts, which states that FERC will consider cumulative impacts "to the fullest extent possible." Where all cumulative impact issues cannot be resolved, FERC will issue licenses with "reopener clauses," enabling the agency to amend the license in the future, pending the relicensing results of other projects in the basin. This policy may theoretically allow for a full consideration of the cumulative environmental impacts of multiple relicensings in a single river basin. However, it threatens to maintain a status quo of existing adverse environmental conditions without a thorough assessment of cumulative impacts.[24]

The Mid-Columbia Agreement

One of the most surprisingly successful uses of the FPA licensing process in terms of Columbia Basin salmon was the Mid-Columbia proceeding. There are five FERC-licensed dams on the Mid-Columbia (see map 1, page 11), one of which, Rock Island Dam, was discussed in the preceding section. In the mid-1970s, state and federal fishery agencies and the Yakama Indian Nation petitioned FERC to modify the dams to require improved flows for salmon spawning and rearing, and to improve juvenile salmon passage at the dams. A long, tortuous administrative process ensued, culminating in a 1980 interim agreement, which led to another interim agreement in 1984, which was finally superseded by a long-term agreement in 1988. The agreement called for ensuring that flows remain low during fall spawning, and for maintaining flows in the winter and spring to ensure that the salmon redds (nests) remain inundated.[25]

With the help of the Mid-Columbia agreement, Hanford Reach fall chinook continue to be the only self-sustaining salmon population in the Columbia Basin. While that success story has often been attributed to the fact that the area is undammed, it is important to also recognize that the flow regime vital for salmon spawning and rearing is a controlled one, not a natural one. Since most human intervention in the name of salmon restoration has failed or backfired, it is useful to recognize and learn from success stories like the Mid-Columbia agreement. Among the lessons to be learned is that the licensing process of the FPA offers opportunities for salmon protection that seem unavailable in the case of federal dams.

Dam Removal

In 1994, FERC adopted a project decommissioning policy in which it stated that it would deny licenses to projects that could not meet requirements of applicable laws. FERC, however, anticipated that denial of licenses in relicensing proceedings "would rarely occur." FERC also contended that it possessed authority to order projects found to be environmentally damaging to be removed, and for the site to be restored to pre-project conditions. This position is, to say the least, at some tension with FERC's position, upheld by the Ninth Circuit, that the proper environmental baseline at relicensing is the river with the dam in place. Although FERC declined to impose the cost of a decommissioning fund on all of its licensees, the agency noted that individual licensees "will ultimately be responsible for meeting a reasonable level of decommissioning costs."[26]

FERC first applied its decommissioning policy in 1997 in the Edwards Dam case. There the agency ordered the removal of the 3.5-megawatt Edwards Dam from the Kennebec River in Maine. FERC agreed with fishery agencies, the state of Maine, and environmental groups that the 160-year old dam should be removed to restore seventeen miles of fish habitat for Atlantic salmon and other fish. FERC's decision was never tested in court because the parties reached a settlement agreement under which the cost of dam removal would be funded by upstream dam operators — in exchange for delays in the imposition of fish passage requirements at their facilities until there were enough fish to warrant fishways — and Bath Iron Works, as mitigation for filling wetlands to accommodate shipyard expansion. The agreement called for the removal of the dam by January 1, 1999, and required the licensee to cede the project site to the local municipality and pay $100,000 to help establish a city park.[27]

FERC's authority to decommission licensed projects is not an insignificant power, although it has yet to receive judicial approval. However, it is likely that more dams will be removed as a result of the imposition of fishway conditions under section 18 of the FPA than FERC's decommissioning authority. Of course, the section 18 conditioning authority cannot directly order dam removal, but the imposition of fishway conditions, which the Ninth Circuit has made clear are the exclusive administrative authority of federal fishery agencies, may make relicensing of many projects economically infeasible. Since those projects may not continue to operate without FERC licenses, and since FERC may not relicense a project without complying with section 18, the real question becomes not whether the dam will be removed, but who will pay the cost. Under FERC's decommissioning policy, "reasonable" costs of removal fall upon the licensee. But as the Edwards Dam case suggests, there may be creative funding opportunities available to share dam removal costs.

One of the first applications of section 18 to produce dam removal was Condit Dam on the White Salmon River in southwest Washington. The river is a potentially important salmon spawning tributary of the Columbia just above Bonneville Dam. When the operator of the dam, PacifiCorp, attempted to obtain a new license for its nearly century-old project, fishery agencies, tribes, and environmental groups objected, calling for dam removal or installation of fish passage measures to restore salmon spawning to the White Salmon. Condit Dam had blocked salmon migration since 1913.

FERC initially rejected dam removal as too expensive, but section 18 gave federal fishery agencies the authority to require installation of fish passage measures as a condition of issuing a new license to the project. Due to the high costs of installing the fishways required by federal fishery agencies and the marginal economic utility of the project, PacifiCorp eventually agreed to remove the project, since removing the dam would be cheaper than installing the fish passage measures. Thus, over a seven-year period, with the assistance of some $17 million in restoration costs paid by PacifiCorp, the dam will come out, restoring salmon spawning to a river reach sealed off for over 80 years. The Condit Dam removal could become the first in a wave of dam removals, prompted by either section 18 fishway conditions or section 4(e) federal land reservation conditions, at least concerning economically marginal projects seeking FERC relicenses. Whether these provisions will prompt removal of economically viable projects, like the Hells Canyon dams — which block Snake River fall chinook from their historic spawning grounds and which must be relicensed in the near future — is less probable.[28]

The Hidden Promise

Through long-ignored provisions like section 18, the FPA offers substantial opportunities to provide important salmon restoration in certain watersheds. Although the FPA is administered by an agency with little sympathy to salmon restoration, the statute assigns significant roles for federal fishery agencies, federal land managers, and state water quality agencies. Sensitive use of those authorities can materially improve salmon passage at FERC-licensed projects and salmon habitat affected by the operation of those projects, and can even produce dam removal. The FPA may therefore be rightfully considered a hidden promise of salmon restoration.

It is not entirely clear how long the FPA will extend this hidden promise, however. In late 2000, the hydropower industry convinced Congress to add a provision to the Energy Act of 2000 which called upon FERC to submit a report, reviewing relicensing procedures and suggesting legislative changes to reduce the cost and time of obtaining a license. This report may encourage Congress and the Bush Administration to reduce the role of federal fishery and land management agencies in the relicensing process, a result that would effectively revoke the FPA's promise of salmon restoration, and perhaps do serious damage to fish, wildlife, and recreational resources throughout the country.[29]

12 – THE ULTIMATE PROMISE? THE TREATY RIGHT TO HABITAT PROTECTION

As indicated in chapter 4, the courts have interpreted the treaty right of taking fish at all usual and accustomed places to mean that tribes have the right to half of the harvestable salmon. In the case that established that principle, *United States v. Washington,* the tribes argued that the treaties also entitled them to 1) half of the harvests of salmon originating from hatcheries, and 2) protection for habitat upon which the harvests depend. Judge Boldt deferred those two issues until the fundamental issue of whether the treaties guaranteed the tribes a share of the harvests was decided. That did not occur until the Supreme Court's affirmance of the Boldt Decision in 1979.[1]

The Orrick Decision

Shortly after the Supreme Court's ruling, the tribes asked Judge Boldt's successor, Judge William Orrick, to decide each of the deferred issues, in what became known as Phase II of *United States v. Washington.* Judge Orrick had little difficulty determining that hatchery fish were indeed included in the equal sharing formula articulated by Judge Boldt and the Supreme Court. This was not an insignificant ruling, given the region's overwhelming commitment to hatcheries as the mitigation option of choice to compensate for habitat damage due to aquatic development throughout the Columbia Basin. In fact, recognition of the close link between hatcheries as compensation for damage to naturally spawning salmon was a chief reason the Ninth Circuit affirmed Judge Orrick's inclusion of hatchery fish in the equal sharing formula.[2]

The most notable aspect of Judge Orrick's decision, however, was his conclusion that the treaty promise of taking fish did imply a right of protection for the habitat necessary to maintain the fish runs, writing that "[t]he most fundamental prerequisite to exercising the right to take fish is the existence of fish to be taken." His decision was a common sense opinion, based on the primary purpose of the treaty, as articulated by the Supreme Court, which was to reserve the right to fish as an economic and cultural way of life. Judge Orrick noted that maintenance of habitat quality was necessary to the survival of the fish. Therefore, he concluded that the treaties must be interpreted to protect that habitat, or the reserved right to fish would be without value. He observed:

> Were this trend [loss of salmon habitat] to continue, the right to take fish would eventually be reduced to the right to dip one's net into the water . . . and bring it out empty. Such a result would render nugatory the nine-year effort in Phase I [of *United States v. Washington*], sanctioned by this Court, the Ninth Circuit, and the Supreme Court, to enforce the treaties' reservation to the tribes of a sufficient quantity of fish to meet their fair needs.[3]

Judge Orrick ruled that the treaties require the state to refrain from degrading or authorizing the degradation of fish habitat if it would interfere with a tribe's "moderate living" needs, a phrase drawn from the Supreme Court's opinion. Further, the Orrick opinion made clear that it would not be easy for the state to prove that a habitat-damaging development would not interfere with a tribe's moderate living needs. When the tribal allocation share was set at 50 percent of the harvest, under Judge Orrick's formula there was a presumption that the tribe's moderate living needs were unmet. Finally, Judge Orrick determined that the burden of satisfying the implied habitat right ran not merely against the state but also against the federal government and private parties.[4]

Judge Orrick's decision made the Supreme Court's moderate living standard the centerpiece of the treaty right to take fish. The Court had suggested that the tribes' harvest share entitled them to no more than a moderate living; Judge Orrick interpreted the treaties to promise them no less. Given the tribes' historic "paramount" dependence on their fisheries, the shared understanding of tribal and federal negotiators that the treaties would safeguard the tribes' commercial fishing livelihood, and the important role that tribal fishing continued to play in the post-treaty economy, the court seemed justified in recognizing that the essential treaty bargain for the tribes was the right to maintain a viable commercial fishing livelihood.[5]

The Appeals

Not surprisingly, the state of Washington appealed the Orrick decision and, in 1982, a three-judge panel of the Ninth Circuit affirmed Judge Orrick on the hatchery fish issue but significantly modified his ruling on the habitat issue. The Ninth Circuit panel replaced the "moderate living" standard with a reasonableness test. Under this formula, the states and the tribes each had to take "reasonable steps commensurate with the resources and abilities of each to preserve and enhance the fishery." Although the panel opinion also suggested that state-approved private developments which discriminated against tribal fisheries would violate the treaty right, the panel ruled without explanation that the right did not burden private parties.[6]

The tribes and the federal government petitioned the Ninth Circuit for a rehearing and, in an unusual procedure, an *en banc* (eleven-judge) panel agreed to hear the case. The *en banc* court affirmed Judge Orrick on the hatchery issue but vacated the district court's habitat ruling, meaning that the lower court's ruling has no effect. A majority of the eleven-judge court believed that articulating the scope of the treaty right in a case with no concrete facts was judicially imprudent, possibly producing legal rules that would be "imprecise in definition and uncertain in dimension." The court noted that the legal standards governing the state's habitat protection duties under the treaty "will depend for their definition and articulation upon concrete facts which underlie a dispute in a particular case." Thus, in 1985, the Ninth Circuit had the question of the implied right of habitat protection before it, and it squarely ducked, preferring to await a specific fact situation in which to decide whether the treaties protected salmon habitat and, if so, how.[7]

The tribes decided against bringing another case with specific facts and instead concentrated their efforts on helping to implement the Columbia Basin Fish and Wildlife Program under the Northwest Power Act (chapter 7) and negotiating and implementing the Pacific Salmon Treaty (chapter 8). As a result, nearly two decades after Judge Orrick's decision, there is no definitive answer about whether the treaties of the mid-19th century include the right of habitat protection, largely because the tribes have chosen to negotiate rather than litigate with state and federal officials. These negotiations produced measures such as the "timber, fish, and wildlife agreement" promising more salmon sensitive forest practices in Washington (chapter 14), and the salmon restoration programs under the ESA (chapter 9) and the Northwest Power Act. Unfortunately, these measures have not proved sufficient to reverse the decline of most Columbia Basin salmon runs.[8]

The Piscary Profit

When the tribes do return to court to vindicate their treaty right to habitat protection, they should be successful. In several cases with specific habitat-damaging facts, lower courts have almost invariably provided the tribes with relief, requiring changes in dam operations, enjoining dam construction and other adverse aquatic developments, and awarding the tribes "prior and paramount" water rights to protect the fish that are the subject of the treaties. Although one court ruled that money damages are unavailable to compensate the tribes for past losses sustained by salmon at the hands of development, it did not deny the existence of a servitude protecting treaty salmon habitat. Those decisions, discussed below, were based on the kind of concrete facts that were lacking in *United States v. Washington*. Collectively, these cases recognize a right to habitat protection for the right of taking fish, which the courts ought to recognize as a *profit à prendre*; that is, the legal right to take and remove a resource from another's land. The fishing right is a *piscary profit*: the right to take and remove fish.[9]

The Shellfish Case

A recent case confirming the treaty right as a *profit à prendre* concerned the shellfish proviso in the Stevens Treaties. The proviso states that the tribes "shall not take shell fish from any beds staked or cultivated by citizens." Uncertainty over the meaning of the words "staked or cultivated" produced three district court and two Ninth Circuit opinions between 1994 and 1998 — not surprising since Washington is second only to Louisiana in national oyster production, and the commercial harvest of clams, mussels, and oysters contributed more than $20 million to the state's economy in 1997. Shellfish owners claimed that the shellfish proviso excluded tribal harvests in any beds "staked or cultivated" by them, using the dictionary definition of those terms. Landowners adjacent to the shellfish beds contended that any privately owned beds were "staked or cultivated," claiming that this was the interpretation of those terms during settlement. The state of Washington argued that the proviso meant that the tribes had only the same rights as other citizens of the state. The tribes and the federal government maintained that "staked or cultivated" meant merely that artificial shellfish beds were excluded from tribal harvests.[10]

The first district court decision agreed with the tribes, interpreting the proviso in light of what the tribes intended at treaty time, which was to continue to fish as they always had, and the local practice at the time involved no staking or cultivating of shellfish beds. As a result, the court interpreted "staked or cultivated" to involve only artificial beds, meaning that natural shellfish beds were subject to the equal sharing principle of the Stevens treaties until the tribes achieve a "moderate living." The court specifically rejected the contention that the tribes had attained a moderate living. In two subsequent decisions, however, the court expansively defined what constituted artificial beds to include any grower-enhancement efforts, such as netting or seeding or predator control measures. The court also imposed on the tribes the burden of surveying tidelands to determine whether natural beds existed and clarified that although the tribes could cross private lands to exercise their rights, they had to demonstrate a need to do so, and that there was no other way to access the shellfish beds.[11]

All parties appealed to the Ninth Circuit, which mostly affirmed the district court, ruling that only artificial beds were "staked and cultivated" within the meaning of the treaty proviso, that the tribes had to demonstrate a need to cross private lands before they could do so, and also approved time, place, and manner restrictions that the lower court imposed on the exercise of the treaty right. However, the appeals court corrected a number of details of the lower court's decision, including 1) imposing the burden on the growers to prove that the beds had been enhanced, rather than imposing the burden on the tribes to show they had not; 2) ruling that unlike private growers, the state's enhancement efforts did not result in an exclusion of tribal harvests; and 3) rejecting the district court's definition of commercial shellfish beds as requiring a minimum density of one-half pound per square foot of clams and ordering a new hearing on the issue. These details aside, the key result of the case was the court's recognition that privately owned shellfish beds were subject to the treaty *profit à prendre*. Private land ownership did not terminate the treaty right; on the contrary, private property and the continuation of the treaty right are entirely consistent with each other. Finally, the measure of the right to harvest shellfish was the tribe's unfulfilled right to a moderate living.[12]

Dam Cases

The first case to recognize the habitat protection potential in the treaties involved a 1971 proposal of two federal water management agencies, the Bonneville Power Administration (BPA) and the Army Corps of Engineers, to change the operation of Columbia Basin dams to increase the dams' capability in order to produce power to satisfy peak load demands. This peaking power proposal was a part of BPA's Hydro-Thermal Power Program, discussed in chapter 5. The two federal agencies wanted to increase daily and weekly water levels and flows in the Lower Columbia and inundate parts of three Indian fishing sites in the reservoir behind Bonneville Dam. The tribes sued to enjoin the program, claiming that the proposed peaking power policy violated their treaty fishing rights.[13]

In 1973, Judge Belloni approved a settlement in the case that forbade the federal agencies from proceeding with peaking operations until there was protection for the fishing sites. He noted that although Congress authorized modifications to the dams for peak power generation, it had not authorized operations that would "impair or destroy any fishing rights . . . secured by Treaty with the Indians." The case could be interpreted as the first judicial recognition that the treaty right to fish could be used to protect salmon habitat.[14]

Four years later, the tribes returned to federal court, seeking to preserve salmon habitat in Catherine Creek in northeastern Oregon's Grande Ronde Basin. The Corps believed it had congressional approval to construct a dam. The government argued that there were no treaty fishing rights on the creek and that, even if there were, a planned fish hatchery would compensate for the lost habitat. Judge Belloni rejected these arguments. He determined that Catherine Creek contained fishing holes that had been used in pre-treaty times by tribal fishers and that would be inundated by the two-and-a-half mile reservoir. Moreover, the government's hatchery was not adequate compensation for the lost fishing grounds. Judge Belloni could find no express congressional recognition that the project would jeopardize treaty fishing rights, and he refused to infer congressional intent to abrogate the tribal rights from the mere authorization of the dam. As a result, he enjoined its construction, and the dam was never built. By affirming the principle that only clear congressional authorization may abrogate fishing rights, the decision protected fish habitat.[15]

The implied right of habitat protection has reached beyond protecting particular tribal fishing sites. In the fall of 1980, the federal Bureau of Reclamation decided to reduce flows from the Cle Elum Dam in the Yakima Basin due to the end of the irrigation season, threatening salmon redds (nests) with dewatering. Salmon had spawned unusually high in the Yakima River that fall because of greater than normal storage releases for irrigation. The Yakama Indian Nation, which had been unable to exercise its fishing rights in the Yakima River for several years due to depleted numbers of returning salmon, requested the basin's watermaster to order the Bureau of Reclamation to maintain the flows needed to protect the redds. The watermaster in turn asked the federal court if he had authority to do so. The district court ordered the master to undertake a number of measures to protect the redds, including 1) releasing storage water, 2) attempting alternative means of preserving the redds, and 3) studying ways to avoid such conflicts in the future.[16]

Irrigation districts served by the dam appealed this decision and, over the course of the next three years, the Ninth Circuit issued three different opinions, all upholding the district court's decision. In the first decision, the appeals court noted that "[t]he parties to a treaty bear a duty to refrain from actions interfering with either the Indians' access to fishing grounds or the amount of fish present there." The court ruled that the tribes' right to adequate water to sustain the salmon redds was not affected by a 1945 consent decree which fixed the Yakama Indian Nation's rights to irrigation water, distinguishing the tribe's water rights for fishing from its irrigation water rights. Although the court made no attempt to quantify the tribe's water rights for fish, it explicitly ruled that dewatering the redds violated treaty fishing rights. While it never wavered in affirming the district court's decision, the Ninth Circuit's subsequent opinions on rehearing became progressively less clear about the nature of the tribe's fishing rights.[17]

In its second opinion, issued in February 1985, the court affirmed the flow releases and other measures ordered by the lower court but stated "we need not decide the exact scope of the treaty fishing right. It is enough to note that the Indian fishing rights are protected and under those circumstances the release of water was justified in order to avoid damage to the redds." This opinion was revoked after the *en banc* Ninth Circuit handed down its Phase II opinion in *United States v. Washington*.[18]

Six weeks after the *en banc* decision, the Ninth Circuit issued a third opinion. The court once again affirmed the trial court, but this time stated merely that there was "no abuse of discretion in the [district] court's decision," and that the lower court's flow directives constituted "reasonable emergency measures" under the circumstances. Although the language in the three Ninth Circuit opinions grew vaguer about the nature of the treaty fishing right, the court upheld the district court's protection of the fish, which the appeals court referred to as a "vital purpose" of the treaty.[19]

Pipelines, Marinas, and Fish Farms

Dams are not the only developments that courts have concluded can violate the treaty fishing right. Construction of the proposed Northern Tier Oil Pipeline, which would have crossed Puget Sound as well as numerous rivers, was challenged for violating environmental statutes and treaty fishing rights. Although the district court determined that the project complied with environmental statutes, Judge Belloni ruled that sedimentation from burying pipelines under rivers could adversely affect salmon and trout populations, including at least two rivers subject to treaty fishing rights. As a result, he ordered a trial on the issue of whether the sedimentation would degrade fish habitat, impair rearing or production potential, or diminish the size or quality of fish runs. The case never went to trial because the project was abandoned when the governor of Washington refused to approve a terminal at Port Angeles due to threats of oil spills and fire in Puget Sound.[20]

Another aquatic development that clashed with treaty fishing rights was a marina in Washington's Elliott Bay. Construction of the marina, which required a federal dredge and fill permit from the Corps of Engineers, would have eliminated part of an off-reservation fishing ground of the Muckleshoot and Suquamish Tribes. In a carefully reasoned opinion, Judge Zilly granted the tribes' request for a preliminary injunction. The court recognized the tribes' right to fish as a "property right which may not be abrogated without specific and express Congressional authority." Judge Zilly concluded that the right of access to a particular fishing site was a separate element of the treaty fishing right from the right to a moderate living from fishing. Thus, even if the tribes' moderate living needs would be unaffected by the marina, as the developer and the Corps argued, the court refused to "collapse[ ] the right of access into the right to a fair share of the fish or to weigh the loss of fishing access against the benefit of the marina, absent an act of Congress." Although the state could restrict fishing in the interest of conservation of the fish, the marina hardly qualified as a fish conservation measure. Consequently, the court enjoined construction of the marina, and in so doing confirmed that the treaty right to access customary fishing sites could protect those sites from habitat destruction. A reconfigured marina was subsequently constructed under a settlement agreement between the tribes and the developer.[21]

A proposed net pen "fish farm" for rearing salmon in the Rosario Strait area of Puget Sound similarly violated the access rights of the Lummi Nation. Like the marina in Elliott Bay, Northwest Sea Farms' net pen would have blocked access to a tribal fishing ground. Unlike the marina, the Corps denied the required federal permit, and Northwest Sea Farms filed suit. The court upheld the Corps' permit denial on the ground that the Corps had a fiduciary duty to consider the tribe's treaty rights, even though the applicable agency regulations made no mention of considering treaty rights in permit decision making. The court observed that the treaty fishing right contained "mutually exclusive protections of the right to access an area for fishing and the right to take a proper quota of fish." Thus, the court rejected the permit applicant's argument that the net pen would have only a minor effect on the tribe's fishing and refused to "conduct a balancing test which views the right to access in relation to the supply of the proper portion of fish." Consequently, the court upheld the Corps' permit denial even though, as with the marina, there was no evidence that the project would have substantially affected the amount of fish available for tribal harvest. According to the court, the Corps lacked authority to make regulatory decisions diminishing treaty rights, as "only Congress has such power."[22]

These cases provide examples of the kinds of habitat-damaging developments that the treaty fishing right can restrain. Where developments block access to traditional tribal fishing grounds, the courts have not hesitated to enjoin them, regardless of their effects on the supply of harvestable fish. Thus, the treaty *piscary profit* has two separate components: an affirmative easement to gain access to tribal fishing grounds and a negative servitude (restriction) limiting activities that jeopardize the supply of fish necessary to furnish the tribes a moderate living.[23]

Water Rights Cases

Like most aquatic developments, the dam construction, pipeline, marina, and fish farm cases dealt with specific locations, and therefore implicated the treaty right to access specific geographic fishing areas. However, water rights cases — like the dam operation cases — involve broader geographic areas and the tribes' right to a moderate living from fishing. As the cases discussed below demonstrate, the reserved water rights doctrine can restrict salmon-damaging activities resulting from the exercise of water rights by other parties. The doctrine also entitles the tribes to a quantified amount of water instream to fulfill the treaties' fishing purposes. The treaties therefore supply the tribes with both a right to a specified amount of water and a right to restrict water uses which damage fish habitat. Quantification of reserved water rights would make clear the obligations of non-

Indian water rights holders and offer the tribes protection against water diversions which damage salmon habitat. But most states do not recognize the ability of unquantified water rights holders to restrain diversions damaging their rights, and few courts have attempted to quantify the amount of water reserved for fishing purposes. Instead, most courts have addressed only the right to restrict habitat-damaging activities in the absence of quantification.

One decision that did quantify the amount of water in the reserved fishing right concerned an adjudication of water rights in Chamokane Creek in Eastern Washington. In that case, the federal district court concluded that a purpose of the Spokane Indian Reservation was to ensure maintenance of fishing in the creek. As a result, the court ruled that the quantity of reserved water was an amount sufficient to preserve fishing in the creek. Because the court determined that native trout propagation required temperatures of 68 degrees Fahrenheit or less, it ordered flows sufficient to maintain that water temperature, and in no case less than twenty cubic feet per second. This decision was the first to marry the amount of reserved water to the quality of that water.[24]

The Chamokane Creek case was more far-reaching than the peaking power or Catherine Creek cases because it extended the scope of the reserved fishing right beyond particular fishing locations to include a right to sufficient water to sustain tribal fishing. The decision prevented state water rights holders from diverting water from the creek if the diversions interfered with environmental conditions necessary to maintain fishing. Thus, the case was one of the first to recognize the potential of the treaty right of taking fish to protect fish habitat throughout a watershed.

While the Chamokane Creek decision recognized a right to maintain environmental conditions necessary to sustain a tribal fishery, another case introduced a restoration component to the treaty right to fish. The Ninth Circuit ruled that the Colville tribes had a right to sufficient water to develop an on-reservation trout fishery to replace their historic salmon runs lost as a result of the completion of construction of the Grand Coulee Dam in 1941. To fulfill the purpose of the tribes' reservation and to preserve its access to fishing grounds, the district court permitted the tribes to use some of their irrigation water to restore streamflows in order to support trout spawning. The Ninth Circuit went further and held that the tribes did not need to use their irrigation water for this purpose because they had distinct reserved water rights "for the development and maintenance of replacement fishing grounds." The court made clear that such a vested property right cannot be divested by "subsequent acts making the historically intended use of water unnecessary." The result indicates that the treaty right to fish includes a restoration as well as a maintenance component.[25]

A different panel of the Ninth Circuit addressed the important issue of the scope of this restoration component in a 1983 case involving the Klamath Tribe's water rights for on-reservation hunting and fishing. The court affirmed a trial court decision, which concluded that the tribe had a "time immemorial" right "to as much water on the Reservation lands as they need to protect their hunting and fishing rights." The appeals court accurately termed the tribal fishing right a negative right, enabling the tribes "to prevent other appropriators from depleting the streams [sic] waters below a protected level in any area where the non-consumptive right applies." However, worried that the implications of the district court decision might be interpreted to impose a "wilderness servitude" on the Klamath Reservation, the Ninth Circuit ruled that restoration of treaty-time (1864) streamflows was not required. Like the district court in *United States v. Washington*, the Ninth Circuit tied the scope of the right to the Supreme Court's "moderate living" standard. Implicit in this standard is the conclusion that the tribes are not entitled to treaty-time fishing levels unless, as the Ninth Circuit noted, "no lesser level will supply them with a living." The moderate living standard gives the treaty fishing right a restoration component, yet eliminates the draconian "wilderness servitude" possibility.[26]

Four years after the Klamath decision, in 1987, the Ninth Circuit recognized another "time immemorial" water right for fish in a case involving the tribes of the Flathead Reservation in Montana. Irrigators served by a reservation irrigation project sued the Bureau of Indian Affairs, seeking to enjoin new project operations designed to provide flows to protect tribal fisheries. The district court granted the irrigators the injunction, ruling that under the 1887 Dawes Act's principle of "just and equal distribution" governing water allocation to irrigators, the Bureau could not protect the fisheries at the expense of the irrigators. The Ninth Circuit reversed, concluding that the "just and equal distribution" language applied only to water rights holders with the same priority date. The water rights for the Flathead reservation were not of equal priority, however, because the tribes had a "time immemorial" priority date for the water reserved for fishery purposes. This date was prior to any reservation irrigation water rights (the reservation had reserved water rights for both irrigation and fish), since the water protected a use that antedated the reservation itself. Therefore, the tribes did not have to share their "prior and paramount fishing water rights" with irrigators who had obtained reservation irrigation rights. The court noted that the exercise of reserved rights "arise[s] without regard to equities that may favor competing water uses." The Flathead case thus made clear that water for the reserved fishing right takes precedence over all irrigation water rights.[27]

The Acquavella Case. An exception to the course taken by most courts in implying a right of habitat protection occurred in a 1990 state court case involving the long-running adjudication of water rights in the Yakima Basin. A Washington trial court ruled that the Yakama Indian Nation had a treaty right to water for fish but determined that the scope of the water right reserved for fish habitat had been diminished substantially by government actions throughout the 20th century. The trial court did conclude, however, that the tribe was entitled to a minimum instream flow to maintain salmon according to annual prevailing conditions. The state supreme court affirmed in 1993, in an unfortunate opinion that created a new category of "diminished" treaty rights, which apparently are not subject to the exacting standards courts require to demonstrate an abrogation of treaty rights.[28]

The Washington Supreme Court purported to recognize the rules of treaty construction by liberally construing the treaty language and interpreting ambiguities in the tribe's favor; the court even applied these rules to actions of administrative agencies. The state court also determined that, like the Flathead Reservation, the Yakama Reservation had both agricultural and fishing purposes, and the tribe possessed reserved water rights for both. However, in the court's effort to avoid the prospect of restoring river flows to treaty-time conditions, the reasoning it used to conclude that the scope of the fishing right was "substantially diminished" was alarming.[29]

The court employed the canons of treaty interpretation to conclude that neither approval of the Yakima Basin Reclamation Project in 1906, nor a 1914 statute which increased the tribe's irrigation water rights, abrogated the treaty right to fish. The court also held that inconsistent government actions in the form of an unspecified series of "congressional, executive, administrative, and judicial acts" from 1905 through 1968 did not abrogate treaty rights in the absence of clear congressional termination. Instead, the federal government recognized the existence of fishing rights by installing fish screens and fish ladders.[30]

Yet in two puzzling sentences the court allowed these same unspecified government actions to "diminish" the Yakama Indian Nation's treaty fishing rights. The court stated, "[w]e conclude, however, that there was encroachment upon and significant damage to the Indians' treaty fishing rights during this period." Thus, although the treaty rights were not extinguished, they were diminished. Under this unprecedented interpretation, government actions inconsistent with the exercise of treaty rights may apparently substantially diminish them, despite a lack of clear congressional intent required to abrogate those rights. This result is particularly regrettable because it invites both federal and state courts to discover such "diminishments" of treaty rights on the basis of subjective judicial interpretations of history. The tribe, perhaps fearing that a hostile Supreme Court would affirm and give the case national implications, decided not to appeal.[31]

The *Acquavella* decision has no support in prior case law interpreting the scope of the treaty fishing right. Unlike the Ninth Circuit in the Klamath case, the Washington Supreme Court made no attempt to link the Yakama Indian Nation's "diminished" treaty fishing rights to the U.S. Supreme Court's interpretation that the treaties promised the tribes a "moderate living." In fact, the state court seemed completely oblivious to that promise. Instead, the court relied on a 1968 settlement of an Indian Claims Commission case as evidence that the tribe's fishing rights had been diminished — even though the commission had no authority to extinguish treaty rights.[32]

Although the Washington Supreme Court's *Acquavella* decision seemed to send a crushing blow to the Yakama Indian Nation's hopes of restoring its salmon runs, subsequent decisions in the Yakima Basin water rights adjudication have minimized its effect. Two trial court decisions in 1995 interpreted the state supreme court's recognition of a limited right of habitat protection "to maintain fish life" in the river to apply to several Yakima River tributaries with treaty fishing grounds and to require fish flows to flush salmon downstream in the spring. The effect was to ratify a "systems operation committee" recommendation of releasing some 600 acre-feet of storage water for fish migration, effectively recognizing the duty of the Bureau of Reclamation to provide flows to "maintain all life stages" of salmon. The Yakama Indian Nation's attorney considered these results to revolutionize project operations in the Yakima Basin, requiring the Bureau to manage water for both irrigation and fish.[33]

The Washington Supreme Court's unfounded "diminished treaty rights" ruling may have been a consequence of the same concerns that led the Ninth Circuit in the Klamath case to opine that the treaty fishing right would not impose a wilderness servitude. Unlike the Ninth Circuit, however, the Washington court failed to see that the way to avoid requiring a return to treaty-time environmental conditions was to articulate the scope of the right in terms of the Supreme Court's "moderate living" standard. Unfortunately, instead of following the Supreme Court's precedent, the Washington court created a novel theory of "diminished" rights which apparently countenances partial abrogation of treaty rights without clear congressional approval.

The Nez Perce Water Rights Case. In another disturbing decision, the Snake River Basin Adjudication (SRBA) court, a special state court established to determine water rights in Idaho's Snake River basin, determined that the Nez Perce Tribe had no water rights for its off-reservation fishing because reserved water rights were confined to reservation lands. The court gave a one-sided interpretation to the purpose of the Nez Perce treaty, concluding that it was intended to facilitate non-Indian settlement, which would be impeded by reserved water rights for fish. In doing so, the SRBA court ignored the U.S. Supreme Court's conclusion that the fishing purpose of the Stevens Treaties aimed to provide the tribes a commercial livelihood.[34]

The SRBA court noted repeatedly that at the time of the treaties, neither the tribe nor the federal government intended to create an implied water right. Yet the lack of specific intent did not prevent the Supreme Court from concluding that the fishing right included 1) an implied affirmative right of access across private property, 2) implied negative rights restricting the state from charging the tribes license fees or enacting legislation discriminating against their fishing, and 3) an implied affirmative right to one-half of the harvests. Presumably, these results were necessary to fulfill the treaties' central purpose of allowing the tribes to pursue a fishing livelihood, but they had no apparent effect on the SRBA court's conclusion that the tribe had no off-reservation water rights.[35]

Central to the SRBA court's decision was its conclusion that the treaty created no property rights in water off the tribe's reservation. The court's reasoning was based on the flawed logic of the federal district court of Idaho which, in an earlier case (the Hells Canyon case discussed below), concluded that since the tribe had no ownership rights in specific fish due to the treaty, Idaho Power Company dams could kill fish and destroy fish habitat with impunity. But in reality the tribe's right of taking fish is a *profit à prendre*, a real property right recognized at common law, and one that has enabled other profit holders to restrain developments damaging habitat necessary to a reasonable exercise of the profit.[36]

Finally, the SRBA court's decision rested on a conclusion that an 1893 agreement in which the Nez Perce agreed to a "present and total surrender of all tribal interests," except as reserved in the agreement, eliminated any possibility of reserved water rights. In convoluted reasoning, the court opined that — despite the fact that the 1893 agreement expressly reserved the tribes' off-reservation fishing rights — there were no off-reservation water rights, basically because the court refused to recognize them. Thus, an agreement diminishing the size of tribe's land reservation necessarily diminished its water rights. To reach this result the court had to confuse proprietary rights (like fishing and water rights) with sovereign powers (like the power to regulate), rely on an irrelevant Supreme Court case concerning sovereignty, and ignore a more recent, relevant Supreme Court case on proprietary rights.[37]

The tenuous reasoning employed by the SRBA court ought to mean that the result will not survive an appeal, and the case is under appeal as of this writing. After the SRBA decision was handed down, the tribe learned that the presiding judge was in fact a water right holder who had a pecuniary stake in his decision, as did his family. Thus, he should have disqualified himself from the case, or at least disclosed his and his family's stakes in the case to the parties. The fact that he did not seems a violation of the state code of judicial conduct.

If the SRBA decision is not revoked due to a breach of judicial ethics, the only courts to which the decision may be appealed are the Idaho Supreme Court and the U.S. Supreme Court. State courts have been historically hostile to tribal reserved water rights, and the U.S. Supreme Court has been antagonistic to almost all Indian rights for nearly two decades. If results like the SRBA decision are upheld, the 21st century will be remembered as a time in which tribes lost their most precious remaining natural resource, their water, through judicial opinions.[38]

Timber Harvests

Timber harvests on steep slopes and in riparian areas can adversely affect fish habitat as much as water diversions, dam operations, or other aquatic developments. Timber harvests are also an important source of employment for small rural communities in the Pacific Northwest. In response to logging restrictions imposed to protect species dependent on forest habitat, particularly restrictions in the Northwest Forest Plan, Congress included in a 1995 appropriations bill a rider with several provisions designed to expedite public land timber harvests, known as the Timber Salvage Rider.[39]

One of the timber harvest authorizations contained in the 1995 Act required federal land managers to release from habitat protection restrictions "notwithstanding any other provisions of law," all uncompleted timber sales which had been subject to an earlier appropriations rider that expired before the sales were finished. Most of those sales were never subsequently offered due to habitat restrictions like those imposed by the Northwest Forest Plan. Consequently, the Timber Salvage Rider directed land managers to complete those earlier timber sales despite the plan's restrictions, including eight sales on the former reservation of the Klamath tribes in south-central Oregon.[40]

The tribes sought to enjoin these revived timber harvests, claiming that the 1995 statute was not intended to abrogate their treaty rights to hunt and fish, and that the timber sales would destroy prime old-growth habitat for mule deer necessary for their subsistence. The tribes also argued that by offering the sales, the Forest Service breached its fiduciary duty to the tribes by failing to manage their former reservation lands to protect their treaty rights. The federal government agreed that the statute did not abrogate the tribes' treaty rights, but maintained that the sales did not offend treaty rights because the Forest Service consulted with the tribes throughout the process of awarding the sales. Timber companies and contractors awarded the sales intervened in the case and claimed that the appropriations rider terminated the tribes' treaty rights with respect to the sales.[41]

The district court agreed with the tribes and enjoined the timber sales in 1996. First, the court concluded that the Timber Salvage Rider did not abrogate the tribes' treaty rights because the statute contained no "clear and reliable evidence" that Congress intended abrogation. Second, the court agreed with both the tribes and the federal government that the government had a fiduciary obligation to consult with the tribes. But the court ruled that the government also had "a substantive duty to protect 'to the fullest extent possible' the tribes' treaty rights, and the resources on which those rights depend." The court therefore enjoined the timber sales until the government "assur[ed], in consultation with the Klamath Tribes on a government-to-government basis, that the resources on which the tribes' treaty rights depend will be protected." By separating the federal government's procedural duties from its substantive duties, the decision clearly indicated that there is a federal duty to protect tribal property rights.[42]

The Hells Canyon Case

The cases discussed above demonstrate that the treaty fishing right has been regularly interpreted to contain an implied right of habitat protection. Unfortunately, while the case law reflects a consistent conclusion that the *piscary profit* gives the tribes some authority to restrain habitat-damaging developments, the courts have been unclear about the scope of the right. In fact, in the case described below, an Idaho federal magistrate completely ignored the Supreme Court's moderate living standard in denying the Nez Perce Tribe's claim for compensation for habitat damages due to Idaho Power Company's Hells Canyon dams.

The Nez Perce sued Idaho Power, alleging that the construction and operation of its three-dam complex in the Hells Canyon reach of the Snake River violated treaty rights by reducing the number of salmon returned to tribal fishing grounds and by inundating those grounds. The tribe argued that it was entitled to damages under section 10(c) of the Federal Power Act. That provision makes each licensee under the Act "liable for all damages" to the "property" of others caused by the construction, maintenance, or operation of its projects.[43]

The decision was written by a U.S. magistrate, whose opinion was subsequently adopted by the federal district court. The magistrate rejected the tribe's claims because he concluded that the tribe had no property rights for which compensation was due, since it did not own the individual fish in a salmon run. Although the magistrate's reasoning misinterpreted treaty rights case law and reflected an extremely unsophisticated view of property rights, the result is actually not entirely inconsistent with the *United States v. Washington* Phase II district court decision, which was limited to prospective, equitable relief — not retrospective, monetary damages. The magistrate's confusion about the nature of the treaty right to fish was a product of his failure to consider most of the decisions discussed earlier in this chapter, his misunderstanding of the few cases he did mention, and his inability to see that the treaties created property rights, a concept the Supreme Court had firmly established nearly 90 years earlier.[44]

The court's basic mistake was its attempt to separate treaty rights from property rights, due in part to Supreme Court precedent suggesting that terminating a tribe's treaty hunting or fishing rights would amount to a governmental taking of property requiring constitutional compensation. Since all parties stipulated that the Snake River salmon runs had "greatly declined since the Hells Canyon Dam Complex was commenced in the mid 1950s," the magistrate distinguished the earlier Supreme Court decision on the ground that there the tribe was seeking damages from a private party, not the federal government. By characterizing the tribe's claim as "treaty rights", not "property rights," the magistrate apparently thought he could limit tribal compensation claims to those against the government. The trouble with this distinction is that it not only ignored the Supreme Court's 90-year old language in *U.S. v. Winans,* it also ignored the results of a number of more recent Supreme Court and lower court decisions making clear that the treaty right is a property right which burdens non-parties to the agreement, including both private parties and subsequently created states.[45]

The magistrate was also convinced that the "tribe owns only an opportunity to exploit" the salmon runs. However, in 1979 the Supreme Court specifically rejected the notion that the treaty fishing right was only an opportunity to harvest fish on a nondiscriminatory basis. According to the Court, the treaty reserved to the tribes more than "merely the chance . . . occasionally to dip their nets into the territorial waters." Moreover, even if the tribe possessed only an equal opportunity to harvest, the magistrate's conclusion that it had no common law remedy for interference with that right hardly follows. As long ago as 1809, English courts recognized that the owner of a duck pond had a cause of action against someone who drove away ducks with gunfire because "he that hinders another in his trade or livelihood is liable . . . for so hindering him." In modern times, fishers have successfully maintained common law actions against those causing environmental damage to fisheries. Even recreational users have been successful. In 1994, for example, the Wisconsin Supreme Court recognized that the owner of a hunting and fishing *profit à prendre* had a right to enjoin a housing development which would have "unreasonably interfered" with the exercise of the profit. Certainly the Nez Perce Tribe, whose treaty fishing right promised the tribe, in the words of the Supreme Court, a "livelihood — that is to say, a moderate living," ought to have at least as much protection as recreationalists without treaty rights.[46]

The magistrate quoted from the vacated Ninth Circuit panel decision in *U.S. v. Washington*, which recognized that the treaty fishing right applied to "the building of dams, factories and highways provided they are State-authorized." But he failed to emphasize that the panel decision also ruled that the treaties imposed an affirmative obligation on federal and state governments to "take reasonable . . . compensatory steps to protect and enhance the fishery" when approving projects "threaten[ing] then-existing harvest levels." There are numerous problems with this articulation of the scope of the treaty duty, including the fact that the vacated panel decision misinterpreted Supreme Court precedent by excluding private parties from treaty-imposed duties. The Ninth Circuit panel also apparently assumed without evidence that the tribes' moderate living needs were satisfied by then-existing harvest levels. Nevertheless, even though it rejected the tribes' claim of damages for the construction and operation of the Hells Canyon complex, by adopting the vacated panel decision the magistrate presumably accepted the fundamental premise of that decision, which affirmed the existence of a habitat protection right.[47]

Perhaps the most problematic aspect of the Hells Canyon decision was the district court's rejection of damages not only for the decline in salmon runs but also for destroying tribal fishing grounds drowned behind Idaho Power Company's reservoirs. This inundation claim was the subject of a separate decision of the magistrate, who concluded that Idaho Power could be held liable for the inundation of the tribe's fishing grounds. But the district court refused the magistrate's recommendation and held that the tribe's right of access was nothing more than a right to cross land to reach the river to fish. The court exaggerated the tribe's claim to amount to a right to prohibit all development of the river banks and responded that the treaty gave the tribe no such protection. The result is inconsistent with a number of other decisions, including the Supreme Court's admonition that the treaty right prevents the tribes from being "crowded out" of their fisheries.[48]

The reasoning of the court in the Hells Canyon case was deeply flawed. At a basic level, the court failed to recognize that the Indian treaty fishing right is a *piscary profit à prendre*; that is, a property right. Some 90 years before the Hells Canyon decision, the Supreme Court described the fishing right as a "servitude" and a "right in land." If there is a defensible justification for enjoining the Winans brothers' exclusion of tribal fishers from Celilo Falls in the 1890s, while refusing compensation in the 1990s for Idaho Power Company's inundation of fishing sites in Hells Canyon, the explanation does not lie in attempting to label the treaty right as something other than a property right. Idaho Power seemed to recognize this reality, paying the tribe over $11 million not to appeal the case.[49]

Although the court's concern about establishing an "absolute" environmental right that would block all development is understandable, its error was in assuming that recognizing the treaty right as a property right would produce such a result. Few property rights are absolute. And remedies for rights violations are contextual, not universal. An understanding of the great flexibility inherent in most property concepts would have allowed the court to avoid the embarrassment of attempting to deny what the Supreme Court had expressly recognized nearly a century earlier. How to articulate the scope of the treaty right in a way that avoids establishing an absolute environmental right that would trump all development, yet is faithful to the Supreme Court's interpretation that the treaty right is a property right, is the subject of the next section.[50]

The Courts' Failure to Come to Grips with the Treaty Right

The uncertain scope of the right of habitat protection has been an overriding concern of the courts that have considered the issue. For example, the *en banc* panel of the Ninth Circuit in *U.S. v. Washington* was leery of articulating a right of habitat protection in a case without concrete facts, possibly because it feared that application of the district court's decision could result in a widespread halting of development throughout the Pacific Northwest. Similarly, the Ninth Circuit's opinion in the Klamath water rights case, the Washington Supreme Court's opinion in the *Acquavella* case, and the Idaho district court's decision in the Hells Canyon case all reflect a judicial reluctance to express the scope of the treaty fishing right in a manner that might require a restoration of conditions that existed at treaty time.

This judicial concern with the specter of establishing a "wilderness servitude," as the Klamath court phrased it, is actually quite detached from reality. Nowhere in the Pacific Northwest do the fish at the center of the treaty bargain — the "res" (the object) of the treaties, as Judge (now Justice) Kennedy once put it, benefit from treaty-time conditions. Moreover, no tribe has argued for restoration of those conditions. The reality is that, far from returning to the pristine environment the judiciary has found worrisome, current conditions threaten several salmon runs with extinction. Judicial predictions about the success of federal and state restoration programs rendering the treaty habitat right unnecessary have proved to be fanciful. The truth is that widespread habitat degradation has been the rule, producing a status quo in which the tribes frequently "dip their nets and come up empty," a condition that the Supreme Court proscribed more than two decades ago.[51]

A second flaw in the courts' opinions is the assumption that because the tribes have a property right to protect the salmon, it necessarily is an absolute right. Not only are few property rights absolute, the tribal "right of taking fish" is an unlikely candidate for an absolute property right, since it is shared "in common with the citizens of the territory." Moreover, the treaty right is a qualified right, subject to regulation to conserve the essential consideration of the treaties, the fish. Non-treaty fishers are subject to the same conservation requirements. Non-treaty *development* should be subject to the same restrictions that burden non-treaty fishing. Surely it should not be more difficult to protect the treaty fishing right by restricting hydroelectric operations or timber harvests than by restricting non-treaty fishing if the damage to the treaty fishing right is otherwise equal.

A third shortcoming in decisions like the *Acquavella* water rights adjudication and the Hells Canyon dam case is the failure to see that, by its very nature as a *profit à prendre,* the treaty fishing right hardly threatens to establish a wilderness servitude. The Supreme Court has made clear that the scope of the right is cabined by the moderate living standard. At common law, the scope of protection afforded *profits à prendre* is "no unreasonable interference" with the exercise of the profit. Applying this "no unreasonable interference" standard to a tribe's moderate living needs obviously would require judicial discretion. But prior case law and administrative orders involving the application of the treaty right against non-treaty fishers have narrowed the scope of that discretion. If the overarching goal is to protect the fish, the "res" of the treaty, the courts — who, in Judge Kennedy's words, have constructive custody of the fish — should apply the same principles to both those who harvest the "res" of the treaties by destroying salmon habitat and those who harvest by hook-and-line.[52]

The Proper Scope of the Treaty Right to Habitat Protection

In defining what constitutes an "unreasonable interference" with the treaty fishing right, the courts ought to draw heavily on the conservation standards laid down in the case law allocating harvest rights between treaty and non-treaty fishers. The first principle that these cases establish is that the preservation needs of the salmon take precedence over competing harvest rights. As Justice Douglas once wrote, the treaties give no one the right to harvest "the last living steelhead," and salmon need not "follow[ ] the fate of the passenger pigeon." Courts have curtailed both tribal and non-tribal fisheries under this principle. Applying this "preserve the res" (to paraphrase Justice Kennedy) priority to development projects which damage fish habitat should be no different than in harvest allocation cases: development activities which threaten the existence of a fish run should be prohibited. In the language of *profit à prendre* law, such developments "unreasonably interfere" with the exercise of the profit *per se*.[53]

But the purpose of the treaty fishing right is not simply to preserve museum-piece fish runs; the purpose is to provide the tribes with "a livelihood . . . a moderate living." Thus, an unreasonable interference with the treaty fishing right should be articulated in terms of the moderate living promise. The contours of the right exist in two court opinions and in a 1997 secretarial order on tribal rights, federal trust responsibilities, and the Endangered Species Act.

The first court opinion outlining the scope of the treaty habitat protection right is Judge Belloni's 1969 "fair share" opinion, which provided a mixture of procedural and substantive protection for treaty harvests. In addition to instructing the state to revise its regulatory policies to ensure that the tribal harvests were considered on an equal basis with non-Indian harvests, he directed the state to allow the tribes to "participate meaningfully" in harvest management decision making and to ensure that restrictions on tribal harvests were "the least restrictive alternative" consistent with preserving salmon for spawning. The Ninth Circuit ultimately ruled that the state's obligation to provide the tribes with a fair harvest share was a separate duty from its obligation to guarantee the tribes access to their fishing grounds.[54]

The second opinion is Judge Reinhardt's concurrence in the *United States v. Washington*, Phase II panel opinion, which also adopted a blend of procedural and substantive protections. As Judge Reinhardt explained:

> If it is inconceivable that the Indians would have agreed to be required
> to fish on the same terms as non-Indians, it is far more inconceivable
> that they would have allowed the State to permit the fishery to be
> destroyed altogether. Merely because the treaty does not provide
> absolute protections, then, does not mean that the rights of the Indians
> to an equal share of fish can be subrogated to other state goals. On the
> contrary, the treaty guarantees that the Indians' supply of fish must be
> safeguarded . . . by every reasonable means.

Like Judge Belloni, Judge Reinhardt called for a demonstration of "due consideration" of the treaty rights throughout the regulatory process and "full participation" of the tribes in making decisions about developments that affect the treaty right. Judge Reinhardt added that development must include an evaluation of feasible alternative locations, incorporation of all reasonable mitigation measures, and a demonstration that the project is "necessary in light of its probable adverse impact on the Indians' fish supply." Unfortunately, Judge Reinhardt also stated that where the fish supply could not "be protected by any other reasonable means, the State may as a last resort require the permittee to pay compensation to the Indians." This misguided interpretation would give states, and presumably federal agencies, unprecedented authority to abrogate treaty rights, authority the courts have wisely limited to Congress, and even then only if Congress is explicit.[55]

A third approach to protecting treaty fishing rights against environmental degradation was provided by a 1997 order issued by the Secretaries of the Interior and Commerce on tribal rights, federal trust responsibilities, and the Endangered Species Act. The order echoed many of the judicially created standards to protect the treaty fishing right. It required that 1) any restrictions imposed on treaty rights must be "reasonable and necessary" for conservation of the species; 2) the conservation purpose served by these restrictions cannot be achieved by reasonable restrictions of non-Indian fishers alone; 3) the restrictions must be the least restrictive alternative in order to achieve the benefits of development; 4) the restrictions cannot discriminate in any way against treaty fishing; and 5) voluntary tribal conservation measures must be inadequate to achieve the conservation purposes before restrictions are imposed.[56]

From these three primary sources, as well as from other case law, the following principles derive. There is an obligation to protect salmon habitat necessary to effectuate the treaty fishing right, but the treaties do not demand a return to the environmental conditions that existed at the time the treaties were signed. The treaty obligations run not merely to the federal and state governments but, as evident from the Supreme Court's 1905 *Winans* decision, to private parties as well. Private parties have no more authority than governments to exclude tribes from their fishing grounds, to deprive them of their fair share of the salmon runs, or to destroy treaty-protected fish. However, private parties requiring government approval for their developments may use the approval process to demonstrate compliance with treaty obligations. State or federal agencies which initiate their own projects, or approve third-party developments, may demonstrate that their actions will not unreasonably interfere with the treaty *piscary profit à prendre* by satisfying the following five requirements:

1. Consider treaty rights, specifically the tribes' right to a moderate living from fishing, throughout the development process;

2. Give tribes the opportunity to participate meaningfully as governments in all development decisions;

3. Ensure that developments do not interfere with tribal moderate living needs;

4. If tribes have not yet attained a moderate living, demonstrate that the development will not "unreasonably interfere" with the attainment of a "moderate living," which would require satisfying six criteria:

    a. showing that the benefits of the development cannot be achieved without adverse effects on treaty fishing rights;

    b. showing that the development is necessary despite those adverse effects;

c. showing that the development does not discriminate, expressly or implicitly, against treaty fishing;

d. showing that the development is the least restrictive imposition on treaty rights available to achieve the benefits of the development;

e. showing that the development incorporates all reasonable measures to reduce the adverse effects on treaty fishing; and

f. showing that, despite the adverse effects of the development, the tribal moderate living needs will be met within a reasonable period of time; and

5. Provide the tribes with "just compensation" for the loss or diminishment of treaty rights if the proposed development satisfies the above criteria but still produces a significant loss of treaty fishing rights which impairs tribal moderate living needs. This compensation must be congressionally approved before the project may proceed.[57]

The "no unreasonable interference" standard that protects common law *profits à prendre*, as defined by the principles articulated above, would avoid the prospect of imposition of a "wilderness servitude" or a return to the environmental conditions that existed at the time the treaties were signed. However, it would promise some restoration, as the above principles would not be limited to new developments but would apply equally to ongoing activities like the operation of Columbia Basin dams. Thus, this property rights approach to the treaty fishing promise would provide meaningful protection and restoration to the remaining salmon runs on which the United States promised tribal members they could pursue their livelihoods, which promise was the basis of the bargain for permitting peaceful settlement of the Pacific Northwest.

Protection of salmon through 19th century Indian treaties is slow, uncertain, and costly, since it involves federal court review. Yet there is no ready alternative, and the judicial process has been at least as successful as alternative administrative and legislative processes, where the tribes were much less likely to obtain fair results. It is instructive to note that both judges who have presided over *United States v. Oregon*, allocating Columbia River salmon harvests — Judges Belloni and Marsh — eventually disqualified themselves as being biased in favor of the tribes. They were not biased when they began to preside over the case, but as they became educated, both decided that the tribes had the superior moral and legal arguments. The judgments of these respected jurists, the product of long-term involvement in treaty rights disputes, should not go unnoticed. Consider these remarks from Judge Marsh after he disqualified himself:

> What remains to be seen is how those treaty rights will be affected by the dwindling sizes [of fish runs] and to what extent those treaty rights may be used as a means of exploring salmon protection measures far beyond what anybody could imagine [under environmental statutes like the ESA]. . . . You can hear why I'm getting off the case.[58]

In January 2001, twenty tribes in Washington state went back to federal court, alleging that the state's poor construction and faulty maintenance of culverts (pipes carrying water under roads and railroad tracks and through embankments) violated their treaty rights. The tribes claimed that improperly designed and maintained culverts block salmon from over 3,000 miles of streams, one reason why they now harvest no more total fish than they did prior to Judge Boldt's 1974 decision. The outcome of this lawsuit may determine, thirty years after the filing of *U.S. v. Washington*, whether the tribes' treaty rights protect the habitat on which salmon depend for their survival.[59]

13 – SAVING SNAKE RIVER SALMON BY BREACHING DAMS

The plight of the Snake River salmon became one of the nation's foremost environmental issues at the dawn of the 21st century, even rising to the attention of the 2000 Presidential candidates. The Snake is the Columbia River's largest tributary, and the Snake Basin, including Idaho's famed Salmon River, contains some of the best remaining salmon habitat in the Columbia Basin. Historically, the Salmon River produced over 40 percent of the spring/summer chinook of the entire Columbia Basin. But, as discussed in chapter 9, all Snake River salmon runs are now on the endangered species list. This is due largely to the fact that Snake River salmon must traverse a series of federal dams along the lower 140 miles of the Snake (see map 10).

These four federal dams — Ice Harbor, Lower Monumental, Little Goose, and Lower Granite Dams — are all operated by the U.S. Army Corps of Engineers. Not only have the four Lower Snake Dams destroyed spawning grounds, they also pose substantial obstacles to both upstream and downstream migrating salmon. Although there are other causes for the decline of Snake River salmon, the overwhelming reason for their listing under the Endangered Species Act was the construction and operation of these dams over the last forty years.[1]

Since approval of the Columbia Basin Fish and Wildlife Program in 1982, restoring Snake River salmon runs has been a regional priority. The Endangered Species Act listings of the 1990s added a federal restoration plan through the ESA's federal consultation process. Neither plan has produced the promised restoration, however, despite reported expenditures as high as $3 billion — although that figure is vigorously challenged by some, who dispute the premise that the primary purpose of the Columbia Basin dams is to maximize hydroelectric revenues. This failure is not altogether surprising given that the NMFS 1995-99 BiOp governing hydroelectric operations authorized dam-related mortalities of up to 86 percent of juvenile sockeye and spring/summer chinook and up to 99 percent of juvenile fall chinook.[2]

Map 10 — The Lower Snake, Hanford, and John Day Reaches

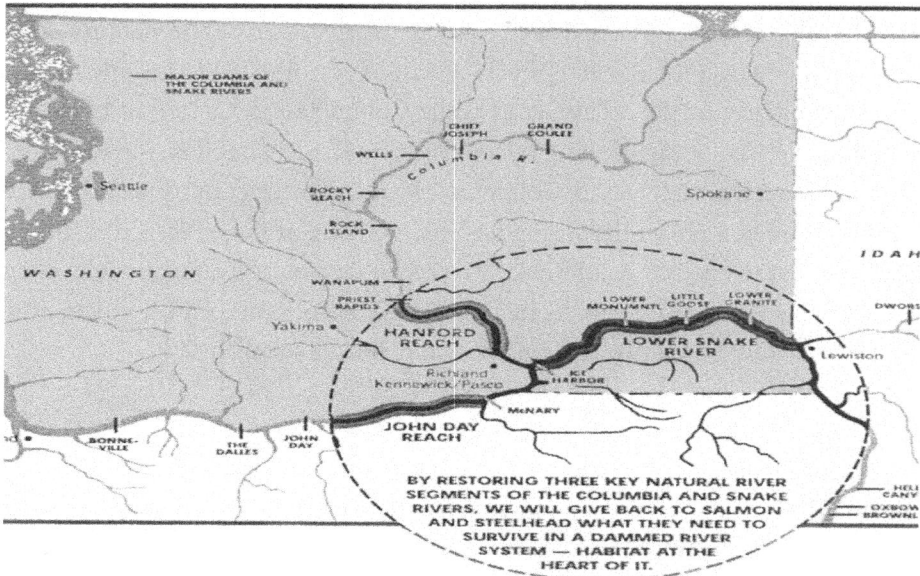

Courtesy of the Save Our Wild Salmon Coalition

Although the 1995-99 BiOp on hydroelectric operations recognized the need for "major modifications" to federal dams, no significant changes ensued. Instead, the centerpiece of the salmon restoration program continues to be a program of trucking and barging juvenile salmon around the dams, a technique that has not survived scientific scrutiny. Although the dam breaching option has substantial scientific support, and studies have shown it to be economically feasible, it generated a wave of opposition throughout the rural Northwest, particularly from elected officials.[3]

The strength of the political opposition to breaching was somewhat surprising since the federal dams on the Lower Snake are hardly an important part of the regional economy. They were authorized in the post-World War II era as make-work projects, despite a cost-benefit ratio of just fifteen cents of benefits for every dollar of costs. They provide no flood control benefits. They produce only small hydropower benefits, which are replaceable. The irrigation they supply serves only thirteen corporate farms. They do supply a navigation channel that makes Lewiston, Idaho, over 450 miles from the ocean, a seaport, but that navigation is some of the most heavily subsidized transportation in the United States. Moreover, there is evidence suggesting that the overall economic benefits of breaching the Lower Snake Dams could substantially outweigh their costs, particularly if the real costs of the dams to the salmon runs are accounted for. One study estimated those costs to be approximately $500 million annually and the loss of 25,000 family- wage jobs in fishing and related industries. This chapter makes the scientific, economic, and legal case for dam breaching.[4]

The Transportation Program

For roughly 25 years, the Corps of Engineers has been transporting salmon smolt by truck and barge to avoid mortalities at the dams and in the reservoirs. This program has created the odd situation of sometimes trucking salmon on Interstate 84, the highway paralleling the Columbia, while grain and other agricultural products float in barges on the river. Although the transportation program has been unable to reverse long-term run size declines, NMFS has continued the transport of juvenile fish under ESA consultation. Since the status quo seems to be a recipe for extinction of several salmon species, in its 2000 BiOp NMFS was basically faced with a choice between improving the transportation program and breaching the four Lower Snake River dams. It chose the former, including improved barging and trucking techniques, structural changes at the dams, and increased flow augmentation to speed the fish to their collection points and to help those which cannot be collected migrate in-river. More flow augmentation, which the 2000 BiOp asks for but does not require, would mean drafting additional amounts of water from Upper Snake Basin reservoirs, with potentially adverse effects on irrigated agriculture, power generation, and resident fish.[5]

Several scientific studies in recent years have called into question the efficacy of continued reliance of truck and barge transportation as the linchpin of Snake River salmon recovery efforts. These reports have suggested that a better alternative would be a program based on restoring natural river conditions. Following is a discussion of eight recent scientific reports.

The Science of Dam Breaching vs. Transportation

The Detailed Fishery Operating Plan (1993). In November 1993, federal and state fishery agencies and treaty Indian tribes, through the interagency Columbia Basin Fish and Wildlife Authority, prepared a comprehensive plan for operating Columbia Basin dams in a manner compatible with salmon migration. The plan advocated seasonal reservoir drawdowns and flow augmentation to help restore more natural river conditions. The fishery agencies and tribes concluded that barge and truck transport of juvenile salmon could not overcome poor river conditions created by the operation of the dams and noted that the transportation program had failed to halt the decline of the Snake River runs. The state agencies recommended restricting use of transportation to a "last resort," to be used only in extremely low flow conditions; the tribes opposed continuing transportation under any circumstances.[6]

The plan called for drawdowns of the Lower Snake River reservoirs to "minimum operating pools" between April 15 and December 1 of each year. This seasonal drawdown plan, which originated in a proposal of Idaho Governor Cecil Andrus at the "Salmon Summit" in 1991 (chapter 9), was subsequently dropped for being of questionable efficacy at high economic cost. The 1993 operating plan also endorsed significant amounts of flow augmentation from both Dworshak reservoir on the Clearwater River and reservoirs in the Upper Snake Basin, calling for 927,000 acre-feet from Upper Snake reservoirs in 1994 and 1.927 million acre-feet by 1998. A 1994 report of the Northwest Power Planning Council's Snake River Basin Water Committee indicated that over a million acre-feet of water, above and beyond the 427,000 acre-feet called for by the Council's 1991 program, was available through a combination of initiatives such as conjunctive ground and surface water management programs, dry year water leases, and land fallowing.[7]

The Independent Peer Review of Transportation (1994). Because NMFS's 1993 hydropower BiOp relied heavily on truck and barge transport — a status quo that caused a federal judge to suggest that salmon recovery efforts need "a major overhaul" — representatives from NMFS, the U.S. Fish and Wildlife Service, state fisheries agencies, and treaty Indian tribes convened a peer review panel to study the scientific issues involved in the transportation program. The ensuing report, completed in May 1994, concluded that the transportation approved by the NMFS BiOp was "unlikely to halt or prevent continued decline and extirpation of listed species of salmon in the Snake River Basin." The report noted that while transportation provides "a temporary respite" from dam-related mortalities, it failed to protect salmon from mortalities associated with river system conditions that exist throughout the salmon life cycle. Therefore, the report explained, "[i]n terms of effecting a program of salmon recovery, it really doesn't matter if the transported salmon survive at a higher rate than untransported salmon, unless the overall survival rate for the population is sufficient to [recover the species]."[8]

The Independent Peer Review criticized the transportation program for proceeding in the absence of a standard for hydroelectric passage survival. The scientists observed that this deficiency made the utility of the transportation program "highly speculative," despite preliminary indications that some salmon species seemed to benefit from transportation under the adverse river conditions existing at the time the transportation experiments were conducted. The report also questioned a key assumption of the preliminary studies, which had claimed apparent benefits from transportation by explaining that "[f]ish appeared to be similarly handled and marked" regardless of whether they were transported or designated for in-river migration. The scientists suggested that the critical premise underlying the studies supportive of transportation — the assumption that juvenile salmon, which were handled and marked and then returned to the river as "control" fish, suffered no mortality as a consequence of this handling and marking — had not been adequately tested and could be seriously flawed. This deficiency, coupled with transportation's potential to induce aberrant homing behavior, adverse genetic effects, and stress resulting in increased vulnerability to predation and disease, led the report to conclude that "[a]vailable evidence is not sufficient to identify transportation as either a primary or supporting method of choice for salmon recovery in the Snake River Basin."[9]

The 1994 Amendments to the Columbia Basin Fish and Wildlife Program. The 1994 amendments to the Northwest Power Planning Council's Columbia Basin Fish and Wildlife Program incorporated a phased approach to Idaho Governor Cecil Andrus's suggested seasonal drawdown plan. The amendments also called for conducting "a mainstem experiment" in which approximately equal numbers of fish would be transported as would be allowed to migrate in-river. This experiment would require a decrease in the number of fish transported in order to allow a legitimate comparison of the ability of transported versus in-river salmon to produce return adults.[10]

Except for the mainstem experiment, the Council voted to restrict transportation to "extremely adverse" river conditions, essentially low water years. Although the Council approved a continuation of transportation in the short term under low flow conditions, it warned that barging and trucking salmon "should not be regarded as a substitute for changes in the river ecosystem" or "as a device to delay substantial improvements in in-river survival conditions."[11]

The Tribal Restoration Plan (1995). In June 1995, the treaty fishing tribes of the Columbia Basin released *Wy-Kan-Ush-Mi Wa-Kish-Wit (The Spirit of the Salmon).* The tribal plan completely eschewed artificial transportation of juvenile salmon, advocating instead gravel-to-gravel salmon management, including dam breaching to restore natural river functions. The tribes called for a long-term goal of achieving "mean historical flows" — defined as flows which would have occurred without water resources development and in the absence of irrigation depletions — during the spring juvenile migration season, and reducing daily and hourly fluctuations in flows occasioned by peak power operations. To help achieve these river flows and to restore ecosystem functions, the tribes called for permanent reservoir drawdowns.[12]

The tribes recommended the immediate termination of artificial transportation, noting that halting transportation would allow the testing of alternative passage measures foreclosed by the transportation program. The tribal position on terminating the transportation program was hardly extreme, as it echoed the Northwest Power Planning Council's earlier call for ending artificial transportation, albeit only in the long term.[13]

The National Research Council Report (1996). In 1992, the National Research Council formed the Committee on Protection and Management of Anadromous Salmon to review the population status, habitat, and environmental requirements of Pacific salmon species in the Northwest. The committee gave only a qualified endorsement to continued transportation in the short run, citing studies showing increased survival of transported salmon compared to salmon migrating in-river. However, the committee failed to consider the fact that, as recognized by the Independent Peer Review of Transportation, salmon migrating in-river suffer stress as a result of marking and handling due to the transportation program, and the committee also seemed to assume that river conditions could never be improved.[14]

One of the reasons the National Research Council overlooked some of the latest scientific information on transportation may have had to do with the composition of the committee, which might have compromised its report. The chief author of the committee's treatment of transportation and its alternatives was Donald Chapman, a biologist who spent his career in the employment of utilities and electricity-intensive industries like aluminum companies. Given the contested nature of salmon science, it was surprising that the National Research Council would choose such an obviously interested scientist. Nevertheless, the report did endorse a policy of reliance on natural river functions in the long run, arguing that:

a pragmatic approach to improving the situation that relies on natural regenerative processes in the long term and the selected use of technology and human effort in the short term . . . rather than on a primary emphasis on substitution, *i.e.*, the use of technologies and energy inputs, such as hatcheries, artificial transportation, and modification of stream channels.[15]

This endorsement of restoring natural river functions would be echoed in subsequent reports, particularly in the Northwest Power Planning Council's Independent Scientific Group report that same year.

The Independent Scientific Group Report (1996). In 1994, the Northwest Power Planning Council established the Independent Scientific Group (ISG). Comprised of eminent scientists and structured to insulate them from political influences, the ISG's purpose was to analyze the science underlying the Council's fish and wildlife program and to suggest a scientific foundation for the program. Two years later, in 1996, the ISG issued its report, which criticized the Council's program for lacking a coherent conceptual foundation and recommended what it called "normative river" conditions, or the restoration of ecological processes consistent with the needs of native fish and wildlife species. The scientists faulted salmon restoration efforts for relying on such failed technological fixes as hatcheries and artificial transport of juvenile salmon, and it suggested that technology was an unlikely substitute for a natural river system. The ISG noted that these technologies were adopted with little or no scientific study and recommended that in the future such measures should bear the burden of proof, implemented only after intensive evaluation.[16]

The report concluded that, even after a quarter-century of experience, "[a]vailable evidence is not sufficient to identify transportation as either a primary or supporting method of choice for salmon recovery in the Snake River Basin." This conclusion was the result of the scientists' finding that artificial transport cannot provide "the minimum survival rates necessary for the maintenance of population levels . . . let alone those survival rates necessary for rebuilding of salmon populations." Rebuilding salmon populations is critical if salmon runs are to become viable components of the region's economy. Instead of barging juvenile salmon around the dams, the ISG report called for restoration of river flows as close as possible to the hydrograph that existed in the pre-dam era and for maintenance and restoration of mainstem spawning habitat like that which exists in the undammed Hanford Reach of the Mid-Columbia River. The Hanford Reach is the last free-flowing stretch of the mainstem Columbia or Snake Rivers which supports self-sustaining salmon populations.

To accomplish mainstem habitat restoration, the ISG recommended permanent reservoir drawdowns, specifically suggesting that the John Day or McNary reservoirs be lowered to expose alluvial reaches that historically supported salmon spawning. The report also noted that drawdowns of the Lower Snake reservoirs would be consistent with its normative river concept. The scientists called attention to the restoration of mainstem habitat, rather than tributary habitat, because it was the mainstem which historically supported "metapopulations" of salmon — large populations which allow for dispersal of spawners to neighboring areas, facilitating recolonization of habitats where extinction has occurred. The ISG argued that restoration efforts should focus on areas that historically were home to metapopulations. Restoring areas that historically supported salmon populations in the mainstem will require permanent reservoir drawdowns and breaching of some dams.[17]

The Idaho Department of Fish and Game Report (1998). In May 1998, the Idaho Department of Fish and Game (IDFG) issued a report on the causes of the decline of Idaho salmon and the available options for recovery. The report concluded that the primary cause of the decline of Idaho salmon was the construction and operation of the federal dams built in the 1960s and 1970s. The report also observed that the transportation program "has not compensated for the dams and is unlikely to provide recovery." The IDFG called for the establishment of a 2 to 6 percent smolt-to-adult survival standard for salmon recovery and embraced the independent scientists' concept of a "normative river" as the best means to achieve this standard. The report observed that "[a]vailable data provide no indication [the current transportation program] can sustain a 2-6% smolt-to-adult survival" and noted that current operations also fail to meet both the 24- and 100-year survival standards.[18]

With the status quo not a viable option, the IDFG report considered two available alternatives: an improved transportation program or restored natural river flows. It rejected transportation for three reasons: 1) uncertainties over the efficacy of untested surface collectors (which would be at the heart of an improved transportation program); 2) the fact that it would take over a decade for surface collectors to be tested and installed; and 3) the fact that an improved transportation program would doubtless require additional water stored in reservoirs in Idaho to flush salmon through the reservoirs to collection stations. The IDFG concluded that existing "data does not indicate flow augmentation can provide enough survival benefits for recovery," citing Idaho's comments to NMFS which claimed that "[h]istorical water velocities cannot be attained with current reservoirs, even using all reservoir storage in the basin." As a result, the IDFG endorsed dam breaching to create natural river conditions, noting that breaching had "a high likelihood of meeting recovery standards." The report concluded that "the natural river option is the best biological choice for recovery of salmon and steelhead in Idaho. This assessment is logical, biologically sound, has the highest certainty of success and lowest risk of failure, and is consistent with the preponderance of scientific data."[19]

The PATH Reports. The Plan for Analyzing and Testing Hypotheses (PATH) was an interagency working group of 25 scientists created by NMFS's 1995 BiOp on hydroelectric operations. The BiOp charged PATH with evaluating alternative models for Snake River salmon recovery in order to help NMFS make a decision, on the basis of the best available science, whether to continue the artificial transportation program or to recommend dam breaching. NMFS created PATH to review the scientific uncertainties affecting salmon survival and "using expert judgment, based on all existing evidence, to quantify the relative degree of belief in . . . conflicting hypotheses about the effects of management actions on stock performances." PATH studies followed scientific procedures developed by scientific consensus and were peer reviewed.[20]

In a March 1998 report, PATH scientists compared three alternatives under three computer models: 1) maintaining the status quo, 2) pursuing maximum transportation, 3) recommending drawdowns to natural river levels. Under one computer model, Fish

Leaving Under Several Hypotheses (FLUSH), developed by the fishery agencies and tribes, the natural river drawdown was the best alternative for salmon recovery. However, another model, Columbia River Salmon Passage (CRiSP), developed by University of Washington scientists and supported by the Bonneville Power Administration, found drawdowns to be the worst alternative.[21]

A revised analysis in August 1998, however, concluded that the natural river drawdown was the best alternative for recovery in the long run, with close to a 100 percent likelihood of recovery over the 48-year and 100-year time periods. The CRiSP model remained considerably more optimistic about short-term (24-year) recovery under the transportation alternative than the FLUSH model (a 61 percent chance of meeting the survival standard versus a 10 percent chance under the FLUSH model), but even the CRiSP model found the natural river alternative superior to transportation (a 76 percent chance versus a 61 percent chance). The FLUSH model, on the other hand, produced a much lower probability of survival under the transportation alternative: just a 10 percent chance of meeting the survival standard in the short run (24-year period), a 12 percent chance of meeting the standard in the mid-term (48-year period), and a 37 percent chance in the long run (100-year period).[22]

After analyzing the August 1998 PATH results, staff of the Idaho Department of Fish and Game determined that, in light of recent smolt-to-adult returns of transported fish of less than one-half percent, survival rates remain four to twelve times below that required for salmon recovery. The staff concluded:

> The natural river option is now the best biological choice regardless of which aggregate hypothesis (model) is used. The natural river option is the only recovery strategy that is robust enough for the fish under both aggregate hypotheses and a variety of assumptions. . . . Under the natural river option, Snake River fall chinook recovery could approach levels evident in the Hanford Reach, which provides a highly productive fishery.[23]

A report from a PATH "weight of the evidence" workshop in September 1998 provided what was the strongest scientific endorsement yet for breaching the Lower Snake Dams. The weight of the evidence process, probably the most difficult chore for the PATH scientists, was an attempt to scientifically assess competing models and theories about alternative management actions on salmon survival. Four PATH scientists, chosen because they had no direct links to the Pacific Northwest, concluded that breaching the Lower Snake Dams would double the chances for recovering Snake River spring/summer chinook populations within 48 years. According to the scientists, dam breaching would improve the recovery chance from 40 percent under current operations to 79 percent. Barging all possible fish would actually reduce the chances of recovery to 35 percent. The Chief of Fisheries of the Oregon Department of Fish and Wildlife concluded that this report showed that the scientific debate was settled in favor of breaching the dams; what remained, he suggested, was whether the region was willing to pay the social and economic costs of breaching.[24]

The final PATH report for 1998 confirmed that Snake River reservoir drawdowns would give all salmon stocks the best chance of recovery. The report concluded that natural river drawdowns would produce a 100 percent probability of recovering fall chinook and a 47-65 percent chance of recovering spring/summer chinook, depending on how soon dam breaching got underway. In contrast, the report estimated the recovery chances under both current operations and under a maximum transportation alternative at just 15-35 percent.[25]

The A-Fish Appendix (1999). With widespread interest in breaching the Lower Snake Dams as a restoration strategy for imperiled Snake River salmon, the U.S. Army Corps of Engineers began an Environmental Impact Statement (EIS) on the issue. In late 1999, the Corps issued a draft EIS which considered several alternatives to improve salmon migration in the Lower Snake, including breaching, but endorsed none. However, the draft EIS did include an appendix (A-Fish Appendix) written by NMFS, which examined the likely effects of hydroelectric system changes on listed salmon.

NMFS's A-Fish Appendix summarized the results of the PATH studies and NMFS's own Cumulative Risk Initiative (CRI), discussed in chapter 9. The PATH studies suggested that dam breaching was more likely than any other change to meet survival and recovery criteria for listed salmon across the widest range of assumptions and variables. Breaching, in short, was the most "risk averse" alternative. But NMFS noted that PATH did not conclude that dam breaching was either necessary or sufficient for salmon recovery.[26]

The A-Fish Appendix contrasted the PATH findings with those of the CRI, which broadened its analysis beyond the hydropower system to include all sources of salmon mortality. The CRI analysis emphasized that in the case of Snake River spring/summer chinook, the species requiring the largest improvements in annual population growth to reduce extinction risk, breaching would not assuredly recover that species unless dam removal nearly doubled survival below Bonneville Dam. The CRI concluded that the best prospects for spring/summer chinook — which faced a "considerable risk of extinction" within a decade — consisted of a combination of habitat restoration, harvest limits and predator control, in addition to hydropower improvements. For Snake River fall chinook and steelhead — species not as imperiled as Snake River spring/summer chinook — the CRI suggested that extinction risks might be adequately reduced through management actions like harvest reductions, improved transportation and fish passage, or dam breaching. But the A-Fish Appendix admitted that the best alternative for increasing fall chinook populations was dam breaching, since it would provide new spawning and rearing habitat for the largely mainstem-spawning species.[27]

The reluctance of the A-Fish Appendix to endorse breaching was a consequence of the CRI's emphasis on the uncertainties involved in what is called delayed mortality of transported juvenile salmon; that is, unexplained mortalities suffered after transported fish are released above Bonneville Dam. The CRI believed that PATH's emphasis on dam breaching was due to high estimates of delayed mortality, which some recent studies hinted may not be warranted. If delayed mortality is lower than estimated by PATH (which based its conclusions on 1994-96 data), breaching may not be significantly better than transportation, especially for spring/summer chinook. Although the A-Fish

Appendix acknowledged the CRI's warning that short-term extinction risks could be as high as 15 percent over the ensuing decade for Snake River spring/summer chinook populations, it seemed to endorse studies to reduce uncertainties on issues such as delayed mortality, the effects of ocean conditions, the potential for improved hatchery operations, and the connections between habitat conditions and salmon productivity, rather than proceeding with dam breaching.[28]

Critics of the A-Fish Appendix — including scientists from the U.S. Fish and Wildlife Service, the states of Idaho, Oregon, and Washington, and the Columbia River Inter-Tribal Fish Commission — faulted its conclusion that transported fish may have higher survival rates than the PATH data indicated. The critics also questioned the Appendix's assumption that the remaining uncertainties in delayed mortality rates could be resolved through years of additional research, and its suggestion that delayed mortality could be attributed to any source other than the hydroelectric system. The Idaho Department of Fish and Game contrasted adult returns in Lower Columbia runs with adult returns in the Snake runs, the former having a rate of five times the latter since the mid-1980s, and also noted that Snake River populations were below replacement levels in 12 of 16 years since mass transportation began. The U.S. Fish and Wildlife Service included a separate appendix to the Corps' draft EIS, Appendix M, which endorsed breaching as a long-term benefit to both resident and anadromous fish as well as wildlife:

> [Breaching] would improve migration conditions for anadromous salmonids and other migratory fish through the area of the four lower Snake River dams, restore riverine habitat and spawning habitat for fall chinook salmon, and improve water quality. Returning the lower Snake River to a free-flowing river would benefit most resident fish native to the area. . . . Overall sportfishing in the study area would be enhanced. With the restoration of a functioning riparian zone and floodplain, habitat critical for many wildlife species would develop and be maintained in the long term.

> While the breaching of the lower Snake River dams would have some short-term adverse impacts to fish and wildlife resources, the long-term benefits would far outweigh the potential impacts.[29]

Despite this strong endorsement by its sister federal fish agency, NMFS proceeded to adopt the A-Fish Appendix approach in its 2000 BiOp, as discussed in chapter 9. The net effect was to impose a high burden of proof on dam breaching: the breaching alternative would not be recommended unless it could be shown to be the only alternative to avoid extinction. On the basis of this burden of proof the breaching alternative was deferred for at least five to eight years.[30]

The scientific studies discussed above show that a significant part of the scientific community believes that the centerpiece of current recovery efforts, the trucking and barging of juvenile salmon, is a failure and unlikely to restore the Snake River salmon runs. The studies also illuminate a growing scientific consensus that breaching the dams to restore natural river conditions is the best option to save Snake River salmon. As the economic studies discussed below indicate, breaching is also an affordable option.

The Economics of Dam Breaching

Historically, there were four reasons for building dams: 1) flood control, 2) hydropower production, 3) irrigation and water supply, and 4) navigation. Although not traditionally a reason for building dams, recreation is now generally regarded as a fifth category of public benefit. Each of these perceived benefits carries with it certain costs. The perceived benefits of dams usually have been fully quantified and overstated, while the costs have been greatly understated or ignored. Traditionally, cost-benefit analysis did not calculate true social costs, such as environmental damage, amortized dam operating and maintenance costs, and support subsidies like those provided navigators and irrigators. Environmental damages were usually not included in the economic cost-benefit balance sheet because their impacts were dispersed or more difficult to quantify than dam benefits. These costs did not disappear, however — they either became a net drain on the regional economy or reappeared as costs to be paid by taxpayers, ratepayers, or fishermen. In the case of the once abundant Columbia Basin salmon runs, the economic costs have been substantial: up to $500 million a year and 25,000 jobs.[31]

The economic benefits associated with the four Lower Snake Dams are considerably less than for many other dams. This is not altogether surprising, given the Corps of Engineers original estimate of the dams' returning only $1.00 in benefits for every $6.67 in costs. Today these dams provide no flood control and little irrigation, and their hydroelectric production is roughly 5 percent of the Northwest's electricity generation. Their chief economic benefit is navigation: they make Lewiston, 465 miles inland, a seaport. But the barge traffic they allow is some of the most heavily subsidized transportation in the country.[32]

With science increasingly pointing toward dam breaching as the best means of restoring Snake River salmon, the chief issue is whether such a course of action is affordable. A series of recent reports suggests that dam breaching is in fact a viable economic option. Following is a discussion of six of those reports.

The Harza Report (1996). Under a contract with the Corps of Engineers, Harza Northwest issued a report in October 1996 on the economic feasibility of various salmon recovery options, including reservoir drawdowns. The report concluded that permanent natural river drawdowns were ten times less costly and three times faster to implement than seasonal drawdowns. Harza estimated that permanently drawing down the four Lower Snake River dams to restore natural river flows would increase salmon survival by about 72 percent over the status quo and run sizes could be doubled if the drawdowns were coupled with passage improvements at the remaining dams on the Lower Columbia.[33]

The report suggested that the cost of natural river drawdowns could be reduced by planning for the drawdowns in stages, drawing down two reservoirs by 2004 and the other two by 2010. This phased approach would allow navigation, recreation, and hydropower users to develop alternatives in an orderly manner. Costs could be further reduced by eliminating expensive studies and measures to improve the artificial transportation program and to maintain the four Lower Snake Dams. Harza estimated that the annual cost of dam breaching would be $75-$153 million. In contrast, Harza estimated the cost of the current transportation, including flow augmentation, is about $200 million per year.[34]

The Idaho Statesman Report (1997). Between July 20 and 22, 1997, the *Idaho Statesman*, a daily newspaper with the largest circulation in Idaho, published a three-day special report on the feasibility of breaching the Lower Snake Dams to re-establish natural river flows. The report concluded that "[b]reaching is an effective way to save taxpayers and electricity ratepayers the expense of maintaining and fixing dams, boost the region's economy by $248 million, end the burden of the Endangered Species Act, protect Idaho water and restore economic balance." The report suggested that breaching the dams would be "an effective way to restore fish runs to the levels of the 1960s, when 75,000 adult salmon returned to Idaho streams and rivers," and that, without breaching, there is a "high probability" that Idaho salmon will disappear. According to the report, breaching would save $98 million per year in subsidies to barge navigation, create a healthy fishery producing $150 million for Idaho's economy, provide another $98 million in income for the Nez Perce Tribe, and aid Idaho irrigation by reducing or eliminating the need for Idaho storage water to flush juvenile salmon to the sea.[35]

The *Statesman* report noted that the four Lower Snake reservoirs produce just 5 percent of the Northwest's electric power, which could be replaced at competitive prices. The dams also supply water to only thirteen heavily subsidized irrigators and provide no flood control at all. Overall, the report estimated the annual costs of breaching the dams to be $509 million, while the annual benefits would be $692 million, a net benefit of $183 million annually. The report concluded that "[c]ivilization progresses by using the experience of the past to make life better for the next generation. With the advantage of three decades of hindsight, it is easy to see that breaching would put the Northwest back on track." Thus, the leading newspaper in the state of Idaho, not known for endorsing extreme environmental policies, adopted dam breaching as the most cost effective solution to recovering Snake River salmon. Most Idahoans did not agree, a reminder that salmon restoration efforts often are not the product of economically rational decisions.[36]

The Breaking the Deadlock Report (1997). In 1997, Cyrus Noe, editor of *Clearing Up*, a weekly report on Northwest energy and fish and wildlife developments, persuaded a group of representatives from diverse groups throughout the Pacific Northwest to meet and discuss the future of Columbia Basin salmon recovery efforts. After six months, the group issued a report that endorsed setting specific biological objectives to guide fish and wildlife recovery efforts and establishing an integrated fish and wildlife plan grounded on sound science.[37]

To understand the economic implications of potential reservoir drawdowns on the Bonneville Power Administration, the region's federal power marketing agency, the group asked the staff of the Northwest Power Planning Council to perform a "reconnaissance level" cost analysis. The staff analyzed a variety of scenarios, including continuation of current operations, drawdown of the Lower Snake reservoirs and John Day reservoir to natural river levels by 2007, and a staggered drawdown that would take place between 2006 and 2018. The report determined that affordability of each scenario correlated less to the costs of reservoir drawdowns than to the market price of BPA power.[38]

If the price of BPA power remains around 20 mills (1/10 cent per kilowatt hour), the report concluded that "[BPA customers] will do well over the long term, whether the five dams are drawn down or not." If market prices fall to 16 mills, however, BPA would lose about $50 million per year, even under current operations. Drawdowns by 2007 under a 16 mill scenario would produce losses less than BPA's annual debt payment to the U.S. Treasury, an average of about $200 million for twenty years, then would yield net benefits of about $80 million thereafter. A staggered drawdown scenario would cut the losses in half during the first decade, then would produce net revenues of about $100 million annually thereafter. At 20 mills, drawdowns by 2007 would produce annual losses during only six of the thirty-year study period, and net benefits would reach nearly $400 million annually during the second decade. The staggered drawdown would produce a benefit almost immediately, averaging around $300 million annually. Thus, only if BPA rates were to drop around 25 percent would BPA experience deficits, which would occur with or without drawdowns.[39]

The Lansing Report (1998). Economist Philip Lansing, who perhaps represents the polar opposite of Donald Chapman's biological advocacy in service of power interests, produced a report for the Oregon Natural Resources Council Fund that explored not just the economic costs of natural river restoration of the Lower Snake but also the "net economic benefits" of restored river flows. The report defined net economic benefits as the economic cost to society after all costs are taken into account. The Lansing report concluded that, when all costs and benefits are considered, natural river flows would save $87 million annually. The report estimated that the actual current cost of Lower Snake dam operations exceeds $236 million annually, including operation and maintenance costs, salmon recovery costs, and navigation and irrigation subsidies. The cost of restoring natural river flows, on the other hand, was estimated at $149.5 million annually, including the costs of providing replacement power, alternatives to navigation, and purchasing farmlands (to retire irrigation diversions).[40]

Although the Lansing report's methodology was endorsed by the Chairman of the University of Montana's Department of Economics, it probably underestimated the cost of reservoir drawdowns, as it did not consider a drawdown of John Day reservoir on the Lower Columbia, and it assumed no flow augmentation would be necessary after the reservoirs were drawn down. The Northwest Power Planning Council's independent economists called into question the Lansing report's conclusion of net economic benefits from dam breaching, criticizing its assumptions that $195 million could be saved in flow enhancement, monitoring, research, and habitat restoration costs; and that replacement electric power could be purchased for 1.6 mills. The advisory board concluded that not all of the $195 million could be saved, and that replacement cost power would likely cost around 2.0 to 2.5 mills, increasing costs by about 50 percent, or around $65 million.[41]

Nonetheless, the Lansing report's main finding remains intact: the net economic benefits of the four Lower Snake River dams are less than their total operational and maintenance costs, associated subsidies to navigators and irrigators, and fish and wildlife mitigation costs. Moreover, the Lansing report made no attempt to quantify recreational benefits from dam breaching, which could be considerable. Nor did the report estimate the "existence value" (the benefit of knowing that a resource exists, even if no use is made of it) of recovered salmon runs which, while difficult to accurately quantify, are real. Of the four major benefits dams typically provide (flood control, hydropower, irrigation, and navigation), Lansing concluded that only navigation benefits are economically significant for the four Lower Snake Dams. But even there, the costs of river transport as a whole (including the costs of dam operation and maintenance, ratepayer subsidies, and salmon mitigation measures) are actually greater than for equivalent transport by rail or truck.[42]

The Goodstein Report (1998). An economic report that was less optimistic about the economic savings associated with dam breaching was produced by Eban Goodstein for the PEW Charitable Trusts. Goodstein, an economics professor at Lewis and Clark College, reviewed the literature on breaching the Lower Snake River dams and, using conservative assumptions, concluded that the economic benefits of breaching the dams would be roughly equivalent to the costs of dam removal. Unlike Lansing, Goodstein did not assume that all of the costs of the current flow enhancement program could be saved.[43]

According to Goodstein, the cost of removing the dams — including lost electricity, extending irrigation pumps, lost navigation to Lewiston, and lost flatwater recreation — will range from $122-$288 million annually. Most of the economic uncertainties concern lost power sales. The economic benefits — including elimination of dam operation and maintenance costs, fish and wildlife costs, and subsidies to navigation, coupled with new revenues from free-flowing river recreational activities and increased fish harvests — would range from $116-$193 million annually. Although Goodstein concluded that the economic costs and benefits would be "roughly comparable," he observed that if the "existence value" of restored salmon runs were included in the equation, the benefits of dam breaching would "clearly overwhelm a hundred million dollars or so of foregone electricity."[44]

The Northwest Power Planning Council Report (1998). In June 1998, the Northwest Power Planning Council refined the reconnaissance level analysis its staff performed for the *Deadlock* report (discussed above), and issued a study on BPA's net revenues under a variety of scenarios, including several involving dam breaching to produce natural river conditions. The report essentially reiterated the conclusion of the earlier reconnaissance study that the chief variable for BPA net revenues is not fish and wildlife scenarios but the market price of power. Under high market prices, BPA would experience positive net revenues under all fish recovery scenarios, including a five-reservoir drawdown scenario (*i.e.*, breaching the four Lower Snake Dams and drawing down John Day reservoir). With medium market prices, BPA would have positive net revenues under all but the most costly scenario (dam breaching coupled with flows and dam modifications necessary to comply with the Clean Water Act). Under low market conditions, BPA would experience negative revenues under any scenario that increased its costs. The report indicated that, with financial reserves of $500 million, under a low-market price scenario BPA could minimize the adverse effects of drawdowns but not eliminate deficits.[45]

The Council report assumed continuation of the numerous subsidies targeted for elimination in the Lansing report. Further, it made no attempt to calculate benefits in order to estimate net social benefits. Nevertheless, the report did indicate that a five-dam drawdown would be affordable under both the high and medium market price scenarios. Only under a persistent low market price scenario — which the report described as "not very likely but possible" — would dam breaching threaten BPA's marketplace competitiveness. The Council report's conclusions were largely confirmed by a subsequent BPA briefing paper on funding the cost of various fish recovery scenarios.[46]

The Corps of Engineers Draft Economic Appendix (1999). The Corps of Engineers draft EIS on the Snake River dams and their effects on juvenile salmon migration included an Economic Appendix, which was the product of the "Drawdown Regional Economic Workgroup" (DREW). DREW estimated the economic effects of maintaining the dams on the Lower Snake as opposed to breaching them.[47]

The Economic Appendix compared existing conditions to two other dam-retention alternatives in addition to dam breaching — "maximum transportation" (reducing spill, which facilitates juvenile fish passage at mainstem dams) and "major system improvements" (focusing on surface collectors to more efficiently divert juvenile fish away from power turbines). However, a rather obvious criticism of the Economic Appendix was that by comparing alternatives to existing conditions, the analysis seemed to suggest that there were no costs associated with maintaining existing conditions. As several of the previously discussed studies indicate, the current system is hardly cost-free — requiring expenditures in excess of $200 million annually.

According to the Economic Appendix, the average annual economic effects of "maximum transportation" and "major system improvements" were minor, both producing small estimated benefits over existing conditions. But each alternative would produce fewer wild salmon returns than existing conditions. On the other hand, the Appendix estimated that dam breaching would produce an estimated net cost of $246 million annually, due to power costs of $271 million. Those estimated net costs would decline about $40 million, to roughly $208 million annually, if the tribes' preferred 0 percent discount rate is employed, instead of the Corps' preferred 6.875 percent rate.[48]

The figures above do not include passive use (or existence) value estimates for recovered salmon runs or for returning the Lower Snake River to a free-flowing condition (independent of any effect on salmon populations). As predicted by the Goodstein report discussed above, use of these existence values overwhelms the other estimates of costs and benefits. The Appendix noted that there is a passive use value associated with wild Snake River salmon increases, but the estimated values vary widely: from a low of $66 million to a high of $879, with a middle range of $142-$508 million. The estimated existence value of a free-flowing Snake River was $420 million. The Northwest Power Planning Council's board of independent scientists quickly challenged the Appendix's use of estimated recreational benefits and existence values: the board acknowledged that they might represent "best available scientific knowledge," but they were not accurate enough (based on contingent value surveys) "to provide useful guidance for the momentous decisions that might be based on them."[49]

The "Going With The Flow" Study (2000).   Because the key costs of dam breaching are due to the loss of approximately 5 percent of the Northwest's hydropower, an environmentalist-funded study analyzed the costs of replacing the loss of 940 average annual megawatts due to breaching (the estimated hydropower costs from breaching when compared to a baseline consisting of improvements in current conditions the environmentalists thought likely). The study, *Going With The Flow: Replacing Energy From Four Snake River Dams*, by the Northwest Energy Coalition and the Natural Resources Defense Council, concluded that the cost of replacement power would amount to $1-$2 per 1,000 kilowatt-hours for 20 years (from 2002-21) if the replacement power was from gas and coal fired sources, and $1-$3 per 1000 kilowatt-hours if replaced by a "zero carbon" scenario consisting of conservation and renewable resources like wind. The latter would produce no rate increase over the former if electric prices are in the medium expected range, and would be cheaper if prices are high.   Another environmentalist-funded economic study concluded that more jobs would be created than lost under a dam breaching scenario: a net gain of over 3,000 new permanent jobs in commercial and sport fishing, operating new power plants and transmission lines, and transportation and shipping.[50]

These economic studies indicate that dam breaching is affordable under the most probable marketplace scenarios, even assuming continuation of the subsidies which the Lansing report identified as amounting to $236 million annually. In fact, both the Lansing and *Idaho Statesman* reports expressly factored in the costs of economic mitigation, such as providing alternative sources of electricity, alternative truck and rail transportation, and alternative means of water diversions. Only if improbably low market conditions persist for extended periods of time is dam breaching of questionable affordability. Even then, if current subsidies to irrigators and navigators were terminated and placed in a contingency reserve, some $4.7 billion could be saved within 20 years, a substantial reserve.[51]

Institution of transmission line charges could also raise significant revenues without making BPA power uncompetitive. Moreover, the Council report's assumption that BPA's rates must cover all fish and wildlife costs under all scenarios may not obtain. It is possible, for example, that a combination of eliminating subsidies, restructuring BPA's payment obligations to the U.S. Treasury, and congressional appropriations could make dam breaching to produce natural river conditions affordable under even the unlikely scenario of low market conditions for 20 years. Even in a worst-case economic scenario for Northwest electric rates, natural river drawdowns would produce only about a 10 percent increase to Northwest ratepayers, who currently pay around 40 percent below the national average.[52]

The Law of Dam Breaching

The initial decision on whether to endorse dam breaching or continued artificial transportation was NMFS's reconsideration of its BiOp on the operation of the Columbia Basin hydroelectric system in 2000. This decision is subject to judicial review under the Endangered Species Act, as are the decisions of the implementing federal agencies on whether to follow the NMFS opinion. Although the ESA continues to dominate the legal landscape, the Northwest Power Act, the Federal Power Act, the Clean Water Act, Indian treaty fishing rights, and the Pacific Salmon Treaty could also affect the drawdown decision.

ESA Decision Making. NMFS's 2000 BiOp on Columbia Basin hydroelectric operations concluded that dam operations would jeopardize the continued existence of listed Columbia Basin salmon without a "reasonable and prudent alternative," which included a non-binding plan of improved hatchery operations and habitat protection and restoration measures. A court can review this BiOp, since it is a final agency action. As the Supreme Court has made clear, a BiOp is "virtually binding" on the agency proposing the action.[53]

The standard of judicial review is quite deferential, since the BiOp must be found to be arbitrary before courts will strike it down. Despite this deferential standard, Judge Marsh struck down the 1993 BiOp on hydroelectric operations, as detailed in chapter 9, because it failed to employ best available science, "focusing more upon [hydroelectric] system capability than the needs of the species" and ignoring "significant information and data from well-qualified scientists . . . from the states and tribes." Yet, three years later, Judge Marsh upheld a revised BiOp, even though it tolerated massive mortalities of juvenile salmon (up to 86 percent of sockeye and spring/summer chinook and 99 percent of fall chinook), and even though the judge expressed doubt about the high level of species risk NMFS chose to tolerate. The court seemed influenced by NMFS's claim that it was implementing an ecosystem approach to salmon recovery, accounting for competing ecological considerations like concern for other species, and the fact that the basin's Indian tribes were not unanimous in challenging the revised BiOp.[54]

NMFS will surely have to defend its 2000 BiOp in court on the basis of using best available science, including consultation with state and tribal biologists, not on the basis of economic savings. Closer judicial review of NMFS's decision may be forthcoming if the tribes can show that the decision was made without careful consideration of the federal trust obligation to undertake protective measures when actions threaten tribal treaty rights. But NMFS's biggest challenge may be to convince a court that its attempt to avoid species jeopardy through reliance on a nonbinding plan, implemented in large measure by non-federal entities, complies with the ESA.[55]

The Effect of Other Federal Statutes. Like the ESA, the Northwest Power Act demands decision making on the basis of best available science. The Ninth Circuit has ruled that this standard, along with another Northwest Power Act provision calling for improved river flows for salmon to meet "sound biological objectives," requires "a high degree of deference" to the biological advice of federal and state fishery agencies and Indian tribes. The court expressly forbade sacrificing fish and wildlife goals in pursuit of what the court termed "the lowest common denominator acceptable to power interests." The 1994 amendments to the Northwest Power Act salmon restoration program called for seasonal drawdowns of two of the four Lower Snake River dams, but that part of the program has not been implemented. The 2000 amendments, which backed away from the reservoir drawdowns and eschewed dam breaching, could run afoul of the Northwest Power Planning Council's obligation to give "a high degree of deference" to the advice of the region's fishery agencies and tribes.[56]

As discussed in chapter 10, water quality in the Lower Snake River remains exceedingly poor, with high temperatures and low levels of dissolved oxygen. The Environmental Protection Agency and state water quality agencies have identified the water quality problems in the Lower Snake River and asked the Corps of Engineers, the operator of the dams, to produce plans to remedy them. Failure to meet water quality standards is a Clean Water Act violation, and environmentalists filed suit. The district court of Oregon subsequently determined that the operation of the dams is in fact a substantial cause of water quality standards violations. However it has yet to order the Corps to develop and implement a remedial plan.[57]

As federal dams, the Lower Snake River dams were congressionally authorized, and therefore not subject to the licensing requirements of the Federal Power Act. But their existence could have a material effect on the relicensing of the Hells Canyon complex, three dams owned and operated by Idaho Power Company, upriver from the Lower Snake Dams (see map 1, page 11). These dams will need to be relicensed shortly, as noted in chapter 11.

Three of the more problematic hurdles Idaho Power will face in getting its projects relicensed are section 7 of the Endangered Species Act, section 401 of the Clean Water Act, and section 18 of the Federal Power Act. Section 7 will require a BiOp on the effect of the operation of the projects on listed salmon downstream. Section 401 will require a water quality certification from the states stipulating that the operation of the Hells Canyon dams primarily for power generation will meet water quality standards applicable to the Lower Snake River. Both requirements could require substantial changes in project operations. Section 18 requires "fishways" at licensed projects, as prescribed by the Interior or Commerce Secretaries. The Ninth Circuit has recently endorsed a broad reading of section 18 authority over the objections of the licensing agency, the Federal Energy Regulatory Commission. Imposing fishway requirements on the Hells Canyon dams designed to reintroduce salmon above the dams would impose staggering costs on Idaho Power. If breaching the Lower Snake Dams were approved as part of a settlement which included relicensing the Hells Canyon dams, all of these hurdles to relicensing, except the loss of Lewiston as an inland seaport, could disappear.[58]

Indian Treaty Rights. As discussed in chapters 4 and 12, Stevens and Palmer treaty tribes have the right to take one-half of the harvestable fish destined to pass their traditional fishing grounds, an uncertain right to habitat protection for the fish, and a right to sufficient water to carry out the purposes of their reservations. The amount of water reserved is also uncertain, but because the purposes of virtually all Indian reservations in the Northwest include allowing the tribes to continue their fishing livelihoods, sufficient water must be made available to support a tribal fishing economy. These instream water rights carry very early priority dates, probably "time immemorial" rights, trumping virtually all competing water claims under Western water law's "first in time, first in right" principle.[59]

In Idaho's Snake River Basin Adjudication, all water rights to the Snake River and its tributaries are being determined in a massive adjudication involving 87 percent of the water rights in the state. The Nez Perce Tribe, and the federal government on its behalf, has made substantial instream flow claims in support of the tribe's treaty fishing right. These claims create substantial uncertainty for virtually every water user in the state, especially agricultural users who irrigate with water stored in Upper Snake Basin reservoirs. This uncertainty has not diminished in the wake of the initial decision denying the tribes' claims, since the SRBA court's opinion in the Nez Perce water rights case was filled with errors and ignored both precedent and bedrock principles of Indian law, as explained in chapter 12. However, it is quite possible that the Nez Perce would reduce its claims for flow augmentation to aid fish migration, which in turn would reduce effects on upstream diverters, in return for breaching the Lower Snake River dams and lowering John Day reservoir, since those measures seem to offer the best opportunity of restoring the tribe's fishing economy. A settlement that promised restored salmon runs through dam breaching could also protect Idaho's irrigation economy and may be in the best interests of all concerned.[60]

Retiring the Lower Snake River Dams

There is no question that breaching federal dams would require congressional approval. First, Congress would have to fund breaching the dams. Second, the Lower Snake River dams were authorized by Congress for navigation, irrigation and, secondarily, power purposes. Breaching the dams would eliminate the navigation channel they create and the power they produce. Therefore, Congress would have to approve retiring the dams and the navigation channel they produce (dam breaching would not necessarily eliminate irrigation).[61]

Congressional approval and funding are usually essential to Indian water rights settlements, so in approving a settlement of the Nez Perce water right claims to the Snake River, Congress could also authorize breaching the dams. While it might seem unlikely that Congress would enact such legislation, if the region's congressional delegation came to realize that this approach is the best way to safeguard both the irrigation economy of Idaho and Eastern Oregon and Washington, as well as to ensure relicensing of Idaho Power's Hells Canyon dams, the chances of congressional action would increase substantially.[62]

Breaching the Lower Snake Dams would create a 220-mile stretch of free-flowing river between the Hells Canyon Dam and the Snake's confluence with the Columbia. In its *Return to the River* report, the Independent Scientific Group of the Northwest Power Planning Council looked closely at protecting and enhancing the Columbia Basin's only stable mainstem-spawning population, the fall chinook of the Mid-Columbia's undammed Hanford Reach. The scientists concluded that drawdowns of McNary and John Day reservoirs on the Lower Columbia would likely restore mainstem-spawning populations as extensions of the Hanford Reach population, since historically the areas now inundated by those reservoirs once supported large salmon populations.

The scientists did not examine the viability of the Lower Snake as mainstem spawning habitat in the absence of the Lower Snake Dams. While it is true that historically the Lower Snake did not provide significant mainstem spawning habitat, the same is also true of the Hanford Reach, which became the most productive mainstem spawning area only when other mainstem spawning areas were successively destroyed by reservoir flooding. Today, the Hanford Reach supports the only spawning population above Bonneville Dam capable of functioning as a core population that could reseed adjacent areas.[63]

Without the four Lower Snake Dams, it appears likely that the newly created 220-mile stretch of free-flowing Snake River would replicate the experience of the now-productive 40-mile stretch of the Hanford Reach. For example, in 1998 fishery officials reported that upriver bright fall chinook, which historically spawned in the Upper Columbia Basin, had begun spawning in great numbers in the lower river in shallow pools below Bonneville Dam because they found suitable habitat there. It seems probable that similar scenarios would be replicated many times over in a free-flowing Lower Snake River, which would be more than five times the size of the Hanford Reach.[64]

Even if a free-flowing mainstem Lower Snake River were ultimately to provide little in viable habitat, it still serves as the gateway to Idaho's Salmon and Clearwater Rivers Basins. Historically, the Salmon alone provided more than 40 percent of the spring/summer chinook produced in the entire Columbia Basin. No basinwide salmon recovery plan can ignore the potential of this area, given its historic abundance and still pristine habitat, comprised largely of national forests and wilderness areas. It seems clear that restoring Snake Basin salmon must be a focal point of any viable salmon recovery program.[65]

Rescuing Snake River salmon from the edge of extinction is now one of the foremost items on the nation's environmental agenda. The existing method of preserving the salmon runs — barging and trucking juvenile salmon around the dams — has failed for over two decades to stem the decline of the species. Considerable scientific evidence suggests that the best way to recover Snake River salmon is to breach the four Lower Snake Dams and drawdown John Day reservoir to restore natural river conditions and produce salmon spawning habitat. In December 2000, over 200 scientists from 27 states signed a letter to the president, endorsing dam breaching in the near term as the best way to recover imperiled Snake River salmon. Economic analyses show that this option will produce net social benefits and is affordable under the most likely electricity price forecasts. Breaching the dams would produce only modest electric rate increases and would sacrifice nothing in flood control. River navigation on the Lower Snake, one of the most highly subsidized transportation systems in the country, can be replaced by affordable rail and truck alternatives. Indeed, the legislation authorizing restoration of natural river flows on the Lower Snake could also provide for economic mitigation to affected river transport interests in the form of improved regional rail and truck infrastructures. Similar sorts of economic mitigation are commonplace in Indian water rights settlements.[66]

If the Lower Snake Dams are not breached, demands for water from Upper Snake Basin reservoirs to restore salmon runs in order to satisfy the Endangered Species Act, the Clean Water Act, or the Nez Perce's water right claims will intensify. One analysis estimated that some 400,000 acres of irrigated agriculture in Idaho could lose water under one flow augmentation plan. Settling this conflict through enactment of federal legislation authorizing dam breaching offers the best chance of restoring the fishing economy of both the Nez Perce Tribe and the state of Idaho, while simultaneously preserving irrigation in Idaho and Eastern Oregon and Washington. The legislation could also remove obstacles to relicensing Idaho Power Company's Hells Canyon dams. An investment in effective salmon restoration would revitalize Idaho's fishing-based tourism and related industries, which could contribute $150 million annually or more to the state's economy. When regional and national politicians begin to understand these realities, they may be led to endorse the science, economics, and law that point toward breaching the Lower Snake Dams and lowering John Day reservoir as the only viable Snake River salmon restoration plan for the 21st century.[67]

14 – ECOSYSTEM MANAGEMENT AND SALMON RECOVERY

Nearly a decade after the first Columbia Basin ESA listings, there is enough experience with that statute and its provisions to suggest that those responsible for implementing the ESA will avoid decisions that might jeopardize entrenched economic activities like navigation on the Lower Snake River. The concept of using ecosystem management to restore salmon runs, while hard to dispute in the abstract, may provide ample discretion for agencies to engage in what Professor Oliver Houck has referred to as "politics with a strong flavor of law-avoidance," allowing difficult decisions to be evaded or deferred. In the case of Columbia Basin salmon, ecosystem management plans can also make it appear that serious salmon restoration strategies are being pursued when in fact the existing activities that produce the lion's share of salmon mortalities are allowed to continue.[1]

The Concept of Ecosystem Management[2]

The origins of ecosystem management can be traced to a 1932 nature sanctuary plan by the Ecological Society of America's Committee for the Study of Plant and Animal Communities, which recognized the importance of protecting both ecosystems and individual species and argued for use of a core reserve/buffer zone approach to natural area protection that factored natural disturbances into management policy. Later, managing to maintain ecosystem integrity became a core element of Aldo Leopold's seminal book, *A Sand County Almanac*. But only a few visionaries took seriously the idea of centering natural resources policy around ecosystems until the early 1990s. Then Secretary of the Interior Bruce Babbitt adopted it as a means to ameliorate the single-species approach of the Endangered Species Act, which he claimed brought on "train wrecks" like the conflict between logging old growth forests and preserving northern spotted owl habitat in the Pacific Northwest.[3]

Ecosystem management has been the subject of endless debate over its goals, the proper scale of its application, and the most appropriate structure for decision making. Perhaps the best description was supplied by Edward Grumbine, who identified ten characteristic themes in the literature on ecosystem management: 1) a "systems perspective" to biodiversity hierarchy; 2) ecological, not administrative, boundaries; 3) total native diversity protection, including species, population, and ecosystem diversity; 4) management that uses ongoing research and data collection; 5) monitoring that provides management with ongoing feedback; 6) management flexibility in the face of uncertainty through use of adaptive management principles; 7) cooperation among governmental entities and between government and private parties; 8) organizational changes in natural resources agencies; 9) recognition of the fundamental role of humans in ecological processes; and 10) dominance of human values in setting policy goals.[4]

Origins of Ecosystem Management in the Columbia Basin

The first real example of an ecosystem management approach in the Columbia Basin was the Northwest Forest Plan, which was the Clinton Administration's response to the 1990 ESA listing of the northern spotted owl and ensuing injunctions of federal timber harvests. The plan, covering some 24 million acres both within and adjacent to the Columbia Basin, brought ecosystem management to federal land planning on a grand scale.

The heart of the plan is an "aquatic protection strategy" (ACS) that aims to restore and maintain the ecological health of watersheds and aquatic ecosystems. The ACS has four main elements: 1) riparian reserves, consisting of roughly 2.6 million acres, or about 11 percent of lands subject to the plan, where timber sales are limited to salvage operations that advance ACS restoration and maintenance objectives; 2) designated key watersheds to serve as refuges for aquatic species, that limit road building; 3) watershed analyses that must precede developments in both riparian reserves and in key watersheds to ensure that ACS objectives are carried out; and 4) a watershed restoration program to improve fish habitat, riparian habitat, and water quality. The National Research Council considered the Northwest Forest Plan to be a "major change in the burden of proof," requiring "relatively high levels of protection for fisheries and other riparian-dependent wildlife species" and clear, well-documented evidence that specific measures are required to protect particular species. Although the plan allows changes in riparian reserves, such changes can take place only with a demonstration of no adverse effects on water quality, wildlife, fisheries, and other aquatic resources.[5]

Watershed analysis, the linchpin of the Northwest Forest Plan's approach to ecosystem management, is a systematic procedure to evaluate current riparian conditions, assess the effect of proposed activities on the watershed, institute monitoring programs, refine the boundaries of riparian reserves, and develop restoration projects. The initial response of the courts to the contents of the Northwest Forest Plan was that its requirements are judicially enforceable and may impose more stringent requirements than the ESA. Federal timber sales must therefore independently satisfy both the ESA and the Northwest Forest Plan before proceeding.[6]

An even broader scale ecosystem planning effort is the Interior Columbia Basin Ecosystem Management Project, which involves some 70 million acres of federal lands east of the Cascade Mountains and extending into Montana and Idaho, an area about three times larger than the Northwest Forest Plan covers. This project was also prompted by ESA litigation, which required the Forest Service and Bureau of Land Management to subject previously approved land management plans to ESA consultation after the listings of Snake River salmon. The consultation resulted in the establishment of interim protections for salmon habitat and a promise to develop an ecosystem-based management strategy for all federal lands east of the Cascades.

In 1997, two draft environmental impact statements were released on the project, both of which devoted a great deal of attention to aquatic ecosystems. But they were attacked by environmentalists for failing to specify management standards or identify conservation reserves in which development activities would be prohibited or curtailed. Development interests, especially grazers and loggers, also opposed the project and nearly succeeded more than once in convincing Congress to remove funding for it. Its future remains uncertain, although revised "supplemental" environmental impact statements are now under preparation. What emerges may include some kind of aquatic conservation strategy resembling that contained in the Northwest Forest Plan. It is at least possible that this could lead to substantial changes in land management practices, emphasizing aquatic protection and de-emphasizing activities, like grazing and timber harvests in riparian areas, which damage fish habitat. This result is hardly certain, however.[7]

Ecosystem Management and the "Normative" River

The National Research Council endorsed watershed analysis in 1996 for salmon restoration. The Council suggested that its watershed analysis was an important means of assessing cumulative effects of developments because it combines habitat-inventory information with environmental-hazard assessments over relatively large areas. However, the Council reported several barriers to successful watershed analysis, including spatial and seasonal variability, dynamic interactions between physical and biological processes, unique attributes of each watershed, and local sensitivities of each watershed and stream reach to management practices. The report recommended habitat restoration and rehabilitation to reestablish self-sustaining conditions that provide some of the ecological requirements of salmon.[8]

A more concrete ecosystem management approach to salmon restoration was proposed by the Northwest Power Planning Council's independent scientists in *Return to the River*, also released in 1996. As discussed in chapter 13, the scientists charged that the Council's fish and wildlife program lacked an adequate conceptual foundation and proposed an alternative "normative river" approach which emphasized the importance of restoring ecological processes needed to sustain salmon populations, not technological substitutes like hatcheries and artificial transport. The report focused on restoring a complex network of interconnected habitat, created and maintained by natural physical and biological processes. It also emphasized the linkage between habitat, environmental diversity, and salmon life history diversity.[9]

Return to the River identified spatially-structured groups of local salmon populations linked by dispersal and interbreeding as a key to salmon recovery. These "metapopulations" can seed or recolonize neighboring populations, but they require salmon "refuges," like the Hanford Reach in the Mid-Columbia, to support core populations that are connected to satellite areas. The scientists criticized Columbia Basin hydroelectric operations for contributing to reductions in stock diversity and suggested ways to minimize these effects. The normative river they espoused was not, however, a natural, undeveloped river, as they took pains to clarify:

> It does not imply that we must return to a pristine, pre-development state. It requires that we learn the critical features of ecosystem and salmon performance and then strive to manage our cultural features (hydropower, irrigation withdrawals, navigation, flood control, etc.) in ways that more closely approximate those normative features. What we actually do will depend on where the actions are to be taken and what amount of alteration has already taken place. . . . Headwater spawning areas can be left pristine. Storage reservoirs already in place can be managed by reregulating to achieve normative features by providing more normal seasonal cycles of flow and temperature. Mainstem reservoirs can be managed to provide habitat, including, in some cases, drawdown or removal of some dams. Areas presently exhibiting normative conditions that are producing salmon (such as the Hanford Reach) can be made into refuges. Mainstem power projects can be designed and operated to more closely mimic key features of the normative river, such as reregulation of flows to stabilize daily fluctuations in flow that allow food web development in shallow water habitats.[10]

Ecosystem Management as a Defense or Complement to ESA Listings

The threat of ESA restrictions has clearly been a principal motivating force in energizing widespread interest in ecosystem management. The paradigmatic example of this phenomenon is the development of the Oregon coho plan, which later evolved into the Oregon salmon plan. The state developed this plan in a vain attempt to ward off a proposed ESA listing for Oregon coho. The state plan sought to achieve coho restoration through agency coordination, private voluntary actions, increased enforcement of existing state laws, and public education. NMFS determined that the state plan required more to avoid a listing. But a memorandum of agreement between the state and NMFS, in which the state promised to implement additional habitat protection measures, including unspecified improvements in forest and agricultural practices, streamflows, and gravel removal regulations convinced NMFS not to list Oregon coho in 1997.[11]

This decision not to list Oregon coho was immediately challenged by a number of environmental groups. In 1998, the federal court in Oregon agreed with the environmentalists that the plan was not sufficient to avoid an ESA listing, because it was based on promises of future regulatory measures, whereas as the ESA requires "existing regulatory measures," which the court interpreted to mean current, enforceable measures. The court therefore refused to allow NMFS to defer a listing based on a patchwork of existing, largely unenforced state laws, promises of new regulations, and volunteerism. The court's ruling convinced NMFS to list Oregon coho under the ESA.[12]*

Although the Oregon plan was unable to prevent an ESA listing, it may still have a role in implementing the ESA, due to the effect of section 4(d) of the Act. That provision authorizes regulations prescribing the conditions under which species listed as "threatened" under the ESA may be taken without violating the statute. Through section 4(d) rules, states and even localities may retain control over certain activities resulting in "takes" of threatened species, thereby gaining a role in salmon recovery, although NMFS must approve of these efforts in its 4(d) rules. Both Oregon and Washington have developed state salmon plans which NMFS may approve under section 4(d), although that is not certain as of this writing. Both states promise improved regulation of private timber harvests under state forest practices statutes, increased enforcement of existing environmental laws, and various restoration efforts. An obvious problem is that state

---

*   As noted in chapter 9, the listing of Oregon coho was struck down by the court in *Alsea Valley Alliance v. Evans*, 2001 WL 11005100 (D. Or. Sept. 10, 2001). However, as suggested there, NMFS could remedy the problem by redefining its ESU concept to deemphasize reproductive isolation.

authority is greatest over habitat damage on private lands and least over hydroelectric operations, with only partial authority over hatchery operations and harvest management. Thus, any state plans approved as part of 4(d) rules would hardly be comprehensive in terms of managing "takes" throughout the salmon ecosystem. Another problem is the states' historic inability to resist habitat-damaging developments; whether state plans approved under the ESA can overcome this traditional bias in favor of development is highly uncertain.[13]

For species listed as "endangered" 4(d) rules cannot authorize takes, although the federal consultation process and incidental take permits under section 10 of the ESA may. Private activities subject to federal approval may be authorized through incidental take "statements" approved as part of the consultation process. Private activities not subject to federal approval may be authorized by incidental take permits, which, as discussed in chapter 9, require the preparation of habitat conservation plans, like those being prepared by two Mid-Columbia public utility districts concerning the operation of their dams.

Ecosystem Management and Judicial Review

One of the first uses of ecosystem management in the context of Columbia Basin salmon concerned a challenge to NMFS's revised BiOp on hydroelectric system operations. As discussed in chapter 9, after NMFS watered down the provisions in its 1995-99 BiOp, a coalition of environmental groups challenged it as being inconsistent with the ESA, particularly its heavy reliance on trucking and barging juvenile salmon. But Judge Marsh, who only three years earlier struck down a NMFS BiOp as arbitrary, this time upheld NMFS's BiOp in part on the basis of ecosystem management claims.

NMFS maintained that its artificial transportation program was necessary to conduct an experiment comparing the survival rates of transported fish with those left in the river to migrate. The agency also noted that other species, like bull trout and sturgeon, might be adversely affected by the higher river flows the environmentalists were seeking for salmon. These ecosystem management claims seemed to convince

Judge Marsh to give greater judicial deference to NMFS than he had three years earlier, when he called for a "major overhaul" in hydroelectric system operations. He did so even though he explicitly questioned NMFS's risk tolerance for salmon extinctions. Thus, one apparent effect of ecosystem management is to reduce the level of judicial scrutiny of BiOps, where the BiOp invokes ecosystem concerns in its decision making.[14]

A more therapeutic effect of ecosystem management on judicial review occurs where there is a discrete ecosystem management plan, with specific requirements, since the courts have ruled that those requirements must be met irrespective of requirements imposed through ESA consultation. That is one lesson from the Umpqua timber sales case, where the court enjoined the sales for violating standards contained in the Northwest Forest Plan, even though NMFS approved the sales in ESA consultation. The ESA therefore does not trump requirements imposed by ecosystem management plans; instead, courts will separately enforce both sets of requirements. In fact, in the Umpqua case, the ESA process became the means to enforce the ecosystem management requirements of the Northwest Forest Plan.[15]

The Basinwide Salmon Strategy

In 1999, with several scientific studies pointing to the efficacy breaching the Lower Snake River dams in salmon recovery, the Army Corps of Engineers released a Lower Snake River draft environmental impact statement (EIS) that compared breaching those dams compared with other ways of improving salmon passage on the Lower Snake River. An appendix to that draft EIS, the A-Fish Appendix, discussed in chapter 13, concluded that dam breaching was more likely to recover Snake River salmon than leaving the dams intact and maximizing artificial transport. However, the A-Fish Appendix also noted that there are enormous uncertainties about both the probabilities of successful fish recovery and the time available to accomplish it, although some of the uncertainties might be reduced by a five- to twenty-year program of studies, experiments, and monitoring. The report specifically recommended studying "differential delayed transportation mortality," or delayed fish mortalities in the lower river due to barging and trucking, suggesting that if these mortalities proved to be low, the dam breaching option might not have such a pronounced advantage over continuing the transportation program. The Appendix did note that the increased risk of extinction due to the time required for additional study was on the average eight percent, higher for some stocks with low populations.[16]

NMFS began altering the conclusions in the A-Fish Appendix almost immediately. Just four months after its release, in August 1999, NMFS scientists issued a draft "cumulative risk analysis" (CRI) as an addendum to the A-Fish Appendix. The CRI reviewed activities other than dam operations adversely affecting the salmon runs, including hatchery operations, harvest controls, and habitat destruction. Expanding the focus to consider many sources of mortality throughout the salmon ecosystem opened up options beyond just dam breaching or continuing artificial transportation. For example, the CRI claimed that breaching might not be necessary to recover spring/summer chinook if improvements in habitat protection and hatchery operations were made. The increased options produced from evaluating hydropower, habitat, hatcheries and harvest management as an integrated system were so welcome that the CRI approach quickly evolved into a federal "all-H" approach (after 4-H clubs objected to its being labeled the "4-H" approach).[17]

In November 1999, nine federal agencies, including NMFS, released an "all-H" working paper that laid out a series of alternative strategies. The agencies offered no preferred alternative, merely a sampling of possible "integrated alternatives," two of which involved dam breaching, two of which relied on continued barging and trucking. However, the U.S. Fish and Wildlife Service broke ranks with the other federal agencies and called for breaching the Lower Snake River dams as the best way of avoiding extinction of the Snake River runs. But the other federal agencies endorsed an "aggressive" habitat protection option, which the CRI claimed would have a high potential for contributing to salmon recovery, although requiring "significantly increased" land and water use regulation by states, localities, tribes, and the federal government. Environmental and fishing groups and Indian tribes claimed that this new "ecosystem approach," while theoretically sound, had the effect of diverting attention from the dams, the cause of 80-90 percent of human-caused salmon mortalities. Industry groups generally welcomed the broader ecosystem approach, no doubt because it offered the promise of preserving the dams and the accompanying salmon transportation program, and perhaps confident that increased state or local regulation of salmon habitat would not materialize.[18]

Not surprisingly, it was the "all-H" approach, now denominated the "Basinwide Salmon Strategy," which was approved by the coalition of federal agencies (the Federal Caucus) in December 2000, as a complement to NMFS's BiOp on hydroelectric operations, discussed in chapter 9. In fact, it was reliance on the basinwide strategy which fueled the BiOp's conclusion that hydroelectric operations would not produce jeopardy to listed salmon in 2001-2005. The strategy's stated priorities — implementing actions with 1) the best chance of being implemented, 2) the most predictable biological benefits, and 3) the broadest benefit to the greatest range of species — allowed the Federal Caucus to look past the conclusions of the A-Fish Appendix about dam breaching being the best recovery option for Snake River salmon. Instead, the caucus devised a strategy which emphasizes a series of performance standards concerning all major sources of salmon.[19]

The centerpiece of the basinwide strategy is protecting and restoring tributary and estuarine habitat through sub-basin plans, improved salmon habitat protection in federal land management, creation of more natural habitat areas along reservoirs, and restoration of estuarine habitat. Many of these measures are under the control of non-federal agencies, so one effect of the strategy is to shift recovery responsibility to the "offsite mitigation" efforts of state, local, and tribal governments. Whether this shifting of responsibility violates the Endangered Species Act is open to question. The strategy also promised hatchery reforms to minimize adverse effects on wild salmon, while still providing fish for harvest, and use of supplementation and broodstock programs as a "safety net" to avoid extinctions. The strategy's harvest measures were largely limited to capping harvests at existing levels and making an effort to increase selectivity of harvests to decrease incidental takes of listed species.[20]

Although the basinwide strategy's hydropower element promised "an aggressive program of improvements at existing dams," few specifics were included. The strategy called for adoption of a systemwide survival standard for juvenile salmon through the hydropower system, but declined to set "hard limits" for survival levels at individual projects. Improved streamflows were also requested, but the means to secure those flows — "potential" storage releases from Canadian reservoirs, "ongoing discussions" that could produce improved Snake River flows, and a flood control study — were left extremely vague. The strategy promised science-based, peer-reviewed evaluations of performance at three, five, and eight-year intervals and will reopen the dam breaching question if progress "is inadequate or the Snake River populations decline."[21]

One might suspect that the real reason for the federal agencies' enthusiasm for the basinwide ecosystem approach is that it seemed more politically palatable than the dam breaching option. Since dam breaching would have to be authorized by Congress, and since powerful U.S. Senators, like Senators Slade Gorton (since retired) and Gordon Smith, declared themselves to be "adamant and inflexible opponents" of dam breaching, there may have been political wisdom in designing a recovery strategy around maintaining the dams, however uneconomical they may actually be. Given the great scientific uncertainties involved in salmon recovery, and the deferential judicial review likely to be accorded to an ecosystem-based recovery plan, the 2000 NMFS BiOp's emphasis on making improvements in non-hydroelectric system sources of salmon mortality, while retaining the Lower Snake Dams, certainly made political sense — even if the result increased the risk of extinction. NMFS has been willing to subordinate biological needs to economic concerns in the past, and it may have done so again.[22]

The Tribal Ecosystem Management Plan

The Basinwide Salmon Strategy, which produced a restoration program to both rescue Snake River salmon and preserve the Lower Snake River Dams, stands in sharp contrast to the 1995 proposal made by the Columbia Basin tribes with Stevens Treaty fishing rights. (See map 7, page ?.) The tribes proposed an ecosystem-based salmon program in 1995 designed to keep the fish in the river and out of barges and trucks. The objective of the tribal plan, titled *Wy-Kan-Mi Wa-Kish-Wit (The Spirit of the Salmon),* was to restore all populations of anadromous fish, including Pacific lamprey and white sturgeon in addition to salmon.[23]

The tribal plan listed four specific goals: 1) restore anadromous fish to the rivers and streams of the Columbia Basin; 2) emphasize restoration strategies that rely on natural production and healthy river systems; 3) protect tribal sovereignty and tribal rights; and 4) reclaim the anadromous fish resource for future generations. The tribes established two means of achieving these goals: halting the decline of salmon populations within seven years and increasing adult salmon returns above Bonneville Dam to four million fish within twenty-five years. The plan also included a series of short- and long-term measures for improving salmon survival, including increased river flows and permanent reservoir drawdowns.[24]

With respect to river flows, the tribal plan did not call for fixed flows based on particular cubic feet per second. Instead, apparently on the belief that it was unrealistic to set flow targets because of a lack of stored water in the Upper Snake Basin and restrictions on Dworshak reservoir, the tribal plan included a volume of water, based on acre-feet, to be set aside for fish flow augmentation as follows: one to three million acre-feet from Upper Snake Basin reservoirs; .45 million acre-feet from Brownlee reservoir; and 1.5 million acre-feet from Dworshak in the spring and another one million acre-feet in the summer. These amounts would be made available to fishery agencies and the tribes to maximize fish benefit, similar to the Northwest Power Planning Council's water budget. On the Columbia, the tribal plan called for sliding-scale flow levels in the spring, ranging from 220,000 to 300,000 cubic feet per second, similar to the fishery agency and tribal recommendations to the Council in 1981. Over the long term, the tribal plan sought to achieve "mean historical flows" — flows that would have existed prior to water resource development — during the juvenile salmon migration period, and reductions in daily and hourly flow fluctuations. These fluctuations are largely due to peak power operations.[25]

The tribal plan called for both short- and long-term reservoir drawdowns to achieve the improved rivers flows it sought. Eschewing the seasonal reservoir drawdowns of the Council's 1991 program, the tribal plan included permanent reservoir drawdowns in order to restore ecosystem functions. In the short run, the plan called for Lower Granite Dam to be drawn down to natural river level and the other three Lower Snake Dams to be drawn down to minimum operating pool, the minimum level at which navigation can continue. In the long run, the tribal plan called for one of three drawdown plans, including one which would draw down John Day and all of the Lower Snake River dams to natural river level, essentially breaching the dams. The tribes expected juvenile salmon survival rates to increase four-fold under this long-term plan.[26]

The tribal plan called for ending juvenile transport by truck and barge altogether, consistent with its goal of keeping fish in the river. The plan also endorsed the use of hatchery supplementation to combat "fragmented and declining" fish populations, at least "where other remedial actions cannot be implemented quickly enough or on a scale that is large enough to halt further population losses." The tribes advocated supplementation techniques simulating natural conditions and managing natural and hatchery fish groups as one gene pool. The goal of the tribes' supplementation program is to establish naturally spawning salmon runs, not simply to maintain harvest levels, as current hatchery operations do. The tribal plan outlined hatchery goals for each sub-basin above Bonneville Dam, with an emphasis on reintroducing salmon to areas from which they had been extirpated. The tribes considered hatchery supplementation to be "an indispensable part of any restoration plan." They claimed that any genetic concerns can be effectively managed — a contested conclusion — and maintained that "the increasing likelihood of species extirpation is in fact the far greater genetic risk."[27]

The tribal plan blasted the approach pursued by NMFS under the ESA, attacking NMFS's failure to "articulate a clear jeopardy standard" and the agency's failure "to give due weight" to the tribes' and state fishery agencies' recommendations. The tribes alleged that the 1995-99 ESA plan failed to meet both survival and recovery standards for Snake River spring and fall chinook, while the tribal plan would achieve survival and recovery of both. The tribes even questioned whether NMFS should have an active role in

Columbia Basin salmon recovery efforts, casting doubt on whether NMFS had played an historically constructive role in recovery of upper basin salmon and charging that the agency had compromised its integrity on hatchery and hydrosystem operation issues.[28]

The Future of Ecosystem Management

Ecosystem management now seems as inevitable as taxes and the internet. Twenty years ago, the Northwest Power Act focused only on the Columbia Basin hydroelectric system and attempted to reduce its effects on salmon. Today, that single-issue approach has been widely repudiated as inadequate and incomplete. It is certainly true that focusing on the entire salmon life cycle is necessary to salmon recovery, and that any approach that does not include protecting and restoring spawning habitat is doomed to failure. But not all life cycle stages are equally perilous to salmon, especially in the Columbia Basin, where the 1995-99 NMFS BiOp authorized hydroelectric dams to "harvest" 80 to 90 percent of juvenile salmon.

Ecosystem management is a concept malleable enough to have been employed to justify continuation of a barging and trucking program, a two-decade old experiment with no proven value. Subsequently, the concept became a central justification for a basinwide recovery strategy built around existing hydroelectric operations, including maintenance of the four Lower Snake Dams, even though those dams are biologically disastrous and economically marginal. Of course, any plan that focused exclusively on the removal of these dams would be incomplete and likely ineffective. But to craft a plan around the dams' continued existence while risking the existence of Snake River runs in the name of ecosystem management makes the concept a defense to status quo operations, which are contrary to sound biology and economics. This is a result that would surprise many advocates of ecosystem management.

15—WILD SALMON IN THE 21ˢᵗ CENTURY

For over 10,000 years, 10 million to 16 million adult salmon returned annually to the Columbia River Basin. In less than a century and a half since the signing of the Stevens and Palmer treaties, the wild salmon runs of the Columbia Basin have been reduced by 99 percent. Some salmon runs have gone extinct; nearly all of the others are now listed under the federal Endangered Species Act.[1]

It is sometimes said that the plight of Columbia Basin salmon in the 20th century reflected society's changing values: from valuing salmon only for harvest to valuing hydropower, flood control, and navigation more than salmon to — at the century's end — questioning the choices of earlier generations. The historical record does not support the perspective that salmon policy has mirrored social values, however, at least not in a deliberative manner. No responsible governmental entity ever declared that Columbia Basin salmon had to be sacrificed in order for civilization to progress. On the contrary, over the years there have been repeated promises that the march of civilization was to occur simultaneously with harvestable runs of Columbia Basin salmon. In typical American fashion the Pacific Northwest was to have it all — developed rivers and harvestable salmon runs without sacrifice or compromise.[2]

The Promises

The first promise concerning salmon was made in the 1850s treaties with the Indian tribes, who were promised that they could maintain their fishing livelihoods in return for ceding to the federal government over 60 million acres in one of the largest peaceful real estate transactions in U.S. history. This first promise — the bedrock of white settlement of the Pacific Northwest — has been honored only in the breach. The tribes have not received the basis of the bargain for which they gave up so much.[3]

A second promise, the notion that developing the waters of the Columbia Basin could proceed without material damage to the salmon runs, has also proved to be illusory. More than a century after their introduction to the basin, hatcheries are still considered to be an experimental technology, with no assurance they will increase run sizes. Moreover, widespread commitment to hatchery production has had pernicious effects on harvest regulation, allowing overharvest of wild salmon in fisheries containing mixed stocks of wild and hatchery fish. Worse, there is now considerable evidence that hatchery fish crowd out wild fish through competition for scarce food and habitat and produce damaging genetic effects. The allure of having salmon without protecting salmon habitat — of having dams and salmon — was another false illusion.[4]

Restoration efforts, which began in earnest two decades ago with the enactment of the Northwest Power Act, have produced many plans, new institutions, litigation, and lots of optimism but few spawning salmon. But the restoration attempts were halting, compromised plans built around maintaining a status quo that favored electric users, navigators, and irrigators — groups that one court referred to as "entrenched river users." Even as the Northwest Power Act program gave way to Endangered Species Act consultation, the ensuing plans were premised on maintaining the status quo as much as possible, or what the same court called "the lowest common denominator." This meant, for example, continuation of an artificial transportation program that, like hatcheries, could show no discernible benefits — even after more than two decades of the experiment. The promise of real salmon restoration remains elusive.[5]

Other promises, like the Pacific Salmon Treaty's promises of reduced salmon interceptions and chinook rebuilding, the Clean Water Act's promise of fishable waters, and the Indian treaty promise of not leaving the tribes with empty nets, remain inchoate, unfulfilled. They apparently will require judicial enforcement, unlikely in the case of an international agreement and uncertain in the other cases. A surprising promise, the Federal Power Act's promise of "fishways" at federally licensed dams, may prompt dam removals — as it has in the case of the Condit Dam — but those are likely to affect only a few dams on Columbia Basin tributary streams. While perhaps significant in terms of restoring those streams, the fishway requirement will not produce basinwide salmon restoration.[6]

A more auspicious salmon restoration initiative, breaching the four federal dams on the Lower Snake River, was a promise not made, despite considerable scientific and economic evidence to support it. The same entrenched river users which compromised other plans have been able to defeat this measure, at least so far. Instead, the region committed to an "ecosystem management" approach, which, while considering all "four H's" of salmon mortalities — the hydrosystem, hatchery, harvest, and habitat — had the effect of deflecting attention from the chief source of mortalities in the Columbia Basin: hydroelectric development and operations. The upshot may be more extinctions of Snake River salmon, as those species might be considered to be on life support, with little time left. If extinctions occur, unlike earlier extinctions which arguably were unknowingly countenanced, these extinctions will be the product of much more willful choices: the Snake River salmon will have been sacrificed to maintain a seaport in Lewiston, Idaho.[7]

The Myths

If the region is ever to establish a viable salmon restoration program for the Columbia Basin, at least eight myths must be recognized and overcome. First, although there is now widespread recognition of the myth that hatcheries can compensate for salmon habitat lost to dams and other river developments, about 40 percent of salmon restoration money in 1999 was spent on hatcheries. There may be a role for hatcheries in a viable Columbia Basin recovery plan, but if there is, hatcheries will not consume 40 percent of total expenditures. And hatchery expenditures almost surely will involve something patterned after the tribes' supplementation plans, which are designed to restore naturally spawning runs, not just maintain harvests, and to have as few adverse effects as possible on spawning salmon while in fact promoting spawning.[8]

Second, an accompanying myth — that the effects of development can be overcome through artificial transport of juvenile salmon — remains a central element in the current salmon restoration program, despite a series of scientific studies that indicate its likely ineffectiveness in recovering Columbia Basin salmon. It took over a hundred years for the hatchery myth to be exposed; the learning curve concerning transportation has to be shorter, since salmon species do not have as long for this scientific reality to be translated into policy. The fact is that technological fixes, like hatcheries and transportation, cannot serve as the basis for viable salmon recovery. This reality was recognized by the independent scientists of the Northwest Power Planning Council in 1996, but was lost in the National Marine Fisheries Service's 2000 decision to continue to rely on barge and truck transport as a key element of salmon recovery.[9]

Third, there is the myth that salmon recovery will require a return to a pre-development river, a "wilderness servitude," as one court put it. The only remaining self-sustaining salmon stock in the Columbia Basin is the Hanford Reach fall chinook of the Mid-Columbia. While it is true that the Hanford Reach is the last undammed stretch of the mainstem Columbia and Snake Rivers, it is hardly a "natural" river. The flows in the Hanford Reach which have allowed salmon to thrive are the product of an artificial environment, albeit one created with salmon in mind. The Mid-Columbia FERC settlement agreement, which governs those flows, was the product of years of contention, litigation, and administrative proceedings. That agreement ought to be a model for creating a viable flow regime in other parts of the Columbia Basin, especially the Lower Snake. The notion that salmon require a pre-development, natural river is a myth; recognizing that myth, the Northwest Power Planning Council's independent scientists called for the creation of "normative" river conditions — restoration of river functions within the existing developed river that would promote salmon recovery without dismantling all development and its benefits.[10]

Fourth, the myth that science will make decisions easy is widespread. Senator Gorton of Washington believed that more science would rein in fish recovery spending under the Northwest Power Act, so he had Congress amend the statute to require scientific review. But scientific review showed that technological fixes like hatcheries and transportation would not restore the fish runs — and helped to reveal their expense.

Senator Gorton learned that science is full of surprises, such as the revelation that the best way to recover Columbia Basin salmon was to draw down mainstem reservoirs to reproduce lost salmon spawning habitat. Science can inform decisions, but it does not, and should not dictate them. Unfortunately, as Will Stelle, former Regional Director of NMFS once observed, most people practice "pick-and-choose . . . agenda-driven science" in which the quality of the science is judged by the apparent results achieved. This is not biological science but political science. The science needs to be separated from the policy, as much as is possible, so that the public is fully informed of the basis for decisions.[11]

Fifth, the myth that the ESA is a draconian, anti-developmental statute remains widespread, despite the fact that the statute has allowed NMFS to sanction continuation of artificial transportation of juvenile salmon instead of repairing salmon habitat. In fact, the ESA's recovery plan for Columbia Basin salmon is less protective of spawning salmon than that of the unenforced plans of either the Northwest Power Planning Council or the Columbia Basin tribes with treaty fishing rights. It is true that the ESA occasionally blocks some developments, like the Inland Land irrigation proposal (discussed in chapter 9), but to suggest that the "ESA block[s] all development," as one recent analysis concludes, is quite inaccurate. Actually, the ESA has sufficient flexibility to have authorized timber harvests that would damage Umpqua Basin salmon habitat (subsequently foreclosed by the Northwest Forest Plan, also discussed in chapter 9). ESA consultation also ratified dredging the Lower Columbia River to deepen the river's navigation channel (subsequently blocked by state water quality concerns), despite the fact that the health of that estuary is a prime reason that NMFS's scientists suggested that breaching the Lower Snake Dams would not by itself recover Snake River salmon. In short, the ESA is hardly draconian in implementation and frequently reaches results that are quite sensitive to economic interests.[12]

A sixth myth is the idea that the restoration of Columbia Basin salmon is a regional issue warranting a regional solution. The notion that Northwesterners should be left to solve the salmon problem has wide currency among regional politicians because it essentially means that they should resolve the issue. But Columbia Basin salmon restoration is a national problem, created in large measure by federal dams and federal subsidies to navigators, irrigators, and electricity users. The cost of maintaining the Lower Snake Dams is currently in excess of $200 million per year, much of it paid by federal taxpayers. The treaties that promised the tribes a fishing livelihood are a federal obligation, as is the trust duty to protect tribal property, as is the obligation to fulfill treaty promises to Canada. So are the requirements to protect endangered species and fulfill international treaties. Calls for a regional solution are usually code phrases at discounting these legitimate federal interests.[13]

Seventh, the rise of ecosystem management as the recovery plan of choice contains the seeds of its own myth. It is certainly true that any program of salmon restoration needs to account for all of the "H's": adverse effects from hydroelectric operations, harvest, hatcheries, and habitat damage. But if ecosystem management is used to justify continuation of trucking and barging salmon — the apparent antithesis of an ecosystem approach — the concept is revealed to be so malleable as to be without substance. If ecosystem management's chief function is to reduce the likelihood of searching judicial review, as in the case of NMFS 1995 BiOp on hydroelectric operations, it is hard to see how salmon will benefit. The new "all H" approach trumpeted by NMFS in its 2000 BiOp seems designed to deflect attention from the salmon mortalities produced by the hydroelectric system, where the lion's share of mortalities occur. By diverting attention away from hydroelectric mortalities to habitat concerns, where states are responsible for most land and water use decisions, the federal government redirected attention away from itself. While an ecosystem perspective to salmon recovery is hard to criticize in theory, in practice it could produce a recovery plan which is badly misdirected.[14]

Finally, the sometimes-mentioned notion that the Columbia Basin salmon problem could be solved if the stakeholders could just talk among themselves is another myth. This idea was tried and found wanting in the "Salmon Summit" of 1990, but it continues to be discussed as if it might produce a viable solution. Such conversations might get the parties to know each other's representatives better, but these conversations seldom produce consensus. Conversations among stakeholders should not be discouraged, for they certainly can produce understanding. But to expect them to produce solutions is to expect too much.[15]

The Future

Making predictions about the future is a hazardous enterprise. The current Endangered Species Act status of the wild salmon of the Columbia Basin is the fruit of more than a century of unwise policies, and it will not be remedied quickly or painlessly. The failed efforts of the Mitchell Act, the Lower Columbia Fishery Development Program, the Lower Snake Compensation Plan, and the Northwest Power Act, ought to counsel against expectations for a quick fix under the ESA. In fact, experience with ESA implementation since 1993 suggests that there will be no dramatic changes in the fortunes of Columbia Basin salmon.

Still, much has been learned in recent years. Perhaps the most important lesson was from the Northwest Power Planning Council's 1996 report, *Return to the River*, which counseled that the mainstem Columbia and Snake Rivers should not be thought of as merely transportation corridors but should be considered potential spawning grounds, as they were before the dams were built. This did not mean, according to the scientists who authored the report, that all the dams should be removed. But they did suggest that some reservoirs should be lowered to permit spawning in historic mainstem spawning areas. The idea would be to attempt to replicate pre-development conditions in as many areas as feasible in light of the developed river.[16]

The "normative river" endorsed by the scientists in *Return to the River* is a worthy model for the 21st century. The way to implement this vision is to decide what is feasible by determining what is affordable. But what is affordable in terms of remaking the Columbia Basin into a fit place for salmon spawning must begin with an examination of the costs of current operations. Reliable estimates exceed $200 million annually, including the costs of current salmon transportation program. Economic analyses like the Corps' draft environmental impact statement on Lower Snake River juvenile salmon migration, which assume that continuation of the status quo is without cost, simply mislead the public and cast doubt on the other figures in the report. Even so, the Corps' estimated $359 million cost of removing the four federal dams should be compared to the $1 billion every four or five years it currently costs to maintain the dams.[17]

If breaching the Lower Snake Dams really costs less than two years of their annual maintenance costs, their breaching ought to be the cornerstone of any serious Snake River salmon recovery plan. Breaching would create a free-flowing Snake River of over 220 miles, more than five times longer than the Mid-Columbia's Hanford Reach, where the basin's only self-sustaining salmon runs now spawn. As the regional director for the U.S. Fish and Wildlife Service stated, in terms of biology the breaching alternative is clearly superior: "a no brainer."

Breaching the Lower Snake Dams may not be sufficient to recover the salmon runs, however. The free-flowing river must still comply with water quality standards, which themselves must be scrutinized to ensure that they meet the Clean Water Act's goal of fishable waters. Hatchery practices need a complete overhaul; where hatcheries are adversely affecting wild stocks, they should be discontinued, and the money reprogrammed to habitat protection. The tribes' supplementation plans, on the other hand, which are designed to produce spawning salmon while avoiding adverse effects on wild stocks, ought to proceed under careful monitoring and evaluation. Harvests also should proceed on the same basis of close monitoring and evaluation. But it ought to be recognized that tribal harvesters have suffered the longest and most severe cutbacks — no commercial harvests of summer chinook since 1964, and no harvests of spring chinook since 1977 — and that the basic premise of white settlement of the Pacific Northwest was that the tribes would maintain their fishing livelihoods, a promise forgotten for most of the past century.[18]

In the wake of the NMFS refusal to recommend dam breaching — and the steadfast opposition of virtually every regional politician not opting for silence, save for Oregon Governor John Kitzhaber and the Seattle City Council — prospects for recovery of Snake River salmon seem bleak. The shame is that the Snake River runs will have been sacrificed for such marginal economic benefits — maintenance of heavily subsidized barge transportation, a small percentage of the region's hydropower, and irrigation to thirteen corporate farms — and the political power of a narrow group of economic interests to resist changes to the status quo. Columbia Basin salmon have been sacrificed for much more in the past. The pity is that they are now being sacrificed for so little.[19]

16 – LESSONS: THE COLUMBIA BASIN AND BEYOND

The saga of Columbia Basin salmon contains lessons that should be useful beyond the confines of the Columbia Basin and for resources other than salmon. Few species are as prized as salmon in the Northwest, although there may be some. But the more than 20-year effort to restore salmon runs, largely unsuccessful thus far despite Indian treaties, federal statutes, an international treaty, numerous scientific and economic studies, and a growing wave of litigation, counsels caution, not optimism. It is much more difficult to restore a wildlife species which has suffered long-term decline than to protect one from prospective harm. Restoring a species whose decline is due to activities with apparent economic benefits is even more daunting, perhaps beyond what can realistically be expected from policymakers.

The development of Columbia Basin streamflows for hydropower, flood control, navigation, and irrigation crippled the basin's salmon runs. But there was never any clear intent to destroy the salmon resource. In fact, the operative assumption was that the region could have both developed rivers and harvestable salmon, a myth that could persist only as long as hatcheries could be viewed as viable substitutes for the habitat lost due to the dams. By the time that the notion that one technology could compensate for the adverse effects of another fell into disrepute in the 1990s, it was very late in the game. The weight of history had coalesced around a developed river of dams, barges, cheap electricity, and irrigated agriculture. That these activities required enormous federal subsidies was less significant than that regional economic interests had come to rely on the developed river. These settled expectations seemed to matter more than the best available science about how to recover the salmon runs, even to a supposedly biologically oriented agency like the National Marine Fisheries Service.

The Northwest Power Act's call for parity between hydropower operations and salmon migration reflected the optimism of 1980. Perhaps influenced by power interests' claims that they were anxious to meet the species' needs, the 1980 statute assumed that operational changes to the hydroelectric system could restore the Columbia's salmon. After passage of the statute, however, those same interests opposed increased river flows for salmon, questioned the authority of the program the statute authorized to require changes in the operation of federal dams, and sought to subject restoration measures to stringent scientific proof and cost-benefit tests. The upshot was years of controversy over the measures in the program, and a persistent reluctance on the part of federal agencies with water management responsibilities to implement the program fashioned by the interstate agency, the Northwest Power Planning Council.

The opposition of what the Ninth Circuit called "entrenched economic river interests" and uncertain federal-state relations burdened the Council's restoration program, causing the Council to resort often to what the court referred to as the "lowest common denominator" and making implementation of the measures the Council approved problematic. Not only did the program include compromised measures such as the water budget, which contained too little water for too short a time to significantly aid salmon migration, but the federal implementing agencies proved reluctant to implement measures they perceived to be inconsistent with their traditional statutory missions. These difficult institutional arrangements ultimately became more significant than the innovations in the 1980 statute, such as redefining the concept of fish and wildlife mitigation to include dam operational changes; deferring to the views of federal, state, and tribal fishery agencies; lowering the burden of proof for remedial action; adopting a systemwide approach to restoration efforts; and funding those efforts with hydropower revenues. The lesson may be that statutory innovations, however conceptually sound, are no substitute for implementation of actual measures. The program's implementation track record in this regard fell well short of its promise.

Implementation problems were not the only shortcoming of the salmon restoration program authorized by the Northwest Power Act. The program had a limited scope of authority: it did not reach water diversions, public land management activities, harvest controls, or hatchery operations not funded by hydropower revenues. The program therefore could not offer a comprehensive approach to salmon restoration. Moreover, since it relied on recommendations from diverse federal, state, and tribal agencies, the program evolved into an eclectic hodgepodge of measures that lacked scientific coherence. All of these problems reduced the program's ability to provide the imaginative and innovative problem solving that Congress expected. Instead, the Northwest Power Planning Council became a negotiator, a broker of deals, which contributed to complaints that the program appealed only to the lowest common denominator. It was no surprise that this interstate program was eclipsed in the 1990s by the listings of salmon under the Endangered Species Act.

When the program authorized by the Northwest Power Act was in its first years, representatives from the U.S. and Canada culminated two decades of negotiations with the signing of the Pacific Salmon Treaty of 1985. The treaty was necessary because of the great geographical scope of the salmon life cycle, in which salmon spawning in the Columbia Basin frequently were harvested in Canadian and Alaskan waters. These relatively uncontrolled distant harvests made a comprehensive approach to salmon restoration impossible. But although the treaty promised equitable harvests between the countries, in practice they could not agree on what equity meant. In fact, the U.S. itself was divided, with Alaskans having a different view than the rest of the delegation. Alaskan harvests of Canadian-spawned salmon produced Canadian retaliation in the form of increased harvests of Columbia Basin-origin salmon. These developments frustrated the treaty promise of preventing overfishing. A 1999 amendment to the treaty introduced abundance-based harvests, which may curtail overharvests, since it links harvest levels to available fish, but the science of estimating available fish is hardly an exact one. Moreover, although the treaty promised to rebuild salmon runs, the long controversy over equitable harvests kept attention riveted on harvests at the expense of habitat protection and restoration. Whether that focus can shift under the new abundance-based harvest scheme is far from clear. Perhaps as in the case of the Northwest Power Act, agreeing to high-minded principles is much easier than implementing them.

The Endangered Species Act (ESA), sometimes referred to as the pit-bull of environmental statutes, was brought to bear on the Columbia Basin salmon crisis in the early 1990s as a result of citizen petitions, not governmental choice. Although the goal of the ESA — prevention of jeopardy to the continued existence of salmon — is more modest than the Northwest Power Act's goal of doubling run sizes, the ESA subjects a much wider range of activities to scrutiny than just hydropower operations, including water withdrawals, salmon harvests, hatchery releases, and public and private land management decisions. The ESA proved to be no panacea for salmon, however. Despite its reputation for ignoring economic consequences, in practice the biological opinions on federal actions that affect Columbia Basin salmon revealed a remarkable sensitivity to economic interests. In fact, the latest biological opinion on hydroelectric operations opted not to recommend breaching of the Lower Snake River dams, even though that clearly is the best biological option for saving Snake River salmon.

Somewhat surprisingly, the marriage of Columbia Basin salmon and the ESA seems to have led to more changes in the implementation of the ESA than in the condition of the salmon. Among the most prominent of the salmon's legacies to the ESA are the definition of salmon stocks subject to ESA protection as evolutionarily significant units, the introduction of multi-year biological opinions for ongoing federal activities, the creation of streamlined procedures which avoid formal biological opinions prepared by NMFS in favor of biological assessments by action agencies, and the use of section 4(d) rules to authorize takes of salmon which are consistent with approved state and local conservation plans. Many of these innovations will be employed in the future far beyond the context of Columbia Basin salmon. Unfortunately, the ESA's legacy to Columbia Basin salmon is hardly as impressive. In fact, the Northwest Forest Plan has imposed greater restrictions on timber harvests than the ESA, and the ESA has not been applied at all to ongoing operations of FERC-licensed projects or to water distribution actions of the Bureau of Reclamation.

Judicial interpretations of the ESA's application to Columbia Basin salmon may also influence activities beyond the Northwest. The initial decision, striking down as arbitrary the biological opinion on hydroelectric operations and calling for a complete system overhaul, interpreted the ESA's mandate of making decisions based on "best available scientific knowledge" to require consideration of the views of other federal, state, and tribal agencies with biological expertise, an innovative interpretation which may make ESA consultation much more open and public than it has been in the past. But the second court decision, upholding a revised biological opinion that relied heavily on artificial transportation rather than improving river conditions to aid salmon migration, illustrated that NMFS could obtain favorable judicial review by invoking ecosystem management principles to defend its chosen course of action. Even though the court questioned the level of species risk NMFS found tolerable, it would not overrule the agency's choice, since the ESA said nothing about what was an acceptable level of risk.

The unwillingness of the court to closely scrutinize NMFS's risk decisions no doubt encouraged the agency to eschew dam breaching and endorse — despite two decades of poor results — a continuation of the program of barging and trucking salmon downstream. To reach this end, NMFS had to discount a series of studies it had commissioned from an interagency team, under the rubric of the Plan for Analyzing and Testing Hypotheses, since those studies indicated that dam breaching was by far the least risky way of restoring Snake River salmon. NMFS then developed a new series of studies, the Cumulative Risk Initiative, authored by its own Science Center, which employed mathematical models to question whether the recovery of Snake River salmon required dam breaching. The new studies thus provided NMFS with scientific cover to continue artificial transportation, along with promised programs of offsite habitat restoration and hatchery reform.

An obvious question is why NMFS, an agency charged by the ESA with rescuing species from the brink of extinction, would prove to be so sensitive to economics in practice. The answer undoubtedly lies in the power of organized interest groups to bring pressure on decision makers to protect a status quo favoring their economic position. Over the past two-and-a-half decades, since completion of the last of the Lower Snake Dams, ports and farmers have come to rely on cheap transportation and, to a lesser extent, cheap power and irrigation water from the developed Snake River. Their intense interest in maintaining the status quo has convinced regional politicians and apparently even NMFS to support their position, an example of the power of concentrated pressure from a minority to maintain a status quo that disserves the majority, even when that status quo requires large-scale federal subsidies.

Beyond the ESA, the Clean Water and Federal Power Acts offer possible remedies for Columbia Basin salmon. Some of these possibilities have yet to be fully explored, but they certainly would not be confined to the Columbia Basin or to salmon. The application of water quality standards to federal dams, the chief killers of Columbia Basin salmon, may produce substantial changes in dam operations. Further, the application of ESA consultation to the water quality standards themselves could produce standards protective of listed species, which would be consistent with the Clean Water Act's goal of providing water quality protective of fish life. The Federal Power Act's provisions requiring fishway conditions and protection of federal land reservations, coupled with required water quality standards certification, should ensure that a new generation of relicensed non-federal projects will be more sensitive to salmon concerns. Moreover, application of these requirements may make the cost of relicensing high enough to make dam removal a viable option, as it was in the case of the Edwards and Condit Dams. Although the Federal Power Act has less universal applicability than the Clean Water Act, in river basins with licensed projects relicensing it can have dominating effects on imperiled species.

Ecosystem management principles may come to dominate Columbia Basin salmon restoration in the early 21st century. This development is hard to dispute theoretically, since attempting to affect only a part of the salmon life cycle through regulation of harvests or hatchery construction produced unsatisfactory results in the past. Single-focused attempts such as these tended to concentrate on the short term and on technological fixes to the salmon problem. The result is a Columbia River in which more than 80 percent of its salmon is of hatchery origin, and where more than half of the upriver juvenile fish are taken out of the river and transported downstream by truck and barge.

A more holistic approach, exemplified by the Northwest Power Planning Council's 1996 *Return to the River* report, was and is badly needed. That study emphasized the importance of habitat protection and restoration, but those measures are long-term in nature: they will not produce an immediate increase in salmon numbers. Even more central to *Return to the River* was the concept of creating habitat conditions suitable for salmon spawning, rearing, and migration, what the report termed a "normative river." A normative river is not a natural river, but a river environment suitable for salmon which can be obtained by changing the operation of the developed river. To an extent, that was precisely the result the drafters of the Northwest Power Act's salmon restoration program intended. Unfortunately, that statute has been interpreted to require creation of suitable conditions for salmon while making no more than minor changes to the hydroelectric system. But it is the hydroelectric system which has the flexibility to accommodate the salmon; the salmon do not have similar flexibility, as the widespread ESA listings show. The normative river concept is one that other river basins may find quite useful.

Ecosystem management, like the ESA, is no panacea. Its holistic approach could encourage diverting attention from the source of 80 percent or more of non-natural salmon mortalities: the hydroelectric system. In fact, NMFS has invoked ecosystem management as a defense to its reliance on barge and truck transportation instead of dam breaching to save Snake River salmon. This invocation produced judicial deference from the same court which had overturned an earlier NMFS decision as arbitrary. If ecosystem management leads to a reduced emphasis on hydroelectric operations, it will retard Columbia salmon restoration in the interest of pursuing an intriguing concept that makes intuitive sense but that cannot succeed if it loses sight of the context of the broader problem it seeks to resolve.

An ecosystem management program worthy of emulation is the tribal restoration plan, which embraces a gravel-to-gravel management philosophy for salmon restoration. The tribes' ability to become major players in salmon restoration decision making just 20 years after the Supreme Court affirmed their property rights in salmon is a remarkable development. They have quickly developed governmental abilities in response to the court's declaration of their property rights, a development that Judge Boldt anticipated when he recognized their governmental rights in 1974. A quarter century later it is the tribes which have the best blueprint for the restoration of Columbia Basin salmon. Tribes in other locations may be able to bring their own governmental expertise to bear on resources on which their livelihood depends.

The ultimate promise to protect salmon may have been that made in the 1850s, in a series of treaties which promised the tribes "the right of taking fish in common with" white settlers. Although the Supreme Court later interpreted this language to promise the tribes a livelihood, and lower courts accorded protection to fish habitat in particular situations, the courts have been reluctant to declare that the treaties include a generic right to protect fish habitat. Because enforcing treaty promises is inevitably dependent on judicial action, enforcement is slow, uncertain, and costly. In the case of Indian treaties, however, there is no real alternative, since the democratic process is not willingly going to enforce promises that seem now to benefit a minority of the population. But, in fact, enforcing the treaty promises has benefited everyone, although most of the benefits to the majority from the largely peaceful settlement of 64 million acres of Pacific Northwest land accrued long ago, while the promise of a viable fishing economy remains elusive 150 years later. The truth is that enforcing the treaty promise of a fishing livelihood will redound to the benefit all who care about Columbia Basin salmon: non-native commercial and recreational harvesters as well as those who believe that now, just as a century-and-a-half ago, harvestable salmon runs are the paramount symbol of the Pacific Northwest.

A NOTE ON THE SOURCES

Over the years, in law review articles, I have written literally thousands of footnotes on Columbia Basin salmon. Even the *Anadromous Fish Law Memo*, which I edited for eleven years between 1979 and 1990, had numerous footnotes in each issue. Over twenty years of footnotes wearied me, so when I read Richard White's *The Organic Machine: The Remaking of the Columbia River* — a book without any footnotes at all — I was inspired to emulate White's example. However, several reviewers discouraged me from pursuing that idea, so the book I wrote has numerous footnotes.

But I did make a diligent effort to limit the number of footnotes by confining them to the end of paragraphs and limiting the references to a few sources. Frequently, the footnotes contain references to my law review articles, which often contain more detailed citations to authority.

Citations conform generally to The University of Chicago Manual of Legal Citation, supplemented by The Chicago Manual of Style, except that references to my law review articles are by short cite only. Those include the following (in alphabetical order):

Amphibious Salmon — *The Amphibious Salmon: The Evolution of Ecosystem Management in the Columbia Basin*, 24 ECOLOGY L.Q. 653 (1997).

Beyond Parity — *Beyond the Parity Promise: Struggling to Save Columbia Basin Salmon in the Mid-1990s,* 27 ENVTL. L. 21 (1997) (with Michael A. Schoessler & R. Christopher Beckwith).

Fulfilling Parity — *Fulfilling the Parity Promise: A Perspective on Scientific Proof, Economic Cost, and Indian Treaty Fishing Rights in the Approval of the Columbia Basin Fish and Wildlife Program,* 13 ENVTL. L. 103 (1982).

Hydroelectric Heritage — *The Northwest's Hydroelectric Heritage: Prologue to the Pacific Northwest Electric Power Planning and Conservation Act*, 58 WASH. L. REV. 175 (1983).

Hydropower vs. Salmon — *Hydropower vs. Salmon: The Struggle of the Pacific Northwest's Anadromous Fish For a Peaceful Coexistence With the Federal Columbia River Power System*, 11 ENVTL. L. 211 (1981).

Implementing Parity — *Implementing the Parity Promise: An Evaluation of the Columbia Basin Fish and Wildlife Program*, 14 ENVTL. L. 277 (1984).

Piscary Profit — *The Indian Treaty Piscary Profit and Habitat Protection in the Pacific Northwest: A Property Rights Approach*, 69 U. COLO. L. REV. 407 (1998) (with Brett M. Swift).

Reviving Parity — *Columbia Basin Salmon and the Courts: Reviving the Parity Promise*, 25 ENVTL. L. 351 (1995).

Saving Idaho's Salmon — *Saving Idaho's Salmon: A History of Failure and a Dubious Future*, 28 IDAHO L. REV. 667 (1992).

Salmon Lessons — *Salmon and the Endangered Species Act: Lessons From the Columbia Basin*, 74 WASH. L. REV. 519 (1999) (with Greg D. Corbin).

The Case For Dam Breaching — *Saving Snake River Water and Salmon Simultaneously: The Biological, Economic, and Legal Case For Breaching the Lower Snake Dams, Lowering John Day Reservoir, and Restoring Natural River Flows*, 28 ENVTL. L. 997 (1998) (with Laird J. Lucas, Don B. Miller, Daniel J. Rohlf & Glen S. Spain).

Unraveling Parity — *The Unraveling of the Parity Promise: Hydropower, Salmon, and Endangered Species in the Columbia Basin*, 21 ENVTL. L. 657 (1991) (with Andy Simrin).

ENDNOTES

Notes to Chapter 1

[1]   TIMOTHY EGAN, THE GOOD RAIN: ACROSS TIME AND TERRAIN IN THE PACIFIC NORTHWEST 22, 181 (Alfred A. Knopf 1990) ("anywhere a salmon can get to," "ritualized fornication"); WILLIAM DIETRICH, NORTHWEST PASSAGE: THE GREAT COLUMBIA RIVER 188 (Simon and Schuster 1995) (Clark quote); ATSUSHI SAKURAI & JOHN N. COLE, SALMON 7 (Alfred A. Knopf 1984) (ocean proteins).

[2]   SAKURAI & COLE (cited in note 1), at 3.

[3]   *Id.* at 4; JOSEPH E. TAYLOR III, MAKING SALMON: AN ENVIRONMENTAL HISTORY OF THE NORTHWEST FISHERIES CRISIS 6-7 (U. Washington Press 1999).

[4]   SAKURAI & COLE (cited in note 1) at 7; ANTHONY NETBOY, THE COLUMBIA RIVER SALMON AND STEELHEAD TROUT: THEIR FIGHT FOR SURVIVAL 16-17 (U. Washington Press 1980); TAYLOR (cited in note 3) at 33 (noting that the First Salmon Ceremony was not universally employed).

[5]   NETBOY (cited in note 4), at 10 (salmon attracted Asian natives); United States v. Washington, 384 F. Supp. 312, 350 (W.D. 1974) (universal dependence); Brief For the Indian Tribes in Washington v. Washington State Commercial Passenger Fishing Vessel Ass'n., 443 U.S. 658 (1979) at 7, quoting Dr. Barbara Lane on native trade) [hereinafter cited as Tribal Brief]; American Friends Service Comm., UNCOMMON CONTROVERSY: FISHING RIGHTS OF THE MUCKLESHOOT, PUYALLUP AND NISQUALLY INDIANS 3 (1970) (richest aboriginals) [hereinafter cited as UNCOMMON CONTROVERSY]; R. J. CHILDERHOSE & MARJ TRIM, PACIFIC SALMON 5 (U. Washington Press 1979) (salmon equivalent to buffalo and reindeer).

[6]   GEORGE WOODCOCK, PEOPLES OF THE COAST 117 (Indiana U. Press 1977) (elaborate procedures); Tribal Brief (cited in note 5), at 6 (bailing canoes); CHARLES F. WILKINSON, CROSSING THE NEXT MERIDIAN: LAND, WATER, AND THE FUTURE OF THE WEST 185 (Island Press 1992); NETBOY (cited in note 4), at 11 (peer pressure, religious taboos); TAYLOR (cited in note 3), at 27-38 (cultural and spiritual norms).

[7]   ROBERT BOYD, THE COMING OF THE SPIRIT OF PESTILENCE: INTRODUCED INFECTIOUS DISEASES AND POPULATION DECLINE AMONG NORTHWEST INDIANS 1774-1874 (U. Washington Press 1999); COURTLAND L. SMITH, SALMON FISHERS OF THE NORTHWEST 5 (Oregon St. U. Press 1979) (1851 estimate); TAYLOR (cited in note 3), at 22-24 (15-mile stretch of river supported over 1,000 people; annual 41 million pounds, relying on Randall F. Schalk, *Estimating Salmon and Steelhead Usage in the Columbia Basin Before 1850: The Anthropological Perspective,* 2 NW ENVTL. J. 19-21 (1986)).

[8]   Tribal Brief (cited in note 5), at 9 (quoting Dr. Barbara Lane); Oregon Territorial Act, 9 Stat. 323 (1848); Oregon Land Donation Act, 9 Stat. 496 (1850).

[9]   Treaty of Medicine Creek, December 26, 1854, 10 Stat. 1132; Treaty of Point Elliot, January 22, 1855, 12 Stat. 927; Treaty of Point No Point, January 26, 1855, 12 Stat. 933; Treaty of Neah Bay, January 31, 1855, 12 Stat. 939; Treaty with the Walla Walla, June 9, 1855, 12 Stat. 945; Treaty with the Yakimas, June 9, 1855, 12 Stat. 951; Treaty with the Nez Perce, June 11,1855, 12 Stat. 957; Treaty with the Tribes of Middle Oregon, June 25, 1855, 12 Stat. 963; Treaty of Olympia, July 1, 1855, 12 Stat. 971; Treaty with the Quinaielts, July 1, 1855, 12 Stat. 971; Treaty with the Flathead, July 6, 1855, 12 Stat. 975. Tribal Brief (cited in note 5), at 23 (salmon as a means of economic self-sufficiency).

[10]   Tribal Brief (cited in note 5), at 17; United States v. Taylor, 3 Wash. Terr. 88 (1887), discussed in chap. 4, text with notes 3-4.

[11]   CHILDERHOSE & TRIM (cited in note 5), at 9; WILKINSON (cited in note 6), at 188; NETBOY (cited in note 4), at 21, 23-24.

[12]   WILKINSON (cited in note 6), at 188 (frenzied free-for-all); Tribal Brief (cited in note 5), at 17-18, 22-24 (proliferation of canneries, new technologies); NETBOY (cited in note 4), at 21 (tribal fishing contributing to canneries).

[13]   NETBOY (cited in note 4), at 19-20 (salmon preserves).

[14]   *Id.* at 34-36.

[15]   On fish wheels, see generally FREDERICK K. CRAMER, FISHWHEELS OF THE COLUMBIA (Binfords & Mort 1971).

[16]   CHILDERHOSE & TRIM (cited in note 5), at 10-11.

[17]   SMITH (cited in note 7), at 74; *Pacific Fisherman* 3 (Aug. 1905) at 20, cited in SMITH, at 74 n.11.

[18]   SMITH (cited in note 7), at 74 (1909 harvest); BRUCE BROWN, MOUNTAIN IN THE CLOUDS: A SEARCH FOR THE WILD SALMON 147 (Simon and Schuster 1982) (1935 harvest; previous harvests averaged 48 million fish).

[19]   DIETRICH (cited in note 1), at 278-79, 310 (Rock Island Dam; Grand Coulee Dam); Bonneville Project Act of 1937, Pub. L. No. 75-329, 50 Stat. 731 (codified as 16 U.S.C. § 832(a), (1994)). On the building of Grand Coulee, see PAUL PITZER, GRAND COULEE: HARNESSING A DREAM (Washington St. U. Press 1994).

[20]   *Hydropower vs. Salmon*, at 228-29 (discussing the 1937 report of the Commissioner of Fisheries); DIETRICH (cited in note 1), at 337-38, (downstream passage problems).

[21]   *Hydropower vs. Salmon*, at 229-34; *Hydroelectric Heritage*, at 205-07.

[22]   *Hydropower vs. Salmon*, at 230 (15% of costs); DIETRICH (cited in note 1), at 339 (5% to 75% mortality). On the efforts to get Congress to authorize construction of the Lower Snake River dams, which began in the early part of the twentieth century, see KEITH C. PETERSEN, RIVER OF LIFE, CHANNEL OF DEATH: FISH AND DAMS ON THE LOWER SNAKE 87-97 (Confluence Press 1995).

[23]   National Marine Fisheries Service, *Biological Opinion on 1995-99 Federal Hydroelectric Operations* 4 (1995) (80% of mortalities); Pub. L. No. 75-502, ch. 193, (codified at 16 U.S.C. § 755) (Mitchell Act).

[24]   DIETRICH (cited in note 1), at 381.

[25]   *Hydropower vs. Salmon*, at 273-74 (Lower Snake hatchery program); 6 WATER AND WATER RIGHTS 89-90 (Robert E. Beck ed. 1994) (hatcheries as a narcotic).

[26]   JIM LICHATOWICH, SALMON WITHOUT RIVERS: A HISTORY OF THE PACIFIC SALMON CRISIS 170-201 (Island Press 1999) (comparing the Columbia and Fraser Rivers); Mathew Evenden, *Fish vs. Power: Remaking Salmon, Science And Society* (Ph.D. Diss. York U. 2000); CHILDERHOSE & TRIM (cited in note 5), at 29, 89-106.

[27]   Federal Power Commission v. Udall, 387 U.S. 428, 437-38 (1967), discussed in Michael C. Blumm & F. Lorraine Bodi, *Commentary*, in NORTHWEST SALMON CRISIS: A DOCUMENTARY HISTORY 129-130 (Oregon St. U. Press 1996) [hereinafter NW SALMON CRISIS].

[28]   Ed Chaney, *A Question of Balance: Water/Energy — Salmon and Steelhead Production in the Upper Columbia River Basin* 13-17 (Northwest Resource Information Center 1978).

[29]   Sohappy v. Smith, 302 F. Supp. 899 (D. Or. 1969) (harvest "fair share"); United States v. Washington, 384 F. Supp. 312 (W.D. Wash. 1974) (half the harvests).

[30]   FAY G. COHEN, TREATIES ON TRIAL: THE CONTINUING CONTROVERSY OVER NORTHWEST INDIAN FISHING RIGHTS 3-17 (U. Washington Press 1986); United States v. Washington, 520 F.2d 676 (9th Cir. 1976); 573 F.2d 1118 (9th Cir. 1978) (affirmances by the court of appeals); Washington v. Passenger Fishing Vessel Ass'n., 443 U.S. 658 (1979) (Supreme Court affirmance); United States v. Washington, 573 F.2d at 1126 (9th Cir. 1978) ("except for some desegregation cases").

[31]   United States v. Washington, 384 F. Supp. at 1032 (2% of harvest).

[32]   Settler v. Lameer, 507 F.2d 231 (9th Cir. 1974).

[33]   United States v. Washington, 506 F. Supp. 187 (W.D. Wash. 1980); United States v. Washington, 759 F.2d 1353 (9th Cir. 1985).

[34]   16 U.S.C. § 839b(h)(10)(A) ("to extent affected"); H.R. Rep. No. 976, 96th Cong. 2d Sess. 49, 56 (1980) ("coequal," "on a par"); 16 U.S.C. § 839b(h)(6) ("best available science," biological outcomes favored, flows for salmon).

[35]   *See* 16 ANADROMOUS FISH LAW MEMO (Nat'l Res. L. Inst. 1982) (700 pages of recommendations); *Implementing Parity*, at 288-351 (overview of 1982 program); *Unraveling Parity*, at 675-677 (water budget).

[36]   Blumm & Bodi (cited in note 27), at 263-264.

[37]   Sohappy v. Smith, 302 F. Supp. 899 (D. Or. 1969) ("fair share"); *see A Plan for Managing Fisheries on Stocks Originating from the Columbia River and its Tributaries Above Bonneville Dam* (February 25, 1977); *Columbia River Fish Management Plan* (October 7, 1988); United States v. Oregon, 699 F.Supp. 1456, 1458 (D. Or. 1988), *aff'd*, 913 F.2d 576 (9th Cir. 1990) (approving an amended comprehensive plan). *See also Piscary Profit*, at 460-462.

[38]   United States-Canada Convention for the Protection, Preservation and Extension of the Fraser River Sockeye Salmon Fishery of the Fraser River System, signed May 26, 1930, T.I.A.S. No. 3867; Blumm & Bodi (cited in note 36), at 275 (startling decline).

[39]   Treaty Between the Government of the United States of America and the Government of Canada Concerning Pacific Salmon, March 18, 1985, T.I.A.S. No. 11091; Blumm & Bodi (cited in note 36), at 276 (failure to restrain habitat damage).

[40]   JOSEPH CONE, A COMMON FATE: ENDANGERED SALMON AND THE PEOPLE OF THE NORTHWEST 36-39 (Henry Holt 1995) (seeds sown in 1987); 54 Fed. Reg. 32,085 (1989) (Sacramento listing).

[41]   55 Fed. Reg. 37,342 (1990) (Snake River petitions); National Marine Fisheries Serv. & Oregon Dept. of Fish and Wildlife, *Past and Present Abundance of Snake River Sockeye, Snake River Chinook, and Lower Columbia river Coho*, 1960-88, at 11 (1989) (6% of 1961).

[42]   JOHN M. VOLKMAN, A RIVER IN COMMON: THE COLUMBIA RIVER, THE SALMON ECOSYSTEM, AND WATER POLICY 85-86 (Western Water Policy Review Advisory Comm'n. 1997) (drawdown proposal and leasing Upper Snake basin water); *Unraveling Parity*, at 725-26 (drawdown proposal).

[43]   Willa Nehlsen, Jack Williams & Jim Lichatowich, *Pacific Salmon At the Crossroads: Stocks at Risk from California, Oregon, Idaho, and Washington*, 16 FISHERIES no. 2, at 4 (1991).

[44]   *Saving Idaho's Salmon*, at 692 (1991 flow requirements); 56 Fed. Reg. 58,619 (1991) (sockeye listing); 57 Fed. Reg. 14,654 (1992) (chinook listing); *Salmon Lessons*, at 528-48 (other listings); Nat'l. Marine Fisheries Serv., *Endangered Species Act Status of West Coast Salmonids*, <http://www.nwr.noaa.gov/salmesa/pubs/pg999pdf>.

[45]   DANIEL J. ROHLF, THE ENDANGERED SPECIES ACT: A GUIDE TO ITS PROTECTIONS AND
IMPLEMENTATION 137-71 (Stanford Envtl. L. Soc'y 1989) (discussing biological opinions); Pacific Rivers
Council v. Thomas, 30 F.3d 1050 (9th Cir. 1994) (federal land management activities subject to the ESA),
discussed in *Salmon Lessons*, at 577-79.

[46]   James L. Buchal, *Some Fallacies About Salmon Restoration*, 25 ENVTL. L. 375 (1995)
(advocating artificial transportation).

[47]   *Salmon Lessons*, at 550-552 (few changes).

[48]   Northwest Resource Information Center v. Northwest Power Planning Council, 35 F.3d 1371
(9th Cir. 1994); Idaho Dep't of Fish and Game v. National Marine Fisheries Serv., 850 F. Supp. 886, 900
(D. Or. 1994) ("seriously . . . flawed").

[49]   National Marine Fisheries Service, *Biological Opinion on Reinitiation of Consultation on 1994-
98 Operation of Federal Columbia River Power System and Juvenile Transportation Program in 1995
and Future Years* 80 (1995), discussed in *Beyond Parity*, at 62-75; *see also id.* at 49-62 (discussing the
1994 amendments to the Columbia Basin Fish and Wildlife Program). The 2000 BiOp is *Nat'l Marine
Fisheries Service, Biological Opinion on Operation of the Federal Columbia River Power System,
Including the Juvenile Fish Transportation Program and 19 Bureau of Reclamation Projects in the
Columbia Basin* at A-3 to A-4 (Dec. 21, 2000) [hereinafter cited as *2000 BiOp*], discussed in chap 9, text
with notes 26-33.

[50]   *Beyond Parity*, at 103-07 ("salmon budget").

[51]   See *id.* at 117-19 (Senator Gorton's science amendment); VOLKMAN (cited in note 42), at 86
(effect of science review); *The Case for Dam Breaching*, at 1012-23 (scientific studies).

[52]   INDEPENDENT SCIENTIFIC GROUP, RETURN TO THE RIVER: RESTORATION OF SALMONID FISHES IN
THE COLUMBIA RIVER ECOSYSTEM xvii, 4-5, 268-69, 509 (Northwest Power Planning Council 1996)
[hereinafter cited as RETURN TO THE RIVER]. A revised version of this report was released by the
Northwest Power Planning Council in late 2000; *see* Doc. 2000-12, available at <www.nwcouncil.org>.

[53]   *The Case for Dam Breaching*, at 1023-31 (citing studies).

[54]   Oregon Natural Resources Council v. U.S. Forest Service, 59 F.Supp.2d 1085 (W.D. Wash.
1999) (failure to perform wildlife surveys); Pacific Coast Federation of Fishermen's Assoc. v. National
Marine Fisheries Serv., 71 F.Supp.2d 1063 (W.D. Wash. 1999), *aff'd* 253 F.3d 1138 (9th Cir. 2001)
(failure to implement aquatic conservation strategy).

[55]   Oregon Natural Resources Council v. Daley, 6 F.Supp.2d 1139, 1159 (D. Or. 1998). *See*
Christine Golightly, *The Oregon Coastal Salmon Restoration Initiative: A Flawed Attempt to Avoid an
ESA Listing*, 7 N.Y.U. ENVTL. J. L. 398 (1999).

[56]   For an overview of the Oregon and Washington approaches, see Mary Scurlock, *Private Forestlands and Salmon Recovery: A Look at Policy Developments Affecting Private Forestry in Oregon and Washington,* 4 BIG RIVER NEWS no. 4, at 5-7 (Nat'l. Res. L. Inst. Spring 1998). Section 4(d) of the ESA, 16 U.S.C. § 1533(d), authorizes NMFS to promulgate conservation regulations for threatened species.

[57]   The "all-H" paper (originally called the "4-H" approach, but changed due to protests from 4-H clubs) is outlined in Jonathan Brinckman & Jim Barnett, *Habitat Gains Emphasis Over Breaching Dams,* THE SUNDAY OREGONIAN, Nov. 7, 1999, at A1; see also Will Stelle, Jr., *Salmon and the ESA in the Columbia River Basin: The NMFS Perspective,* 6 BIG RIVER NEWS no. 2, at 1 (Nat'l. Res. L. Inst. Winter 2000).

Notes to Chapter 2

[1]   DIETRICH (cited in chapter 1, note 1), at 324 (sources of human wonderment and human wealth); *see generally* CORNELIUS GROOT AND LEO MARGOLIS, EDS., PACIFIC SALMON LIFE HISTORIES (U. British Columbia Press 1991) [hereinafter cited as PACIFIC SALMON LIFE HISTORIES].

[2]   LICHATOWICH (cited in chapter 1, note 26), at 11-12 (freshwater origin, ocean cooling); SAKURAI & COLE (cited in chapter 1, note 1) at 3 (freshwater flush).

[3]   SAKURAI & COLE (cited in chapter 1, note 1), at 3 (two distinct species); ANTHONY NETBOY, SALMON: THE WORLD'S MOST HARASSED FISH 32 (Winchester Press 1980) (more extensive ocean migrations).

[4]   SAKURAI & COLE (cited in chapter 1, note 1), at 4-5 ("brights"); CHILDERHOSE & TRIM (cited in chapter 1, note 5), at 31.

[5]   NETBOY (cited in note 3), at 36-37 (weight); SAKURAI & COLE (cited in chapter 1, note 1), at 5-6 (chum salmon characteristics).

[6]   SAKURAI & COLE (cited in chapter 1, note 1), at 6-7; CHILDERHOSE & TRIM (cited in chapter 1, note 5), at 32-34.

[7]   CHILDERHOSE & TRIM (cited in chapter 1, note 5), at 32-34.

[8]   SAKURAI & COLE (cited in chapter 1, note 1), at 7-8; CHILDERHOSE & TRIM (cited in chapter 1, note 5), at 37-38.

[9]   LICHATOWICH (cited in chapter 1, note 26), at 164, 234 (two types of chinook); PACIFIC SALMON LIFE HISTORIES (cited in note 1), at 314 (below 56th parallel); CHILDERHOSE & TRIM (cited in chapter 1, note 5), at 37-42.

[10]   National Marine Fisheries Serv., *Biological Opinion on 1994-98 Operation of Consultation of Federal Columbia River Power System and Juvenile Transportation Program in 1995 and Future Years* 68-69, 91 (1995) (in worst-case conditions, mortalities up to 96% for sockeye and spring/summer chinook, up to 97% for fall chinook).

[11]   CHILDERHOSE & TRIM (cited in chapter 1, note 5), at 43.

[12]   NETBOY (cited in note 3), at 33.

[13]   PACIFIC SALMON LIFE HISTORIES (cited in note 1), at ix (two Asian species).

[14]   BROWN (cited in chapter 1, note 18), at 62 (Elwah); LICHATOWICH (cited in chapter 1, note 26), at 21 (spawning preference).

[15]   LICHATOWICH (cited in chapter 1, note 26), at 233-34 (least abundant, two types of chinook); DIETRICH (cited in chapter 1, note 1), at 325 (spring chinook).

[16]   UNCOMMON CONTROVERSY (cited in chapter 1, note 5), at 48-49 (tribal reliance on fall chinook); Eric Lemelson, Brett Swift & Shauna Whidden, *Difficult Choices Face Policymakers on Future of Hanford Reach*, 2 BIG RIVER NEWS no. 1, at 1 (Nat'l. Resources L. Inst. Fall 1995) (Hanford Reach); *Salmon Lessons*, at 530-36 (chinook listings).

[17]   LICHATOWICH (cited in chapter 1, note 26), at 234 (coho life history); UNCOMMON CONTROVERSY (cited in chapter 1, note 5), at 149 (coho).

[18]   PACIFIC SALMON LIFE HISTORIES (cited in note 1), at 400.

[19]   LICHATOWICH (cited in chapter 1, note 26), at 207-08, 212 (coho harvests); 62 Fed. Reg. 24,588 (1997) (codified at 50 C.F.R. § 227.4(i)); 63 Fed . Reg. 24,588 (1997) (Northern California/Southern Oregon coho); 64 Fed. Reg. 42,587 (1998) (Oregon Coast coho). Central Califomia coho were listed in 1996, 61 Fed. Reg. 56,138 (1996), but Sacramento River coho went extinct in the mid-1980s without ESA intervention.

[20]   UNCOMMON CONTROVERSY (cited in chapter 1, note 5), at 149; PACIFIC SALMON LIFE HISTORIES (cited in note 1), at 99 (reduced interaction).

[21]   NETBOY (cited in note 3), at 29 (sockeye); PACIFIC SALMON LIFE HISTORIES (cited in note 1), at 5 (range to Sacramento River); Thomas Jensen, *The United States-Canada Pacific Salmon Interception Treaty: An Historical and Legal Overview*, 16 ENVTL. L. 363, 374 (1986) (1930 Convention); 56 Fed. Reg. 58,612 (1991) (sockeye listing); UNCOMMON CONTROVERSY (cited in chapter 1, note 5), at 149 n.2.

[22]   LICHATOWICH (cited in chapter 1, note 26), at 235; UNCOMMON CONTROVERSY (cited in chapter 1, note 5), at 150; NETBOY (cited in note 3), at 29, 33.

[23]   NETBOY (cited in chapter 1, note 4), at 41; PACIFIC SALMON LIFE HISTORIES (cited in note 1), at 286.

[24]   CHILDERHOSE & TRIM (cited in chapter 1, note 5), at 91-92; PACIFIC SALMON LIFE HISTORIES (cited in note 1), at 121.

[25]   NETBOY (cited in chapter 1, note 4), at 41-42 (spawn more than once, from December to June); UNCOMMON CONTROVERSY (cited in chapter 1, note 5), at 150 (4-year life cycle); LICHATOWICH (cited in chapter 1, note 26), at 235 (steelhead range); *see* <www.nwr.noaa.gov/salmon/salmesa/sthswit.htm> (10 steelhead runs listed); 63 Fed. Reg. 13,347 (1998), 64 Fed. Reg. 14,517 (1999) (steelhead listings).

[26]   See chapter 4's discussion of the *Puyallup* cases, text accompanying notes 18-20; NETBOY (cited in chapter 1, note 4), at 41 (Columbia Basin greatest producer).

[27]   LICHATOWICH (cited in chapter 1, note 26), at 22 ("central themes," habitat and salmon inextricably linked).

[28]   W.E. Ricker, *The Stock Conception in Pacific Salmon, in* HEREDITARY AND ENVIRONMENTAL FACTORS AFFECTING CERTAIN SALMONID POPULATIONS 19-160 (U. British Columbia Press 1972); Nehlsen *et al.* (cited in chapter 1, note 43), at 5-6.

[29]   BROWN (cited in chapter 1, note 18), at 80, 87 (reporting the late spawning fall run was wiped out due to irrigation practices).

[30]   NATIONAL ACADEMY OF SCIENCES, UPSTREAM: SALMON AND SOCIETY IN THE PACIFIC NORTHWEST 148, 319-20, 304-14 (1996) [hereinafter cited as UPSTREAM].

[31]   Nehlsen *et al.*, (cited in chapter 1, note 43), at 11 (depleted stocks).

[32]   RETURN TO THE RIVER (cited in chapter 1, note 52), at 70, 72-74.

[33]   *Id.* at 76-77.

[34]   *Id.* at 80.

[35]   UPSTREAM (cited in note 30), at 164; RETURN TO THE RIVER (cited in chapter 1, note 52), at 131; United States v. Washington, 506 F. Supp. at 203.

[36]   UPSTREAM (cited in note 30), at 180-99, 201.

[37]   *Id.* at 2, 75-76.

[38]   *Id.* at 2-3, 76-77.

39   *Id.* at 87-89.

40   *Id.* at 103-105.

41   56 Fed. Reg. 58.612, 58,619-22 (1991).

42   57 Fed. Reg. 14,653, 16,659 (1992). Although environmentalists petitioned NMFS to list spring and summer chinook, NMFS decided to combine them into one "evolutionarily significant unit," citing genetic similarities and difficulty in clearly demarcating life history distinctions between the two runs. *Id.* at 14,654-55.

43   *Id.* at 14,660.

44   *Id.* (hydropower the chief cause); 59 Fed. Reg. 42,529, 42,530-31 (1994) (emergency interim rule). In 1998, NMFS ultimately decided not to classify the species as endangered, citing increased adult returns. 63 Fed. Reg. 1807, 1809-10 (1998) (spring/summer chinook numbers up to 6500 in 1997 from 1116 in 1995; fall chinook up to 726 from 350 in 1995).

45   On ocean conditions, see *Oregon and the Management of Columbia River Salmon: Proceedings of a Symposium* (Northwest Power Planning Council Doc. 99-11, Gustavo A. Bishal, ed. July 1, 1999). For an example of an opponent of freshwater restoration efforts, see Buchal (cited in chapter 1, note 46).

46   National Marine Fisheries Service, *Biological Opinion for 1995 to 1998 Hatchery Operations in the Columbia Basin* 36 (1995) [hereinafter cited as *1995-1998 Hatchery BiOp*]; National Marine Fisheries Service, *Biological Opinion on Artificial Propagation in the Columbia Basin* (March 29, 1999) [hereinafter cited as *1999 Hatchery BiOp*].

47   *Id.* at 43,942-44.

48   *See* 64 Fed. Reg. 14,308 (1999) (Upper Columbia spring chinook); 64 Fed. Reg. 14,508 (1999) (Columbia River chum); 64 Fed. Reg. 14,528 (1999) (Mid-Columbia steelhead).

49   UPSTREAM (cited in note 30), at 101; 62 Fed. Reg. 43,937 (1997) (Upper Columbia and Snake River listings); 63 Fed. Reg. 13,347 (1998) (Lower Columbia listing); 64 Fed. Reg. 14,517 (1999) (Mid-Columbia and Upper Willamette listings).

50   UPSTREAM (cited in note 30), at 101-03; 63 Fed. Reg. 11,774, 11,775, 11,780 (1998).

51   Institute for Fishery Resources, *The Cost of Doing Nothing: The Economic Burden of Salmon Declines in the Columbia River Basin* 2 (1996) [hereinafter cited as *The Cost of Doing Nothing*] ($500,000 annual costs, 25,000 jobs); *Beyond Parity*, at 126 (quoting Chairman Ted Strong); on the judicial interpretation of the Columbia Basin's Indian treaties, see chapters 4 and 12.

Notes to Chapter 3

[1]   *The Case for Dam Breaching*, at 1023-31 (citing studies).

[2]   TAYLOR (cited in chapter 1, note 3) at 23 (41 million pounds, more sustainable); Northwest Power Planning Council, *Compilation of Information on Salmon and Steelhead Losses in the Columbia River Basin* 81-83 (1986) (42 million pounds); LUTHER SHEELEIGH CRESSMAN, PREHISTORY OF THE FAR WEST: HOMES OF VANISHED PEOPLES 1-2 (U. Utah Press 1977); COURTLAND SMITH, SALMON FISHERS OF THE COLUMBIA 5-14 (Oregon St. U. Press 1979) (fishing at falls); Dale Goble, *Introduction to the Symposium on Legal Structures for Managing the Pacific Northwest Salmon and Steelhead: The Biological and Historical Context*, 22 IDAHO L. REV. 417, 446 n.117 (1986) (three distinct cultural groups); Joint Statement Regarding the Biology, Status, Management, and Harvest of the Salmon and Steelhead Resources of the Puget Sound and Olympic Peninsula Drainage Areas of Western Washington, compiled by Washington Dept. of Fisheries, U.S. Fish and Wildlife Service, and Washington Dept. of Game for United States v. Washington, Civil No. 9213 (W.D. Wash., May 14, 1973) (coastal tribes); Stephen Dow Beckham, *Ethnohistorical Context of Reserved Indian Fishing Rights: Pacific Northwest Treaties, 1851-1855*, (report prepared for United States v. Washington, Civil No. 9213B, Phase 1, Determination Re: Accounting for the Non-Treaty Catch 42-54 (Sept. 1, 1984)) (fishing practices).

[3]   ROBERT H. RUBY & JOHN A. BROWN, THE CHINOOK INDIANS: TRADERS OF THE LOWER COLUMBIA 21-22 (U. Oklahoma Press 1976) (salmon exchanged for manufactured goods); Tribal Brief (cited in chapter 1, note 5), at 18-20 (Quiniper and Vancouver, ownership of sites); COURTLAND SMITH, FISH OR CUT BAIT 12 (Oregon Sea Grant 1979) (in excess of 5 million pounds); Charles F. Wilkinson & Daniel Conner, *The Law of the Pacific Salmon Fishery: Conservation and Allocation of a Transboundary Common Property Resource*, 32 U. KANS. L. REV. 7, 29 (1983) (dipnet platforms); TAYLOR (cited in chapter 1, note 3), at 36-37 (individual and village rights).

[4]   UNCOMMON CONTROVERSY (cited in chapter 1, note 5), at 10-14 (half-century before buffalo; cordial relations with fur traders); United States v. Washington, 384 F. Supp. 312, 352 (W.D. Wash. 1974) (exports); U.S. Dept. of the Interior, Office of Indian Affairs, Div. of Forestry and Grazing, *Report on the Source, Nature, and Extent of the Fishing, Hunting and Miscellaneous Related Rights of Certain Indian Tribes in Oregon and Washington* 35 (July 1942) (compiled by Edward Swindell, Jr.) [hereinafter cited as *Swindell Report*] (little fishing by whites).

[5]   United States v. Washington, 384 F. Supp. at 353-54 (W.D. Wash. 1974) (by treaty, not force); Act of Aug. 14, 1848, 9 Stat. 323 (Oregon Territorial Act); Act of Sept. 27, 1850, 9 Stat. 496 (Oregon Land Donation Act); Washington v. Washington State Commercial Passenger Fishing Vessel Ass'n, 443 U.S. 658, 664 (1979) [hereinafter cited as *Passenger Fishing Vessel*] (80 percent population decline); TAYLOR (cited in chapter 1, note 3), at 41 (1841 population estimate); *see generally* ROBERT BOYD, THE COMING OF THE SPIRIT OF PESTILENCE: INTRODUCED INFECTIOUS DISEASES AND POPULATION DECLINE AMONG NORTHWEST COAST INDIANS, 1774-1874 (U. Washington Press 1999).

[6]   UNCOMMON CONTROVERSY (cited in chapter 1, note 5), at 16-17.

[7]   DIETRICH (cited in chapter 1, note 1), at 377 (64 million acres for $1.2 million); Judith V. Royster, *The Legacy of Allotment*, 27 ARIZ. ST. L.J. 1, 13-14 (1995) ("surplus lands"); JANET A. MCDONNELL, THE DISPOSSESSION OF THE AMERICAN INDIAN, 1887-1934 (Indiana U. Press 1991).

[8]   UNCOMMON CONTROVERSY (cited in chapter 1, note 5), at 21 (more removal than Indians wanted).

[9]   *See* Paul S. Wilson, *What Chief Seattle Said*, 22 ENVTL L. 1451 (1992) (discussing the differences between what Chief Seattle actually said, and how the media has distorted his speech).

[10]   *Swindell Report* (cited in note 4), at 340-41, 353.

[11]   *Id.* at 355, 417.

[12]   United States v. Washington, 384 F. Supp. at 354-55 (creating new political entities); BARBARA LANE, POLITICAL AND ECONOMIC ASPECTS OF INDIAN-WHITE CULTURAL CONTACT IN WESTERN WASHINGTON IN THE MID-NINETEENTH CENTURY 28 (1973), at 28 (appointment of chiefs).

[13]   United States v. Washington, 384 F. Supp. at 355-56 (Chinook jargon); UNCOMMON CONTROVERSY (cited in chapter 1, note 5), at 23-24 (Stevens' interpreter, George Gibbs); Tribal Brief (cited in note 1), at 17-18 (treaty language); LANE (cited in note 12), at 28 (no precedent for legal documents, nor alienation).

[14]   United States v. Washington, 384 F. Supp. at 350 (dependence on salmon); *Swindell Report* (cited in note 4), at 351-52 ("fish in common with the whites").

[15]   Joint Biological Appendix (cited in note 1), at 327 (quoting Commissioner of Indian Affairs); *Passenger Fishing Vessel*, 443 U.S. at 666 n.8 (1979) ("catch most of our fish").

[16]   *Swindell Report* (cited in note 4), at 351.

[17]   *Id.* at 348 (emphasis added) (Stevens' quote from treaty negotiations); Jack Landau, *Empty Victories: Indian Treaty Fishing Rights in the Pacific Northwest*, 10 ENVTL. L. 412 (1980) (64 million acres); Tribal Brief (cited in chapter 1, note 5), at 25 (Stevens' quote to Senate); U.S. COMM'N ON CIVIL RIGHTS, INDIAN TRIBES: A CONTINUING QUEST FOR SURVIVAL 64 (1981) (concern about small reserves).

[18]   DIETRICH (cited in chapter 1, note 1), at 156 (Stevens' broken promise); BROWN (cited in chapter 1, note 18) at 132 (Northwest Indian War); UNCOMMON CONTROVERSY (cited in chapter 1, note 5), at 34-39 (delayed treaty ratification).

[19]   *Passenger Fishing Vessel*, 443 U.S. at 664 (most fish harvested and sold by natives); Tribal Brief (cited in chapter 1, note 5), at 26 (tribal role in frontier economy).

[20]   Wilkinson & Conner (cited in note 3), at 30-31.

[21]   Tribal Brief (cited in chapter 1, note 5), at 27; TAYLOR (cited in chapter 1, note 3), at 63 (Columbia River canneries).

[22]   Joseph Evans Taylor, III, *Steelhead's Mother Was His Father, Salmon: Development and Declension of Aboriginal Conservation in the Oregon Country Salmon Fishery* 312 (1992) (unpublished Master's thesis, University of Oregon) (on file with University of Oregon); Tribal Brief (cited in chapter 1, note 5), at 28-30.

[23]   LICHATOWICH (cited in chapter 1, note 26) at 33-37; TAYLOR (cited in chapter 1, note 3), at 27-28 (native custom, kinship, ceremonies, and taboos created an inherent check on harvests).

[24]   TAYLOR (cited in chapter 1, note 3), at 44-45.

[25]   LICHATOWICH (cited in chapter 1, note 26), at 44-47.

[26]   TAYLOR (cited in chapter 1, note 3), at 23, 63-65.

[27]   *Id.* at 59.

[28]   *Id.* at 46-59 (effects of white development on salmon habitat).

Notes to Chapter 4

[1]   Washington v. Washington State Commercial Passenger Fishing Vessel Ass'n., 443 U.S. 658, 684 (1979) [hereinafter cited as *Passenger Fishing Vessel*].

[2]   Taylor (cited in chapter 3, note 22), at 312.

[3]   United States v. Taylor, 13 P. 333, 335-36 (Wash. Terr. 1887). The injunction against the Taylors was affirmed after Washington statehood in United States v. Taylor, 44 F. 2 (D. Wash. 1890).

[4]   Taylor (cited in chapter 3, note 22), at 242-43.

[5]   United States v. Alaska Packers Ass'n., 79 F. 152 (D. Wash. 1897); Jones v. Callvert, 32 Wash 610, 73 P. 701 (1903) (Tulalip case); Taylor (cited chapter 3, note 22), at 243-44; on the Lummi Indians, see DANIEL BOXBERGER, TO FISH IN COMMON: THE ETHNOHISTORY OF LUMMI INDIAN SALMON FISHING (U. Nebraska Press 1989).

[6]   Taylor (cited in chapter 3, note 22), at 246-47.

[7]   *Id.* at 247; United States v. Winans, 73 F. 72 (D. Wash. 1896).

[8]   United States v. Winans, 198 U.S. 371, 380-81 (1905).

[9]   *Id.* at 382-84.

[10]   Winters v. United States, 207 U.S. 564 (1908). *See* JOHN SHURTS, THE WINTERS DOCTRINE: ORIGIN AND DEVELOPMENT OF THE INDIAN RESERVED WATER RIGHTS DOCTRINE IN IT'S SOCIAL AND LEGAL CONTEXT (U. Oklahoma Press 1999).

[11]   Seufert Bros. Co. v. United States, 249 U.S. 194, 197-99 (1919).

[12]   Tulee v. Washington, 7 Wash. 2d 124, 109 P.2d 280 (1941), *rev'd*, 315 U.S. 681, 685 (1942).

[13]   State v. Tulee, 109 P.2d 280, 285 (Wash. 1941) ("profit à prendre").

[14]   State v. Towessnute, 89 Wash. 478, 481-82, 154 P. 805, 807 (1916).

[15]   Tribal Brief (cited in chapter 1, note 5), at 39-40.

[16]   Makah Tribe v. Schoettler, 192 F.2d 224 (9th Cir. 1951) (state failed to demonstrate conservation necessity); Maison v. Confederated Tribes of the Umatilla Reservation, 314 F.2d 169, 173-74 (9th Cir. 1963) (ban designed to protect non-Indian fisheries; echoing the *Tulee* case); *see* Landau (cited in chapter 3, note 17), at 435.

[17]   Dept. of Game v. Puyallup Tribe, 70 Wash. 2d 245, 422 P.2d 754 (1966), *aff'd*; Dept. of Game v. Puyallup Tribe, 391 U.S. 392, 398, 401-03 (1968) (*Puyallup I*); Ralph W. Johnson, *The States Versus Indian Off-Reservation Fishing: A United States Supreme Court Error*, 47 WASH. L. REV. 207, 208-09 (1972).

[18]   Dept. of Game v. Puyallup Tribe, 414 U.S. 44, 48-49 (1973) (*Puyallup II*).

[19]   Puyallup Tribe v. Dept. of Game, 433 U.S. 165, 176-77 (1977) (*Puyallup III*); *see also* United States v. Washington, 496 F.2d 620 (9th Cir.), *cert. denied*, 419 U.S. 1032 (1974) (Puyallup reservation not extinguished).

[20]   *Puyallup II*, 414 U.S. at 48-49.

[21]   Sohappy v. Smith, 302 F.Supp. 899, 905 (D. OR. 1969).

[22]   *Id.* at 908-911; Sohappy v. Smith, No. 68-409, slip. op. at 2-3 (D. Or. Oct 10, 1969) (unpublished judgment). *See also* Timothy Weaver, *Litigation and Negotiation: The History of Salmon in the Columbia Basin*, 24 ECOLOGY L.Q. 677, 680-81 n.12 (1997) (reprinting a portion of Judge Belloni's unreported opinion); Penny H. Harrison, *The Evolution of a New Comprehensive Plan for Managing Columbia River Anadromous Fish*, 16 ENVTL. L. 705 (1986).

[23]   United States v. Washington, 384 F. Supp. 312, 338-39 n.26 (W.D. Wash. 1974) (off-reservation treaty rights not detrimental to the perpetuation of any species of anadromous fish), 393 (permitting commercial net fishing on same runs of fish), 403 (regulatory scheme discriminated against

native fishing) (W.D. Wash. 1974); Tribal Brief (cited in chapter 1, note 5), at 54.

24   *Id.* at 343, 386 (required allocation); Tribal Brief (cited in chapter 1, note 5), at 57-59 nn. 202-07, n.209 (exclusions from equal sharing formula; 18% of total Washington harvest).

25   United States v. Washington, 520 F.2d 676 (9th Cir. 1975), *cert. denied*, 423 U.S. 1086 (1976); Tribal Brief (cited in chapter 1, note 5), at 64-69 nn.229-61 (shooting threats); Puget Sound Gillnetters Ass'n v. Moos, 88 Wash. 2d 677, 565 P.2d 1151 (1977); Purse Seine Vessel Owners Ass'n v. Tollefson, 89 Wash. 2d 276, 571 P.2d 1393 (1977). Puget Sound Gillnetters v. U.S. District Court, 573 F.2d 1123 (9th Cir. 1978) (quote).

26   *Passenger Fishing Vessel*, 443 U.S. at 676, 682, 686-87 (1979). For a discussion of how the "moderate living" standard became part of the Supreme Court's decision, see David H. Getches, *Conquering the Cultural Frontier: The New Subjectivism of the Supreme Court in Indian Law*, 84 CAL. L. REV. 1573, 1637-39 (1996) (citing Justice Marshall's papers, which indicate that the standard was a consequence of a successful eleventh-hour attempt by Justice Stevens to keep a majority of the Court from rehearing the case and perhaps overruling *Puyallup II*'s broadening of the scope of the treaty right beyond a mere access right).

27   *Passenger Fishing Vessel*, 443 U.S. at 687-89.

28   Sohappy v. Smith, 302 F. Supp. 899, 910-11 (D. Or. 1969); Sohappy v. Smith, No. 68-409 (D. OR. May 8, 1974) (order dissolving temporary restraining order).

29   However, the advent of tribal management capability hardly signaled an era of peace and equity. *See* Russell L. Barsh, *Backfire From Boldt: The Judicial Transformation of Coast Salish Proprietary Fisheries Into a Commons*, 4 WESTERN LEGAL HISTORY 85 (1991).

30   United States v. Washington, 384 F. Supp. at 403; Settler v. Lameer, 507 F.2d 231 (9th Cir. 1974) (tribes as regulators).

31   A Plan for Managing Fisheries on Stocks Originating from the Columbia River and Its Tributaries Above Bonneville Dam (Feb. 28, 1977); *see* United States v. Oregon, 699 F. Supp. 1456 (D. Or. 1988), *aff'd*, 913 F.2d 576 (9th Cir. 1990) (approving as amended comprehensive plan); Confederated Tribes v. Baldridge, No. C80-342T (W.D. Wash. Aug. 4, 1981); COHEN (cited in chapter 1, note 30), at 127-32; Don Sampson, *One Tribe's Perspective on "Who Runs the Reservoirs,"* 26 ENVTL. L. 681, 686 (1996). On the ESA and Columbia River allocation, see chap. 9, text with notes 77-79; on the tribal suit over culverts, see chap. 12, text with note 59.

Notes to Chapter 5

1   DIETRICH (cited in chapter 1, note 1) at 45. For figures on the size of the Columbia, see Bonneville Power Administration, *et al.*, *The Columbia River: The Inside Story* 4-6 (1991) [hereinafter cited as *BPA Inside Story*].

2   U.S. General Accounting Office, *Region At the Crossroads, The Pacific Northwest Searches for New Sources of Electric Energy* (1978).

3   DIETRICH (cited in chapter 1, note 1), at 46.

4   *BPA Inside Story* (cited in note 1), at 6-7 (18,500 megawatts); 6 WATER AND WATER RIGHTS 59 (Robert E. Beck, ed. 1994) (6% of streamflows irrigate 7.8 million acres); TIM PALMER, THE SNAKE RIVER: WINDOW TO THE WEST 54, 90, 245 (Island Press 1991) (13.5 million acre-feet of storage, 3.8 million irrigated acres, 73% above Milner Dam). *See generally* MARK FIEGE, IRRIGATED EDEN: THE MAKING OF AN AGRICULTURAL LANDSCAPE IN THE AMERICAN WEST (U. Washington Press 1999).

5   Russell Thurow, U.S. Forest Service, *quoted in* Paul Koberstein, *Summer Salmon Reader*, CASCADIA TIMES, July 1996, at 9 (2%).

6   Except as otherwise noted, this section is adapted from *Hydroelectric Heritage*; and sources cited therein. *See especially* SAMUEL P. HAYS, CONSERVATION AND THE GOSPEL OF EFFICIENCY: THE PROGRESSIVE CONSERVATION MOVEMENT, 1890-1920 (Atheneum Press 1959).

7   On public power before the New Deal, see JAY BRIGHAM, EMPOWERING THE WEST: ELECTRIC POLITICS BEFORE FDR (U. Kansas Press 1998).

8   RICHARD WHITE, THE ORGANIC MACHINE: THE REMAKING OF THE COLUMBIA RIVER 50 (Hill and Wang 1995) (The Dalles Dam generating 13 times the demand of Portland); on the Progressive dream of the capability of hydropower to liberate the human spirit by destroying monopolies and concentrated wealth, cleanse polluted cities, and restore prosperity to rural America, LEWIS MUMFORD, TECHNICS AND CIVILIZATION (Harcourt Brace & Co. 1934) may be the paradigmatic work. *See* WHITE, at 55-56; DIETRICH (cited in chapter 1, note 1), at 258-60 (Rufus Woods); *see also* ROBERT E. FICKEN, RUFUS WOODS, THE COLUMBIA RIVER AND THE BUILDING OF MODERN WASHINGTON (Washington St. U. Press 1995).

9   *Hydropower vs. Salmon*, at 224-25; WHITE (cited in note 8), at 55 (boosters' dreams); PETERSEN (cited in chapter 1, note 22), at 77 (Corps' 308 reports).

10   Adapted, except where noted, from *Hydroelectric Heritage*, at 191-202 (used by permission of the Washington Law Review).

11   DIETRICH (cited in chapter 1, note 1), at 260, 266, 278-79.

12   *Id.* at 266-69.

13   United States v. Arizona, 295 U.S. 174, 186-92 (1935) (ruling that funding of projects under the National Industrial Recovery Act was not sufficient authorization).

14   *Hydropower vs. Salmon,* at 226-28.

[15]   16 U.S.C. § 832 (Bonneville Project Act); DIETRICH (cited in chapter 1, note 1), at 285-87.

[16]   Adapted, except where noted, from Blumm & Bodi, (cited in chapter 1, note 36), at 103-05 (used by permission of Oregon Sea Grant and Oregon State University Press). The Commissioner of Fisheries Report was reprinted in Sen. Doc. No. 87, 75th Cong., 1st Sess. (1937).

[17]   TAYLOR (cited in chapter 1, note 3), at 228-29 (Grand Coulee transplantation).

[18]   Sen. Doc. No. 87 (cited in note 16), at 76.

[19]   Pub. L. No. 75-502, ch. 193, 52 Stat. 345 (1938) (current version at 16 U.S.C. § 756); 16 U.S.C. § 756 (all activities necessary to conservation of salmon). The Secretary of Commerce was substituted for the Secretary of Interior in 1970, due to the creation of the National Oceanic and Atmospheric Administration.

[20]   Michael L. Goodman, *Preserving the Genetic Diversity of Salmonid Stocks: A Call for Federal Regulation of Hatchery Programs*, 20 ENVTL. L. 111, 151 (1990) (*citing* S. Leider, J. Loch & P. Hulett, *Studies of Hatchery and Wild Steelhead in the Lower Columbia River* (Wash. Dept. of Wildlife Rep. No. 87-8, 1987)); LICHATOWICH (cited in chapter 1, note 26) at 207-21.

[21]   Adapted, except where noted, from *Hydroelectric Heritage*, at 202-12 (used by permission of the Washington Law Review); and Blumm & Bodi (cited in chapter 1, note 36), at 109-10 (used by permission of Oregon Sea Grant and Oregon State University Press).

[22]   DIETRICH (cited in chapter 1, note 1), at 284.

[23]   Flood Control Act of 1944, ch. 665 §§ 1-8, 58 Stat. 887; Rivers and Harbors Act of 1945, ch. 19, 59 Stat. 10.

[24]   Rivers and Harbors Act of 1945, ch. 19, § 2, 59 Stat. 22 (adequate provision for spawning salmon).

[25]   On the habitat-protection promises in the Lower Columbia River Development Program, *see* LICHATOWICH (cited in chapter 1, note 26), at 191-92; Federal Power Comm'n v. Oregon, 349 U.S. 435 (1955); City of Tacoma v. Taxpayers of Tacoma, 357 U.S. 320 (1958) (licensing projects over the opposition of state agencies).

[26]   Adapted, except where noted, from *Hydroelectric Heritage*, at 215-19 (used by permission of the Washington Law Review); and Blumm & Bodi (cited in chapter 1, note 36), at 125-27 (used by permission of Oregon Sea Grant and Oregon State University Press). *See also* NEIL SWAINSON, CONFLICT OVER THE COLUMBIA: THE CANADIAN BACKGROUND TO AN HISTORIC TREATY (McGill-Queens U. Press 1979); Ralph W. Johnson, *The Canadian United States Controversy Over the Columbia River*, 41 WASH. L. REV. 676, 711-12 (1966); Albert Utton, *The Columbia River Treaty and Protocol*, 1 LAND & WATER L. REV. 181, 182-83 (1964); KAI LEE, DONNA KLEMKA & MARION MARTS, ELECTRIC POWER AND THE FUTURE OF THE PACIFIC NORTHWEST 54-58 (U. Washington Press 1980).

[27]   Treaty Between the United States and Canada relating to Cooperative Development of the Water Resources of the Columbia River Basin, 15 U.S.T. 1555, T.I.A.S. No. 5638 (1964).

[28]   Columbia River Treaty (cited in note 27), at VIII(4), reprinted in *Hydropower vs. Salmon*, at 224, n.174 (allowing reduction of Canadian benefits when water is not used to generate power in the U.S.).

[29]   Pacific Northwest Coordination Agreement, Contract No. 14-02-4822, § 15 (1964) (priority to nonpower uses).

[30]   Public Works Appropriation Act of 1965, Pub. L. No. 880-571, 78 Stat. 682 (1964) (authorization for Intertie); Pub. L. No. 88-552, 78 Stat. 756 (1964) (codified at 16 U.S.C. §§ 837-837h) (surplus power sales).

[31]   Adapted, except where noted, from *Hydroelectric Heritage*, at 221-28 (used by permission of the Washington Law Review); and 6 WATER AND WATER RIGHTS (cited in note 4), at 82-85 (used by permission of The Michie Company, a division of Mathew Bender & Co., Inc. © 1994 by Michie). *See, e.g.,* GUS NORWOOD, COLUMBIA RIVER POWER FOR THE PEOPLE: A HISTORY OF THE POLICIES OF THE BONNEVILLE POWER ADMINISTRATION, 24, 258, 274-75 (Bonneville Power Admin. 1981); LEE *et al.* (cited in note 26), at 36-41, 76-83, 102-03, 118-20, 130-32, 135, 140, 172, 175. Jeffrey Foote, *et al., Bonneville Power Administration: Northwest Power Broker,* 6 ENVTL. L. 831, 843-47 (1976).

[32]   Port of Astoria v. Hodel, 8 Envt'l Rep. Cas. 1156 (D. Or. 1975), *aff'd*, 626 F.2d 134 (9th Cir. 1980); Natural Resources Defense Council v. Hodel, 435 F. Supp. 590 (D. Or. 1977), *aff'd*, 626 F.2d 134 (9th Cir. 1980).

[33]   NORWOOD (cited in note 31), at 262 (notices of insufficiency).

[34]   LEE *et al.* (cited in note 26), at 131, *citing* S.B. 320, 1977 Oregon Legislature; *id. citing* City of Portland v. Hodel, Civ. Nos. 77-928, 77-929 (D. Or. 1977).

[35]   *Id.* at 172 (bills beginning in 1977).

[36]   WHITE (cited in note 8) (organic machine). After 1970, implementation of the Mitchell Act was the responsibility of the Secretary of Commerce; see above note 19.

[37]   *See Beyond Parity*, at 103-07 (discussion of BPA's "cost cap," referred to as a "budget"); *see also* VOLKMAN (cited in chapter 1, note 42), at 151-52; Idaho Dept. of Fish and Game v. NMFS, 850 F.Supp. 886, 900 (D. Or. 1994) ("deficit situation").

[38]   *Saving Idaho's Salmon*, at 672, *citing* Paul Shaffer, *Build Dams and the Hell With the Fish*, HIGH COUNTRY NEWS, Apr. 22, 1991, at 13 (shadow policy); F. Lorraine Bodi, *Protecting Columbia River Salmon Under the Endangered Species Act*, 10 ENVTL. L. 349 (1980).

Notes to Chapter 6

[1]   Bill Bakke & Joseph Cone, *Commentary*, in NORTHWEST SALMON CRISIS (cited in chapter 1, note 36), at 47 (first hatchery). For good historical overviews of the region's reliance on hatcheries, *see* LICHATOWICH (cited in chapter 1, note 26) at 123-50, 207-221; TAYLOR (cited in chapter 1, note 3), at 6-7, 77-132; and Ernest Brennon, *et al.*, *Review of Artificial Production of Anadromous and Resident Fish in the Columbia Basin*, App. I of Northwest Power Planning Council, *Artificial Production Review* 64-92 (Doc. 99-15, 1999) [hereinafter cited as *Artificial Production Review*].

[2]   *Problems with Hatcheries*, in NORTHWEST SALMON CRISIS (cited in chapter 1, note 36), at 131-38; RETURN TO THE RIVER (cited in chapter 1, note 52), at 389-398; Northwest Power Planning Council, *Artificial Production Review*, (cited in note 1), at iii (still an experiment).

[3]   Livingston Stone, *The Artificial Propagation of Salmon on the Pacific Coast of the United States, With Notes on the Natural History of the Quinnat Salmon*, BULLETIN OF THE UNITED STATES FISH COMMISSION (1896), reprinted in NORTHWEST SALMON CRISIS (cited in chapter 1, note 36), at 53-54; Bakke & Cone (cited in note 1), at 46 (random theory of salmon migration).

[4]   Stone (cited in note 3), at 54-55; TAYLOR (cited in chapter 1, note 3), at 93 (map of hatcheries at the turn of the century).

[5]   George Staley, *Artificial Propagation in Oregon*, reprinted in NORTHWEST SALMON CRISIS (cited in chapter 1, note 36), at 40-41; Bakke & Cone (cited in note 1), at 46 (Anderson's notion of salmon stocks); TAYLOR (cited in chapter 1, note 3), at 217-18 (federal scientists' studies).

[6]   *See* TAYLOR (cited in chapter 1, note 3), at 70-72 (on George Perkins Marsh). *See also id.* at 89 (". . . [T]he core assumption of fishery managers in the nineteenth century [was that] habitat destruction was an unfortunate cost of 'civilization', but fish culture would ameliorate change. If salmon continued to decline despite fish culture, then fishers were solely to blame.").

[7]   *See id.* at 222.

[8]   U.S. Commissioner of Fisheries report, S. Doc. No. 87, 75th Cong., 1st Sess. (1937), reprinted in NORTHWEST SALMON CRISIS (cited in chapter 1, note 36), at 100-02.

[9]   16 U.S.C. § 755-57 (the Mitchell Act) (now administered by the Secretary of Commerce, see chapter 5, note 19).

[10]   Rivers and Harbors Act of 1945, ch. 19, § 2, 59 Stat. 10, 21-22 (1945).

[11]   Act of August 8, 1946, 60 Stat. 932 (1946) (Mitchell Act Amendments); Columbia River Inter-Tribal Fish Commission, *The Mitchell Act: An Analysis* 4, 9, 11-12 (1981); Leo Laythe, *The Fishery Program in the Lower Columbia River*, 48 TRANSACTIONS OF THE AMERICAN FISHERIES SOCIETY 78 (1948), reprinted in NORTHWEST SALMON CRISIS (cited in chapter 1, note 36), at 112-13 (Lower Columbia Fishery Development Program); Robert C. Lothrop, *The Misplaced Role of Cost-Benefit Analysis in*

Columbia Basin Fishery Mitigation, 16 ENVTL. L. 517, 523 (1986) (24 hatcheries).

[12]   H.R. Doc. No. 531, 81st Cong., 2nd Sess. (1950), reprinted in NORTHWEST SALMON CRISIS (cited in chapter 1, note 36), at 116-19; Lothrop (cited in note 11), at 523 (100 million hatchery fish).

[13]   Lothrop (cited in note 11), at 526, 528.

[14]   This section draws on Michael L. Goodman, *Preserving the Genetic Diversity of Salmonid Stocks: A Call For Federal Regulation of Hatchery Programs,* 20 ENVTL. L. 111, 126-128, 134-41 (1990); and John L. Dentler & David V. Buchanan, *Are Wild Fish Worth Conserving?* (Or. Dept. of Fish and Wildlife Rep No. 86-87), at 4-7 (1986) (importance of reproductive isolation; mixed stock fisheries).

[15]   Jack K. Sterne, Jr., *Supplementation of Wild Salmon Stocks: A Cure for the Hatchery Problem or More Problem Hatcheries?* 23 COASTAL MGMT. 123, 124-25 (1995).

[16]   Richard Neuberger, *The Great Salmon Mystery,* SATURDAY EVENING POST (Sept. 13, 1941), at 21-22, 44, reprinted in NORTHWEST SALMON CRISIS (cited in chapter 1, note 36), at 197-98; Brennon (cited in note 1), at 69 (1999 assessment of the results of Grand Coulee reprogramming).

[17]   Douglas W. Dompier, *Commentary,* in NORTHWEST SALMON CRISIS (cited in chapter 1, note 36), at 199.

[18]   Sterne (cited in note 15), at 125; Columbia Basin Fish and Wildlife Authority, *Integrated System Plan for Salmon and Steelhead Production in the Columbia River Basin* 199 (June 1991).

[19]   Sterne (cited in note 15), at 124, 130-31.

[20]   National Fish Hatchery Review Panel, *Report of National Fish Hatchery Review Panel* (Conservation Foundation 1994), discussed in Brennon (cited in note 1), at 98-99.

[21]   Columbia Basin Fish and Wildlife Authority, *Draft Programmatic Environmental Impact Statement, Impacts of Artificial Salmon and Steelhead Production Strategies in the Columbia River Basin* 1 (purpose), 6 (quote), 16-18 (generic basinwide approach), 22-24 (adverse effects), 36-40 (rejected alternatives), 41-42 (preferred alternative) (December 10, 1996).

[22]   RETURN TO THE RIVER (cited in chapter 1, note 52), at 377, 388, 396.

[23]   *Id.* at 397-401.

[24]   UPSTREAM (cited in chapter 2, note 30), at 314-20.

[25]   *Id.* at 321-23.

[26]   This discussion draws from Brennon (cited in note 1), at 99-102.

[27]   The first two paragraphs of this subsection are adapted from *Salmon Lessons*, at 560-62 (used by permission of the Washington Law Review), discussing *1995-1998 Hatchery BiOp* (cited in chapter 2, note 46).

[28]   *1995-1998 Hatchery BiOp* (cited in chapter 2, note 46), at 8-11.

[29]   *1999 Hatchery BiOp* (cited in chapter 2, note 46), discussed in chapter 9, text accompanying notes 39-40.

[30]   Columbia River Inter-Tribal Fish Commission, *Wy-Kan-Ush-Mi Wa-Kish-Wit (The Spirit of the Salmon)* vi-v, 5B-24 (1995) [hereinafter cited as *Tribal Restoration Plan*].

[31]   *Id.* at v (quote); Sterne (cited in note 15), at 129-130; Letter of Phil Mundy, Columbia River Inter-Tribal Fish Comm'n, to Merritt Tuttle, National Marine Fisheries Service 3 (Feb. 19, 1991).

[32]   Energy and Water Development Appropriations Act of 1997, Pub. L. No. 104-206, § 512 (1996) (amending § 4(h)(10) of the Northwest Power Act, 16 U.S.C. § 839b(h)(10)); *Artificial Production Review* (cited in note 1).

[33]   *Artificial Production Review* (cited in note 1), at 2-3.

[34]   *Id.* at 16-21. *See also* Ray Hilborn & John Wilton, *Lessons From Supplementation of Chinook Salmon in British Columbia*, 14 NORTH AMERICA J. OF FISHERIES MGMT. 1 (1994) (experimental nature of hatcheries); Russell E. Foerster, *Restocking Depleted Sockeye Salmon Areas By Transfer of Eggs*, 6 J. OF FISHERIES RESEARCH BD. OF CANADA 483 (1946) (importance of locally adapted broodstocks).

[35]   *Artificial Production Review* (cited in note 1), at 22-29.

[36]   Independent Scientific Advisory Board, Scientific Review Team, *Review of Artificial Production of Anadromous and Resident Fish in the Columbia Basin* (Northwest Power Planning Council Doc. No. 99-4, April 1999); Northwest Power Planning Council, *Columbia River Basin Fish and Wildlife Program, Fiscal Year 2000 Annual Implementation Plan* 28-29, 107-08 (March 2000).

[37]   Gary K. Meffe, *Techno-Arrogance and Halfway Technologies: Salmon Hatcheries on the Pacific Coast of North America*, 6 CONSERVATION BIOLOGY 351 (1992), reprinted in NORTHWEST SALMON CRISIS (cited in chapter 1, note 36), at 135, 138 ("halfway technology"); Joseph Cone, *Commentary*, in NORTHWEST SALMON CRISIS (cited in chapter 1, note 36), at 139 (expense of hatcheries).

[38]   William H. Miller *et al., Analysis of Salmon and Steelhead Supplementation* iii (report to Bonneville Power Admin., 1990).

[39]   *Id.* at iii-iv, 1; Goodman (cited in note 14), at 111, 126-43.

Notes to Chapter 7

[1]   43 Fed. Reg. 45,628 (1978) (biological status review); 16 U.S.C. §§ 839 *et seq.* (Northwest Power Act); H.R. Rep. 976, 96th Cong., 2d Sess, pt. 1, at 49, 56-57 (1980) (co-equal partnership).

[2]   16 U.S.C. §§ 839b(h)(6)(E) (improved passage at dams and improved flows); 839(b) (substantially obtainable from existing system).

[3]   *See* DANIEL A. FARBER & PHILIP FRICKEY, LAW AND PUBLIC CHOICE: A CRITICAL INTRODUCTION (U. Chicago Press 1991) (narrow, focused interest groups can usually preserve a status quo that is not beneficial to the broad public).

[4]   LEE *ET AL.* (cited in chapter 5, note 26), at 130-32 (bills in Congress); James O. Luce, *When the Walls Come Tumbling Down: The Demise of the Northwest Power Act*, 3 WEST-NORTHWEST 299, 304-06 (1996) (customers' suspicions).

[5]   S. 885, 96th Cong., 1st Sess. (1979) (bill that passed Senate in 1979); U.S. General Accounting Office, *Impacts and Implications of the Pacific Northwest Power Bill* (1979).

[6]   Pub. L. No. 96-501, 94 Stat. 2697 (1980) (codified at 16 U.S.C. §§ 839 *et seq.*).

[7]   Adapted, unless otherwise noted, from *Hydroelectric Heritage*, at 231-33 (used by permission of the Washington Law Review).

[8]   16 U.S.C. §§ 839c(h) (widespread use), 839e(a)(1) (sound business principles), 839e(e) (lowest possible rates).

[9]   16 U.S.C. §§ 839b (Council), 839e (involvement of states, local governments, and the public); 16 U.S.C. §§ 839d(c) (Council veto) 16 U.S.C. § 839b(e)(3)(D) (power plan to include electric forecasts); 16 U.S.C. § 839f(e) (authorizing judicial review of final agency actions).

[10]   16 U.S.C. § 839(1); 16 U.S.C. § 839b(h).

[11]   Adapted, except where noted, from *Unraveling Parity*, at 666-70 (used by permission of Environmental Law). *See also* Roy Hemingway, *The Northwest Power Planning Council: Its Origins and Future Role*, 13 ENVTL. L. 673 (1983); *Symposium on the Constitutionality of the Northwest Power Planning Council,* 17 ENVTL. L. 767-999 (1987); Kai N. Lee & Jody Lawrence, *Adaptive Management: Learning From the Columbia River Basin Fish and Wildlife Program,* 16 ENVT. L. 431 (1986); John M. Volkman & Kai N. Lee, *Within the Hundredth Meridian: Western States in a Time of Transition*, 59 U. COLO. L. REV. 551, 562-69 (1988).

[12]   16 U.S.C. §§ 839b(h)(1)(A), (h)(10)(A); *id.* § 839b(h)(6)(E)(i)-(ii); H.R. Rep. 976 (cited in note 1), at 56-57 (co-equal partnership; anxious to meet fish and wildlife needs).

[13]   16 U.S.C. §§ 839b(h)(1)(A) (systemwide program); *Id.* 839b(h)(1)(A), (h)(2)(B), (h)(5), (h)(6)(E)(i) (changed operations); *id.* § 839b(h)(8)(A) (offsite enhancement); *id.* § 839b(h)(6)(B) (best available science); *id.* § 839b(h)(6)(C) ("minimum cost alternatives" relevant only where they achieve the "same sound biological alternative"); *id.* § 839b(h)(5), (h)(6)(A), (h)(7) (program to "complement existing and future activities" of fish agencies and Indian tribes and to give "due weight" to their "recommendations, expertise, and legal rights and responsibilities"); *id.* § 839b(h)(10)(A) (BPA to use its financial authorities "in a manner consistent" with the program); *id.* § 839b(h)(8)(B) (electric ratepayers to pay fish and wildlife costs attributed to hydroelectric development and operation).

[14]   *Id.* §§ 839b(h)(2), (h)(4)(A), (h)(5)-(7), (h)(11)(B) (tribal role in formulating the program); on the Pacific Salmon Treaty, see chapter 8.

[15]   16 U.S.C. §§ 839b(h)(10) (BPA to use its financial and legal authorities "in a manner consistent" with the Council's program), (h)(11)(A)(ii) (federal water managers to take the Council's program "into account to the fullest extent practicable" at each relevant stage of their decision making); 126 Cong. Rec. H29,810 (daily ed. Nov. 17, 1980) (remarks of Rep. Dingell) (no super fish and wildlife agency).

[16]   RETURN TO THE RIVER (cited in chapter 1, note 52), at xxi-xxii, 43-44.

[17]   Northwest Resource Information Center v. Northwest Power Planning Council, 35 F.3d 1371, 1395 (9th Cir. 1994) (entrenched river users).

[18]   Adapted, except where noted, from *Unraveling Parity,* at 670-702 (used by permission of Environmental Law); and 6 WATER AND WATER RIGHTS 96-102 (Robert E. Beck ed. 1994) (used by permission of The Michie Company, a division of Mathew Bender & Co. Inc., © 1994 by Michie).

[19]   NORTHWEST POWER PLANNING COUNCIL, 1 RECOMMENDATIONS FOR FISH AND WILDLIFE PROGRAM UNDER THE PACIFIC NORTHWEST ELECTRIC POWER PLANNING AND CONSERVATION ACT 167-69, 679, 686-718 (1981).

[20]   H.R. Report 976 (cited in note 1), at 57 (innovative, imaginative approaches).

[21]   16 U.S.C. § 839b(h)(6)(E)(i)-(ii) (improved salmon passage).

[22]   Northwest Power Planning Council, *1982 Columbia Basin Fish and Wildlife Program* §§ 701 (wild stock preference), 1204 (hydroelectric conditions), 604 (adult passage), 504 (ocean harvest), 904 (Yakima Basin), 1304(e)(2) (most expeditious means of funding). For a discussion of the 1982 program, see *Implementing Parity*, at 288-351.

[23]   16 U.S.C. §§ 839b(h)(10)(A) (in a manner consistent with the program); *Id.* (h)(11)(A)(ii) (take program into account); 1982 Program (cited in note 21) § 1304(e)(5) (agencies must explain why implementation is impracticable).

[24] The discussion of program amendments from 1984-91 is adapted from *Unraveling Parity*, at 679-702 (used by permission of Environmental Law).

[25] 16 U.S.C. § 839b(h)(6)(E)(i) (calling for improved fish passage at mainstem dams).

[26] Northwest Power Planning Council, *Compilation of Information on Salmon and Steelhead Losses in the Columbia Basin* 4-5 (1986) (7-14 million salmon lost); Northwest Power Planning Council, *Hydropower Responsibility for Salmon and Steelhead Losses in the Columbia River Basin* 1 (1986) (hydropower losses of 8 million annually).

[27] Northwest Power Planning Council, *Protected Areas Summary and Response to Comments* (1988).

[28] Idaho v. Herrington, No. 87-7704 (9th Cir. 1987); National Wildlife Federation v. Bonneville Power Administration, No. 87-7705 (9th Cir. 1987) (lawsuits challenging transmission line upgrade); H.R. Rep. 976 (cited in note 1), at 57 (innovative, imaginative solutions).

[29] Northwest Power Planning Council, *Amendments to the Columbia Basin Fish and Wildlife Program (Phase Two)* 44 (Dec. 1991) [hereinafter cited as *1991 Amendments*] (reservoir drawdown on Lower Snake River).

[30] *1991 Amendments* (cited in note 29), Response to Comments 33 (Jan. 15, 1992) ("However, the Council does not believe that these measures are enough").

[31] Northwest Power Planning Council Chairman, Ted Hallock, as quoted in TROUT & SALMON LEADER 6 (Jan. 15, 1992).

[32] Northwest Resource Information Center v. Northwest Power Planning Council, 35 F.3d 1371, 1375, 1377-78, 1389 (9th Cir. 1994), *cert. denied*, Pacific Northwest Generating Co-op v. Northwest Power Planning Council, 516 U.S. 806 (1995).

[33] *Id*. at 1394 (citing 16 U.S.C § 839b(h)(5)) (high degree of deference).

[34] *Id*. at 1389, 1391.

[35] Adapted from *Beyond Parity* at 51-62 (used by permission of Environmental Law).

[36] UPSTREAM (cited in chapter 2, note 30), at 210.

[37] RETURN TO THE RIVER (cited in chapter 1, note 52), at xvii-xviii, 5-7, 19-20.

[38] *Id*. at 4-5, 18-20, 508.

[39] *Id*. at 268-69, 509, 513.

[40]   *Id.* at 510.

[41]   Energy and Water Development Appropriations Act of 1997, § 504, 110 Stat. 3005-06 (Sept. 30, 1996) (adding a new § 4(h)(10)(D)(vi) to the Northwest Power Act).

[42]   *See Beyond Parity*, at 118 (redundancy of cost-effectiveness requirement); John M. Volkman, *How Do You Learn From a River? Managing Uncertainty in Species Conservation Policy*, 74 WASH. L. REV. 719, 735-36 (1999) (describing the overwhelming uncertainty about oceanic effects); chapter 6, text with notes 32-36 (Council's review of hatcheries).

[43]   Volkman (cited in note 42), at 754-55; Northwest Power Planning Council, *Report and Recommendations of the Northwest Power Planning Council upon Review of the Corps of Engineers' Columbia River Fish Mitigation Program* 5 (Doc. No. 99-5, April 28, 1999).

[44]   16 U.S.C. § 839b(h)(11)(A)(ii); Confederated Tribes v. FERC, 746 F.2d 466, 473 (9th Cir. 1984) (substantive requirement); PUD No. 1 of Douglas County v. BPA, 947 F.2d 386, 392-94 (9th Cir. 1991) (BPA has substantive obligation to give equitable treatment to fish and wildlife independent of the Council's program).

[45]   *See* Northwest Environmental Defense Center v. BPA, 117 F.3d 1520, 1526-27 (9th Cir. 1997).

[46]   *Id.* at 1533-34.

[47]   RETURN TO THE RIVER (cited in chapter 1, note 52), at 18-25; Multi-Species Framework, Columbia River Basin Multi-Species Framework: Helping Define the Future of the Columbia River, discussed in Volkman (cited in note 42), at 757-58.

[48]   Volkman (cited in note 42), at 759.

[49]   Northwest Power Planning Council, *Columbia River Basin Fish and Wildlife Program*, 13 (Doc. 2000-19, n.d.) [hereinafter cited as *2000 Program*]; Bill Randolph, *It's Unanimous! Power Council Approved New F & W Program*, CLEARING UP, Oct. 23, 2000, at 11-12; Barry Espenson, *Council OK's Amendment; Funding Plan Still Blank*, COLUMBIA BASIN BULLETIN, Oct. 20, 2000 <http:cbbulletin.com>.

[50]   *Id.*; Barry Espenson, *Council: Taxpayers, Ratepayers Should Share ESA Burden*, COLUMBIA BASIN BULLETIN, Oct. 20, 2000 <http:cbbulletin.com>.

[51]   *2000 Program* (cited in note 49), at 13.

[52]   *See* Jonathan Brinckman, *BPA Power Crisis Might Put Salmon At Risk*, OREGONIAN, Jan. 19, 2001; Eric Sorenson, *Salmon Must Pay In Power Crunch*, SEATTLE TIMES, Jan. 19, 2001; Bill Virgin, *BPA Acts in Face of Power Crisis*, SEATTLE POST-INTELLIGENCER, Jan. 19, 2001.

Notes to Chapter 8

[1]   For the classic description of "the tragedy of the commons," see Garrett Hardin, *The Tragedy of the Commons*, 162 SCIENCE 1243 (1968). *See also* Barton H. Thompson, *Tragically Difficult: The Obstacles to Governing the Commons*, 30 ENVTL. L. 241 (2000).

[2]   For discussion of the history of U.S.-Canadian relations leading to the Pacific Salmon Treaty, see Thomas C. Jensen, *The United States-Canada Pacific Salmon Interception Treaty: An Historical and Legal Overview*, 16 ENVTL. L. 363, 369-400 (1986). On the Fraser River runs, see JOSEPH E. TAYLOR III, THE HISTORICAL ROOTS OF CANADIAN-AMERICAN SALMON WARS, in ON BROTHERLY TERMS: CANADIAN-AMERICAN RELATIONS WEST OF THE ROCKIES (U. Washington Press, forthcoming).

[3]   United States-Canada Convention for the Protection, Preservation, and Extension of the Sockeye Salmon Fishery in the Fraser River System, signed May 26, 1930. 8 U.S.T. 1058, T.I.A.S. No. 3867, 50 Stat. 1355 (1930). *See* JOZO TOMASEVICH, INTERNATIONAL AGREEMENTS ON CONSERVATION OF MARINE RESOURCES, WITH SPECIAL REFERENCE TO THE NORTH PACIFIC (Stanford Food Research Inst. 1943); KURKPATRICK DORSEY, THE DAWN OF CONSERVATION DIPLOMACY: U.S.-CANADIAN WILDLIFE PROTECTION TREATIES IN THE PROGRESSIVE ERA (U. Washington Press 1998).

[4]   16 U.S.C. §§ 1801-82 (establishing a U.S. 200-mile zone of jurisdiction over fisheries; now known as the Magnuson-Stevens Fishery Conservation and Management Act). Canada's extension of jurisdiction over offshore fisheries to 200 miles is explained in Barbara Johnson, *Canadian Foreign Policy and Fisheries,* in CANADIAN FOREIGN POLICY AND THE LAW OF THE SEA (Barbara Johnson & Mark W. Zacher, eds. 1977).

[5]   Jensen (cited in note 2), at 383, n.53 (citing National Marine Fisheries Service, *Columbia River Fisheries Development Program, 1980 Annual Report* (1980)).

[6]   *Id*. at 384-86.

[7]   *Id*. at 396-400 (on treaty negotiations); Confederated Tribes v. Kreps, No. 79-541 (D. Or. Sept. 10, 1979) (subjecting ocean harvests to treaty allocation); Confederated Tribes v. Baldrige, No. C80-342T (W.D. Wash., May 12, 1982) (approving a motion to add Alaska as a defendant in treaty rights case); Treaty Between the Government of the United States of America and the Government of Canada Concerning Pacific Salmon, March 18, 1985, T.I.A.S No. 11,091 [hereinafter cited as Pacific Salmon Treaty].

[8]   Pacific Salmon Treaty (cited in note 7), Art. III, ¶ 1(a-b).

[9]   Pacific Salmon Treaty Act of 1985, Pub. L. No. 99-5, 99 Stat. 7, 16 U.S.C. § 3631-44; 16 U.S.C. § 3632(a), (c).

[10]   Confederated Tribes and Bands of Yakima Indian Nation v. Baldridge, 605 F. Supp. 833, 835 (W.D. Wash. 1985).

[11]   United States statement at the First Plenary Session, February 10, 1989, in Pacific Salmon Commission, *Fourth Annual Report* 11, 12 (1989); Canadian Statement at the First Plenary Session, Feb. 10, 1989, in Pacific Salmon Commission, *Fourth Annual Report* 14, 15 (1989).

[12]   Marlyn Twitchell, *Implementing the U.S.-Canada Pacific Salmon Treaty: The Struggle to Move from "Fish Wars" to Cooperative Fishery Management*, 20 OCEAN DEV. & INT'L L. 409, 417 (1989). *See* Letter to the Honorable George P. Schultz from C. Wayne Shinners (Mar. 25, 1987); ANCHORAGE DAILY NEWS, June 14, 1987, at C7.

[13]   Pacific Salmon Commission, News Release (Feb. 25, 1988) at 1; Letter from Timothy Wapato to Sec. of State (Feb. 19, 1988); Canadian Statement at the First Plenary session of the Pacific Salmon Commission, February 10, 1989, in Pacific Salmon Commission, *Fourth Annual Report* 15 (1989); Executive Summary of the Meeting of the Standing Committee on Research and Statistics, September 13-14, 1988, in Pacific Salmon Commission, *Fourth Annual Report* 24 (1989); Statement of the Canadian Section at the First Plenary Session, December 10, 1991, in Pacific Salmon Commission, *Seventh Annual Report* 6 (1992); United States Statement at the Third Plenary Session, December 12, 1991, in Pacific Salmon Commission, *Seventh Annual Report* 13, 14, 16 (1992).

[14]   Agreement between the Government of the United States of America and the Government of Canada on the Establishment of a Mediation Procedure Regarding the Pacific Salmon Treaty, Sept. 11, 1995, Hein's No. KAV 4421, State Dep't No. 95-211 at Art. III; *Salmon Talks Hit Impasse*, FINANCIAL POST, March 6, 1996, at 22; David Bedford, *The Equity Principle: Will the Pacific Salmon Treaty Collapse Under Pressures for Reallocation of Fish?* 67 (Fall 1996) (unpublished paper, submitted in the Pacific Salmon Seminar at Northwestern School of Law of Lewis and Clark College).

[15]   *See* Richard Louv, *U.S., Canada Make Good in Their Fishery Pact*, SAN DIEGO UNION TRIBUNE, July 7, 1999, at A3; British Columbia v. U.S., No. C97-1464C (W.D. Wash. Jan. 30, 1999).

[16]   Agreement Between the United States and Canada Amending Annex IV to the Treaty Concerning Pacific Salmon, with attachment, Aug. 12, 1998; Agreement Between the United States and Canada Amending Annex IV to the Treaty Concerning Pacific Salmon, with attachments, June 3, 1999 [hereinafter cited as *1999 Treaty Amendments*]. *See* Karol de Zwagger Brown, *Truce in the Salmon War: Alternatives For The Pacific Salmon Treaty*, 74 WASH. L. REV. 605, 688-695 (1999) (discussing the 1999 amendments).

[17]   *1999 Treaty Amendments* (cited in note 16), at Annex IV, chap. 3, ¶ 2(b)(ii) & 4 (e).

[18]   *Id.* at Annex IV, chap. 4, ¶ 2(d) & (e); Bureau of Oceans and International Environmental and Scientific Affairs, *Summary of the Pacific Salmon Agreement*, June 3, 1999 (buy-back and Indian share).

[19]   *1999 Treaty Amendments* (cited in note 16), at Annex IV, chap. 1, ¶ 2; chap. 5, ¶ 4-12; chap. 6, ¶ 1, 9; Brown (cited in note 16), at 689-92.

[20]   *1999 Treaty Amendments* (cited in note 16), at Attachments C, D, E.

[21]   British Columbia Ministry of Fisheries, Review of New Arrangements under the Pacific Salmon Treaty (June 14, 1999); Columbia Basin Bull., No. 46 (June 11, 1999) <http://www.nwpcc.org/bulletin/bull_46.htm#2> (quoting Dale Kelley, Executive Director of the Alaska Trollers Ass'n).

[22]   Paul Koberstein, *Shipwreck! Is the Pacific Salmon Treaty Lost at Sea?*, 3 BIG RIVER NEWS no. 1, at 1, 3, 6 (Nat'l. Res. L. Inst. Fall 1996) (discussing Alaskan harvests and conservation failures).

Notes to Chapter 9

[1]   Columbia Basin Fish and Wildlife Authority, *Proposed Mainstem Flows for Columbia Basin Anadromous Fish* (1990), reprinted in *Unraveling Parity*, at 708.

[2]   Nehlsen, *et al.* (cited in chapter 1, note 43), at 4-5, 7-8.

[3]   Salmon Summit, *Status of Salmon Summit Deliberations on Mitigation and Survival Issues* (1990).

[4]   National Marine Fisheries Service & Oregon Department of Fish and Wildlife, *Past and Present Abundance of Snake River Sockeye, Snake River Chinook, and Lower Columbia Coho* (1990).

[5]   56 Fed. Reg. 58,619, 58,622 (1991).

[6]   57 Fed. Reg. 14,653-60 (1992).

[7]   16 U.S.C. § 1532(16) (definition of species); 56 Fed. Reg. 58,612, 58,618 (1991) (evolutionarily significant units); Daniel J. Rohlf, *There's Something Fishy Going On Here: A Critique of the National Marine Fisheries Service's Definition of Species Under the Endangered Species Act,* 24 ENVTL. L. 617, 636-51 (1994).

[8]   56 Fed. Reg. 29,553 (1991) (Lower Columbia River coho); 58 Fed. Reg. 23,390 (1993) (Illinois River winter steelhead); 65 Fed. Reg. 20,915 (2000) (Umpqua River cutthroat); *Umpqua Cutthroat to be Combined with Larger ESU, Removed From List*, ENDANGERED SPECIES & WETLANDS REP., Feb. 1999, at 6.

[9]   16 U.S.C. §§ 1533(b)(3) (citizen petition process); 1532(6) (definition of endangered species); 1532(20) (definition of threatened species).

[10]   Northwest Power Planning Council, *1987 Columbia River Basin Fish and Wildlife Program* 5 ("possibly, the most ambitious effort in the world to save a biological resource").

[11]   16 U.S.C. § 1538(a)(1)(B); 50 C.F.R. § 17.3 (definition of take); upheld in Babbitt v. Sweet Home, 515 U.S. 687 (1995); 16 U.S.C. §§ 1536(a)(2) (no jeopardy); 1536(b) (biological opinion), 1536(a)(2) (best available science); Bennett v. Spear, 520 U.S. 154, 169, 178 (1997) (BiOps "virtually binding").

[12]   16 U.S.C. § 1533(d) (section 4(d)); *see* chapter 14, text accompanying note 13 (discussing 4(d) rules).

[13]   Nat'l Marine Fisheries Service, *Endangered Species Act Section 7 Consultation/ Conference Biological Opinion: 1992 Operation of the Federal Columbia River Power System* (1992). On the 1991 amendments to the Columbia Basin Fish and Wildlife Program, see chapter 7, text with notes 29-30.

[14]   U.S. Dept. of Commerce, *Biological Opinion on 1993 Operation of the Federal Columbia River Power System* 10-11, 15 (1993).

[15]   Idaho Dept of Fish and Game v. NMFS, 850 F.Supp. 886, 893 (D. OR. 1994).

[16]   *Id*. at 893, 897-900.

[17]   *Id*. at 900 (emphasis in original).

[18]   Most of the remainder of this chapter is adapted from *Salmon Lessons*, at 552-86 (used by permission of the Washington Law Review), which contains more detailed citations to authorities.

[19]   Nat'l Marine Fisheries Serv., *Biological Opinion on Reinitiation of Consultation on 1994-98 Operation of the Federal Columbia River Power System and Juvenile Transportation Program in 1995 and Future Years* 95, 98-101, 103-04, 113 (1995) [hereinafter cited as *1995 Hydro BiOp*]. For more detail on the changes NMFS made between the draft and final BiOp, see *Salmon Lessons*, at 552-56.

[20]   *Id*. at 80, 92-94, 112. On the history of the transportation program, *see* RETURN TO THE RIVER (cited in chapter 1, note 52), at 575-78; Lisa Mighetto & Wesley Ebel, *Saving the Salmon: A History of the U.S. Army Corps of Engineers' Efforts to Protect Anadromous Fish on the Columbia and Snake Rivers* 119-23 (report to the U.S. Army Corps of Engineers 1994).

[21]   American Rivers v. NMFS, No. 96-384-MA, at 26 (D.Or. Apr. 3, 1997).

[22]   *Id*. at 5-7, 11, 26, *aff'd*, American Rivers v. NMFS, No. 97-36159 (9th Cir. March 8, 1999).

[23]   U.S. Army Corps of Engineers, *Draft Lower Snake River Juvenile Salmon Migration Feasibility Report/Environmental Impact Statement, Appendix A-Anadromadous Fish* (written by the National Marine Fisheries Service) [hereinafter cited as *NMFS A-Fish Appendix*].

[24]   *Id*. at A4-23 (spring/summer chinook), A5-20 to 21 (fall chinook), A6-11 to 13 (steelhead), A7-12 (sockeye).

[25]   *Id*. at A ES-5 to A ES-8, A4-23 to A4-27; Barry Espenson, *Scientists Stress Action For Looming Fish Extinctions*, COLUMBIA BASIN BULLETIN, April 7, 2000 <http://cbbulletin.com> (discussing non-Snake River stocks at risk).

[26] *2000 BiOp* (cited in chapter 1, note 49); The Federal Caucus, *Conservation of Columbia Basin Fish: A Conceptual Recovery Plan* (Dec. 2000) [hereafter cited as *Caucus Recovery Plan*]. The Federal Caucus consists of the U.S. Army Corps of Engineers, the Bonneville Power Administration, the Bureau of Indian Affairs, the Bureau of Land Management, the Environmental Protection Agency, the U.S. Fish and Wildlife Service, the U.S. Forest Service, and the National Marine Fisheries Service.

[27] *2000 BiOp* (cited chapter 1, note 49), chap. 9 (describing the draft BiOp's "reasonable and prudent alternative").

[28] *Id.* at 9-11 to 9-15, 9-53 ("the best the hydrosystem can do without dam breaching . . .").

[29] *Id.* at 9-76 to 9-78.

[30] *Id.* at 9-55 to 9-76.

[31] *Id.* at 9-133 to 9-141 (habitat), 9-143 to 9-150 (harvest), 9-151 to 9-160 (hatcheries).

[32] *Id.* at 9-5, 9-6, (breach triggers); Jonathan Brinckman, *Unreleased Federal Plan Calls For Dam Breaching*, OREGONIAN, Nov. 18, 2000 (describing the unreleased draft BiOp).

[33] *See Scientists Say NMFS' BiOp Lacks Collaboration*, COLUMBIA BASIN BULLETIN, Sept. 15, 2000 <http://cbbulletin.com>; *States, Others Want Major Changes in Federal Recovery Plan*, COLUMBIA BASIN BULLETIN, Oct. 6, 2000 <http://cbbulletin.com/cbb>; Bill Rudolph, *Region Gets 4,000 Pages of Dam Studies, But No Answers Yet*, CLEARING UP, Dec. 27, 1999, at 12 ("no brainer").

[34] *1995-1998 Hatchery BiOp* (cited in chapter 2, note 46), at 36, 64 (1995); Nat'l Marine Fisheries Serv., *Proposed Recovery Plan for Snake River Salmon* V-4-1 to V-4-49 (1995) [hereinafter cited as *NMFS Proposed Recovery Plan*].

[35] *Tribal Restoration Plan* (cited in chapter 6, note 30), at 5B-14; *see* Sterne (cited in chapter 6, note 15), at 123, 127 (discussing the cautious reception to supplementation among NMFS, the Northwest Power Planning Council, and environmentalists).

[36] *See* Nat'l Marine Fisheries Serv., *Biological Opinion on Nez Perce Tribal Hatchery, 1998-2002 Hatchery Operations* 7-8, 28 (1997) [hereinafter cited as *Nez Perce BiOp*]; *Power Council Funds New Hatchery, Hears Debate Over Value*, CLEARING UP, Dec. 13, 1999, at 12 (scaled back proposal funded); Barry Espenson, *Snake River Supplementation Project Shows Promise*, COLUMBIA BASIN BULLETIN, Oct. 20, 2000 <http://cbbulletin.com> (discussing 1999 returns).

[37] *Nez Perce BiOp* (cited in note 36), at 9-12, 23-25, 28.

[38] *Artificial Production Review* (cited in chapter 6, note 1), discussed in chapter 6, text accompanying notes 32-35.

[39] *1999 Hatchery BiOp* (cited in chapter 2, note 46), at 118.

40   *Id.* at 1 (percentages), 118 (Nez Perce hatchery), 135-41 (jeopardy finding and conditions).

41   On harvest restrictions accounting for other sources of salmon mortality, see UPSTREAM (cited in chapter 2, note 30), at 254.

42   On incidental takes, *see NMFS Proposed Recovery Plan* (cited in note 34), at ES-6; on continuing declines of salmon numbers, see UPSTREAM (cited in chapter 2, note 30), at 257. Incidental takes are authorized as part of the consultation process by 16 U.S.C. § 1536(b)(3)-(4); incidental take permits outside of the consultation process with habitat conservation plans are authorized by *id.* § 1539(a)(1)(B).

43   The Magnuson-Stevens Act appears at 16 U.S.C. §§ 1801-1854; secretarial approval is required by § 1854; see Ramsey v. Kantor, 96 F.3d 434, 444-45 (9th Cir. 1996), on the Secretary of Commerce's role under the Magnuson Act.

44   Nat'l Marine Fisheries Serv., *Biological Opinion on the Fishery Management Plan for Commercial and Recreational Fisheries off the Coasts of Washington, Oregon, and California of the Pacific Fishery Management Council* 10-12 (1996) [hereinafter cited as *Ocean BiOp*]; Pacific Fishery Management Council, *Preseason Report III: Analysis of Council-Adopted Management Measures for 1995 Ocean Salmon Fisheries* 13-14 (1995).

45   *Ocean BiOp* (cited in note 44), at 15-17, 32-34.

46   Pub L. No. 64-123, 40 Stat. 515 (1918) (Columbia River Compact); A Plan for Managing Fisheries on Stocks Originating from the Columbia River and its Tributaries above Bonneville Dam (1977, amended 1988) upheld by the courts in United States v. Oregon, 699 F. Supp. 1456 (D. Or. 1988), *aff'd,* 913 F.2d. 576 (9th Cir. 1988); *see* Harrison (cited in chapter 4, note 22); Weaver (cited in chapter 4, note 22).

47   Courtenay Thompson, *Steelhead Suggestion Limits Tribal Harvests,* THE OREGONIAN, Apr. 13, 1998, at B1 (on Stelle's suggestion); United States v. Oregon, No 68-513-A at 3-4 (Sept. 3, 1998); Nat'l Marine Fisheries Serv., *Biological Opinion on Impacts to Listed Steelhead Resulting from 1998 Fall Season Fisheries Conducted Under the Columbia River Fish Management Plan and 1996-98 Management Agreement* 4 (1998) [hereinafter cited as *Comprehensive Plan BiOp*] (concerning the low numbers of returning wild steelhead).

48   United States v. Oregon, at 5-6 (citing 16 U.S.C. §1536(a)(2), for the ESA's broad definition of federal agency action).

49   *Comprehensive Plan BiOp* (cited in note 47), at 11-15.

50   U.S. Depts. of Interior and Commerce, *Secretarial Order on American Indian Tribal Rights, Federal-Tribal Trust Responsibilities, and the Endangered Species Act,* para. 3(C)(iii)(1997), reprinted in 72 WASH. L. REV. 1089, 1095-96 (1997), discussed in Charles F. Wilkinson, *The Role of Bilateralism in Fulfilling the Federal-Tribal Relationship: The Tribal Rights-Endangered Species Secretarial Order,* 72

WASH. L. REV. 1063 (1997).

[51]   U.S. Dept. of Agriculture, *Streamlining Consultation Procedures Under Section 7 of the Endangered Species Act-February 1997 Procedure Guidance* (1997); 15 C.F.R. § 402.14(h) (biological consultation procedures).

[52]   Pacific Rivers Council v. Robertson, 854 F.Supp. 713, 722-23 (D. Or. 1993).

[53]   Pacific Rivers Council v. Thomas, 30 F.3d 1050, 1053-57 (9th Cir. 1994); Pacific Rivers Council v. Thomas, 873 F.Supp. 365, 372 (D. Idaho 1995). The injunction was later dissolved when the consultation was completed. Pacific Rivers Council v. Thomas, 897 F. Supp. 454, 455 (D. Idaho 1995).

[54]   On the Columbia Basin Ecosystem Management Project, see *Amphibious Salmon*, at 672-74. On land management changes produced by ESA consultation, see *Salmon Lessons*, at 578-79, nn. 412, 414; on NMFS's determination that habitat protection on federal lands supplies inadequate salmon protection, see 63 Fed. Reg. 11,482, 11,499 (1998); on the Columbia River Inter-Tribal Fish Commission's perspective on PACFISH, consider the following electronic mail from Jim Weber (then a Policy Analyst for the Columbia River Inter-Tribal Fish Commission) to author, stating:

> You asked for some evidence that PACFISH and the ESA aren't working. Attached are some memoranda and correspondence regarding the Summit timber sale on the Malheur National Forest in the Middle Fork John Day country. This is bull trout and spring chinook habitat. Our hydrologist Jon Rhodes visited the timber sale area in April 1999, the first spring after the logging had been initiated and found a muddy mess. He took approximately 180 photographs of what he found. We presented about 40 of these photos to Rick Applegate and Randy Tweten of NMFS, and Ron Rhew, of the USFWS. From there, we set up a field trip on the Forest, including Forest Service reps, to look over the site (this occurred in June 1999). We then waited for something to happen, some report to be made. Nothing happened. We wrote to NMFS and USFWS in September and included some suggestions. No response. Nothing has happened. Both NMFS and USFWS concede that this sale was not implemented properly. Even the Forest Service concedes implementation problems. Nothing has been done to ensure that they won't recur. Nothing has been done about the basic issue that you simply can't do projects like this without causing damage.
>
> On August 5, 1999, I spoke with Ron Rhew, USFWS, who was one of the guys on the field trip. I reiterated that we had ample photographic evidence of road and landing related sediment and of it being routed into streams (the project was promised to be a no sediment impact project). He didn't feel like there was much they could do on the sediment issue because there wasn't enough 'background' information to determine whether the project had resulted in any new sediment delivery. If that is true, then the section 7 [biological consultations] process (and adaptive management) are incapable of functioning on that forest.

[55]   55 Fed. Reg. 26,114 (1990) (spotted owl listing); Seattle Audubon Society v. Lyons, 871 F.Supp. 1291, 1322, 1324 (W.D. Wash. 1994), *aff'd*, 80 F.3d 1401 (9th Cir 1996), upholding U.S. Depts. of Agriculture & Interior, *Record of Decision for Amendments to Forest Service and Bureau of Land Management Planning Documents Within the Range of the Northern Spotted Owl and Standards and Guidelines for Management of Habitat for Late-Sucessional and Old-Growth Forest Related Species Within the Range of the Northern Spotted Owl* (1994).

[56]   Nat'l. Marine Fisheries Serv., *Biological Opinion and Conference Opinion on Implementation of Land and Resource Management Plans (USFS) and Resource Management Plans (BLM)* 3, 49 (1997); 61 Fed. Reg. 41,514, 41,517-20 (1996) (Umpqua cutthroat trout listing).

[57]   Pacific Coast Fed'n of Fishermen's Assns. v. NMFS, No. C97-775 R (W.D. Wash. May 29, 1998), at 27-31, discussed in Patti Goldman, *Endangered Species Act Duties*, Big River News, at 1, 3 (Spring 1998). On the motivation for the Northwest Forest Plan, see *Amphibious Salmon*, at 669.

[58]   Letter from William Stelle, Jr., NMFS Regional Administrator, to Cary Osterhaus, Roseburg Bureau of Land Management District Manager 10-14, 21-23 (Dec. 18, 1998).

[59]   Pacific Coast Federation of Fishermen's Associations v. National Marine Fisheries Service, 71 F.Supp.2d 1063 (W.D. Wash. 1999), *aff'd*, 253 F.3d 1138 (9th Cir. 2001). *See* Lauren M. Rule, *Enforcing Ecosystem Management Under the Northwest Forest Plan: The Judicial Role,* 12 Fordham Envtl. L.J. 211 (2000)

[60]   Nat'l Marine Fisheries Serv., *Biological Opinion on Inland Land, Inc., Columbia River* 2, 10, 15 (1997).

[61]   *Id*. at 8-10.

[62]   *Id*. at 12-16.

[63]   Bill Crampton, *NMFS Takes Heat Over Water Policies*, Columbia Basin Bulletin, Sept. 4, 1998 <http://www.nwppc.org/bulletin/bull_12.htm#2> (discussing charges made by members of Congress, state legislators, and irrigators at a hearing of the House Resources Committee held in Pasco, Washington on September 2, 1998). The ESA-water right cases are Riverside Irrigation Dist. v. Andrews, 758 F.2d 508 (10th Cir. 1985); U.S. v. Glenn-Colusa Irrigation Dist., 788 F.Supp. 1126 (E.D. Cal. 1992); Sierra Club v. City of San Antonio, 112 F.3d 789 (5th Cir. 1997). The Bureau of Reclamation cases are O'Neill v. United States, 50 F.3d 677 (9th Cir. 1995); and Natural Resources Defense Council v. Houston, 146 F.3d 1118 (9th Cir. 1998).

[64]   Southwest Ctr. for Biological Diversity v. FERC, 967 F. Supp. 1116 (D. Ariz. 1997) (exclusive jurisdiction in courts of appeal); American Rivers v. FERC, 170 F.3d 896 (9th Cir. 1998) (FERC order a prerequisite for judicial review); Platte River Whooping Crane v. FERC, 876 F.2d 109 (D.C. Cir. 1989) (requiring FERC consideration of fish and wildlife in annual licenses). A subsequent decision clarified that FERC's authority to impose new protective conditions in ongoing licenses was limited to situations in which it had reserved the authority to change conditions in the original license. *See* Platte River

Whooping Crane v. FERC, 962 F.2d 27 (D.C. Cir. 1992). Such reserved authority exists concerning most Columbia Basin projects.

[65]   American Rivers *et al.*, *Notice of Intent to Sue for Violations of the Endangered Species Act* 3 (1997) (6.5 million acre-feet of water); National Marine Fisheries Serv., *Draft Biological Opinion on Bureau of Reclamation Operations and Maintenance of Its Projects in the Snake River Basin Above Lower Granite Dam* (Apr. 8, 1999) <http://www.nwr.noaa.gov/1hydrop/page.pdf>; *see also* Natural Resources Defense Council v. Houston, 146 F.3d 1118 (9th Cir. 1998) (holding that the Bureau of Reclamation's failure to complete section 7 consultation prior to renewing water supply contracts violated the ESA, and that the trial court acted within its discretion in ordering that the contracts be rescinded); O'Neill v. United States, 50 F.3d 677 (9th Cir. 1995) (ruling that Bureau contract language absolved the government of liability for its failure to deliver the full contractual amount of water due to a shortage caused by statutory environmental mandates).

[66]   *See* 16 U.S.C. § 1540(g) (ESA citizen suit provision).

[67]   16 U.S.C. §§ 1532(19) (definition), 1539(a) (taking prohibition); 50 C.F.R. § 17.3, upheld in Sweet Home v. Babbitt, 515 U.S. 687 (1995).

[68]   16 U.S.C. § 1539(a).

[69]   61 Fed. Reg. 63,854 (1996), codified at 50 C.F.R. §§ 17.3, 17.22, 17.32, 222.3, 222.22, challenged in Spirit of the Sage v. Babbitt, No. 98-1873 (EGS), (D.D.C.).

[70]   Habitat Conservation Plan Factsheet, available at <http://www.chelanpud.org/ FISHWILD.html>; email interview with Janet Sears, Public Affairs, National Marine Fisheries Service (Sept. 15, 1999).

[71]   Rocky Reach Anadromous Fish Agreement and Habitat Conservation Plan, §§ Introduction (c), I, III(1) (March 25, 1998); National Marine Fisheries Serv., Questions and Answers about the Mid-Columbia Habitat Conservation Plan (June 27, 1998), available at <http://www.nwr.noaa.gov/1press/062798_3.htm>; Albert Gore, Jr., Statement of Vice President Gore on Columbia River Salmon Restoration (June 27, 1998), available at <http://www.nwr.noaa.gov/1press/062798_4htm>.

[72]   16 U.S.C. § 1539(a)(2)(B)(ii) and (iv) (incidental take permit standards); Nicole Cordan & Starla Roels, *Mid-Columbia HCPs and the Implications of the No Surprises Policy*, 5 BIG RIVER NEWS no. 3, at 8-9 (Nat'l. Res. L. Inst. Spring 1999) (discussing tribal comments).

[73]   Cordan & Roels (cited in note 72), at 8, citing 16 U.S.C. § 1536(a) (authorizing incidental takes through the federal consultation process); Nat'l. Marine Fisheries Serv., *Endangered Species HCP Handbook*, at 1-4.

[74]   16 U.S.C § 1533(d) (Section 4(d)); 65 Fed. Reg. 42,422 (2000) (to be codified at 50 C.R.F. § 223) (4(d) rules).

[75]   65 Fed. Reg. at 42,423, 42,480 (2000).

[76]   *See* Barry Espenson, *Federal Lawsuit Challenges NMFS' 4(d) Rules*, COLUMBIA BASIN BULLETIN (Sept 15, 2000), <http://cbbulletin.com> (describing the environmentalists' suit); Mike O'Bryant, *Coalition Challenges Salmon Recovery Premises*, COLUMBIA BASIN BULLETIN (Oct. 6, 2000) <http://cbbulletin.com> (describing the developers' suit).

[77]   *See* chapter 4, text with notes 17-20 (discussing the Supreme Court's treatment of conservation in the *Puyallup I* and *II* cases).

[78]   *See* U.S. Depts. of Interior and Commerce, *American Indian Tribal Rights, Federal-Tribal Trust Responsibilites, and The Endangered Species Act*, Sec. Order No. 3206, at 6 (June 5, 1997).

[79]   United States v. Oregon, Civ. No. 68-513 (D. Or. Oct. 13, 1998).

[80]   This section and the last one in this chapter are drawn from *Salmon Lessons*, at 599-602 (used by permission of the Washington Law Review), which contains citations.

[81]   *See* TAYLOR (cited in chapter 1, note 3), at 220; ARTHUR F. MCEVOY, THE FISHERMAN'S PROBLEM: LAW AND ECOLOGY IN THE CALIFORNIA FISHERIES, 1850-1980, at 187-206 (Cambridge U. Press 1986).

Notes to Chapter 10

[1]   33 U.S.C §§ 1251(a) (national policy), 1319 (penalties), 1342 (permit program for point source discharges), 1362(7), (12), and (14) (definitions of "navigable waters," "discharge of a pollutant," and "point source").

[2]   *Id.* §§ 1288, 1329 (nonpoint source programs); 1315(b)(1)(E) (annual reports by states to include non-point sources and controls). *See also* U.S. General Accounting Office, *The Federal Role in Addressing and Controlling Nonpoint Source Pollution* (Feb. 26, 1999).

[3]   *Id.* §§ 1301(b)(1)(C) (permits must meet water quality standards), 1313 (water quality standards); Pub. L. No. 89-234, 79 Stat. 903 (1965) (Water Quality Act of 1965).

[4]   On TMDLs, *see* Oliver A. Houck, *TMDLs IV: The Final Frontier*, 29 ENVIRO. L. REP. 10,469 (1999), and earlier articles in the series; Robert W. Adler, *New TMDL Litigation Leaves Many Unanswered Questions*, 6 RIVERS 269 (1998); Nina Bell, *TMDLs: The Key to Unlocking the Clean Water Act*, 5 BIG RIVER NEWS no. 4, at 1 (Nat'l. Res. L. Inst. Fall 1999).

[5]   The author was an attorney for EPA in the late 1970s when the agency's reaction to the National Wildlife Federation's petition was under consideration. On the water quality problems dams cause, see National Wildlife Federation v. Gorsuch, 530 F.Supp. 1291, 1297-1303 (D. D.C. 1982).

[6]   National Wildlife Federation v. Gorsuch, 693 F.2d 156, 165-66 (D.C. Cir. 1982), *rev'g* 530 F.Supp. 1291, 1306-13 (D.D.C. 1982).

[7]   National Wildlife Federation v. Consumers Power Co., 862 F.2d 580, 589 (6th Cir. 1988), *rev'g* 657 F. Supp. 989 (W.D. Mich. 1987).

[8]   33 U.S.C. § 1251(a) (goal of the Clean Water Act).

[9]   33 U.S.C. §§ 1313(c)(2)(A) (purpose), 1313(c)(3)-(4) (federal oversight), 1313(c)(1) (review every three years), 1301(b)(1)(C) (permits to achieve water quality standards), 1323(a) (federal activities to achieve water quality standards), 1341(a) (water quality certification for federally licensed and permitted activities).

[10]   *Id.* § 1313(c)(1)(2)(B) (contents of a water quality standard); PUD No. 1 of Jefferson County v. Washington Dept of Ecology, 511 U.S. 700, 712-720 (1994), discussed in 4 WATERS AND WATER RIGHTS § 40.08(e)(2) (Robert E. Beck, ed., 1996 ed.).

[11]   See the sources cited in note 4 on the TMDL litigation and its significance.

[12]   *See* Washington Dept. of Ecology, *Ecology's 1998 Candidate List of Impaired and Threatened Waterbodies—the 303(d) List,* <http://www.wa.gov/ecology/wq/303d> (visited Oct. 20, 1999); Comments of Nina Bell, Northwest Environmental Advocates to author (Jan. 13, 2000) (Washington's restrictive criteria for listing non-complying waterbodies; significant sublethal effects in urban estuaries).

[13]   National Marine Fisheries Serv., *Biological and Conference Opinion on Approval of Oregon Water Quality Standards for Dissolved Oxygen, Temperature, and pH,* at 15 (July 7, 1999) [hereinafter cited as *BiOp on Oregon Water Quality Standards*].

[14]   *Id.* (data on half of streams); *see* notes 25-33 and accompanying text in this chapter on NMFS's questioning the adequacy of Oregon water quality standards.

[15]   Personal communication between Mike Edmondson, Idaho Div. of Environmental Quality and Melissa Powers (Oct. 22, 1999); Comments of Nina Bell (cited in note 12), at 3 (temperature as a surrogate for other water quality problems).

[16]   *BiOp on Oregon Water Quality Standards* (cited in note 13), at 19 (dissolved oxygen), 26 (temperature).

[17]   *Id.* at 19 (sediment), 45 (pH).

[18]   Bell (cited in note 4), at 3 (discussing the cases).

[19]   *Id.* at 3-4.

[20]   Idaho Sportsmen's Coalition v. Browner, 951 F.Supp. 962 (W.D. Wash. 1996) (invalidating the state's list of impaired waters and ordering EPA to identify them); Idaho Conservation League v. Browner, 968 F.Supp. 546 (W.D. Wash. 1997) (upholding EPA's decision on the inadequacy of the state's water quality standards); *see* Arthur D. Smith, *Introduction to the 1998 Idaho Water Quality Symposium,* 35 IDAHO L. REV. 431 (1999).

[21]   Discussed in Stephanie M. Parent, *Water Quality Standards: A Necessary Step for Snake River Dams and a Healthy River,* 5 BIG RIVER NEWS no. 4, at 5-6 (Nat'l. Res. L. Inst. Fall 1999); 33 U.S.C. § 1323(a) (federal activities resulting in the discharge or runoff of pollutants must meet state water quality standards). The most recent of four cases finding that Forest Service timber sales violated state water quality standards was Idaho Sporting Congress v. Thomas, 137 F.3d 1145, 1153 (9th Cir. 1998) (citing Oregon Natural Resources Council v. United States Forest Service, 834 F.2d 842, 852 (9th Cir. 1987)). *See also* Marble Mountain Audubon Soc'y v. Rice, 914 F.2d 179, 182-83 (9th Cir. 1990) ("The judicial review provision of the Administrative Procedure Act, 5 U.S.C. §§ 701-706, permits private citizens to sue for alleged state water quality control violations from nonpoint sources"); Oregon Natural Resources Council v. Lyng, 882 F.2d 1417, 1424-25 (9th Cir. 1989) ("The CWA also requires states to implement water quality standards with which federal agencies must comply"). For an able critique of the reasoning of the *Idaho Sporting Congress* case, see Robin Kudis Craig, *Idaho Sporting Congress v. Thomas and Sovereign Immunity: Federal Facility Nonpoint Sources, the APA, and the Meaning of 'In the Same Manner and to the Same Extent as any Non-governmental Entity,'s* 30 ENVTL. L. 527 (2000) (arguing that the Clean Water Act requires federal facilities to comply with state water quality standards only when the state would impose similar requirements on non-federal nonpoint sources).

[22]   Wash. Admin. Code §§ 173-201A-130(98)(a-b) (temperature), 173-201A-030(2)(c)(iii) (dissolved gas), 173-201A-030(2)(a-b) (narrative standard for class A waters), 173-201A-070(4) (antidegradation policy concerning class A waters).

[23]   *See* Mike O'Bryant, *EPA Gives Corps Snake River EIS a Failing Grade,* Columbia Basin Bulletin (April 28, 2000) <http://cbbulletin.com>; U.S. Environmental Protection Agency, *Columbia River Temperature Assessment: Simulation Methods* (Feb. 1999) (EPA finding); 40 C.F.R. § 1508.27(b)(10) (NEPA regulation requiring consideration of whether a proposed action threatens a violation of federal, state, or local law); Lynn Francisco, *EPA Still After Corps Over Alleged Clean Water Act Violations,* CLEARING UP, Aug. 14, 2000, at 11 (discussing a July 31, 2000 letter of EPA to the Corps).

[24]   National Wildlife Fed'n v. Army Corps of Engineers, 92 F. Supp.2d 1072 (D. Or. 2000).

[25]   *BiOp on Oregon Water Quality Standards* (cited in note 13), at 15-16.

[26]   *Id.* at 9-10 (lack of implementation, adverse effects, EPA's conditional approval), attachments 2 (letter expressing EPA's conditional approval), 3 (conservation measures which the state will implement), 4 (regional temperature criteria project).

[27]   *Id.* at 20-22.

[28]   *Id*. at 19, 23-24.

[29]   *Id*. at 25-26.

[30]   *Id*. at 29-36.

[31]   *Id*. at 37-39.

[32]   *See* 60-day Notice of Intent to Sue on Behalf of Northwest Environmental Advocates for Failure to Perform Mandatory Duties Under the Clean Water Act and Endangered Species Act (July 10, 2000).

[33]   33 U.S.C. § 1251(a)(2) (national goal of water quality protecting the propagation of fish, shellfish, and wildlife).

Notes to Chapter 11

[1]   The Federal Power Act is codified at 16 U.S.C. §§ 791-825. Jurisdiction under the FPA extends to traditionally navigable waters and post-1935 projects affecting interstate commerce. See 4 WATERS AND WATER RIGHTS § 40.03 (Rob't. E. Beck, ed., 1996 ed., 2000 supp.).

[2]   16 U.S.C. §§ 797(e) (section 4(e)), 803(a) (section 10(a)). Section 10(a)(2) contains the directive to consider plans prepared by others.

[3]   First Iowa Hydroelectric Corp. v. FPC, 328 U.S. 152 (1946) (FERC licenses may ignore most state laws); California v. FERC, 495 U.S. 490 (1990) (reaffirming *First Iowa*); PUD No. 1 of Jefferson County v. Washington Dept. of Ecology, 511 U.S. 700 (1994) (state water quality standards may condition FERC projects); 33 U.S.C. § 1341 (water quality certification conditions); 16 U.S.C. §§ 797(e), 803(j), 811 (federal land management conditions, fish and wildlife recommendations, fishway conditions).

[4]   16 U.S.C. § 799 (maximum 50-year terms); H.R. Rep. No. 934, 99th Cong., 2d Sess. 22 (1986) ("new look"); American Rivers v. FERC, 201 F.3d 1186, 1195-1199 (9th Cir. 2000); 16 U.S.C. §§ 807 (federal takeover), 808(f) (non-power licenses).

[5]   16 U.S.C. § 803(j) (section 10(j)); H.R. Rep. 507, 99th Cong., 2d Sess. 30 (1986) (legislative history of 1986 amendments).

[6]   56 Fed. Reg. 61,137, 61,139 (Dec. 2, 1991) (Indian tribes do not qualify under section 10(j)); 18 C.F.R. §§ 4.34(e) (60-day time period), (e)(3) (substantial evidence requirement).

[7]   On FERC's interpretation of section 10(j), see 4 WATERS AND WATER RIGHTS § 40.09(c) (cited in note 1); American Rivers v. FERC, 201 F.3d 1186, 1202-1205 (9th Cir. 2000).

[8]   16 U.S.C. §§ 796(2) (prohibiting licenses in national parks and monuments), 797(e) (section 4(e)).

[9]   Escondido Mutual Water Co. v. LaJolla Band of Mission Indians, 466 U.S. 765, 772, 776-87 (1984).

[10]   18 C.F.R. § 4.34(b) (FERC regulations); Southern California Edison v. FERC, 116 F.3d 507, 518 (D.C. Cir. 1997); Mega Renewables, 44 F.E.R.C. ¶ 61,395 (1988) (acknowledging that 4(e) requires FERC to include the conditions or deny the license); Camille E. Held, 42 F.E.R.C. ¶ 61,032 (1995) (concerning a requirement that the licensee obtain a Forest Service special use permit); Boise-Kuna Irrigation Dist., 46 F.E.R.C. ¶ 61,385 (1989) (concerning a Forest Service reservation of authority to approve changes to the project).

[11]   16 U.S.C. § 811 (section 18); Puget Sound Energy, Inc., 81 F.E.R.C. ¶ 61,354 at 62,656 (1997) (state fishery agencies do not have section 18 conditioning authority).

[12]   56 Fed. Reg. 23,108, 23,146 (1991) (FERC's original definition); 56 Fed. Reg. 61,137, 61,140-45 (1991) (FERC's revised definition); Pub. L. No. 102-486, § 1701(b), 106 Stat. 3008 (vacating FERC's definition).

[13]   On FERC's interpretation of section 18, see 4 WATERS AND WATER RIGHTS § 40.09(b) (cited in note 1). The 60-day time limit is imposed by 18 C.F.R. § 4.34(b).

[14]   American Rivers v. FERC, 201 F.3d at 1187, 1210 (9th Cir. 2000), quoting from Bangor Hydro-Electric Co. v. FERC, 78 F.3d 659, 663 (D.C. Cir. 1996).

[15]   33 U.S.C. §§ 1341(a)(1), (d); on the FPA's preemption of state laws, see 4 WATERS AND WATER RIGHTS § 40.07 (cited in note 1); 18 C.F.R. §§ 4.38(f)(7)(iii) (amendments to original license applications), 16.8(f)(7)(iii) (amendments to re-licensings).

[16]   PUD No. 1 of Jefferson County v. Washington Dept. Of Ecology, 511 U.S. 700, 709-721 (1994).

[17]   American Rivers v. FERC, 129 F.3d 99, 107, 110-11 (2d Cir. 1997) (the state's conditions involved a reservation of state authority to review and approve any significant changes to the project and all maintenance activities; construction deadlines concerning fish passage and canoe portage facilities; and operational conditions concerning minimum water levels and peak water flows). The substantial evidence standard is imposed by 16 U.S.C. §§ 803(a), 825(*l*).

[18]   Southwest Center for Biological Diversity v. FERC, 967 F. Supp. 1166 (D. Ariz. 1997) (jurisdiction only for appeals courts); American Rivers v. FERC, 170 F.3d 896 (9th Cir. 1998) (FERC order a prerequisite for judicial review), discussed in chap. 9, text accompanying note 64; Pacific Rivers Council v. Thomas (existing land management plans subject to ESA consultation), discussed in chap. 9, text with notes 52-53.

[19]   16 U.S.C. § 1536(a)(2) (all federal actions "authorized, funded, or carried out" subject to ESA review); 15 C.F.R. 402.3 (all federal discretionary actions).

[20]   18 C.F.R. §§ 4.38 (consultation), 4.41(f), 4.51(f) (Exhibit E). An abbreviated Exhibit E is required of small projects (1.5 megawatts or less, or 5 megawatts or less at existing dams). *Id.* § 3.60(d)(2).

[21]   62 Fed. Reg. 59,802, 59, 811 (Nov. 5, 1997) (amending 18 C.F.R. § 4.34(i)).

[22]   4 WATERS AND WATER RIGHTS § 40.10 (c)(1) (cited in note 1); Confederated Tribes v. FERC, 746 F.2d 466, 470-71, 476 (9th Cir. 1984).

[23]   American Rivers v. FERC, 201 F.3d 1186, 1197 (9th Cir., 2000), citing 54 Fed. Reg. at 23,776 (1989).

[24]   59 Fed. Reg. 66,714, 66,718 (1994), codified at 18 C.F.R. § 2.23.

[25]   The background and early implementation of the agreement is traced in F. Lorraine Bodi, *FERC's Mid-Columbia Proceeding: Ten Years and Still Counting*, 16 ENVTL. L. 555 (1986); *see also* VOLKMAN (cited in chapter 1, note 42), at 71-72.

[26]   60 Fed. Reg. 339, 340 (1995), codified at 18 C.F.R. § 2.24.

[27]   Edwards Manufacturing Co., 81 F.E.R.C. ¶ 61,255, at 62,208-09 (1997); 4 WATERS AND WATER RIGHTS § 40.13 (cited in note 1); American Rivers v. FERC, 201 F.3d 1186, 1210 (9th Cir. 2000) (fishway conditions are within the discretion of federal fishery agencies, not FERC).

[28]   Charlton H. Bonham, *The Removal of Condit Dam: A Matter of Economics*, 5 BIG RIVER NEWS no. 4 at 7 (Nat'l. Res. L. Inst. Fall 1999); Charlton H. Bonham, *The Condit Dam Removal and Section 18 of the Federal Power Act: A Coerced Settlement*, 14 J. ENVTL. L. & LITIG. 97 (2000); Jonathan Brinckman, *Utility Plans to Remove Condit Dam*, THE OREGONIAN, Sept. 23, 1999, 1999 WL 28262512 ($13.7 million for dam removal, $2 million for permits and mitigation, and $1 million for the Yakama Indian Nation's Fishery Enhancement Fund).

[29]   Energy Act of 2000, Pub. L. No. 106-469 § 603, 114 Stat. 2029.

Notes to Chapter 12

[1]   See discussion of the Supreme Court's decision, in chapter 4, text with notes 26-27.

[2]   United States v. Washington, 759 F.2d 1353, 1360 (9th Cir. 1985), *aff'g* 506 F.Supp. 187, 197 (W.D. Wash. 1980). For an earlier Ninth Circuit affirmance on the hatchery issue, see United States v. Washington, 694 F.2d 1374, 1379-85 (9th Cir. 1982).

[3]   United States v. Washington, 506 F.Supp. at 203-04 (W.D. Wash. 1980).

[4]   *Id.* at 208, citing Washington v. Washington State Commercial Passenger Fishing Vessel Ass'n, 443 U.S. 658, 686-87 (1979) [hereinafter *Passenger Fishing Vessel*].

[5]   *See* United States v. Washington, 384 F.Supp. 312, 350 (W.D. Wash. 1974) (paramount dependence on fishing); on the understanding of treaty negotiators, see chapter 3, text with notes 9-17; on the role of tribal fishing in the post-treaty economy, see chapter 3, text with note 19.

[6]   United States v. Washington, 694 F.2d 1374, 1381 n. 15, 1387, 1389 (9th Cir. 1985) criticized by *Piscary Profit*, at 416-417 n.40. The affirmance on the hatchery issue is at 694 F.2d at 1379-85.

[7]   United States v. Washington, 759 F.2nd 1353, 1357 (9th Cir. 1985). The *en banc* panel first ruled that it possessed no jurisdiction to decide the case because the district court's rulings were on partial summary judgment in No. 81-3111, slip. op. 5397 (9th Cir. Dec. 17, 1985), but the court reversed itself with the opinion cited first in this note.

[8]   On the timber, fish and wildlife agreement, see KAI N. LEE, COMPASS AND GYROSCOPE: INTEGRATING SCIENCE AND POLITICS FOR THE PROTECTION OF THE ENVIRONMENT 120-24 (Island Press 1993).

[9]   1 RESTATEMENT OF THE LAW OF PROPERTY (SERVITUDES) § 1.2(2) (2000); 8 THOMPSON ON REAL PROPERTY § 65 (David A. Thomas, ed., 1994); Gary D. Meyers, *United States v. Washington (Phase II) Revisited: Establishing an Environmental Servitude Protecting Treaty Fishing Rights*, 67 OR. L. REV. 771, 783-84 (1988). Most of the remainder of this chapter is adapted from *Piscary Profit*, at 463-502 (used by permission of the University of Colorado Law Review), which contains more extensive citations to authorities.

[10]   United States v. Washington, 873 F.Supp. 1422, 1431-32 (W.D. Wash. 1994) (*Shellfish I*); Mariel J. Combs, *United States v. Washington, The Boldt Decision Reincarnated*, 29 ENVTL. L. 683, 698-700 (1999).

[11]   *Shellfish I*, 873 F.Supp. at 1435-37, 1441-42, 1445-46; *Shellfish II*, 898 F.Supp. at 1461-62, 1472-73; *Shellfish III*, 909 F.Supp. at 792.

[12]   United States v. Washington, 135 F.3d 618, 634-40 (9th Cir. 1998), *amended by* 157 F.3d 630 (9th Cir. 1998).

[13]   *See* ROBERTA ULRICH, EMPTY NETS: INDIANS, DAMS, AND THE COLUMBIA RIVER (Oregon St. U. Press 1999).

[14]   Confederated Tribes of the Umatilla Indian Reservation v. Callaway, No. 72-211, slip. op. at 5-7 (D. Or. Aug. 17, 1973).

[15]   Confederated Tribes of the Umatilla Indian Reservation v. Alexander, 440 F. Supp. 553, 555-56 (D. OR. 1977).

[16]   Kittitas Reclamation Dist. v. Sunnyside Valley Irrigation Dist., 763 F.2d 1032, 1034 (9th Cir. 1985) (discussing the district court's unpublished opinion).

[17]   Kittitas Reclamation Dist. v. Sunnyside Valley Irrigation Dist., No. 80-3505, slip. op. at 5-7 (9th Cir. Sept. 10, 1982).

[18]   Kittitas Reclamation Dist. v. Sunnyside Irrigation Dist., 752 F.2d 1456 (9th Cir. 1985), withdrawn after United States v. Washington, 759 F.2d 1353 (9th Cir. 1985).

[19]   Kittitas Reclamation Dist. v. Sunnyside Irrigation Dist, 763 F.2d at 1035.

[20]   No Oilport! v. Carter, 520 F.Supp. 334, 372-73 (W.D. Wash. 1980).

[21]   Muckleshoot Indian Tribe v. Hall, 698 F.Supp. 1504, 1505-06, 1512-14, 1517, 1522-23 (W.D. Wash. 1988).

[22]   Northwest Sea Farms v. United States Army Corps of Eng'rs, 931 F.Supp. 1515, 1518-22 (W.D. Wash. 1996).

[23]   The Ninth Circuit affirmed the two separate elements of the treaty fishing right in United States v. Oregon, 718 F.2d 299, 304 n. 6 (9th Cir. 1983).

[24]   United States v. Anderson, 6 Indian L. Rep. F-129, F-131 (E.D. Wash., July 23, 1979). This decision concerned a land reservation created by Executive Order, not a Stevens or Palmer Treaty, and involved an on-reservation fishing right. The results were adopted by another district judge (the previous judge having died), and left undisturbed by the Ninth Circuit. United States v. Anderson, 591 F.Supp. 1 (E.D. Wash. 1982), *aff'd*, 736 F.2d 1358 (9th Cir. 1984).

[25]   Colville Confederated Tribes v. Walton, 460 F.Supp. 1320, 1330 (E.D. Wash. 1978), *aff'd*, 647 F.2d 42, 46, 48 (9th Cir. 1981). In a subsequent decision, the Ninth Circuit reversed the district court's determination allocating only about half of the 350 acre-feet of water per year needed for the tribal fishery after granting Indian and non-Indian irrigators their full amount of water. The Ninth Circuit ruled that the tribe should get its full amount of 350 acre-feet, subject to a *pro-rata* reduction when insufficient water was available, apparently recognizing a reservation date priority for the replacement fishery. Colville Confederated Tribes v. Walton, 752 F.2d 397, 404-05 (9th Cir. 1985).

[26]   United States v. Adair, 723 F.2d 1394, 1411, 1414-15 (9th Cir. 1983), *aff'g* 478 F.Supp. 336, 345 (D. Or. 1979).

[27]   Joint Bd. of Control of the Flathead, Mission, and Jocko Irrigation Dists. v. United States, 832 F.2d 1127, 1131-32 (9th Cir. 1987), *rev'g*, 646 F.Supp. 410, 426 (D. Mont. 1985). The Dawes Act, designed to promote the allotment and irrigation of Indian lands, states in part: "In cases where the use of water for irrigation is necessary to render the lands within any Indian reservation available for agricultural purposes, the Secretary of the Interior is authorized to prescribe such rules and regulations as he may deem necessary to secure a just and equal distribution . . ." Dawes Act, 24 Stat. 388 (1887) (codified in relevant part at 25 U.S.C. § 381 (1994).

[28]   State Dept. of Ecology v. Acquavella, Civ. No. 77-2-01484-5, at 2 (Wash. Sup. Ct. Oct. 22, 1990), *aff'd*, State Dept. of Ecology v. Yakima Reservation Irr. Dist., 850 P.2d 1306, 1317-19 (Wash. 1993).

[29]   850 P.2d at 1316-19, 1329.

[30]   *Id*. at 1319-23.

[31]   *Id*. at 1323.

[32]   *Id*. at 1323-25.

[33]   Order Re: Treaty Reserved Water Rights at Usual and Accustomed Fishing Places, State Dept. of Ecology v. Acquavella, No. 77-2-01484-5 (Wash. Sup. Ct. Mar. 1, 1995); Order Re: "Flushing Flows," State Dept. of Ecology v. Acquavella, No. 77-2-01484-5 (Wash. Sup. Ct. Apr. 13, 1995); Timothy Weaver, *Remarks at the Northwest Water Law and Policy Project* (Portland, Or., May 20, 1995).

[34]   In Re SRBA, Nez Perce Tribe Instream Flow Claims, Case No. 39576 (Idaho Dist. Ct. Nov. 10, 1999) *slip op*., at 39-40, 47, ignoring Washington v. Washington Passenger Fishing Vessel Assn., 443 U.S. 658, 686 (1979), discussed in chapter 4, text with notes 27-28.

[35]   SRBA decision (cited in note 34), at 31-33; the Supreme Court cases of *Winans* (affirmative access right), *Tulee* (no license fees), and *Puyallup II* (no discriminatory regulations) are discussed in chapter 4, text with notes 7-10, 12, 18; the harvest share decision is cited in note 34 above.

[36]   SRBA decision (cited in note 34), at 34-37, relying on Nez Perce Tribe v. Idaho Power Co., 847 F.Supp. 791 (D. Idaho 1994), discussed below text accompanying notes 43-50; on the fishing right as a *profit à prendre*, see this chapter text with notes 45-46, 52.

[37]   SRBA decision (cited in note 34), at 44-46, relying on South Dakota v. Yankton Sioux Tribe, 522 U.S. 329 (1998) and ignoring Minnesota v. Mille Lacs Band of Chippewa Indians, 526 U.S. 172 (1999); for a more detailed criticism of the SRBA decision, *see* Michael C. Blumm, Dale D. Goble, Judith V. Royster & Mary Christina Wood, *Judicial Termination of Treaty Water Rights: the Snake River Case*, 36 IDAHO L. REV 459 (2000).

[38]   On the Supreme Court's antagonism to Indian rights, see Getches (cited in chapter 4, note 26).

[39]   Emergency Supplemental Appropriations for Disaster Relief and Recissions Act, Pub. L. No. 104-19, 109 Stat. 194 (1995); U.S. Dept. of Agriculture, Forest Service, *Record of Decision for Amendments to Forest Service and Bureau of Land Management Planning Documents Within the Range of the Northern Spotted Owl* (1994), discussed in *Amphibious Salmon*, at 668-72.

[40]   On the 1995 rider, see Slade Gorton & Julie Kays, *Legislative History of the Timber and Salvage Amendments Enacted in the 104th Congress: A Small Victory for Timber Communities in the Pacific Northwest*, 26 ENVTL. L. 641 (1996); Michael Axline, *Forest Health and the Politics of*

Expediency, 26 ENVTL. L. 613 (1996).

41   Klamath Tribes v. United States Forest Service, No. 96-381-HA (D. Or. Oct. 2, 1996). The Klamath Reservation was terminated by Congress in the Klamath Reservation Termination Act of 1954, 25 U.S.C. § 564, but the tribes' hunting and fishing rights survived the termination of the reservation. Kimball v. Callahan, 493 F.2d 564 (9th Cir. 1974). Since the tribes now exercise their hunting and fishing rights on lands ceded (mostly) to the federal government, they resemble the off-reservation fishing rights reserved in the Stevens Treaties.

42   Klamath Tribes v U.S. Forest Service (cited in note 41), at 21, 24-25. On the federal fiduciary duty, see Mary Christina Wood, *Fulfilling the Executive's Trust Responsibility Toward the Native Nation's on Environmental Issues: A Partial Critique of the Clinton Administration's Promises and Performance*, 25 ENVTL. L. 733 (1995).

43   Federal Power Act, 16 U.S.C. § 803(c). The tribe filed suit because the statute of limitations was about to run on its claims. The 1982 Indian Claims Limitation Act extended the statute of limitations for pre-1966 tribal damage claims against private parties, allowing these claims to be submitted to the Bureau of Indian Affairs for determination of which claims the Department of Justice would pursue. In December 1991, the bureau informed the Nez Perce that it would not recommend the Justice Department pursue its claim against Idaho Power because damages would be difficult to prove. As a result, the tribe had until December 20, 1992, to pursue its claims in court, which it did.

44   Nez Perce Tribe v. Idaho Power Company, 847 F.Supp. 791, 794, 809-12 (D. Idaho 1994) [hereinafter *Nez Perce Tribe*]; United States v. Winans, 198 U.S. 371, 381, 384 (1905), discussed in chapter 4, text with notes 7-10.

45   *Nez Perce Tribe*, 847 F.Supp. at 794, 811-12; Menominee Tribe of Indians v. United States, 391 U.S. 404, 413 (1968); on the prior case law burdening private parties, see chapter 4, text with notes 9, 11 and this chapter, text with notes 10-12, 26-27.

46   *Passenger Fishing Vessel*, 443 U.S. at 679, 686 (1979) (no empty net dipping); Keeble v Hickeringill, 103 Eng. Rep. 1127, 1128 (K.B. 1809) (duck pond case); Union Oil Co. v. Oppen, 501 F.2d 558, 568 (9th Cir. 1974) (allowing a damages action against oil companies by commercial fishers damaged by an oil spill); Figluizzi v. Careajou Shooting Club of Lake Koshkonong, 516 N.W.2d 410 (Wisc. 1994) (awarding an injunction to recreationalists); Allen H. Sanders, *Damaging Indian Treaty Fisheries: A Violation of Tribal Property Rights?*, 17 PUB. LAND & RESOURCES L. REV. 153, 162-67 (1996) (collecting other cases); *Passenger Fishing Vessel*, 443 U.S. at 686 (moderate living).
        The magistrate did not completely reject the right to habitat protection, however. Relying on the vacated panel decision of the Ninth Circuit in Phase II of *United States v. Washington*, he decided that the habitat protection right applies only to a development that was "part of a pattern of discrimination against treaty fishing runs." Nondiscriminatory "reasonable development," the magistrate opined, "should be borne fifty/fifty by treaty and non-treaty fishermen." *Nez Perce Tribe*, 847 F.Supp. at 809, relying on United States v. Washington, 694 F.2d 1374, 1389 (9th Cir. 1982), (The magistrate recognized that the *en banc* Ninth Circuit vacated the panel opinion in 1985. Nevertheless, he treated the vacated panel opinion as non-binding but well-reasoned authority and found its reasoning "persuasive" on the nature of the tribes' treaty right to habitat protection. 847 F.Supp at 808). How the tribes could show

discriminatory development neither the magistrate nor the vacated opinion on which he relied said. But the Hells Canyon dams — indeed all of the Columbia Basin dams — no doubt damaged treaty fishing more than non-treaty fishing, particularly if the non-treaty ocean harvest is considered.

[47]   *Nez Perce Tribe*, 847 F.Supp. at 809, relying on United States v. Washington, 694 F.2d at 1382-83, n. 17, 1385, 1389, while overlooking United States v. Winans, 198 U.S. 371 (1905) (applying treaty burdens to private parties). For other criticisms of the magistrate decision, *see Piscary Profit*, at 487 n. 400.

[48]   Order on Second Report and Recommendation and Dismissing Action, Nez Perce Tribe v. Idaho Power Co., No. 91-0517-S-HLR, slip op. at 5-8 (D. Idaho Sept. 28, 1994), ignoring Kittitas Reclamation Dist. v. Sunnyside Valley Irrigation Dist., 763 F.2d 1032 (9th Cir. 1985) (affirming an injunction preventing the inundation of salmon redds); Confederated Tribes of the Umatilla Indian Reservation v. Alexander, 440 F.Supp. 553 (D. Or. 1977) (enjoining construction of a federal dam that would inundate tribal fishing grounds); *Passenger Fishing Vessel*, 443 U.S. at 676 (no "crowding out").

[49]   United States v. Winans, 198 U.S. 371, 381 (1905). The Nez Perce appealed the case to the Ninth Circuit, but before the court heard the case, the parties reached a settlement in which Idaho Power agreed to pay some $16.5 million to the tribe, $11.5 of which was to settle the case, and $5 million of which was for the tribe's "full support" of Idaho Power's attempt to relicense its three Hells Canyon dams. The $5 million is not payable to the tribe until the dams receive new licenses.

[50]   The error of the Hells Canyon case was compounded when its reasoning was adopted by another judge in the federal district of Idaho in a companion case concerning damages caused the Nez Perce by two Washington Water Power dams in the Clearwater Basin, which had been removed in 1963 and 1973 but which had damaged the tribe's fish runs and its fishing sites. Nez Perce Tribe v. Washington Water Power, Civ. 91-0518-S-HLR (D. Idaho Mar. 28, 1996). On the flexibility of property concepts and the contextual nature of remedies, see *Piscary Profit*, at 498 nn. 410-11.

[51]   *Passenger Fishing Vessel*, 443 U.S. at 667, 684 (1979) (no empty net dipping); United States v. Oregon, 657 F.2d 1009, 1015 (9th Cir. 1982) ("res" per Judge Kennedy); United States v. Adair, 723 F.2d 1394, 1411 (9th Cir. 1983) ("wilderness servitude").

[52]   United States v. Oregon, 657 F.2d at 1016 (Judge Kennedy on judicial constructive custody); 1 RESTATEMENT (THIRD) OF PROPERTY: SERVITUDES § 4.9 (2000) (no unreasonable interference standard for servitudes); *see id.* § 1.1(2) (servitudes include *profits à prendre*).

[53]   Department of Game of Wash. v. Puyallup Tribe, Inc., 414 U.S. 44, 49 (1973) (*Puyallup II*) (Justice Douglas quotes); Puyallup Tribe, Inc. v. Department of Game of State of Wash., 433 U.S. 165, 175-77 (1977) (*Puyallup III*) (tribal fishing subject to conservation regulations); United States v. Oregon, 657 F.2d (upholding an injunction against a tribal fishery for conservation purposes); Hoh Indian Tribe v. Baldridge, 522 F.Supp. 683 (W.D. Wash. 1981); Confederated Tribes v. Kreps, Civ. No. 79-541 (D. Or. Sept. 10, 1979) (applying conservation regulations to non-tribal ocean fisheries).

[54]   Sohappy v. Smith, 302 F.Supp. 899, 908-11 (D. Or. 1969); United States v. Oregon, 718 F.2d 299, 304 n.6 (9th Cir. 1983).

[55]   United States v. Washington, 694 F.2d at 1389-91 (Reinhardt, J., concurring); County of Oneida v. Oneida Indian Nation, 470 U.S. 226, 247-48 (1985) (explicit statutory language required for abrogation); Charles F. Wilkinson & John M. Volkman, *Judicial Review of Indian Treaty Abrogation: "As Long as Water Flows, or Grass Grows upon the Earth" How Long a Time is That?*, 63 CAL. L. REV. 601, 610-11 (1975).

[56]   American Indian Tribal Rights, Federal-Tribal Trust Responsibilities, and the Endangered Species Act, U.S. Dept's of Interior and Commerce, Sec. Order No. 3206 and Appendix 6 (June 5, 1997), discussed in Wilkinson (cited in chapter 9, note 50).

[57]   Citations providing precedents for each of the criteria may be found at *Piscary Profit*, at 497-99 nn.453-64. For an alternative approach to implementing the Stevens Treaty promise of habitat protection, one calling for rebuilding salmon runs to their approximate historic levels and money damages payable to the tribes until that goal is accomplished, see Mary Christina Wood, *The Tribal Right to Wildlife Capital (Part II): Asserting a Sovereign Servitude to Protect Habitat of Imperiled Species*, 25 VERMONT L. REV. 355 (2001).

Some elaboration of the moderate living standard is warranted here, however. Although this standard has received a good deal of critical commentary, if defined properly, it is a useful criterion. First, the standard reflects the Supreme Court's recognition that the treaties' basic promise to the tribes was that they could continue to pursue their livelihood as commercial fishers; the promise was not just that the tribes retained ceremonial and subsistence fishing rights. Second, while the equal sharing formula imposes a ceiling on the tribal right, the moderate living test provides a floor, and is at least as consistent with the likely contemporaneous tribal understanding of the meaning of the treaty as the equal sharing formula. Third, the moderate living test, if interpreted to require a significant change in circumstances (the Supreme Court mentioned few tribal fishers or abandoning fishing) as a prerequisite and use of a multi-factor test (including per capita income from fishing, the percentage of tribal members below the poverty line, the health circumstances of tribal members, and tribal unemployment rates) like that suggested by the district court in United States v. Washington, 873 F.Supp. 1422, 1446 (W.D. Wash. 1994) and endorsed by the Ninth Circuit, 157 F.3d 630, 651-643 (9th Cir. 1998), would probably protect the tribes from arbitrary reductions in their share, so long as the central premise of the treaties — that the tribes could continue as commercial fishers — is part of the analysis. *See also* Lac Courte Oreilles Band of Lake Superior Chippewa Indians v. State, 686 F.Supp. 226, 228-30 (W.D. Wisc. 1988) (attempting to translate treaty-time lifestyles into modern income requirements and concluding that about $20,000 per household in 1986 dollars would be required for the tribes in question; the court concluded that even if the tribes harvested all of the resources in their hunting and fishing grounds, they would not attain this standard of living). At any rate, the issue is quite academic at this point, when the average tribal fisherman on the Columbia River loses money; *Beyond Parity*, at 126 (quoting Columbia River Inter-Tribal Fish Commission Chairman Ted Strong to the effect that the average tribal fisherman loses about $7000 per year). Finally, the moderate living test supplies an answer to those worried about the treaties requiring restoration of treaty-time environmental conditions and an end to all development. Instead, the treaties require only habitat conditions necessary to fulfill the treaties promise of a viable fishing economy.

[58] *See* Michael Lancaster, *Treaties May Trump ESA, Judge Says*, CAPITOL PRESS, Nov. 3, 2000 (quoting Judge Marsh).

[59] *See* Lynda V. Mapes, *Another Potential Lightning Boldt*, SEATTLE TIMES, Jan. 17, 2001; Robert McClure, *Tribes Reignite Legal Battle Over Fish Catch: Suit Could Give Indians Control Over Wide Range of Activities*, SEATTLE POST-INTELLIGENCER, Jan. 17, 2001.

Notes to Chapter 13

[1] RETURN TO THE RIVER (cited in chapter 1, note 52), at 90 (Salmon River productivity); on the factors causing the decline of Snake River salmon, see *The Case For Dam Breaching*, at 999-1000 n.4.

[2] *1995 Hydro BiOp* (cited in chapter 9, note 19), at 72 (estimated mortalities); Jim Yustavitch, *Breaching, Drawdowns, and the Art of Salmon Recovery*, TROUT, Summer 1998, at 12, 18, ($3 billion estimate). Many conservationists dispute the estimated expenditures, however, since the estimates usually include "foregone hydropower revenues," which is controversial since it assumes that the primary purpose of the federal dams is to produce hydropower, and that is not the primary purpose for which the dams were authorized. *See Beyond Parity*, at 103-04.

[3] *1995 Hydro BiOp* (cited in chapter 9, note 19), at 81 (need for major dam modifications). On the political opposition, see *The Case For Dam Breaching*, at 1004 nn. 25-26 (citing articles). Breaching a dam would involve a slow lowering of reservoir levels to prevent erosion, removing the earthen embankment, and leaving the concrete locks and powerhouses in a drydock state. Engineers claim that breaching a dam would be considerably simpler than building one. Breaching all four Lower Snake Dams likely would take four to seven years, including time for engineering studies. Bill Lotus, *How to Breach a Dam*, LEWISTON MORNING TRIBUNE, June 7, 1998, at 1D.

[4] *Saving Idaho's Salmon*, at 672 (dams' original cost-benefit ratio); *The Case For Dam Breaching*, 1023-24, 1027 (dam's current benefits) (citing studies); *The Cost of Doing Nothing* (cited in chapter 2, note 51), at 51 (cost of $500 million annually and 25,000 jobs).

[5] On the origins of the Corps' transportation program, see Meghetto & Ebel (cited in chapter 9, note 20), at 119-20, 123.

[6] Columbia Basin Indian Tribes and State & Federal Fish and Wildlife Agencies, *Detailed Fishery Operating Plan, With 1994 Operating Criteria* (1993) [hereinafter cited as *Detailed Operating Plan*]. The Columbia Basin Fish and Wildlife Authority, formed in 1985, is a coalition of federal, state, and tribal fish and wildlife agencies which facilities interagency coordination on issues of regional significance. The authority not only formulated the detailed operating plan but also a schedule of biologically based river flows to facilitate salmon migration and a integrated basinwide plan aimed at doubling the salmon runs. *See* 6 WATERS AND WATER RIGHTS 133 (Robert E. Beck ed., 1994).

[7] *Detailed Operating Plan* (cited in note 6), at 6-8; Bookman-Edmonston Engineering, *Report of the Snake River Basin Water Committee, Water Management Opportunities within the Snake River Basin* 8-9, 12 (1994). On the "Salmon Summit" proposal, see chapter 9, text with note 3.

[8]   Phillip R. Mundy, *et al.*, *Transportation of Juvenile Salmonids from Hydroelectric Projects in the Columbia River Basin: An Independent Peer Review* 3, 83, 116 (1994). On the "major overhaul," see Idaho Dept. of Fish and Game v. NMFS, 850 F.Supp. 886, 900 (D. Or. 1994), discussed in chapter 9, text with notes 15-17.

[9]   Mundy (cited in note 8), at 32, 84, 101-02, 108-09, 114, 117-18.

[10]   Northwest Power Planning Council, *Columbia River Basin Fish and Wildlife Program* 5-32 (1994) [hereinafter cited as *1994 Council Program*]. For an insightful interplay between the salmon restoration plans of the Council and NMFS under the ESA, see VOLKMAN (cited in chapter 1, note 42), at IV-41 to IV-50, IV-65 to IV-71.

[11]   *1994 Council Program* (cited in note 10), at 5-46.

[12]   *Tribal Restoration Plan* (cited in chapter 6, note 30), at 5B-24 to 5B-31; *see* Melissa Powers, *The Spirit of The Salmon: How the Tribal Restoration Plan Could Restore Columbia Basin Salmon*, 30 ENVTL. L. 867 (2000).

[13]   On the Council's program, see this chapter, text with notes 10-11.

[14]   UPSTREAM (cited in chapter 2, note 30), at vii, 241.

[15]   *Id.* at 4; on the influence and background of Chapman, see Paul Koberstein, *Fishy Science: How Scientists Endanger the Salmon*, CASCADIA TIMES, Jan. 1996, at 10, 13.

[16]   RETURN TO THE RIVER (cited in chapter 1, note 52), at xvii, 5, 19, 506, 510.

[17]   *Id.* at xx, 268-69, 328, 509, 513. On metapopulations, see *id.* at 29-30, 76.

[18]   Idaho Dept. of Fish & Game, *Report to the Director, Idaho's Anadromous Fish Stocks: Their Status and Recovery Options* 6, 8, 11-13 (1998).

[19]   *Id.* at 13-17.

[20]   *1995 Hydro BiOp* (cited in chapter 9, note 19), at 6; *Plan for Analyzing and Testing Hypothesis (PATH), Preliminary Decision Analysis Report on Snake River Spring/Summer Chinook* ii (D.R. Marmorek & C.N. Peters eds., 1998) [hereinafter cited as *PATH Report*].

[21]   *PATH Report* (cited in note 20), at vi-vii, 59, 65.

[22]   Memorandum from PATH Planning Group to Implementation Team, Corrections to the PATH Preliminary Report ix, table E-1 (Aug. 4, 1998).

[23]   Idaho Dept. of Fish & Game, *Salmon & Steelhead Recovery Update* 2 (Aug. 13, 1998).

24 Conclusions and Recommendations from the PATH Weight of the Evidence Workshop 18-19 (Sept. 8-10, 1998); Jonathan Brinckman, *Scientists Say Dam Removal is Key*, OREGONIAN, Oct. 1, 1998, at B1, B6 (statement of Oregon Chief of Fisheries).

25 Plan for Analyzing and Testing Hypotheses (PATH), *PATH Final Report for Fiscal Year 1998*, at 24 (D.R. Marmorek *et al.* eds. 1998).

26 U.S. Army Corps of Engineers, *Draft Lower Snake River Juvenile Salmon Feasibility Report/Environmental Impact Statement, Appendix A* (by the National Marine Fisheries Service), at A ES-7 (1999); on the PATH studies and the CRI, see chapter 9, text with notes 23-24.

27 *Id.* at A ES-5 to A ES-6, A ES-8.

28 *Id.* at A ES-7 to A ES-8, A4-23 to A4-271 (spring chinook).

29 See Rob Masonis, *The Scientific Case for Lower Snake River Dam Removal*, THE OSPREY (newsletter of the Federation of Fly Fishers), Jan. 2000, at 4-5 (surveying critics of the A-Fish Appendix); U.S. Army Corps of Engineers (cited in note 26), at M ES-13 (quote).

30 On 2000 BiOp, see chapter 9, text with notes 26-33.

31 *The Cost of Doing Nothing* (cited in chapter 2, note 51), at 51.

32 On the dams' original cost-benefit ratio, see text accompanying note 2; U.S. Army Corps of Engineers, *Columbia River System Operation Review* 3-3, 5-1 to 5-2 (1995) (no flood control, little irrigation, 5% of region's electricity).

33 Harza Northwest, Inc., *Final Report: Salmon Decision Analysis: Lower Snake Feasibility Study* 1-9 to 1-10 (1996).

34 *Id.* at 1-10 to 1-11, 1-14.

35 Susan Whately & Rocky Barker, *Breaching: A Natural River Saves Fish and Money*, IDAHO STATESMAN, July 20, 1997, at 12A [hereinafter *Idaho Statesman Report*].

36 *Id.* at 13A.

37 Witt Anderson, *et al.*, *Fish and Wildlife Recovery in the Pacific Northwest: Breaking the Deadlock* (Nov. 18,1997) <http://www.newsdata.com/enernet/xpan/deadlock/fwreport.html>.

38 *Id.* at 8, app. B, at 1-2.

39 *Id.* at app. B, at 3-5.

[40]   Philip S. Lansing & Eve Vogel, *Restoring the Lower Snake River: Saving Snake River Salmon and Saving Money* 2-4 (n.d.) [hereinafter cited as *Lansing Report*]. The Lansing report estimated the following annual costs: $194.4 million for salmon restoration (*id.* at 13, 26-29), $114 million for irrigation and navigation (*id.* at 25), and $11.2 in electric power rate subsidies for 13 agribusiness irrigators pumping water from Ice Harbor reservoir). The report also estimated that navigation cost shippers $1.23 per ton, while electric ratepayers and taxpayers pay an additional $12.66 per ton (*id.* at 19-21, 30-32).

[41]   Letter from Thomas M. Power, Professor and Chair, University of Montana, to Ken Rait, Oregon Natural Resources Council (Apr. 24, 1998); Independent Economic Advisory Board Review, *Comments on Restoring the Lower Snake River: Saving Snake River Salmon and Saving Money* (presented at the Council's meeting on Nov. 4-5, 1998).

[42]   *Lansing Report* (cited in note 40), at 19.

[43]   Eban Goodstein, *Dam Economics: Overview and Application to the Lower Snake River* C-3, C-15 to C-20, in Fred Munson & Scott Highleyman, *Dam Removal as a Tool for Anadromous Fish Restoration: An Assessment* (report to the PEW Charitable Trusts 1998).

[44]   *Id.* at C-8 to C-18. Goodstein reported that a study in connection with the proposed removal of the Elwah Dam in Olympic National Park suggested that the "existence value" to the public across the U.S. of restored salmon runs was extremely high: on the order of $3-6 billion. *Id.* at C-17.

[45]   Northwest Power Planning Council, *Analysis of the Bonneville Power Administration's Potential Future Costs and Revenues* 6-8 (1998).

[46]   *Id.* at 4, 9, 35, 39, 47; Bonneville Power Admin., *Revised Briefing on Fish Funding Options* 21-22 (1998).

[47]   U.S. Army Corps of Engineers (cited in note 26), at *Appendix I – Economics*.

[48]   *Id.* at I ES-16, I ES-17 (fewer wild salmon) , I 10-3 to I 10-4.

[49]   *Id.* at I4-8; Independent Economic Analysis Board, *Review of Economic Appendix I of the Corps' Lower Snake Feasibility Study* 5 (June 21, 2000).

[50]   *See NWEC: Snake Dams Can Be Replaced With Clean Energy Resources*, CLEARING UP, April 17, 2000, at 11-12 (discussing the NWEC/NRDC study, *Going With The Flow: Replacing Energy From Four Snake River Dams* (April 2000)); *Study: Dam Breaching Would Boost Employment*, COLUMBIA BASIN BULLETIN, July 14, 2000 <http://cbbulletin.com> (discussing a study by American Rivers).

[51]   *Lansing Report* (cited in note 40); *Idaho Statesman Report* (cited in note 35).

52 Use of transmission charges was endorsed by former BPA Administrator Randy Hardy, see *Beyond Parity*, at 110-11; F. Lorraine Bodi, *Salmon in the Balance, in Competing for the Mighty Columbia River: Past, Present, and Future: The Role of Interstate Allocation* (Apr. 30-May 1, 1998) (10% rate increase).

53 *2000 BiOp* (cited in chapter 1, note 49); *Caucus Recovery Plan* (cited in chapter 9, note 26); 50 C.F.R. § 402.029(h) (authority to promulgate reasonable and prudent alternatives); Bennett v. Spear, 520 U.S. 154, 177-178 (1997) (virtually binding nature of BiOps).

54 See text following note 33, chapter 9 on the vulnerability of the 2000 BiOp. Idaho Dept. of Fish & Game v. NMFS, 850 F.Supp. 886, 893, 900 (D. OR. 1994); American Rivers v. NMFS, No. 96-384-MA (D. Or. Apr. 3, 1997), discussed in chapter 9, text with notes 21-22.

55 On the federal trust obligation to Indian tribes, see Mary Christina Wood, *Reclaiming the Natural Rivers: The Endangered Species Act as Applied to Endangered River Ecosystems*, 40 ARIZ. L. REV. 197, 255-67 (1998); see also chapter 12, text with note 42.

56 16 U.S.C. §§ 839b(h)(6)(B) (best available science), (E)(ii) (improved flows to meet sound biological objectives); Northwest Resource Info. Ctr. v. Northwest Power Planning Council, 35 F.3d 1371, 1388, 1391-93 (9th Cir. 1994); *see* chapter 7, text with notes 31-34.

57 33 U.S.C. §§ 1313, 1323(a); Letter from Chuck Clark, EPA Regional Administration for Region 10, to Brigadier General Robert H. Griffin, Commander, North Pacific Division, U.S. Army Corps of Engineers (Dec. 9, 1997); Nat'l Wildlife Fed'n v. Army Corps of Engineers, 92 F.Supp.2d 1072 (D. Or. 2000). On the suit, see chapter 10, text with notes 21-24.

58 33 U.S.C. § 1341 (section 401 of the Clean Water Act, construed in American Rivers v. FERC, 129 F.3d 99 (2d Cir. 1997)); 16 U.S.C. § 1536 (section 7 of the Endangered Species); 16 U.S.C. § 811 (section 18 of the Federal Power Act, broadly construed in American Rivers v. FERC, 201 F.3d at 1186 (9th Cir. 2000)).

59 On Indian reserved water rights, see 4 WATERS AND WATER RIGHTS, § 37.02 (Robert E. Beck ed., 1996 ed. & 2000 supp.).

60 On the Nez Perce water rights case, see chapter 12, text accompanying notes 34-37; on water use in the Snake Basin, see MARK FIEGE, IRRIGATED EDEN: THE MAKING OF AN AGRICULTURAL LANDSCAPE IN THE AMERICAN WEST (U. Washington Press 1999). The argument for a settlement is made in greater detail in *The Case for Dam Breaching*, at 1045-46, 1053-54, an article whose co-authors included one of the Nez Perce Tribe's attorneys.

61 The Lower Snake Dams were authorized in the Act of March 2, 1945, Pub. L. No. 14 , 79th Cong., 1st Sess. (1945), discussed in *Hydropower vs. Salmon*, at 233-34.

62 For a sampling of Indian water rights settlements, see 4 WATERS AND WATER RIGHTS, § 37.04(c)(1) (Robert E. Beck ed., 1996 ed. & 2000 supp.).

[63]   RETURN TO THE RIVER (cited in chapter 1, note 52), at xx, 79, 90; Telephone conversation between Don Miller, Native American Rights Fund and Chip McConnaha, Northwest Power Planning Council (Sept. 29, 1998) (on the history of the Hanford Reach).

[64]   *See* Margaret Holenbach, *Feds Reject Proposal to Aid Spawners Below Bonneville*, COLUMBIA BASIN BULL. (Oct. 23, 1998)<http://www.nwpcc.org/bull_19.htm>.

[65]   RETURN TO THE RIVER (cited in chapter 1, note 52), at 90 (Salmon River 40 percent of basin's productivity).

[66]   *See* Don B. Miller, *Of Dams and Salmon in the Columbia/Snake Basin: Did You Ever Have to Make Up Your Mind*, 6 RIVERS 69 (1997); *Lansing Report* (cited in note 40), at 19-20, 30-32 (navigation on the Snake costs shippers only 9 percent of its total costs; they pay only $1.23 per ton out of a total cost of $13.89 per ton); on the scientists' letter, see Brent Hunsberger, *Scientists Send Letter Asking Clinton To Breach Lower Snake Dams*, Oregonian, Dec. 19, 2000 at D5, 2000 WL 27113285; on Indian water right settlements, *see* 4 WATERS AND WATER RIGHTS § 37.04(c)(1) (1996 ed. & 2000 supp.).

[67]   *See* Barry Espenson, *Bureau Mulls Million Acre-Feet Flow Augmentation*, COLUMBIA BASIN BULL. (Aug. 28, 1998) <http://www.nwpcc.org/bull_11htm> (discussing a preliminary estimate by the Bureau of Reclamation of a loss of 400,000 irrigated acres).

Notes to Chapter 14

[1]   Oliver A. Houck, *On the Law of Biodiversity and Ecosystem Management*, 81 MINN. L. REV. 869, 975-77 (1997).

[2]   Adapted from *Amphibious Salmon*, at 658-60 (used by permission of University of California, Berkeley, Ecology Law Review © 1997). *See generally* R. Edward Grumbine, *What Is Ecosystem Management*, 8 CONSERVATION BIOLOGY 27 (1994); Robert B Keiter, *Beyond the Boundary Line: Constructing a Law of Ecosystem Management*, 65 U. COLO. L. REV. 293 (1994).

[3]   Victor E. Shelford, *Report of the Committee For the Study of Plant and Animal Communities and the Committee on the Preservation of Natural Conditions* (Dec. 28, 1932), 14 ECOLOGY 229 (1933); ALDO LEOPOLD, A SAND COUNTY ALMANAC AND SKETCHES FROM HERE AND THERE (Oxford U. Press 1949).

[4]   R. Edward Grumbine, *What is Ecosystem Management?*, 8 CONSERVATION BIOLOGY 27, 28-29 (1994).

[5]   U.S. Dept. of Agriculture, Forest Service, *Record of Decision for Amendments to Forest Service and Bureau of Land Management Planning Documents Within the Range of the Northern Spotted Owl and Standards and Guidelines for Management of Habitat for Late-Successional and Old-Growth Forest Related Species with the Range of the Northern Spotted Owl* 7, B-18, B-20, B-30, B-87-89, C-30-32 (1994); UPSTREAM (cited in chapter 2, note 30), at 224-25 ("major change in burden of proof").

[6]   Pacific Coast Federation of Fishermen's Associations v. National Marine Fisheries Service, 71 F.Supp.2d 1039 (W.D. Wash. 1999), *aff'd* 253 F.3d 1138 (9th Cir. 2001), discussed in chapter 9, text with note 59.

[7]   *Amphibious Salmon*, at 672-73.

[8]   UPSTREAM (cited in chapter 2, note 30), at 206-11.

[9]   See the discussion of RETURN TO THE RIVER in chapter 13, text with notes 16-17.

[10]   RETURN TO THE RIVER (cited in chapter 1, note 52), summarized in 28 ENVTL. L. 503 (1998); the quote is from 28 ENVTL. L. at 514.

[11]   *Salmon Lessons,* at 546.

[12]   Oregon Natural Resources Council v. Daley, 6 F.Supp.2d 1139, 1152-55 (D. Or. 1998); 63 Fed. Reb. 42,587 (1998) (Oregon coho listing).

[13]   16 U.S.C. § 1533(d) (section 4(d) of the ESA); <http://www.oregon-plan.org> (Oregon plan); <http://www.governor.wa.gov/esa/strategy.htm> (Washington Strategy for Salmon).

[14]   *See* chapter 9, text with notes 17 (major overhaul) 21-22 (questioning soundness of NMFS risk tolerance, but affirming).

[15]   *See* chapter 9, text with note 57.

[16]   *Salmon Lessons*, at 602-03; Barry Espenson, *A-Fish Report Stresses Uncertainties*, COLUMBIA BASIN BULLETIN (April 16, 1999) <http://www.nwppc.org/bulletin/bull_39.html>.

[17]   Barry Espenson, *Feds Offer Their "Four H" Approach*, COLUMBIA BASIN BULLETIN (Nov. 19, 1999) <http://www.nwppc.org/bulletin/bull_62.htm>; *Scientists Evaluate NMFS' Extinction Analysis* (Nov. 19, 1999) <http://www.nwpcc.org/bulletin/bull_62htm>.

[18]   Barry Espenson, *Reaction Varied on Fed's 4-H Message*, COLUMBIA BASIN BULLETIN (Nov. 19, 1999) <http://www.nwppc.org/bulletin/bull_62.htm>; Four-H Fact Sheet (Nov. 16, 1999) <http://nwr.noaa.gov/1press/four-h/factsheet.html>; Jonathan Brinckman, *U.S. Agency Suggests Breaching Four Dams*, OREGONIAN, Dec. 17, 1999, at A1.

[19]   *Tribal Restoration Plan* (cited in chapter 6, note 30), at 1-1; *Caucus Recovery Plan* (cited in chapter 9, note 26).

[20]   *Tribal Restoration Plan* (cited in chapter 6, note 30), at 5-8.

[21]   *Id.* at 3, 42, 55.

[22]   *See Gorton, Smith Assure Irrigators on Breaching*, COLUMBIA BASIN BULLETIN (Dec. 3, 1999) <http://www.nwppc.org/bulletin/bull_63.htm>; *see also Salmon Lessons*, at 552-56, for examples of NMFS favoring economic over biological concerns.

[23]   *Tribal Restoration Plan* (cited in chapter 6, note 30), at 1-1. *See Beyond Parity*, at 75-80, for a summary of the tribal restoration plan.

[24]   *Id*. at 1-4, 5B-2 to 5B-3, 5B-37 to 5B-43.

[25]   *Id*. at 5B-40.

[26]   *Id*. at 5B-41 to 5B-43. The tribes had three different long-term drawdown plans: 1) John Day and Ice Harbor draw down to natural river levels; 2) John Day to be drawn down to spillway crest level (the minimum level at which adult fish ladders still operate) and Ice Harbor and Lower Monumental drawn down to natural river levels; or 3) John Day and all four Lower Snake Dams drawn down to natural river level. The tribes estimated that survival rates would increase three-fold under option 1; 3.4 times under option 2; and four-fold under option 3. *Id*.

[27]   *Id*. at 5B-39 (end to transportation), iv-v, 5B-24, 5B-35 (hatchery supplementation).

[28]   *Id*. at 4-15, 4-27 n. 135, 5C-3 to 5C-4.

Notes to Chapter 15

[1]   Northwest Power Planning Council, *Compilation of Information on Salmon and Steelhead Losses in the Columbia River Basin* 4 (1986) (historic run sizes of 10 to 16 million salmon).

[2]   See, for example, the conversation between Colin Fogarty and Bill Lunch, on *Oregon Considered* (Oregon Public Broadcasting television broadcast, Dec. 30, 1999) (salmon as a mirror of society's values); *see also* Alvin Anderson, *Shall We Have Salmon, Dams, or Both, in* TRANSACTIONS OF THE FIFTEENTH NORTH AMERICAN WILDLIFE CONFERENCE 449 (1950).

[3]   On the treaty promises, see chapters 3, 4, and 12.

[4]   On the false hope of hatcheries, see chapter 6.

[5]   Northwest Resource Info. Ctr. v. Northwest Power Planning Council, 35 F.3d 1371, 1395 (9th Cir. 1994) ("entrenched river users", "lowest common denominator"); on the Northwest Power Act program, see chapter 7; on the Endangered Species Act program, see chapter 9.

[6]   On the Pacific Salmon Treaty, see chapter 8; on the Clean Water Act, see chapter 10; on the Federal Power Act, see chapter 11. 16 U.S.C. § 811 contains the "fishway" requirement.

[7]   On breaching the Lower Snake River dams, see chapter 13; on ecosystem management, see chapter 14.

[8]   Electronic mail from John Shurts, Northwest Power Planning Council General Counsel, to author (Nov. 3, 2000) (explaining that 40% of the Council's fiscal year budget for the "direct program budget" — which funds BPA's activities like off-site mitigation for hatcheries and habitat restoration, monitoring, research, and management coordination — was devoted to hatcheries, mostly projects on tribal lands. The 40% figure does not include BPA's reimbursement payments to the federal treasury for appropriations funding passage improvements at Corps of Engineer dams, for example).

[9]   RETURN TO THE RIVER (cited in chapter 1, note 52), at 5 ("Despite decades of effort, the present condition of most populations in the Columbia River Basin demonstrates the failure of technological methods to for substitute lost ecosystem functions"); *2000 BiOp* (cited in chapter 1, note 49), at 9-59 (describing juvenile transportation as a "reasonable and prudent alternative").

[10]   United States v. Adair, 723 F.2d 1394, 1414 (9th Cir. 1983) ("wilderness servitude"); on the Mid-Columbia settlement agreement, see Bodi (cited in chapter 11, note 25); on the "normative river," see RETURN TO THE RIVER (cited in chapter 1, note 52), at xvii, 5, 7, 19-20; see also *Beyond Parity,* at 112.

[11]   On the Gorton science amendment, Pub. L. No. 104-206, § 504, 110 Stat. 2984, 3005-06 (adding a new § 4(h)(10)(D)(iv) to the Northwest Power Act), see *Beyond Parity,* at 117-19; on drawdowns of mainstem reservoirs to restore salmon spawning habitat, see RETURN TO THE RIVER (cited in chapter 1, note 52), at 268-69, 513; William Stelle, Jr. *Overcoming the Seven Myths of Columbia River Salmon Recovery,* 28 ENVTL. L. 493, 499 (1998) ("pick-and choose" science).

[12]   For a comparison of the three salmon plans, see *Beyond Parity,* at 80-83; on the Inland Land proposal, *see* chapter 9, text accompanying notes 60-63; TAYLOR (cited in chapter 1, note 3), at 257 ("The Endangered Species Act reversed the equation by blocking all development that threatened salmon . . ."); on the ESA's authorization of timber harvests that were blocked by the Northwest Forest Plan, see chapter 9, text accompanying notes 55-59; on the approval of the dredging of the Columbia, see Mike O'Byrant, *NMFS Issues No Jeopardy on Dredging,* COLUMBIA BASIN BULLETIN (Dec. 17, 1999) <http://www.nwpcc.org/bull/bulletin_65.htm#4>; Jonathan Brinckman, *Agency OKs Dredging Columbia,* OREGONIAN, Dec. 16, 1999, at B1.

[13]   *See* Stelle (cited in note 11), at 500 (myth of a regional solution); *Congress to Hold Hearings on all Hs,* COLUMBIA BASIN BULLETIN (Dec. 17, 1999) <http://www.nwpcc.org/bulletin/bull_65.htm#3> (Senator Mike Crapo (R-Id) claiming that the Northwest "still has the responsibility to sort out the science and craft its own recovery plan"); for estimates of the current costs of the dams in excess of $200 million annually, see chapter 13, text with notes 40-44.

[14]   For the case affirming the barging program in part on ecosystem management grounds, see chapter 9, text with notes 21-22; on the "all H's approach, see Barry Espenson, *Feds Release Salmon Recovery Documents,* COLUMBIA BASIN BULLETIN (Dec. 17, 1999) < http://www.nwppc.org/bulletin/bull/_65.htm#1> (discussing the federal "all Hs" working paper); Sue Safford, *Seattle Seminar Calls for Basin Decisions,* COLUMBIA BASIN BULLETIN <http://www.nwppc.org/bulletin/bull_65.htm.#8> (Donna Darm, NMFS Assistant Regional Director, raising questions about regulation of non-federal lands; harvests by Alaskans, Canadians, and tribes; and state water law).

[15] On the Salmon Summit, see chapter 9, text with note 3; TAYLOR (cited in chapter 1, note 3), at 237-57 (cautioning against telling simple stories; advocating understanding a complex history).

[16] RETURN TO THE RIVER (cited in chapter 1, note 52), at xvii, 5, 19. *See also* Independent Scientific Group, *Return to the River: An Ecological Vision for the Recovery of the Columbia River Salmon,* 28 ENVTL. L. 503, 507-14 (1998) (discussing the "Normative Salmon Ecosystem").

[17] On the $200 million cost, see chapter 13, text with notes 40-44; on the Corps' draft EIS, see Espenson (cited in note 14).

[18] *See* Espenson (cited in note 14) (quoting U.S. Fish and Wildlife Service Regional Director, Ann Badgley); *Tribal Restoration Plan* (cited in chapter 6, note 30), at 2-8 (1964, last year of commercial summer chinook harvests), 2-10 (1977, last year of commercial spring chinook harvests).

[19] Brent Hunsberger, *Kitzhaber Calls for Breaching Snake Dams,* OREGONIAN, Feb. 19, 2000, at A1; Kitzhaber's speech calling for dam breaching was delivered to American Fisheries Society, and was reprinted by the Oregonian on Feb. 19, 2000 at <http://cbbulletin.com; http://www.oregonlive.com/ege-bin/printer/printer.egi>; *see also* John Kitzhaber, *Memo to Jack Roberts: If Not Dams, What?* OREGONIAN, Feb. 25, 2000, at D7; *Seattle Endorses Lower Snake Dam Breaching,* COLUMBIA BASIN BULLETIN, Sept. 1, 2000 <http://cbbulletin.com>; Natalie M. Henry, *Northwest Governors Criticize Kitzhaber Over Dam Removal,* LAND LETTER, Feb. 29, 2000; *Bush and New BiOp: An Iffy Proposition At Best,* CLEARING UP, Nov. 20, 2000, at 12 (noting that Columbia River Alliance (an organization of power and water users) director Bruce Lovelin claimed that the BiOp would be "dead on arrival" in a Bush presidency); *Seattle Endorses Lower Snake Dam Breaching,* Columbia Basin Bulletin, Sept. 1, 2000 <http://cbbulletin.com>; Jim Brunner, *City's Dam Stand Makes Waves,* SEATTLE TIMES, Sept. 7, 2000.

TABLE OF CASES

United States v. Winans, 73 F. 72 (C.C.D. Wash. 1896), *rev'd* 198 U.S. 371 (1905), ch 4, nn 7, 8-9; ch 12, nn 35, 44, 47, 49

Washington v. Washington State Commercial Passenger Fishing Vessel Ass'n, 443 U.S. 658 (1979), ch 1, nn 5-6, 8, 10,12, 30; ch 3, nn 5, 15, 19; ch 4, nn 1, 26-27; ch 12, nn 4, 34, 46, 48, 51

Winters v. U.S., 207 U.S. 564 (1908), ch 4, n 10

INDEX